Sammy Marks ♩10

'*A well-written, carefully researched, original and valuable work which . . . will rightly come to occupy a prominent place in South African historiography. . . . Richard Mendelsohn has not only provided us with a remarkably vivid and extremely honest portrait of a hitherto frustratingly elusive character in the gallery of South African historical actors, but also managed to cast light on a dark and neglected period of our economic history.*' – Professor Charles van Onselen, African Studies Institute, University of the Witwatersrand.

D1613121

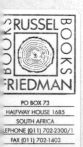

RUSSEL BOOKS
BOOKS FRIEDMAN

PO BOX 73
HALFWAY HOUSE 1685
SOUTH AFRICA
TELEPHONE (011) 702-2300/1
FAX (011) 702-1403

SAMMY MARKS

'The Uncrowned King of the Transvaal'

RICHARD MENDELSOHN

David Philip · *Cape Town*
Ohio University Press · *Athens, Ohio*
In association with
Jewish Publications–South Africa

First published 1991 in southern Africa by David Philip Publishers (Pty) Ltd,
208 Werdmuller Centre, Claremont 7700, and by Jewish Publications–South Africa,
Kaplan Centre for Jewish Studies, University of Cape Town, Rondebosch 7700,
Cape Town

Published 1991 in the United States of America by Ohio University Press, Scott
Quadrangle, Athens, Ohio 54701

© 1991 Richard Mendelsohn

ISBN 0-86486-188-5 (David Philip, paper)
ISBN 0-86486-164-8 (David Philip, cloth)
ISBN 0-8214-0998-0 (Ohio University Press, cloth)
ISBN 0-8214-0999-9 (Ohio University Press, paper)

Printed and bound by Creda Press, Solan Road, Cape Town

Library of Congress Cataloging in Publication Data:

Mendelsohn, Richard.
    Sammy Marks: the uncrowned king of the Transvaal/by Richard
Mendelsohn.
        p.   cm.
    Includes bibliographical references and index.
    ISBN 0-8214-0998-0 (cloth). – ISBN 0-8214-0999-9 (paper)
    1. Marks, Samuel, 1845-1920.   2. Jewish businessmen – South Africa –
Biography.   I. Title.
HC905.M36M46 1991
338.092 – dc20
    [B]   90-28333
                                                             CIP

Contents

	Preface	vii
I.	Beyond the Pale, 1844–1882	1
II.	Founding the First Factory in the Transvaal, 1882–1885	23
III.	Gold, Gin and Coal, 1885–1895	38
IV.	The Transvaal from Within, 1896–1899	65
V.	Courting Kruger: Sammy Marks and the President	86
VI.	A Country House on the Highveld: Zwartkoppies in the 1890s	101
VII.	Between the Lines, 1899–1902	110
VIII.	Keeping the Peace, 1902–1908	140
IX.	Reconstructing the Business, 1902–1908	155
X.	The Gilded Cage: Zwartkoppies after the War	181
XI.	Sammy Marks the Jew	197
XII.	Senator and Steelmaker, 1908–1919	215
XIII.	Sammy Marks: The Haimisher Mensh, 1844–1920	234
XIV.	Epilogue: 'Overtaken by Nemesis'	249
	Genealogy	263
	References	264
	Bibliography	291
	Index	300

Preface

Shortly after the end of the South African War, W. T. Stead, one of the most renowned English journalists of the day, visited the Transvaal to report on the British Empire's most recent and painful acquisition. Among those he interviewed was a short, grey-haired and heavily weathered Russian-born Jew of close to 60. 'One of the most remarkable men in South Africa', he wrote afterwards, 'is Mr. Samuel Marks, of Messrs. Lewis and Marks. Sammy Marks, as he is familiarly known, is a Russian Jew, who many years ago came to South Africa with a pedlar's pack, and who is now many times a millionaire. He has sent his son to Harrow to be educated, but he himself can neither read nor write. But he can read South Africa as a book, and his local reputation is such that he is jocularly known as the uncrowned king of the Transvaal.'[1]

The king was physically unprepossessing and alien in bearing. A local journalist described him as 'a scrub faced little man with a big head, and a face criss-crossed with many lines, a head fringed with a hearth rug of iron-grey hair and a bristly beard. A short, stout, uncompromisingly alien-looking person, alien in speech and alien in manner, to whom frock coats and fancy waistcoats are still foreign abominations.'[2] And yet despite his plainness and his strangeness, he greatly impressed the distinguished English visitor. Why was W. T. Stead so taken with this pedlar turned millionaire? How had this 'remarkable' man acquired his large and 'royal' local reputation? Who was this supposedly illiterate Russian Jew with a son at Harrow?

The answer has been attempted before but never in a properly documented full-length work. Marks has figured in numerous popular accounts of the period as well as in a handful of serious academic studies. Many of the former are inaccurate, with error recycled from text to text, while the latter are restricted in scope, dealing only with limited areas of Marks's business career. Marks has become encrusted in myth, a larger-than-life, mock-heroic figure, the subject of comic anecdote. There are jokey tales of Marks's intimate but combative friendship with Paul Kruger, of bags of gold coins poured out before credulous Boer landowners to induce them to part with their farms, and of nouveau riche ignorance. A fable I encountered again and again in Johannesburg, Cape Town and Pretoria has Marks ordering a copy of the Venus de Milo and then complaining to the railways that one of the arms had broken off in transit.

Families have their cherished Marks legends which have all been improved in the telling. While this biography was being written four approaches were made by people claiming a connection to Marks. One had Marks working as a young man on her greatgrandfather's farm in the Fransch Hoek valley. One had a gold watch that Marks supposedly bartered for a mule and cart at roughly the same time. One claimed that a grandfather was a half-brother of Marks, one that a grandmother was an illegitimate daughter. None of these claims are documented, none are likely, none can bear close scrutiny. All are evidence of the propensity of families to romanticise their pasts.

Myth flourished over the years in the apparent absence of documentation. It seemed more than likely that Marks, whose command of written English was reputedly slight, had committed little to paper, and that there were no Marks papers of the sort that a Percy FitzPatrick or a Jan Smuts, two of his highly literate contemporaries, had left to posterity. In 1984 this belief was dramatically refuted. Through an arrangement between the Samuel Marks Trust and the Kaplan–Kushlick Foundation a huge cache of papers was transferred from Zwartkoppies, Marks's country home twelve miles east of Pretoria, to the University of Cape Town. This was the first historians knew of the existence of a remarkable collection. For more than half a century the papers had been carefully preserved in a dry strongroom, reminiscent of a small bank-vault, off the great kitchen of the house. Now they were to be meticulously sorted and catalogued and then stored in a controlled environment where temperature and humidity were held constant.

The nucleus of the collection consisted of 40 letterbooks, averaging 500 pages in length. For almost four decades Marks's secretaries had painstakingly copied all of his private outgoing correspondence into these with the aid of letterpresses, one of which still survives at Zwartkoppies. Dampened blotting paper, bound flimsy and original letter were sandwiched together tightly and evenly by the press; the blotting paper drew the ink of the original onto the flimsy. Thousands of letters were copied in this way. They document in considerable detail both Marks's private life and his business and political career between 1880, when he was a young man of 36, and his death in 1920. The great majority are in English though many of the early ones are in Yiddish, the German dialect spoken by the Jews of Eastern Europe. Translation of these is no easy task. Some of the letters are smudged, making it difficult to identify the Hebrew characters. Marks's idiosyncratic use of language further complicates matters. His Yiddish letters are an entertaining hybrid of English and Yiddish words that would baffle even Leo Rosten, the author of *The Joys of Yiddish*, a popular seriocomic lexicon of the Yiddish language.

Marks's English letters are less problematic. The early ones are in the immaculate copperplate of his secretaries; his later ones, from the mid-1890s onwards, are typewritten. As early as 1896, when the typewriter was still as novel and as exciting as the bicycle, the electric light and the Kodak camera, Marks ordered 'one of the very latest and best typewriters', together with a stand

and a supply of ribbons and carbon paper. In his childhood Marks had been taught to write in Hebrew characters; in his later life, he found the forming of English characters very difficult, as his crabbed signature attests. Consequently he relied on dictation when writing in English. First he would dictate his letters 'slowly word for word' to his confidential secretary or to a clerk in his office. Then, as he once explained to his partner, Isaac Lewis, 'before having them sent off I read them and if, in my way of thinking, I find anything in them that is not correct, I have them re-written. So therefore, the people who type my letters are not responsible one way or the other for anything expressed in them.'[3]

The convenience of this procedure encouraged Marks to write reams of letters to a wide range of acquaintances and friends. He also wrote weekly letters to his children who were sent to England for their schooling, but these are often formal and laconic, usually little more than half a typed page in length. By contrast his weekly letters to his partner Isaac Lewis in London are intimate and richly detailed, often running to as many as ten or more typed pages. The biographer can only be thankful that in the age before air travel and trunk-calls full and honest reporting in writing was indispensable if a business partnership was to flourish. Isaac Lewis's lengthy replies form part of a large but far less complete set of the letters Marks received from his correspondents, who included many of the most prominent business and political personalities of his time. Besides this, the collection contains a long but broken run of Marks's financial records – his cashbooks, ledgers, journal and balance sheets. There are also title-deeds, agreements and promissory notes, reports on mines and businesses, household orderbooks and a box filled with household receipts which would delight a social historian reconstructing the upper-class Victorian household. Marks's thrifty habits and his reluctance to discard anything are a biographer's dream.

The present project grew out of the enthusiasm of three people. It was conceived originally by Neill Maisels, Sammy Marks's oldest grandson and the chairman of the Marks Trust. Neill was committed from the start to the publication of a thoroughly researched and fully documented study of his grandfather which would sweep away the cobwebs of legend and myth that surrounded his memory. Throughout the gestation of the biography he encouraged the author to make it as accurate and comprehensive as possible, warts and all. Mendel Kaplan of Johannesburg, industrialist, philanthropist and Jewish communal leader, acted as the facilitator of the project, arranging for the transfer of the Sammy Marks Collection to Cape Town and for the preparation of the biography. Sally Frankental, director of the Isaac and Jessie Kaplan Centre for Jewish Studies at the University of Cape Town, provided the vital institutional support, many cups of coffee, and much canny advice. The Anglo American and De Beers Chairman's Fund and Jewish Publications South Africa gave very generous financial support, while the University of Cape Town granted the necessary extended leave.

My sincere thanks to all of these, and to those most supportive and sympathetic of archivists, Leonie Twentyman-Jones and Etaine Eberhard of the Manuscripts and Archives Division of the Jagger Library at the University of

Cape Town. Ultimately this study rests on Leonie's superb arrangement of the Sammy Marks Collection. Many thanks to Lozer Karabelnik, Naomi Bloch and Lilian Dubb for their Yiddish translations, and to Edward Isaacs for information about Sheffield Jewry. Thanks too to the staff of the State Archives in Pretoria and of the South African Library in Cape Town, to Barbara Conradie and Letitia Theunissen at the Standard Bank Archives in Johannesburg, to Maryna Fraser at the Barlow Rand Archives, to Beth MacFarlane at Anglo American, to Edgar Price at Johannesburg Consolidated Investment, to Baby Deyzel and Lisel Meyer at the Vaal Teknorama, Marie vanVuuren of the City Council of Pretoria, Mike Scholes of the Transvaal Provincial Administration, and the staff of the National Cultural History Museum, Pretoria, for their assistance with the photographs.

I am very grateful as well to Elsie and Rayme Rabinowitz, Peter and Hilda Schwartz, Neill and Ethne Maisels, and Gavin and Colleen Lewis who sheltered and fed me in the Transvaal, and to Noel Garson, Jeffrey Butler, Charles van Onselen, Milton Shain, Howard Phillips, Elizabeth van Heyningen, Arthur Davey and Vivian Bickford-Smith who gave me advice and a sympathetic audience.

Finally, my love and appreciation to my wife Odette without whose constant encouragement and cheerful acceptance of my long absences in the Transvaal – and in my study at night – this book would not have been possible.

Sammy Marks and his father, Mordechai Feit Marks, once an itinerant tailor, later a public benefactor in his home town of Neustadt by courtesy of his wealthy son (Photo: Sammy Marks Museum)

*Bertha Marks
(Photo: Mrs Dolly Maisels)*

*Bertha Marks and children. From
left: Dolly, Louis, Phil, Joe,
Bertha, Girlie. In front: Ted.
(Photo: Sammy Marks Museum)*

Zwartkoppies, Marks's country house (Photo: Sammy Marks Museum)

A tennis party at Zwartkoppies, with Bertha on the left (Photo: Marks Museum)

The white domestic staff at Zwartkoppies (Photo: Sammy Marks Museum)

Sammy, Bertha and Dolly, with a group of friends, including Dr Kay seated on the left, at Zwartkoppies (Photo: Sammy Marks Museum)

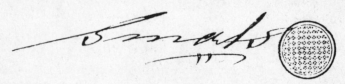

Sammy Marks at Zwartkoppies in a characteristic pose (Photo: Mrs Dolly Maisels)

I

Beyond the Pale, 1844–1882

Samuel Marks was born on 11 July 1844 in Neustadt, a small Russian frontier community on the border between the Tsarist empire and East Prussia. To St Petersburg, it was an obscure town in the Lithuanian region of the empire. But to its Jewish inhabitants, it was a *shtetl*, a Jewish township, within the notorious Pale of Settlement, the crescent of territory on the western margin of Russia to which they had been confined by Tsarist decree.

The Jews of Lithuania were unwilling subjects of the Tsar. The presence of the Marks family and of their Neustadt neighbours in the Russian empire was an accident of history. Marks's ancestors had migrated eastwards at the end of the Middle Ages to escape persecution and despoliation at the hands of the rapacious princes of Western Europe. They had been welcomed by the rulers of Lithuania and Poland who were eager to capitalise on their commercial skills which were then at a premium in undeveloped Eastern Europe. But with the partition of the Polish–Lithuanian union between its overbearing neighbours – Prussia, Russia and Austria – at the end of the eighteenth century, the Jews of Lithuania had found themselves unwelcome subjects of an antisemitic Russian empire which had previously forbidden them entry. The Jews were the unwanted legacy of Tsarist territorial ambition in Eastern Europe: their new masters accepted their presence very grudgingly and through the nineteenth century hedged their lives around with restrictions great and small.

Marks's birthplace, Neustadt, was a tiny part of the spoils of the partition of Poland–Lithuania. It passed in 1795 to Prussia but was ceded in 1815 to Russia. Its chequered past was reflected in its names of which it had at least three: its Jewish inhabitants knew it as Neustadt; St Petersburg and the Russian officials who were stationed in the town knew it as Vladislavov; while the Lithuanian peasants who lived in the surrounding countryside called it Naumiestis, the name by which it is officially known today. Neustadt was surrounded on three sides by river. On the west lay the Schirwindt, a sluggish stream which separated the Russian town from a Prussian town of the same name. Schirwindt (now Kutuzovo) was connected to Neustadt by a bridge. Across this came the German customers of the Jewish artisans and merchants of Neustadt. On its

northeastern flank Neustadt was circled by the Sheshupe River, across which lay
a small suburb. Few Jews lived here. Instead they clustered together in the old
town around their *shul* – their synagogue – and their *bet midrash* – their
communal house of study. A mile outside town lay the Jewish cemetery and
four miles away the Paroshnewer forest where the long history of Neustadt
Jewry was to end abruptly and savagely less than a hundred years after Marks's
birth. On Tuesday 1 July 1941, all but a handful of the Jewish men of Neustadt
were shot in the cemetery by the Nazis; on Tuesday 16 September 1941, all but
a few of the Jewish women and children were murdered in the forest. As a
frontier town Neustadt faced both east and west. Some 43 miles to the northeast
lay Kovno (now Kaunas), one of Lithuania's few sizeable towns, a commercial
centre as well as one of the great centres of traditional Jewish learning in Eastern
Europe. To the west, on the Baltic coast, lay the Prussian city of Königsberg
(now Kaliningrad), a six-centuries-old trading city which exported Russian
staple products – grain, flax and hemp – to an industrialising Western Europe.[1]

Mid-nineteenth-century Lithuania was a backward region of a backward
empire, its Jewish inhabitants an ethnic underclass whose legal oppression was
fully matched by their economic deprivation. 'The Jews live in great congestion,
very often several families live in one small room,' a Russian observer wrote of
life in the Pale. 'The Jew's expenses are quite small. In the morning he eats
radishes, onions, garlic fish or herring with bread. . . . There are tradesmen
whose families fast the whole day till the bread-winner comes home and brings
his earnings.' Samuel's father, Mordechai Feit Marks, might well have been one
of these. An itinerant tailor, he was forced by circumstances to leave his wife
Miriam, his sons Samuel (Sammy), Ellia and Joseph, and his daughters Fanny
and Krena, and travel in search of work. As a Jewish contemporary wrote: 'The
tradesmen and small traders, who operated with a capital of from 50 to 100
ruble, were hardly able to earn their bitter livelihood. Not being able to find in
the . . . "Shtetl" the opportunity to use their abilities and their knowledge of
trades, many such inhabitants of the "Shtetlech" would go out of their provinces
in search of a livelihood. They would leave their families to God's will and to the
soft hearts of the neighbours.'[2]

Poor though it was, the *shtetl* nevertheless supported a rich and complex
infrastructure of cultural, religious and educational institutions. One of these
was the *cheder*, the elementary school, where the young Marks acquired a basic
literacy in Hebrew, the *loshen kodesh*, the sacred tongue which was strictly
reserved for study and worship. (Yiddish, the language of everyday usage, a
German dialect written in Hebrew characters, was acquired at home rather than
formally taught in the *cheder*.) The boys of the *shtetl* (but not their sisters, whose
education was a low priority) often started *cheder* when they were no more than
3 years old. Their classroom, shared by children ranging widely in age, would
probably have been a partitioned-off section of the main room in the *melamed*'s,
or teacher's, modest house; at the far end of the room, behind a screen, the
teacher might have had his bedroom and kitchen. The *melamed* was poorly paid
and had a lowly status in the community. He would have had no formal training
in pedagogy. His teaching methods and materials, such as they were, would

have made few concessions to the youth of his charges. They learnt Hebrew, the language of prayer rather than of conversation; their texts were the adult prayer book, the Bible and the rabbinical commentaries on it, and the Talmud, the body of Jewish law. There were no special primers for young readers. First the boys were taught the Hebrew alphabet, then reading, before finally turning to the Bible at the ripe old age of 5 or 6.[3]

The intense and thorough grounding in the Bible which followed left an enduring impression on those who experienced it. The biblical stories that Marks, for example, studied in *cheder* as a child provided a wealth of reference which he drew on throughout his life. 'When I read certain letters,' he wrote many decades later, 'it reminds me of what I read about Jonah and his gourd when I was a little Boy!!!' Again, long after leaving the *shtetl*: 'I remember as a schoolboy reading in the Bible about Moses, the Ten Commandments and the Golden Calf.'[4]

After *bar mitzvah*, the traditional coming of age at 13, a privileged few would have continued to the more advanced form of education the Jewish community provided, the *yeshivah* or talmudical academy. There is nothing to indicate that Marks, who came from a poor family, went beyond elementary school or *cheder*, and indeed he was to express his regret in later life about his limited schooling. But while the young Marks's formal education might have been restricted, his informal education was less so. His curious and receptive mind seems to have drawn a range of important lessons from the physical and social milieu in which he grew up. The *shtetl* provided Sammy Marks with a set of values which shaped his conduct long after he left his birthplace. The *shtetl* valued hard work – 'Work, and God will help' – as well as diligence, self-control and sobriety. It esteemed learning, charity and devotion to family. In Eastern Europe, family even more than synagogue was the focal point of *shtetl* life. Cardinal importance was attached to family ties. Jewish parent and child were bound together by an enduring web of obligations that stretched well beyond childhood, beyond even support in old age to the grave itself; a son's ultimate duty was to say *kaddish*, the mourner's prayer, on the anniversary of his parents' death. There was also a binding, lifelong obligation to aid one's siblings and their offspring if assistance was needed and if one could at all afford to do so.

Beyond the family the *shtetl* placed a great value on mutual support. *Tsdokeh* – charity – 'saved from death'; it was seen as the prime virtue, the essence of Jewishness, a cardinal duty and a joy, and served as a source of social prestige second only to learning. In a mid-nineteenth-century *shtetl* like the Neustadt of Sammy Marks's childhood, learning still meant traditional religious learning, but even here the *Haskalah* – the Jewish enlightenment which had begun further westwards in Germany a century before – had begun to cast its secularising shadow. As a result Marks experienced little difficulty in shedding the larger part of traditional Jewish observance once he left the *shtetl*, while at the same time clinging tenaciously to the fundamentals – the values – that lay behind the practice.[5]

The physical landscape of his youth, like the spiritual and cultural, seems to have played an important part in forming the adult Marks. Mid-nineteenth-

century Lithuania was still a land of forests. Its great oak trees remained the focus
of folk customs that had survived the coming of Christianity many centuries
before. These sprawling virgin forests, like the Paroshnewer four miles outside
Neustadt, seem to have made an indelible impression on the young Marks. They
left him with a lifelong passion for trees and forests. Long after his departure
from Eastern Europe he tried to recreate on a treeless stretch of the South African
Highveld the forests he must have so vividly remembered from his youth.
Scattered through the countryside were vodka stills and taverns which slaked
the thirsts of the local peasantry. Many of these were run by Jews, an ironic
circumstance given that they themselves placed a cultural premium on
abstemiousness. The seed might well have been planted here for what was to be
Marks's principal activity in his middle years: the distilling of liquor on the
Highveld for black migrant workers on the mines of the Witwatersrand.

Marks's childhood world was bounded by the Prussian border which ran
alongside Neustadt. Unlike the barbed wired and mined frontiers of Cold War
Eastern Europe, this was a very porous boundary. Smugglers, many of them
Jewish, regularly slipped across into Prussia and returned with contraband
goods. The Russian border guards were paid to look the other way. As a child
growing up in a town on the frontier Marks would have learnt at a very young
age that in many societies officials have their price, a lesson he would apply very
successfully many years later in Paul Kruger's Transvaal. Across the border
were the great estates of Prussia's aristocratic landlords. In the mid-nineteenth
century, as Marks grew up, the Junkers were busily improving their estates and
turning these to account. Mills, breweries and distilleries were built on estates
which increasingly specialised in crops destined for the market. This model of
agricultural development might well have been the inspiration for his own
pioneer efforts decades later to establish a great commercial farming enterprise
at the Vaal River.

Marks grew up at a very difficult time in the history of Jewish settlement in
Russia. His childhood, like that of his boyhood friends, was overshadowed by
the threat of conscription into the Tsarist army. In 1827, seventeen years before
Marks's birth, Tsar Nicholas I had decreed that Jews, who had traditionally been
exempt from military service, should now serve in the Russian army. The terms
imposed on them were far more severe than those imposed on their gentile
neighbours. Jews could be drafted at the age of 12. These child recruits were then
placed in cantonist battalions, special military units for those under the age of 18.
Once they achieved their majority they were transferred to regular units where
they served a further 25 years. Each Jewish community was held responsible for
supplying its quota of recruits. Faced with this unenviable but unavoidable task,
the leaders of the community inevitably saw to it that the burden of conscription
fell most heavily on poor families like Sammy Marks's. Communities employed
khappers, snatchers, to pressgang children for military service. Many of those
who were seized were well below the minimum age of recruitment. Some were
as young as 8 or 9. Their fate was miserable. Alexander Herzen, the Russian
revolutionary, describes meeting a convoy of Jewish recruits deep in the interior
of Russia, far from the areas of Jewish settlement:

They brought the children and formed them into regular ranks: it was one of the most awful sights I have ever seen, those poor, poor children! Boys of twelve or thirteen might somehow have survived it, but little fellows of eight and ten. . . . Not even a brush full of black paint could put such horror on canvas.

Pale, exhausted, with frightened faces, they stood in thick, clumsy soldiers' overcoats, with stand-up collars, fixing helpless, pitiful eyes on the garrison soldiers who were roughly getting them into ranks. The white lips, the blue rings under their eyes bore witness to fever or chill. And these sick children, without care or kindness, exposed to the raw wind that blows unobstructed from the Arctic Ocean, were going to their graves.[6]

Those who survived the ordeal found that their Jewishness was under constant assault, both physical and emotional, for Tsar Nicholas saw child conscription as a means of converting the Jews. Thousands of children succumbed to these unbearable pressures and converted. To escape this fate – conscription and conversion – parents hid their children in the forests or sent them across the frontier. In desperation fingers or toes were amputated to avoid the draft.

In the four years before Marks turned 12, the danger increased as the authorities stepped up the rate of recruitment. While we have no documentation, his parents' anxiety can be imagined. The effect on the young child of the dark fears that his parents must have harboured for his safety can only be guessed at. These parental nightmares seem to have cast their shadow over Marks in later life. When he himself became a parent many years after, he was intensely anxious about his children's well-being. His exaggerated fears for their safety and health possibly stem from his own childhood insecurities. Conscription hung like a sword over an impoverished household where father was frequently away on business.

Sammy turned 12 on 11 July 1856. Six weeks later, on 26 August 1856, Tsar Alexander II, who had succeeded his father Tsar Nicholas the year before, abolished the cantonment system with its dreaded child recruitment. Jews were now to be conscripted on the same basis as for the rest of the population, as young adults rather than as children. The relief in the Marks household must have been immense.[7]

Marks's fearful childhood left him with an abiding hatred of Tsarist Russia. When many years later, in 1905, the Russians suffered a 'terrible defeat' at the hands of the Japanese at Port Arthur on the Pacific, Marks was quietly pleased; it 'does not cause me a single regret,' he wrote to a friend. Years before, moreover, he had cheerfully predicted the revolutionary disturbances that followed the defeat: in 1901 he had written that he ' thought there would be a revolution before many years passed and have no doubt good will result from it'.[8]

Before he turned 18, Sammy left home and family and departed for England. Leaving the *shtetl* took some courage. 'When I left our native country,' Marks later recalled, 'I had no one to look after me.' Nor, he might have added, had he any means or useful skills. Yet he, like the generations of Russian Jewish emigrants that followed, took with him an irrepressible optimism. Despite the material deprivation and oppression the *shtetl* endured, it was not a demoralised community; it endowed its departing children with a sense of hope, a buoyancy and resilience, born of the intense vitality of its cultural and communal life.[9]

In 1861 Marks sailed for Hull, probably from Königsberg in East Prussia, with a consignment of Russian horses bound for the industrial city of Sheffield in northern England. His arrival coincided with a critical moment of transition in the economic life of the town: long the hub of the traditional English cutlery trade, with its small workshops and rudimentary technology, Sheffield had just embarked on a new course, as the cradle of the modern English steel industry. Only a few years before Marks came to Sheffield, Henry Bessemer had persuaded a local steelmaker to adopt the 'converter', his revolutionary invention for the mass production of steel. The expansion of both the old and the new industries drew thousands of newcomers to the city, amongst them a small number of Eastern European immigrants like Marks, who were the forerunners of the great Jewish exodus from Russia at the end of the century.[10]

Marks was welcomed to Sheffield by a kinsman who had recently set up shop in the city as a jeweller. He, it seems, supplied the seed-money Sammy needed to go peddling, which was then the common resort of young Jewish immigrants without skills and with very limited means. Between trips Marks lodged with a prominent member of the Sheffield Jewish community, Tobias Guttmann, variously described as a jeweller, hawker and cutler. Guttmann became the young man's mentor. As Marks fondly recalled years later, he 'coached me how to succeed'.[11]

Guttmann's advice was that Marks should try his luck in South Africa, an increasingly attractive destination, like Australia and America, for young men of wide ambition but narrow means. When Marks objected that he had not the money for the fare, Guttmann offered to pay his passage to Cape Town and presented him with a large case of knives. 'This was my capital,' Marks gratefully recollected long afterwards.[12] Marks sailed for the Cape in 1868 at the age of 24. Though he had spent only a few years in England, these seem to have been decisive. Sheffield, in the heartland of the industrial revolution, made a profound impression on a young man who had grown up in a poor village in a remote province of an economically retarded empire. It inspired an ambition he was to pursue for much of the rest of his career – the creation of a South African Sheffield on the veld. The Sheffield years also gave him an enduring regard for England, the English and Englishness, which conditioned many of the choices he was to make later in life. Liberal England had extended to Marks and his fellow Russian Jewish immigrants the tolerant welcome denied them by their country of birth.

As at Sheffield, Marks arrived at the Cape at a moment of historical transition. The year before, 1867, a large diamond, the Eureka, had been discovered on a remote farm in the northern reaches of the colony; within a year, a further discovery, the Star of South Africa, led to a rush to the Vaal River and the beginnings of an industry that was to revolutionise a sub-continent still predominantly pastoral and agrarian. Marks was not immediately involved. Instead, as in England, he began as a pedlar, an occupation known locally as smousing. He hawked Guttmann's knives about Cape Town, and to his pleasant surprise, made a neat profit. He reinvested this in goods he bought on the Parade, the city's open-air market, and then peddled these in the suburbs of Cape Town. He was joined shortly afterwards by a distant cousin, Isaac Lewis, who had come from the same *shtetl* in Lithuania. They formed a partnership which rapidly prospered, if in a modest way: living very frugally, they soon accumulated enough cash to buy a horse and cart, then a second horse and cart. With goods on credit from Cape Town wholesale merchants, they extended their 'beat' into the Boland, the city's rural hinterland.[13]

Meanwhile the search for diamonds had continued unabated, moving away from the Vaal to a promising cluster of farms some 25 miles from the river. In July 1871 news of the discovery of a major diamond pipe on one of these set off a frenzied rush throughout the Cape Colony to what was to become the famed Kimberley mine. Marks and his partner were caught up in the general excitement. They loaded their two carts with goods and set off at once for Colesberg Kopje, the site of the discovery. But long before they reached it, they had sold every article they carried to the poorly equipped hopefuls making their way northwards. Turning about, Marks and Lewis returned to Cape Town, and loaded up once again, taking with them this time a prefabricated store made of wood. When they eventually arrived at the diggings after their double journey, they sold off cart and horse and opened shop. With goods in short supply, they made a handsome profit. Payment was mostly in diamonds, and Lewis and Marks soon found that dealing in these was more profitable even than trading in scarce general goods.[14]

Lewis and Marks rapidly established a reputation for square dealing, which set them far apart from the dubious 'kopje wallopers', petty diamond buyers, who scuttled around the claims at the Kimberley mine, gulling credulous diggers. Within a short time Lewis and Marks, and a handful of other diamond merchants, came to dominate the local diamond trade, acting as intermediaries between Kimberley and the great diamond centres of Europe. Diamonds were brought for sale to Lewis and Marks's corrugated iron offices in New Main Street, between the Albion bar and the Diggers Arms; the partners would examine these, make their selection and ship them off to diamond merchants in London, Amsterdam and elsewhere.[15]

In time Sammy and Isaac were joined on the diamond fields by their younger brothers, Barnet and Joseph Lewis and Ellia and Joseph Marks. Barnet Lewis, who impressed Kimberley with his daily gallops through the mining camp on a striking white mount, was taken in by Sammy and Isaac as their third partner. Joseph Marks, Joseph Lewis and Ellia Marks set up their own shortlived partnership of Lewis and Marks Junior. While they were never formally part of the senior partnership, they were extensively aided by their older siblings, for the *shtetl*'s emphasis on family solidarity held sway as much in Africa as it had in Russia.[16]

The Marks and Lewis brothers were part of a sizeable Jewish contingent on the diamond fields. Unlike Sammy, Isaac and their kin, who had come from Eastern Europe, the majority of these Jews were of German or English origin. The great Russian Jewish exodus was only to commence in the next decade. By the mid-seventies Marks and his co-religionists had established a congregation and had built a 400-seat synagogue which they crowded only on the High Holidays. For the rest Marks and his fellow Jewish pioneers on the diamond fields practised a diluted orthodoxy: the central observance of the Jewish faith, the holy Sabbath, was, a Kimberley pioneer recalls, 'rarely observed with any strictness'.[17]

Kimberley and Neustadt were not only at a great spiritual remove, but also at a great physical remove. The diamond fields could not have seemed less like Marks's birthplace. The nearest river, the Vaal, was leagues away, while the surrounding countryside was sear and treeless. Visiting in October 1877, the novelist Anthony Trollope found Kimberley 'a most detestable place'. Though it was not yet high summer temperatures soared during his stay to 96 in the shade and 160 in the sun. The landscape was droughtstricken and quite bare: 'I do not think that there is a tree to be seen within five miles of the town,' he complained, '. . . I doubt whether there was a blade of grass within twenty miles. Everything was brown. . . .' Trollope gagged on 'an atmosphere of dust and flies . . . of dust so thick that the sufferer fears to remove it lest the raising of it may aggravate the evil, and of flies so numerous that one hardly dares to slaughter them by the ordinary means lest the dead bodies should be noisome.' The locals told him with masochistic pride that the flies and dust were worse still in mid-summer, December through February.[18]

All this Marks and his kinsmen stoically endured in search of their fortunes. In the mid-seventies the two partnerships, Lewis and Marks Senior and Lewis and Marks Junior, began to invest heavily, like other Kimberley diamond merchants, in diamond mining, which seemed to offer a better rate of return in the long term than simply trading. Sammy and Isaac had bought their first mining claims as early as 1872, but had been prevented from adding to these at the time by a regulation which placed a strict limit on claim ownership of two per digger. As the Kimberley mine had gone deeper, this restriction became increasingly unworkable. With hundreds of diggers pressing upon each other in the confined space of the mine, an anarchic situation had arisen. Diggers constantly encroached upon one another's pocket-sized claims; the roadways separating these began to collapse as the claims beneath them grew deeper; and water accumulated in the depths of the mine. If the Kimberley mine was to be worked in a rational fashion, if expensive machinery was to be introduced, if capital was to be invested, the restriction on claim ownership had to go.[19]

Though there were some who hoped to keep the Kimberley mine a small man's diggings, economic necessity won the day. The restriction was eased in 1874, when claimholders were allowed ten claims apiece, and then finally removed in 1876, opening the way to substantial capital investment in the mine and to the aggregation of sizeable claimholdings. Once the restriction was lifted, Lewis and Marks, and the other diamond merchants who had accumulated capital through trading in rough stones, began speculating feverishly in claims on the Kimberley mine. Spectacular capital gains were possible through buying and selling; besides, investment in production seemed to promise a better rate of return than trading. In the first quarter of 1877, for example, soon after the removal of the restriction, Lewis and Marks spent close to £20,000 on claims. Much of this was the profit they had made from selling other claims to Jules Porges, a London diamond merchant, who was amongst the first major overseas investors in the diamond fields.[20]

The net effect of the lifting of the restriction, and of the speculative investment by the diamond merchants, was to concentrate ownership of the claims on the Kimberley mine. The number of claimholders fell from 1,600 in 1872, when Lewis and Marks acquired their first claims, to 300 in 1877. Fewer than twenty claimholders controlled over half these claims, while four, the Lewis and Marks partnership, the Paddon brothers, Jules Porges and J. B. Robinson, owned a quarter of the mine between them.[21]

Lewis and Marks and the Paddon brothers, Samuel and William, young and successful diamond merchants like Isaac and Sammy, combined their claims to form the Kimberley Mining Company, one of the earliest mining companies on the fields. An unlimited company, it was described by the Standard Bank in 1877 as a 'well managed concern' which paid 'handsomely'. The Paddons held half of its capital of £82,000, Lewis and Marks the remainder. By 1879 its capital had been increased to £200,000 (of which Lewis and Marks still held half), and it was now producing an average of £1,000 of diamonds per week, equal to an annual gross return on capital of over 25 per cent. Early in the year, Sam Paddon and Barnet Lewis went to England and negotiated their company's merger with the claims that Jules Porges held in the Kimberley mine.[22]

Porges, who had strong connections in both English and French financial circles, floated the new combined company, the Compagnie Française des Mines du Diamants du Cap, in Paris at the end of the year. A joint stock company with a nominal capital of fourteen million francs or £560,000, it was the largest mining concern in Africa, holding nearly one quarter of the richest diamond mine on the Cape diamond fields and, indeed, in the world.[23] The 'French Company' was the first South African diamond mining company to be placed before the investing public in Europe. Its flotation was a great success, and by mid-1880 its shares were trading freely at a high premium over their issue price . This prompted many other claimholders on the diamond fields to follow suit: claims were converted into joint stock companies with heady abandon, and the shares offered to excited investors, caught up in a 'share mania'. By early 1881 some 66 companies had been launched, with a total nominal capitalisation of well over seven million pounds, a figure out of all proportion to the inherent value of the shares, for, unlike the French Company, many of these new concerns were simply 'swindles'.[24]

During the 'share mania', Lewis and Marks off-loaded a large part of their holding in the French Company on Cape Town and Kimberley buyers, and promptly reinvested their gains in further speculation, largely on the diamond fields, but also in the Transvaal, Free State and the Cape. The Standard Bank considered them 'about the most wealthy firm on the Fields'. The partners were 'shrewd and careful men' who 'have been amongst the most successful people on the Fields'. They 'had a considerable interest in nearly every good thing which has been floated in connection with the Mines here', and were worth at least £300,000. Marks was the wealthiest of the partners: 'he cannot be worth less than £150,000.'[25]

With an ironic symmetry, Lewis and Marks invested a substantial part of their profits from the sale of shares to Cape investors, in property at Cape Town. With a view to its future development, they bought land in the rapidly growing suburb on the slopes of the mountain immediately above the city. Their prize purchase was Leeuwenhof, a gracious if run-down Cape Dutch homestead, which was assigned later to Isaac Lewis when the partners decided to divide their Cape holdings. [26]

Most of their profits were reinvested, though, on the diamond fields. Lewis and Marks transferred their attentions from the Kimberley mine to one of its lesser satellites, the Dutoitspan mine, some two miles east of the Big Hole. Though it had been discovered shortly before the Kimberley mine, it had not developed at anything like the same pace during the 1870s. While some of the most valuable stones were buried in Dutoitspan, there was not the same abundance as at the Kimberley mine. 'Nature', a modern scholar writes, 'was generous to Dutoitspan in quality but it was miserly in quantity.' But this was no obstacle during the 'share mania' of 1880–1. Speculators, like Lewis and Marks, who had made large profits by selling their stakes in the Kimberley mine, were on the *qui vive* for fresh opportunities for speculative gain. The neglected Dutoitspan mine, with its undeveloped and apparently underpriced claims, seemed one of these.[27]

Lewis and Marks, and other Kimberley investors, bought heavily at Dutoitspan in 1880–1, pushing up the prices of claims astronomically. By February 1881, the partners had already invested over £200,000 in a mine they hoped would soon rival the Big Hole. As a token of their hopes, they resurrected the Kimberley Mining Company at Dutoitspan, this time as a private company with a nominal capital of £200,000, of which £70,000 was paid up by late 1881. Their other interests at Dutoitspan included the inaptly titled Phoenix company and the Incorporated company; the latter was split in two in 1881 and refloated in London as the Anglo–African, with a bloated capitalisation of £650,000, second highest on the diamond fields, and as the more modest Anglo–French company.[28]

The practical supervision of these mining interests was left to Sammy Marks, when on account of the diamond boom the partners decided to reorganise their operations. Isaac Lewis, who had a flair for finance, was sent to England to set up a London office to handle company promotion and share trading; Barnet Lewis, dour and unimaginative, remained behind in Kimberley and took charge of the firm's original activity of diamond buying, now greatly reduced in importance; Sammy Marks, physically energetic and the most practically minded of the partners, took on the management of the Kimberley Mining Company and general responsibility for the firm's interests at Dutoitspan. He also undertook the development of the firm's new interests beyond the diamond fields.

The most important of these lay 230 miles to the north, on the banks of the Vaal River. Some four years before, in December 1876, the government of the

Orange Free State (caught up in the general excitement about South Africa's hidden riches) had commissioned George William Stow, a self-taught geologist, pioneering copyist of rock art and ethnologist of the San, and failed businessman, to conduct a geological survey of its northern districts. In 1878, after almost a year of exploration, Stow had arrived at the confluence of the Taaibosspruit with the Vaal River, opposite today's Vanderbijlpark. Spotting an outcrop of coal, he sank a 24-foot shaft and struck a solid seam, some 15½ feet thick. Further test sinkings a few miles to the east convinced him that he had found a major coal-field, rivalling earlier discoveries in Natal and the Eastern Cape.

Stow's employers in Bloemfontein were less impressed. What they had hoped to discover were precious metals and minerals, not a remote coal-field a couple of hundred miles from the nearest possible market. Stow's contract was not renewed. For a while he busied himself in Bloemfontein with his magnum opus on the San and his pioneering collection of rock art, and then left for Kimberley, where he and Sammy Marks met.[29]

Unlike the government of the Free State, Marks was very excited about Stow's discovery. As a mine manager, he was painfully aware of the high cost of fuel on the diamond fields. The introduction of large numbers of steam engines on the mines since the late 1870s had meant that Griqualand West, and a wide swath of territory beyond, were stripped of their trees, driving up the price of firewood to prohibitive levels, so much so that by the early 1880s fuel constituted as much as 30 per cent of the total working costs of the diamond companies. It seemed to Marks that if coal could be brought to Kimberley at a competitive price, the suppliers would profit handsomely. Cheap coal would obviously be a popular substitute for expensive wood.[30]

Lewis and Marks rounded up a weighty consortium of investors to acquire and exploit the coal-bearing farms Stow had discovered. These included the prominent local diamond merchants and claimholders Thomas Lynch and Samuel Paddon, the Parisian brokers Herz, Fils et Compagnie, the wealthy Anglo–French diamond merchant and company promoter Jules Porges, as well as his partner Julius Wernher. In 1880 they formed the South African and Orange Free State Coal and Mineral Mining Association, a private partnership with a nominal capital of £75,000. As the discoverer, George Stow was allotted 10 of the 75 shares, while shares went as well to Marks's younger brothers, Ellia and Joseph. Sammy was always very much the concerned older brother.[31]

Stow was sent back to the Vaal coal-field to buy up promising farms. During 1881 he and John Fraser, a one-time ship's doctor turned influential Bloemfontein lawyer, bought a large bloc of properties on both the Free State and Transvaal banks of the river. These ranged in price from the considerable sum of £15,500 paid to the old Voortrekker 'Kwaai Augus' Pistorius for the farm Klipplaatdrift, to the bargain price of £310 (£60 down) paid for Klipfontein to a Boer who urgently needed just this sum to pay a creditor.[32]

Two white miners followed Stow in April 1881, with a wagon-load of tools and supplies and instructions to forward a trial consignment of coal to

Kimberley. Marks was very optimistic about the prospects: 'I myself have the
same belief in it', he wrote to Julius Wernher, 'as I had with the Kimberley Mine,
though the profits may be a little smaller and we may have to wait a little longer
for returns, but come they must.' He calculated that even if the coal cost £2 a ton
to mine and £8 to freight to Kimberley by ox-wagon, the Association would still
make a reasonable profit on the transaction, for he had already been offered as
much as £15 a ton by the French Company, the leading concern in the Kimberley
mine.[33]

In August 1881 Marks paid his first visit to the region which was to be his
stamping-ground for the rest of his career. During his stay, he made personal
contacts and conceived ideas which were to shape his life for at least the next two
decades. He left Kimberley on the 1st, in the company of Jerôme Dumont, a
Parisian visitor to the diamond fields, who represented a syndicate of French
banks in search of investment opportunities in South Africa. Marks took him
along on the trip, hoping to interest him and his principals in the new coal
venture. After a six-day journey, Marks and Dumont arrived at their remote
destination, the Vaal River coal-fields, to find that George Stow, 'an old
gentleman' nearing 60, who had been forced to sleep under a bucksail
throughout the Highveld winter, was desperately ill. Marks sent him at once by
wagon to Kroonstad, some 85 miles away, to see a physician.

While waiting for him to recover and return to show them around the
property, Marks and Dumont decided to visit Pretoria. Here, once again, Marks
arrived at a critical historical juncture. Only the week before, British and Boer
representatives had met to sign a convention which formally concluded the
short, sharp struggle that restored the Transvaal Republic's independence,
snatched away by Britain four years before. Founded by the Voortrekkers, who
had first crossed the Vaal River in the late 1830s, the Republic had struggled
through decades of political division and economic bankruptcy before succumb-
ing tamely to the British in a bloodless coup in 1877. The humiliation of
annexation had roused the Boers from their lethargy, and led by Paul Kruger
they had first protested peacefully, then taken up arms in December 1880,
inflicting a stinging defeat on the British in February 1881 at Majuba. The
Pretoria Convention, signed just days before Sammy Marks's arrival, formally
resurrected the Boer Republic.

The declared purpose of Sammy's visit to Pretoria was to make practical
arrangements for the Vaal River coal estates. The mine's most pressing need was
wagon transport for its coal. Marks was referred to Fox, the contractor who had
supplied all government transport needs during the British administration; he
agreed to provide at least 200 wagons to run between the coal-fields and
Kimberley once he had surveyed the route and decided on his tariff. The mine
also needed durable, water-resistant timber for its shafts and underground
galleries. Since there was nothing suitable within a radius of 120 miles of the
fields, Marks arranged for a trial consignment of boekenhout (South African
beech) from the Pretoria district. At the same time he applied to the government
for nothing less than the indigenous forests of the Transvaal. While his
audacious offer to buy these was turned down because the government was

reluctant to alienate a public resource which it reckoned was worth hundreds of thousands of pounds, his investigation into the local supply of wood might well have been the genesis of the grand scheme of afforestation he later implemented on the Vaal River in the 1890s.[34]

The undeclared purpose of the Pretoria visit was to look into the possibilities for doing business in the Republic. Both Lewis and Marks had felt for some time that once peace was restored, the Transvaal, with its virtually untapped mineral and agricultural potential, would be a very rewarding field for speculative investment. With this in mind, Marks approached the Boer leaders while he was in Pretoria and explained that he was eager to invest in their country as he believed that it had a great future. Paul Kruger, nineteen years older than Sammy and soon to be elected president of the restored Republic, seems to have formed a favourable impression of his visitor, and promised that as long as he kept faith with the Republic, he could rely on government support and protection for his ventures. After a decent interval, discussion inevitably strayed beyond the strictly official. Kruger, a shrewd and successful land speculator, and, like his guest, a man with a keen eye for opportunity, offered to sell Marks Vyffontein, a farm he owned close to the Coal Association's Vaal River holdings. Eager to please, Marks promised that Stow would examine the ground and make an offer.[35]

During his stay in Pretoria Marks had one other encounter of special significance for the future. He was approached by a Hungarian gentleman, whose name he had some difficulty grasping (Marks refers to him successively as Mappings, Nelmapalus and Nelmapus), who offered him a partnership in a liquor concession he proposed to obtain from the Transvaal government. Marks must have been quite taken with the idea, for once Alois Hugo Nellmapius – a Hungarian Jewish adventurer who had made his way to the Pilgrim's Rest gold-fields in the early seventies and had subsequently endeared himself to Kruger – had actually secured the concession some two months later, Marks invited him to Kimberley to discuss a possible deal.[36]

Nellmapius would have been one of the few Jews Marks would have met in Pretoria. The Jewish population of the Boer capital was minuscule compared to Kimberley's and as yet there was no organised Jewish communal life. Pretoria had less than half the general population of Kimberley. It was a small town of single-storeyed buildings, of vacant lots and of unmade roads which turned into slush when it rained. It was a remote outpost, far from the commercial centres of the coast. Its links with the outside world were a telegraph line built during the British occupation and a weekly mail coach from Kimberley. The arrival of the coach was the most exciting event of the week. The second most exciting event, according to a friend of Sammy Marks, was the daily gathering on Church Square to watch the time-ball – erected by the British on a tall pole on top of a nearby hill – drop at noon. 'Watches were adjusted and the excitement for the day was over.' Many of the excited onlookers would have been English or German or Hollander. Though it was the capital of the restored Boer Republic, its commercial, cultural and professional life was dominated by Uitlanders. Merchants like Thomas Beckett – later a good friend and business associate of Sammy Marks – and Edmund Bourke served on its fledgling town council and formed its chamber of commerce. They and their fellow Uitlanders were the mainstays of the capital's cultural and social life. Despite its remoteness, Pretoria had all the conveniences of Victorian small-town life – a gentleman's club (predecessor of the Pretoria Club); a turf club; a public library, open from 4 to 8 p.m. daily except on Wednesdays, which charged an annual subscription of £1; a botanical garden, 176 acres in extent; a masonic lodge (which would have welcomed Marks who had joined a lodge in Kimberley); and two newspapers – the thrice-weekly *Transvaal Argus* and *De Volksstem* which appeared alternatively in English and Dutch. Marks would have stayed in one of Pretoria's three small hotels – the European (which advertised its 'good stabling' and 'attentive groom'), the Royal ('The Best Liquors Billiards . . . Stables') or possibly the Edinburgh.

Marks must have found Pretoria an oasis after the harshness and heat of Kimberley. The verdant Transvaal capital with its pleasant climate would have made the same favourable impression on him as it had on Anthony Trollope some four years before. Pretoria was 'both picturesque and promising', the English novelist had written. 'Down many of the streets of the town . . . little rivulets flow, adding much to the fertility of the gardens and to the feeling of salubrity. . . . The town gardens are large, fertile and productive. . . . The streets are broad and well laid out, with a fine square in the centre . . . . Perhaps the most peculiar feature of the place is the roses. There are everywhere hedges of roses, hedges which are all roses, – not wild roses but our roses of the garden though generally less sweet to the smell. And with the roses, there are everywhere weeping willows, mourning gracefully over the hitherto unaccomplished aspirations of the country.'[37]

Marks was more positive about the prospects of the Transvaal than the earlier visitor. After thoroughly exploring Pretoria's possibilities, Marks and Dumont, his French travelling companion and potential backer, set off once more for the Vaal River. The route between Pretoria and the coal-fields ran across the Witwatersrand, a sparsely populated farming district of little apparent consequence. While travelling through it, Marks passed up an opportunity he was later to regret profoundly. He was offered all of a farm called Driefontein for what was even then a trifling sum, a mere £800. As Marks was about to close the deal, Dumont intervened. 'Oh! you have got ground enough already!' he carped. Good-naturedly, Marks deferred to Dumont's judgement and so, unwittingly, threw away a golden chance to take possession of a lengthy section of the Witwatersrand Main Reef which straddled the farm. 'Do you think', he exploded years later, 'I could get that farm for £800 today? No!!!'[38]

Arriving again at the coal-fields, Marks found that Stow had not yet returned, and that, annoyingly, the two white miners had not completed the four trial shafts he had instructed them to sink at varying distances from the river during his absence in Pretoria. Only one had been finished, but it was enough to convince Marks that this was a coal deposit 'sufficient . . . to last South Africa for 50 and perhaps 100 years'. Marks was not exaggerating; the property, the first coal mine on the Highveld, is still being mined today. 'As far as the banks of the river are concerned, from end to end of our property coals are creeping out . . .,' he later reported. In the one completed shaft a layer of coal 6¹/₂ feet thick had been struck only 23 feet beneath the surface; elsewhere Marks saw a seam which was all of 13 feet thick. The shallow depth and thickness of these seams, characteristic features of the Highveld's coal deposits, meant that the cost of extraction would be significantly lower than in the much deeper British pits.

Before leaving, Marks measured out ground for two buildings to be constructed with the copious local stone. One was a store: the sight of the mining material he had sent from Kimberley lying all over the veld offended his love of order. The other was an office and dormitory for the three white employees. 'I found it was impossible', he reported, 'for any European to live in a tent up there in that climate.' Marks had Stow in mind. On the way home he stopped off at Kroonstad to visit his ailing manager, and was informed by the doctor that 'if he got over it, it would be a very narrow escape indeed'. While in the dorp, Marks also made arrangements to recruit labour for the mine. An agent was hired to 'entice' all the blacks he could, 'even if they all don't work for the Association, so as to make the location as large as possible'.

Marks's return to Kimberley after this trail-blazing tour was delayed for three days through 'very heavy weather', which made the rough roads of the Free State impassable. This was only one of a series of trials that Marks and Dumont, like other travellers in the interior, had to endure. Their wagon broke down twice and had to be repaired at the roadside. They were also forced to buy a horse at an inflated price when their mule collapsed and died.[39]

On his return Marks reported to a meeting of the Association in Kimberley and wrote to its members in Paris and London. Having now seen the coal-fields, his enthusiasm was quite unbounded. This was 'a splendid speculation', indeed 'one of the finest in South Africa', ranking alongside mighty Kimberley itself. 'I think if it is followed up, it will perhaps turn out a little better than diamond mining,' he wrote; 'if it were in Europe it would be worth as much as half of the Kimberley mine today.'[40]

This was not merely hyperbole to excite his chief investors; Marks was willing, in fact eager, to back his judgement with his own money. He urged Lewis to sell off part of their holdings on the diamond fields and reinvest instead in the coal-fields, arguing that if a further £50,000 or £60,000 were invested over and above the purchase price of the farms, the venture 'would pay A1' – and not only because of the coal it would sell.

There are several things which could be made, provided the money be laid out, as for instance, as much paraffin could be made as would supply the whole country, tar also, and all kinds of iron work. Besides this within a radius of 40 miles of our property we could get grain very cheap, viz:- mealies, wheat and potatoes at less than one half of the prices ruling in Cape Town. If so don't you think a good distillery for making spirits would pay for fire and water would cost you nothing you may say, and you would be in the very centre of the country for the articles required. You may think this rather a foolish idea, but before you commence laughing at it ask someone if it is so very absurd.[41]

Meanwhile though, there was a major obstacle that had to be overcome first if the coal-fields were to achieve their full potential. Coal is a very bulky, low-value commodity; if it is to be marketed profitably, cheap and plentiful transport is essential. And here, of course, lay the rub: the coal-fields were all of 230 miles from their intended market, Kimberley, and the only means of transport available at the time was the ox-wagon which was ill-suited to the task. It was both expensive and unreliable, and its availability depended on the whim of its farmer-owner and, beyond that, on the weather and the state of the veld. While transport would be plentiful during the Highveld summer, it could not be relied upon during the dry Highveld winter when grazing for the oxen would be sparse.

As a child of the railway age, Marks's solution was to build a tram or railway connection between the diamond fields and the coal mine, a very ambitious scheme given that neither Kimberley nor Bloemfontein, deep in the interior of the country, was connected yet by rail with the coast. If the Orange Free State could be persuaded to grant a concession and financial support, a line could be built linking Kimberley with Bloemfontein, and then running on via Winburg, Kroonstad and Heilbron to the Transvaal. In discussion with Dumont, a figure of no less than £1,500,000 was tossed around as the likely outlay, but Marks felt confident that this would yield a return of more than 6 per cent per annum. 'You may think', he wrote to Isaac Lewis, 'I am taking very great views on the question and no doubt you are right, but when one travels together with a man like Du Mont, who says he represents 6 or 8 bankers in Europe, one can't help falling into many of his views to some extent.' The success of the railway would be guaranteed by Kimberley's apparently insatiable appetite for fuel. Should the line be constructed, Marks wrote to Lewis some time later, 'then we are the masters of the fuel of Griqualand West and you know yourself that fuel is a very very big item. . . .'[42]

Marks's ambitions went still further. A railway connection would need iron rails, and so would the colliery. He knew that imported rails cost as much as £40 a ton at Kimberley because of heavy transport charges, and that if these were brought on to the Vaal by ox-wagon, the cost would become quite prohibitive. Reports of an iron-ore deposit a mere ten miles from the coal mine gave him an inspiration: why not establish a foundry at the Vaal to produce pig iron 'on the spot', which could then be used for manufacturing inexpensive rails? For between £50,000 and £80,000 an iron works of the sort he had seen in Sheffield in his youth could be erected on the Free State–Transvaal border; this would be ideally placed to supply the growing inland market with iron, 'which is the most important article South Africa wants after water'. Even if the firm lacked sufficient capital at present to finance this exciting venture, there would surely be little difficulty in persuading English manufacturers to provide the additional funds. Marks had estimates prepared by Robey and Company, a Lincoln firm that supplied much of his mining equipment, and was encouraged by these. The figures seemed to suggest that the project was not only viable, but would be 'very cheap'. He was not to know that Vaal River coal was unsuitable for metallurgical purposes, and that the nearest economically viable iron deposit, as yet undiscovered, lay many miles distant.[43]

But before Marks could do anything about these grand schemes, he had to grapple with the more immediate difficulties facing the firm's diamond-mining interests in Dutoitspan. The 'share mania' had petered out by the middle of 1881, leaving mine managements dangerously exposed. The new companies floated during the boom were desperately short of working capital. Company promoters had spent heavily on buying inflated claims and on ordering the latest steam-driven machinery, but had made inadequate provision for meeting development and running expenses. The new companies lacked the financial reserves needed to tide them over any difficulties that might occur. The collapse of the share market in June 1881, and the consequent evaporation of investor confidence in diamond shares, made it impossible to go back to the market for additional capital. Local investors had been very badly shaken, and in any case were now very hard-up, while foreign investors who had previously toyed with the idea of a flutter on the diamond mines were frightened off.

The over-rapid expansion of diamond production as a result of the creation of a myriad of new companies and of investment in the poorer mines had brought in its train other problems as well. It had greatly increased the demand for labour, which had inevitably pushed up wages and working costs; similarly, it had also increased demand for fuel, confronting companies with soaring fuel costs which they were financially ill-equipped to absorb. Then there were the perennial problems of the diamond fields: illicit diamond buying (IDB) and the poverty of the satellite mines.

Try as he might, Marks could not raise the level of productivity of the firm's holdings in the Dutoitspan mines to a satisfactory level: 'if they are not there, I cannot go and place them there . . . ,' he rebuked his partners, when they complained about the meagre yield of diamonds from their Dutoitspan claims. Marks, like other mine managers, laid most of the blame for this on diamond theft. Diamond theft and illicit diamond buying were, in the words of a contemporary, 'the custom of the country'. Like poaching in eighteenth-century England or speeding on the modern motorway, it was a widely practised 'popular' crime, winked at by many, the obvious exceptions being those who were its victims. Marks estimated that as much as one-third of the white population of the diamond fields engaged in the illicit trade, and that diamond theft was rife throughout the workforce: 'not one in twenty overseers in all the Mines is honest,' he complained. 'The Kaffirs now don't seem to trouble much about the small diamonds[;] they are beginning to go for the big ones.'[44]

The losses to the diamond-mining companies, possibly more than a third of their total yield Marks suspected, were clearly unsustainable, particularly at a time when companies were barely profitable. The solutions Marks proposed to the problem and to the related issues of labour control and costs, ranged from a new and startling dress code for his black workers who either worked naked or in a special (presumably pocketless) garment that he designed, through far-reaching changes in the law, to a radical restructuring of the workforce.[45]

Marks felt that the law needed drastic amendment. As it stood, convictions were difficult to secure, while the recovery of stolen diamonds was very troublesome as Marks discovered when he struggled to repossess a 461 carat giant, equivalent to a week's dividends, which had been pilfered from the Kimberley Mining Company. Marks and the other mine-owners were against trial by jury for diamond offences. Given the permissive popular view of illicit diamond buying, the state would be hard put to secure a conviction from a jury of the accused's peers. Marks and his colleagues also believed that the burden of proof in diamond cases should be shifted from the state to the accused, a complete reversal of a basic principle of English law.[46]

Marks, always an innovative manager, also considered ways of reshaping the workforce to ensure a constant supply of labour and to curb diamond theft. One possibility was to substitute white unskilled labour for black. Marks had experimented with this in mid-1881 when black labour was almost unobtainable, but had found the results very disappointing. 'I engaged fifty white men as labourers, but it would not answer, they worked one day and got drunk the next. You can always depend on the Kafirs.' When the idea was revived later on by John X. Merriman, the Cape politician, Marks objected on the grounds of expense and of labour discipline: 'white labour . . . would not be practicable. 1st because it is impossible for Europeans to live here on 30/- per week be he ever so rough and common. 2nd because it is impossible to keep down Europeans in the same way that you can the natives.' White labour would expect at least £4 a week, and at that rate of pay, 'you might just as well close up the diggings.'[47]

The ultimate solution, Marks felt, to both the labour and the IDB problems was to recruit a new workforce of 8,000–10,000 men in China. Not only would the scheme cut the cost of labour by 50–75 per cent, but it would also guarantee the participating companies 'a steady and constant supply of labor [sic] all the year round', instead of the wildly fluctuating supply of the present, where 'for a couple of months you are perhaps overstocked with Boys, and then for the next 3 or 4 months you cannot get a sufficient supply to carry on your works.' Crucially, the scheme would also protect the companies against diamond theft. Opportunities to pass on stolen diamonds would be minimised. On recruitment the Chinese labourers 'must be made to understand that they will be treated as soldiers are, that is to live in barracks, to be marched to and from the barracks to work, in working clothes, which would be afterwards laid aside.' The barracks would be linked directly with the mines and would be guarded by white constables.

State support was vital if the scheme, which anticipated the closed compound system introduced later in the decade, was to be given effect. If the diamond mines were to secure this stable, cheap, and regimented workforce, the government would have to guarantee that the Chinese 'would be kept in check'. Marks was hopeful that the government would agree. But state support was never solicited. Though Marks felt the scheme 'a very feasible idea', it was never put to the test: fearing that 'Chinese labour would be very troublesome', his partners vetoed the proposal. Had it been implemented, it might have had far-reaching consequences not only for the shaping of the South African mining industry, but of the society at large. A successful experiment with Chinese labour at Kimberley in the early 1880s might have substantially altered the way in which the Rand mining industry met its labour requirements in the 1890s. It might have persuaded the Randlords to draw on Chinese labour at this early stage rather than rely on large-scale black labour migrancy. The social and economic consequences of such a decision would have been profound.[48]

Besides replacing black with Chinese, Marks also proposed substituting a fresh batch of British and Continental workmen for the mines' existing overseers and artisans. As he complained bitterly, 'all the white overseers are lazy, and take no interest in the work as they used to do, some of them even trying to steal the diamonds'. It was 'impossible to get more than one half of the work we used to get from skilled workmen'. Marks sensed correctly that this was tied up in some way with the shift from individual claimholding to company ownership of the mines. 'The chief reason', he suggested, for the workmen's reluctant performance of their duties, 'is that all the ground is now the property of Companies. . . .' What he was encountering, it appears, was the resentment of men who had recently been claimholders themselves, or at least independent contractors, and who were now reacting against their reduction in status to employees.

Marks's solution was to import honest British workmen, for whom he, like many of his colonial contemporaries, had a high if somewhat exaggerated regard. After an encouraging discussion in late 1881 with John X. Merriman, the most effective member of the Cape ministry, who promised state support, Marks arranged assisted passage for 37 Cornish miners to the Cape, free rail tickets to the diamond fields, and company housing and medical care when they arrived in Kimberley. The experiment was anything but a success. At first Marks was prepared to give Cousin Jack the benefit of the doubt. 'The Cornishmen sent out have proved rather troublesome,' he wrote after two months of service, 'but no doubt they will get broken in, in time.' Within a month of this, though, his Kimberley Mining Company had run out of patience. No further Cornish overseers were to be sent out, the company secretary instructed. 'It will be a good thing for the KMC when their time is up. There is every week three or four sick, and with two or three exceptions, for supervisors, they are useless.'[49]

In late 1881, Marks received a welcome distraction from all his Kimberley difficulties. Two months after his first visit to the Transvaal he received a wire from the Hungarian gentleman who had approached him in Pretoria about establishing a distillery in the Republic. Alois Hugo Nellmapius had now obtained a concession from the government and was eager to deal.[50]

Despite his transparent lack of means – Nellmapius was chronically hard-up – he had been awarded a concession on very attractive terms. In its eagerness to promote the development of what it knew was no more than an economic backwater, the Transvaal government was willing to grant very generous terms to prospective industrial investors and to overlook their lack of solid credentials. Nellmapius was awarded the exclusive right for a fifteen-year period, from 1882 to 1897, to produce liquor from grain, potatoes and other locally grown products, with the exception of 'treefruits' and grapes. No government would dare interfere with the Boer's sacred right to distil *mampoer* or firewater! Nellmapius was required to exercise the right without delay. A distillery would have to be up and running by July 1882; failure to meet this deadline would mean forgoing a deposit of £1,000. Beyond this the state demanded very little: the concessionaire would have to pay an annual fee of £1,000 but would be exempted from any further taxation, the state surrendering the right to impose excise duties on the distillery's products. To sweeten the deal still further, the government also threw in the exclusive right to produce sugar from mealies, kaffircorn, sugarbeet and other local products, with the exception of sugar-cane which, like fruit, was excluded to protect Boer cottage industry. To ensure the saleability of the concession, Nellmapius was given explicit permission to take partners; these he now came down to Kimberley to recruit.[51]

Marks was certainly attracted, yet he hesitated. Nellmapius seemed such a slippery fellow, 'able to talk and say what is not quite the truth'. Besides, Marks felt so ignorant about the distilling business and Barnet Lewis, the partner resident in Kimberley, was so discouraging. With some reluctance Marks decided to 'let it slip', warning his partners that 'it may be we have lost a good thing'.[52]

Undiscouraged, Nellmapius and an equally dubious associate, Edward Cohen, an English Jew who later became a Portuguese peer, the Viscount Matalha, returned to the Transvaal to continue their hunt for government concessions. 'I believe their intentions', Marks wrote, 'are to get about a million and a half of concessions from Government for anything from making a needle to an 80 ton boat to go down the Vaal River as far as Barkly!!! Powder they are going to make for government, . . . a tramway *pro bono publico*, and iron for a Railway to go right and left of the country, weaving factories for the wool etc. . . . if it please God all these things should succeed, I think the Transvaal will be able to export more goods than the whole of Great Britain.' Shortly after their departure, Marks sent a message to the Transvaal government not to grant too many concessions to any single individual or firm; this, he warned, would deter other investors.[53]

Despite his scepticism about Nellmapius, Marks – a risk-taker and entrepreneur to his core – found the liquor proposition irresistible, and within a month had reversed his decision and taken the concession under offer, at the same time advancing Nellmapius the not insignificant sum of £2,000, to Isaac Lewis's consternation.[54]

In December 1881 Nellmapius left for England to make further arrangements with Isaac Lewis, the firm's financial expert. By the same mailship, Marks sent a warning to his partner to remain calm, however irritated he might be by his loquacious visitor. 'Nellmapius . . . is a gentleman who talks a great deal, and I may say more than a great deal, and has put me out of patience many times with talking so much, therefore I warn you not to take any notice of it. I think as well as others he has a very good business in hand.' A while later, a second caution followed: 'as far as management goes . . . I have no doubt that you have arranged it that it shall all rest with us, so that this gentleman will have no control over anything.'[55]

This proved impossible. Nellmapius insisted on taking part in the direction of the new concern, which was to be a partnership between himself and Lewis and Marks. A third would belong to Nellmapius, two-thirds to Lewis and Marks; the latter would provide the cash while Nellmapius would chip in his concession. Nellmapius also insisted that the works be established at Hatherley, a farm he had recently acquired some eleven miles east of Pretoria. Marks had hoped that the distillery would be part of the industrial complex he dreamed of establishing on the Vaal River coal-fields.[56]

While Lewis and Nellmapius negotiated in England, Marks continued his struggle with the partners' failing Kimberley operations. 'I am so busy digging all day so have no time for much else,' he wrote in late 1881; 'there is only 10 working hours in a day and in digging there is so much to look after.' The demands on a manager's attention at Dutoitspan were almost too much for a single individual:

If a head manager sees if each working man is in his proper place, and does his work in a proper manner and sees that no labour is wasted, and trys [sic] to get as much out of each man as the Company pays for, besides seeing that all the machinery is in proper working order, I am certain he has not time to do all this once in a day because a day has only 10 working hours. Now if there is a little office work to do besides, stores and cattle to look over, and to see that the Overseers do not try to keep the diamonds found in the Claims for themselves, and to plan out what shall be done tomorrow or in a week, and writing reports to the Board, then I say it is impossible for one to do it all.[57]

Little wonder then that when Marks reordered boots from England in late 1881, he instructed his bootmakers to allow more room for his corns![58]

Under severe strain at work, Marks found the Kimberley summer of 1881–2 particularly oppressive. 'Hot weather is not agreeable even if you are used to it,' he grumbled; 'I don't want to have to run about next summer in the Mine as I cannot stand it. This summer I have not yet had a week's good health. . . .' Shortly after reporting that sickness was rife in the mining town (many were down with the ubiquitous 'camp fever') he himself succumbed. For a fortnight in March 1882 he lay dangerously ill, while his brother Joe deputised at the Kimberley Mining Company. When, in early April, he had passed through the worst of the crisis, he left to convalesce in Cape Town, presumably on doctor's orders: Kimberley physicians then believed that a spell at the seaside was the best way of ensuring a complete return to health. [59]

Marks's stay at the Royal Hotel was less restful than he had hoped. It coincided, quite fortuitously, with the convening of a parliamentary select committee on ways and means of combating the illicit diamond traffic. This was chaired by the 29-year-old member for Barkly West, Cecil John Rhodes. Nine years Sammy's junior, he had arrived on the diamond fields at much the same time, and like him, had rapidly built a speculative fortune, which he – unlike Sammy, who had no political ambition – now hoped to convert into political power. As a director and manager of a string of mining companies and, by repute, one of the wealthiest men in Kimberley, Marks was Rhodes's star witness – a spokesman for mining capital at Kimberley.

Rhodes carefully led Marks through his lengthy testimony. Drawing on extensive personal experience, Marks provided graphic evidence of the depredations of the illicit diamond traffic which he warned would be the 'ruination' of Kimberley. Ever practical, he tabled a series of draconian measures that he, and his fellow mine-owners, believed would curb the traffic. Bolstered by the telling testimony of Sammy and other witnesses, Rhodes's select committee recommended 'exceptional and stringent legislation' against IDB. This took the form of the Diamond Trade Act of 1882, a far-reaching measure which, as Marks had suggested, placed the onus of proof on the accused while providing for trial without jury and for banishment from the diamond fields. In the wake of this Act, and the appointment of additional detectives, the much-hated trap system, which Sammy had staunchly defended before the committee, was practised more vigorously than ever. But closed compounds, the panacea proposed by Marks and the mining industry for their IDB and labour control problems, came only in the mid-decade, by which time his interest in the Kimberley diamond industry had waned.[60]

As matters turned out, Marks's testimony before Rhodes's select committee in April 1882 was his swansong as a Kimberley mining man. Illness and his stay in Cape Town gave him an opportunity for reflection about the future. After over a decade of its heat, squalor and clamour, he had no desire to return to Kimberley. He was sure that his health would not stand another season on the diamond mines. Cape Town seemed an attractive alternative, and Marks toyed with the idea of taking over the Leeuwenhof estate from the partnership and refurbishing it for his own use. Meanwhile, though, before any final decision could be taken, there was business to attend to in the Transvaal. [61]

Tobias Guttmann of Sheffield,
Marks's early mentor
(Photo: Sammy Marks Museum)

II

Founding the First Factory in the Transvaal, 1882–1885

When Marks returned to Kimberley from Cape Town in May 1882, he stayed long enough only to announce his intention of resigning his mine managership. Within days he set off again, for Pretoria this time, to make the final arrangements for launching the proposed distilling company.[1] Marks had to see to the local registration of the new company, De Eerste Fabrieken in de Zuid-Afrikaansche Republiek, a task complicated by the inadequacies of Transvaal company law. He also had to arrange the transfer of Nellmapius's concession to the new company and negotiate a price for Hatherley, the farm on which the distillery was to be erected. This, Marks reported to his partner in London (who had recently experienced the Hungarian's loquacity), was 'good hard work, as you can imagine when Nellmapius has got a man in his own town. . . .' To Isaac Lewis's chagrin, Marks agreed to pay Nellmapius £8,000 for a farm which had been acquired only two years previously for £1,400. Nellmapius was also to receive a further £1,000: £500 for the government and £500 for 'general expenses'.[2]

Marks was hopeful that he would be able to work with Nellmapius despite his qualms about him. Partly because of these, he felt it essential to remain in Pretoria to supervise operations, at least while the factory was being put into working order. The Hungarian could not be trusted to do this alone. From 'what I can see of Nellmapius himself', Marks wrote, 'he would not be particular to give a friend of his £2 for an article worth only £1'.[3]

Marks was very optimistic about the factory's future, and professed to be unconcerned about the large investment that was required. 'I am not frightened about the amount of Capital in the least,' he reassured Isaac Lewis, after estimating that the project would cost the Lewis and Marks partnership somewhere between £40,000 and £50,000 before the distillery was in working order. Once it was in operation, he insisted, profits would flow in immediately; within a year, the full capital outlay would have been recouped, and all further expansion would be funded by retained profits rather than out of the pockets of Lewis and Marks.[4]

Marks was convinced that his gin and brandy would be able to compete successfully with imports from the Cape and overseas. Early experiments indicated that Transvaal grain was of an equivalent quality to European, and that liquor could consequently be produced for as little as 7d. a bottle, less than it cost to transport a bottle of liquor from the coast. Given this competitive edge, and the present and potential size of the market, the distillery would be able to dispose of its products easily and profitably. Marks was confident that it would capture the 'white' trade of the Transvaal. This was already a sizeable market: per capita consumption was 'very large', with the inhabitants of Pretoria alone consuming some £20,000 of liquor a year. And it was bound to grow rapidly. The country was 'opening up': a succession of gold discoveries in the eastern Transvaal was drawing a stream of thirsty diggers, all prospective customers of the distillery. Besides, the distillery would also win a share of the 'native' trade of the Transvaal (supplied at that time by traders from the Cape), a share of the trade of the neighbouring Free State and possibly even a small portion of the diamond field market. As a token of his confidence, Marks opposed the sale of scrip till the company was working and had demonstrated its great worth. His partners were free to sell their holdings, but not his, for this was an 'A1 business', not only 'the best we have ever had', but 'one of the best businesses that was ever started in South Africa'.[5]

Once transfer was taken of the concession, Marks set to making the practical arrangements for establishing the first factory in the Transvaal. Managerial work of this kind was his speciality within the firm, just as finance was Isaac Lewis's forte, and diamond dealing Barnet Lewis's. This was no small matter given the remoteness and backwardness of the Republic, and Marks was soon to complain about 'the amount of trouble that I have had in a semi-wild country like this to get things into proper order'.[6]

First Marks had to settle in Schuster, the German distiller Nellmapius had recruited in Europe to prepare Cognac, Hollands (gin), Chartreuse, Ginger Brandy, Curaçao, Rosewater and Goldwasser.[7] Secondly, workmen had to be recruited. Marks attempted to hire artisans locally but found that 'all the blacksmiths here are not fit to be strikers in Kimberley, drunkards, and don't know their work at all', while the local masons and bricklayers were incompetents whose experience was limited to building small houses. Marks was forced to send off to Potchefstroom and Kimberley for bricklayers, masons and carpenters. 'I am not particular of what nation or colour they are,' he wrote, 'as long as they are good steady working men. . . .' Though more competent than the locals, the Kimberley workmen were not necessarily more sober and reliable. Of three bricklayers Barnet Lewis sent up, only two arrived at the building site; 'the other one, his friends left in the Trunk [*tronk* or gaol] at Pretoria, he offering to take charge of the Transvaal flag in the principal square there, as drunk as a lord.' Marks proposed to pay these workmen £6 per month plus board (including tobacco and a bottle of beer once a week) and lodging (which was essential since the building site was well out of town).[8]

He also planned on hiring about 50 black labourers at 30s. per month plus food. Again, rather than recruiting locals, Marks took on Shangaan or Tsonga who arrived in a half-starved condition after tramping 300 miles from the east coast with minimal supplies. Before being put to work they were fattened up with mealie meal for three days; then, for a week or two, set to 'light work': sitting on the ground in a row and passing bricks. After this no further concessions were made. Marks was soon nicknamed 'chow-chow' from his pronunciation of '*che-che*', 'be quick', a nickname that accurately reflected his sense of urgency. 'Everyday means a loss,' he lamented to his partner.[9]

The third contingent of workmen – cooper, carpenter, coppersmith and locksmith recruited in Germany by the distiller – was the most troublesome and left Marks with a life-long prejudice against their fellow countrymen. The 'dirty Germans' were 'always quarrelling and fighting amongst themselves', and Marks was eager to get rid of them as soon as he could. It was very difficult to communicate with them since they could speak no English, while his German was negligible.[10]

Besides recruiting a workforce, Marks also had to see to equipment and supplies, a difficult task when little was stocked locally and orders placed in Europe took as much as seven months to arrive. Wagonloads of machinery, bought by Isaac Lewis in Germany and England, came up from Durban to Hatherley and were assembled by a German engineer specially imported for the purpose. Building materials were ordered from Potchefstroom and Kimberley, timber felled in the indigenous forests to the north, and stones quarried near the site. Over one million bricks were made by hand and burnt on the property.[11]

Marks's difficulties were compounded by the wilfulness of his resident co-director who was jointly responsible for the building operations. Marks was rapidly disabused of his initial illusion that he could work with Nellmapius. The Hungarian was quarrelsome and took offence very easily; he very soon fell out with Schuster, the German distiller he had himself recruited; and bickered with Lewis and Marks about the interest on the money the partners had advanced him. Marks was constantly apologising for the behavior of the Hungarian, who needed endless humouring and appeasing. Replying, while briefly in Kimberley, to an angry letter, which also contained the news that Nellmapius had been appointed a Justice of the Peace, Marks gently teased: 'I am glad to hear of you getting the Commission as a JP. The only thing is in thinking it over it makes me feel rather queer, especially if when I return we might have a few words and then you might make use of your power upon me. However I can leave this to your generosity.'[12]

Nellmapius was also extravagant and unbusinesslike: 'Mr. N. would rather pay £3 for an article that he can get for £2, as he is too charitable and too good natured for my money. . . . The business is good enough, but you must not forget, if you open the doors of the Bank of England, it will also get empty.' What is more, Nellmapius was shortsighted and given to cutting corners: 'as to fixing machinery he does that on the supposition that all factories should be built to last three years only. . . .' He was also wholly untrustworthy: 'With Mr. Nellmapius I can look for nothing as I do not put any faith at all in his declarations. . . .'[13]

Worst of all, he pretended to expertise he did not possess, interfered with the builders and spurned the advice of experts with near disastrous consequences. While Marks was on a brief visit to Kimberley, Nellmapius, who claimed that he had had wide architectural experience, made alterations to the design of the factory that dismayed the German engineer and the artisans. Marks received word that windows and a door Nellmapius had designed broke all the rules of sound building and would not last a year; and that the distiller refused to enter the cellar for fear it would collapse. When the distiller and engineer brought their misgivings to Nellmapius's attention, he lost his temper and refused to budge. The net result was that it cost the company ' a good many thousands' to repair the damage.[14]

For all his failings, Marks did not dislike Nellmapius. Nellmapius was 'not a bad fellow', Marks explained to one of the Hungarian's victims, he was merely a confounded nuisance. 'Most men have some folly or other and Mr. N's is I think that he believes he knows everything. But after all is said, he is not one of the worst men one can meet with.'[15]

Nor was he without his uses. Nellmapius, who knew his way around the *voorkamers* of power in Pretoria, tutored Marks in the less than subtle art of building influence amongst the Boers. When the Boers prepared for war in the eastern Transvaal in late 1882 against Mampuru, the Pedi leader, and his Nzundza Ndebele allies, Nellmapius, who was appointed the government's procurement agent for munitions, enlisted Marks's assistance: 'it is as much in your interest as it is in mine, to do so . . .,' he argued. Marks arranged the shipment from Kimberley of dynamite (later used by Nellmapius himself to blast the Ndebele out of their cave strongholds) and of 250 boxes of gunpowder, so that the Boers could fight a war which he privately considered 'just the usual Boer game, a sort of cattle stealing arrangement'. But while Marks learnt useful lessons from Nellmapius, he himself was not a complete novice when it came to the art of earning goodwill: he had purchased Kruger's farm near the Vaal for the Coal Association, over objections by his joint managing director that the company was short of funds and had more than enough land already. Marks insisted it was 'worth the Company's while' for Kruger '*will most likely remain President for two or three years to come*'.[16]

However useful Nellmapius was as a lobbyist, Marks was nevertheless delighted and relieved when he began to lose interest in the distillery and devote himself instead to establishing a gunpowder factory in the Transvaal, yet another of his concessions from the government, and a project which was to fail dismally.[17]

Marks's problems in setting up the distillery left him with little time for much else. The outside world and Kimberley in particular seemed increasingly remote as the factory absorbed all of his energy and attention. He was reluctant to venture off, even the short distance to the Vaal River collieries, 'as I must be away from here as little as possible'. Besides, the factory increasingly seemed more promising than the colliery.[18]

For a brief while earlier in 1882, the coal company had appeared to prosper. Its coal was in great demand in Kimberley as more and more steam engines were installed, for even though the coal sold at close to £15 per ton, it was still 25 per cent cheaper than wood. So great was the demand that Marks believed the coal company could sell three times the quantity were it available, the inhibiting factor being the supply of ox-wagons. Even in summer transport was at a premium. Stow, the discoverer and manager of the coal mine, was quoted the 'exorbitant' rate of £11 per ton for a steady supply of wagons for the 14-day, 230-mile journey to Kimberley. After taking the costs of production into account, this would have left an unacceptably narrow profit margin.[19]

Stow, gravely ill the year before, passed away in March 1882. His death coincided with a serious deterioration in the company's fortunes. Without his personal supervision the quality of the coal forwarded to Kimberley declined; and mining companies refused to accept the 'rubbish' – the coal mixed with shale – they were offered. Customers reverted to using wood which, under the pressure of competition from coal, had fallen in price.[20] Marks cast around for ways of minimising costs at the colliery and of increasing revenue. The cost of labour could possibly be reduced if the workforce, already some 100 strong in mid-1882, could be supplied with cheap provisions. This might be achieved, Marks felt, if the vast acreage which the Association had accumulated on both banks of the Vaal could be turned to account.[21]

In May 1882, Marks spent some days examining the Association's farms on the banks of the Vaal River and was very impressed with their agricultural potential. 'There is ground and water enough, and good ground too, to cultivate and plough, and produce thousands of mudes [sic] of grain. . . . There are lots of farms in the Transvaal, but there is always some drawback – some are short of water, some have poor ground, then again the farmers are poor and lazy, but here we have about 100,000 morgen with plenty water everywhere, the ground beautifully level, and no stones, which we can plough with machinery, as we have fuel and water for nothing.' Contrary to Boer complaints, farm labour too would be plentiful and cheap – 'we can't go by what the farmers say, as they are always ready to have Kaffers but pay them nothing for their work; but you can have plenty Kaffers for about 1/6 a day with food.'[22]

So taken was Marks with the estate that he flirted with the idea of renting farm land from the Association and working it himself. Since this was not really practical because Marks needed to devote most of his attention to the distillery at Hatherley, he suggested instead that the Coal Association invest a couple of thousand pounds in farming and irrigation. They might consider sending out three or four 'A1' English farmers to take the property in hand, 'for to get good farmers in this country is simply impossible, and it is not worthwhile having bad ones, as they will spoil the Company's property'. If the Association invested in irrigation, farm machinery and a flour mill, 'a great production would follow', and they would surely win a share of the local grain market which was presently dominated by Australian and American imports.[23]

Nothing came of these ambitious ideas. Marks's associates saw their Vaal River investment as primarily one in coal-mining. In the days before the discovery of the Witwatersrand, and the development of a large market in the interior, Highveld farming held little attraction for hard-nosed Cape or

European investors. Besides, the Association was increasingly hard-pressed to keep even its coal operation afloat and had no cash to spare for risky farming ventures. Overproduction of diamonds at Kimberley had created an over-supply of this luxury item and had led to a collapse of the diamond price in late 1882. This was a devastating blow to Kimberley mining companies, already desperately short of working capital and struggling with high costs, poor yields and narrow profit margins. The Vaal River colliery suffered along with its customers, the diamond-mining companies. Demand for fuel dried up as companies closed down or curtailed their operations. Marks's coal company was left with heaps of unsold coal, unpaid accounts it stood little chance of collecting, a forbidding overdraft at a bank which was threatening to withdraw the facility, and the very real prospect of bankruptcy.[24]

Matters were made still worse by 'the fearfully expensive mode of working' at the colliery. Despite Marks's suggestion that the less efficient white workers be replaced by less expensive blacks, the manager was unable to reduce costs significantly, confirming Marks's view that 'whenever you leave your work in Strangers hands, they are bound to make a mess of it, you may pay them any salary you like, all they look after is the 1st of the month to get their cheques'.[25]

To the dismay of Marks and his co-directors, the Association found itself selling coal at less than the cost of production and transport, with little hope of improvement. Rather than run it at a loss, the directors decided to close the colliery in December 1882, just sixteen months after Marks's first, auspicious visit to the Vaal River coal farms. For the time being, tenant farming would be the sole source of revenue from the estate.[26]

Without the injection of capital Marks had proposed, the Vaal River property was farmed in much the same way as the neighbouring Boer properties. It was occupied by a sprinkling of *bywoners* – poor white tenants – and by a larger number of black sharecroppers, who surrendered as much as half of their harvest to the company by way of rent, which was then sent on to Kimberley or to the distillery at Hatherley. Black tenants were actively recruited on Marks's instructions and provided with seed, for sharecroppers, like 'Jan Doctor' and 'Englishman', who worked their allotments intensively, drawing on the labour of their households and the assistance of their kinsmen and neighbours, were often more productive than Boer *bywoners*. These knew more of pastoralism than of ploughing and found it socially demeaning to draw on the labour of their womenfolk and children.[27]

For the time being though, the Vaal River estate took second place to the distillery. After a spell in a disagreeable Pretoria hotel, Marks established himself on the factory premises, sharing quarters with his secretary and with Schuster. Marks had a bedroom built and properly floored to suppress the swarms of fleas of summer, then furnished it with a chest of drawers, brass bedstead and sprung mattress brought up by wagon from Kimberley. In the evenings Marks would read and study, and reminisce about his youth and the early years in Kimberley. Always an energetic autodidact, he sent off for a primer so that he could teach himself German and so communicate with his German staff who could speak no English. He sent also for the best books in English on distilling. He was acutely conscious of his ignorance of the business he controlled. Ordering the books, he explained 'I find myself devoid of even any theoretical knowledge of a business in which I take great interest.' He needed the books so that he could follow the technical discussions at management meetings and avoid the embarrassment of 'asking or putting any questions in such a manner as to display my want of knowledge [of] the subject'.[28]

Over the months Marks's uncertainty about his future, fanned originally by illness and the decline of the diamond industry, had receded. When he had come up to the Transvaal in May 1882 it had been for a limited period of time only, to set up the factory; he had soon found that Pretoria was 'a lovely place' with a 'splendid climate', where he felt healthier and heartier than he had for months before in Kimberley. He had gradually come to the conclusion too that the success of the factory depended on his continuing presence. By November 1882 he had given up all thought of moving to Cape Town, or of returning to Kimberley, and had instead resolved to settle permanently in the Transvaal: 'as far as this business goes here, I have made up my mind, to remain here, as long as my heart will allow, to see that this is a success.' The firm's failing Kimberley business he now left entirely in Barnet Lewis's hands.[29]

While Marks's feelings of uncertainty faded, his partners' anxieties grew apace. By December 1882 the factory had become a serious source of dissension within the partnership: costs had already exceeded Marks's original estimates and the building was not yet finished. And Marks kept making additional requests for fresh spending on equipment and building. His explanation – 'This being a new business we hardly yet know what we do want; but every day we learn more of our requirements' – was by no means reassuring.[30]

Nor were his endlessly repeated expressions of faith in an enterprise which even he had to concede 'has eaten up at present a good deal of our money'. They need have no further fear, he insisted, that the liquor would not sell, their great anxiety from the start. Storekeepers were already clamouring for the factory's products, even though these were not yet freely available – 'the common stuff that I am now distilling which is only raw spirit is sold as fast as I can make it in town.' Consumer reaction to these trial batches, which were 'of the very roughest kind', was, he claimed, overwhelmingly favourable: in the Zoutpansberg 'even the white men' were drinking it although it was only 'Kaffir Brandy'. Once the distillery began to make 'good stuff', competition would be impossible, and once it went into full production, it would not be able to keep up with demand. Hence further expenditure was fully warranted.[31]

The partners were not persuaded. Barnet Lewis in particular, who had been sceptical from the start about the liquor business and who was struggling with a sinking diamond market, was increasingly reluctant – and unable – to forward funds from Kimberley to complete the factory. This infuriated Marks: 'You keep on telling me I must not draw; do you want me to leave off the building and allow it to stand idle; because I cannot coin money here; and money I must have to complete it.' Again, a few days later: 'I am not wasting one penny and am spending money only when absolutely needed. I have quite enough to do with all the anxiety, trouble and worry that I have had with the work here without hearing any complaints or being annoyed on the score of money.'[32]

Two months after this salvo, and nine weary and anxious months after Marks's arrival in the Transvaal, the distillery was at last operational, much to Marks's great relief and satisfaction. 'Unless you had been here and seen the work executed,' he wrote to Isaac Lewis, 'you can form no idea of the difficulties I have had to surmount in erecting such a building and fixing the machinery in the short space of 9 months.'[33]

With the distillery completed, Marks's fertile mind turned to other projects, other possibilities. This was by no means a random process, resting on chance and sudden inspiration. Instead Marks seems to have relied on associative thinking, on constructing chains of related ideas. There were usually clear linkages between the projects he proposed, one leading logically to the next. Thus, for example, he now conceived the idea of establishing a glass factory in the Transvaal as a logical extension of the distillery business. The original intention was to sell liquor in casks, but it was soon apparent that at least some of the customers preferred their booze, especially their gin, in bottles. To satisfy this preference, Marks ordered bottles from the coast, but found that the heavy costs of transporting a bulky item long-distance made this an expensive business. His thoughts soon turned to the feasibility of making bottles locally. What would it cost, he wrote to a foundry near Sheffield, to erect and operate a small furnace and 'blowing apparatus' capable of producing up to 1,200 bottles a day of 'rough construction', as well as glass tumblers? The raw material was readily available: there was plenty of sand in the neighbourhood.

Anticipating serious objections from his more cautious partners, Marks put the idea to Isaac Lewis very tentatively. 'I might write more on this subject,' he explained, 'but as a rule my views go further than yours and I would not like to upset you with fresh ideas.' As he had feared, his partners were unimpressed. They were far less receptive than he to new ideas: they were more worried about money, more anxious about keeping the partnership on an even financial keel in difficult times, more directly involved in the problems of raising funds during a recession, more fearful of failure, altogether more hesitant and cautious.[34]

Consequently nothing came of the idea at this stage, or of a scheme to manufacture sugar, which had been part of the original concession to Nellmapius. Times did not warrant the additional investment. The recession at Kimberley had backwashed over the entire region, and the Transvaal in particular seemed a very poor risk. As Marks later recalled, during a more prosperous age, 'In the Transvaal, at the time I speak of, people were frightened to invest one shilling where they would now put in a thousand or two.'[35]

An added disincentive to further investment was the disappointing perfor-mance of the new distillery. Contrary to Marks's confident predictions that the distillery would speedily corner the Transvaal market, sales in the early months were only 'fair' rather than exciting. The distillery's brandy and gin very swiftly encountered serious consumer resistance and rejection. The decision to release the factory's products before the liquor had been adequately refined – a business tactic aimed at generating some income while the distillery was being put in order – misfired badly. The rough spirits which the Zoutpansbergers had reportedly enjoyed, repelled more discriminating tipplers, and gave Eerste Fabrieken brandy and gin a poor reputation that it would labour under for years. As Marks ruefully admitted later on, he had allowed himself to be persuaded by Nellmapius that the Transvaal public was undiscriminating and 'that we could make any kind of common brandy and it would sell well. We did so and the result was a failure. People stated that the stuff was not worth drinking and neither was it.'[36]

Marks's solution was to recruit fresh talent, an Englishman, Stokes, who knew more about the art of 'mixing' than Schuster, the German distiller. Before making the appointment, though, Marks had to resist an offer of assistance from the irrepressible Nellmapius, who once again pretended to an expertise he lacked. Nellmapius as the 'mixer', Marks warned, 'would mean ruination to the business'.[37]

The disappointing sales meant that despite Marks's original prediction that the distillery would rapidly become profitable and self-sustaining, his partners were called upon to inject further working capital into the factory. When Barnet balked, threatening not to honour further drafts, Marks could hardly contain his exasperation: 'I must plainly tell you', he wrote, 'that if this kind of thing goes on much longer I shall lose my senses altogether.'[38]

An added complication was the relatively short duration of the concession the government had granted Nellmapius. Lewis and Marks felt that fifteen years was insufficient time to recover and adequately reward their considerable capital outlay on the factory. Consequently Marks lobbied members of the government and Volksraad for an extension of the concession for a further ten years, taking special care when stocking up with mealies for the distillery to buy from a wide range of their constituents rather than from the leading Pretoria merchants.[39]

As part of this campaign, Nellmapius and Marks decided to throw a large party cum public tasting at the distillery in the guise of a formal opening ceremony. Justifying the expenditure, Marks explained to his cost-conscious and prissy partner in Kimberley that the company could expect 'to derive directly and indirectly many advantages' from the party. The formal opening of the Eerste Fabrieken on Wednesday 6 June 1883 was used to promote the distillery's products and to woo the Boer notables upon whose support the extension of the concession depended. All members of the Executive Council and the Volksraad were invited to the 'christening' of the distillery, as were the general public by means of an open invitation in the press. Pretoria, the newspapers wrote, was ' a deserted village' on the day of the opening. Among the large crowd who came were many blacks, 'well clothed and clean . . . who came from great distances to witness the ceremony and who mixed freely amongst us just at sufficient distance to show respect'.

The festivities began just before 11 in the morning with President Kruger's grand entry into the factory premises through a triumphal arch spanning the roadway. After a 21-gun salute, the presidential party was escorted around the factory by Marks and Schuster. The Boer dignatories were greatly impressed; many of them had never seen steam-driven machinery in operation before.

The 'christening' ceremony took place at 12 on a platform at the foot of the factory chimney, the tallest structure in the Transvaal. After a droll introduction – 'Burghers, brothers, friends and enemies . . .' – Kruger launched into a lengthy historical recitation – 'related with much graphic force' – about the travails of the Voortrekkers, the stated purpose of which was to defend the Boer's right to the land. Having proved to his own satisfaction that the charge that the Transvaal had been seized from the native inhabitants by violent and dishonourable means was false, Kruger went on to defend his controversial industrial concessions policy against its free-trade critics. If the Republic was to bolster its cherished independence, it would have to exploit its natural resources more effectively. To attract the investment necessary to do so, it would have to provide adequate protection, for without this the new enterprises would not survive. The distillery was the first fruit of this policy, a first step in the direction of true independence. Accordingly, he now christened it De Volkshoop, the People's Hope, a title seldom used afterwards: the distillery would be more popularly known as Hatherley or Eerste Fabrieken. In keeping with a tradition with which he was clearly unfamiliar, Kruger then broke a bottle of champagne, dry *monopole*, against the chimney; instead of swinging, he jabbed, cutting his hand badly and dousing himself in champagne.

The public was then invited to sample the distillery's wares. These, the *Transvaal Advertiser* reported, were 'freely dispensed to all who desired to test their quality, and we need not say that curiosity was very general, and that many came and came again, until they could drink no more.' Suitably refreshed, 300 guests then adjourned upstairs for a sumptuous luncheon. The banqueting-hall was a converted store-room with appalling acoustics, but this did nothing to discourage Nellmapius, who proposed a toast to the President in a long and inaudible speech, delivered in broken Dutch 'with great vehemence and spirit', while Marks, more reticent, saw that the guests' glasses were kept filled with French wines and Hatherley spirits.[40]

A fortnight after this Boer bacchanalia, the Volksraad extended the liquor concession for a further fifteen years on the government's recommendation.[41]

Despite the success of the launching party, the distillery continued to struggle with the problem of the poor public image of its liquor, known derogatorily as 'Nellmapius' or 'Mapius'. Strenuous efforts were made for years after to dispel this negative perception, but with only limited results. Quality control was tightened – Stokes, the new English distiller, 'will not send out a drop until he has satisfied himself' – and advertisements were regularly placed in the press.

Besides plugging the medicinal properties of the distillery's products – Hatherley Ginger Brandy was 'the great preventive of Choleraic attacks, also the remedy for Indigestion, and safeguard against Dysentery' – the advertisements also stressed their purity. Much play was made of the medals and diplomas Eerste Fabrieken won at international expositions and of an analytical report by a professor at Halle University in Germany which declared 'the Spirits perfectly Faultless, First-class Products, free from all impurities, and notably free, moreover from any admixture of Fusil Oil', a nauseating byproduct of alcoholic fermentation.[42]

Rather than establishing a rapid and easy ascendancy in the Transvaal and in the neighbouring territories, as Marks had initially expected, the distillery faced the hard grind of developing a sales network and building a market for its products. Marks worked energetically at pushing on sales. Regional agents were appointed, including his brother Joe in the northern Free State who sold brandy below cost to build up custom. Boer farmers were sent out with wagonloads of liquor to sell on commission, and barrels were delivered to thirsty British troops on a military expedition across the Republic's western border.

For all Marks's strenuous efforts, the Fabrieken continued to battle. The distillery not only worked well below capacity – Marks estimated 'that we can produce treble the amount we have been doing if we had only the market for it' – but also suffered severe cash-flow problems. Its customers, the storekeepers, struggling themselves to stay afloat, paid their accounts very slowly and Marks felt 'it inadvisable to push [them] too much'. Meanwhile, the distillery had to find money to meet its working costs, and to pay for the mealies supplied by black and white farmers, as well as the rye and barley grown with seed Marks specially imported from England and distributed amongst the Boers. So hard-up was Eerste Fabrieken that at one point Marks was forced to lend his own money to the distillery, money he had earmarked for the purchase of a farm for his private use.[43]

Since his arrival in the Transvaal, Marks had lived in makeshift accommodation, first in a Pretoria hotel, then, while the distillery was being built, in bachelor quarters at the factory, shared with senior members of his staff. Once the factory was completed and operational, Marks had a little more time to devote to his personal affairs. In late 1883 he decided he would buy a farm, not on the partnership's but on his own account. The farm he chose was known as Christienen Hall and belonged to Charles William Rufus Cockcroft of Dordrecht in the Cape Colony. Some 902 morgen in extent, it was a portion of a farm called Zwartkoppies which adjoined Hatherley. It was undeveloped and, as Marks later recalled, 'so swampy in parts that my horse sank up to the saddle'. Its farmhouse, for all the grandeur of its title, was simple and tumbledown and bore the scars of a skirmish at the site during the recent Boer–Brit struggle when it had been pierced by a shell. Marks paid £1,400 and took transfer in March 1884. The farm reverted to the original name of Zwartkoppies – Christienen Hall was clearly unsuitable for a Jewish owner.[44]

Marks took an even more momentous personal decision later that year. A 40-year-old bachelor, he returned to England to marry Bertha Guttmann, one of the daughters of Tobias Guttmann, Marks's mentor and friend in Sheffield, who had paid his passage to South Africa sixteen years before and provided his initial capital, a large case of knives.

Marks gave little hint of his intentions in his prior correspondence. There are no letters to the young lady, who was eighteen years his junior. The Marks papers are frustratingly circumspect about the circumstances of this match, which was probably an arranged marriage. Instead there is bachelor banter with his fellow diamond magnate Julius Wernher, another late-marrying Victorian. 'You ask me why I don't get married. I think as you are at home you have the best chance and that I ought to ask you the same question'. And there is joshing with his future sister-in-law, Frederica Lewis, his partner Isaac's sister, whose courtship with Ellia Marks is often referred to in the letters. 'Many thanks for having looked me out a young lady with such a good dowry,' he wrote to 'Freddy' a year before his marriage. 'If you could arrange to send me the money, and the young lady to a School, I should be very well pleased.'[45]

Sammy and Bertha were married, out of community of property, in Sheffield on 16 December 1884, almost exactly five years after the death of Bertha's mother Louisa. The day before their wedding they signed a marriage settlement, a common practice amongst the propertied classes in Victorian England, which provided that within six months of the solemnisation of the marriage, Marks was to pay £16,000 to trustees who would see that it was invested in approved securities. The annual income was to be paid directly to Bertha, thus assuring her of a more than modest independent income for life. Marks had some difficulty in raising the necessary cash, which is symptomatic of his shortness of ready funds at this difficult time in his business career. He was forced to reclaim substantial loans to his brothers Joe and Ellia and to pass a bond over the Zwartkoppies farm in Bertha's favour.[46]

Marks returned to Africa and his factory on the veld with his 22-year-old English bride in March 1885. The inevitable culture shock for a young girl from a great industrial city and a protected, middle-class, Anglo–Jewish environment arriving at a remote farm in an alien countryside can only be imagined. Her reactions, unfortunately, are not recorded. They moved into the old farmhouse on Zwartkoppies temporarily while arrangements were made for more comfortable accommodation, better suited to their position in society. A week after his return Marks sent his agents in Durban an indent for building material: 'I am anxious to get on with it immediately,' he wrote, 'therefore I desire the goods to be sent forward without any delay. . . . Further I desire to get the benefit of all discounts allowed by the people from whom you purchase.' The agents were to see that the goods were very carefully packed: a mantelpiece recently sent for use at Eerste Fabrieken had arrived damaged. They were also to see that all the wagons came via the Highveld road to avoid passing through Pretoria. Marks did not want the local storekeepers to discover that he had bypassed them and purchased directly from Durban: while he was keen to minimise the cost of the building materials, he was also anxious to avoid offending the merchants who retailed his gin and brandy.[47]

The agents were instructed to forward the mountain of furniture and household goods which the couple had acquired before leaving England. A surviving receipt in the Marks papers, issued by a brass foundry, R. W. Winfield and Company of Holborn Viaduct, London, indicates that this included a 5 foot x 6 foot 6 inch 'Massive Brass French Bedstead' (costing £30. 10s.) with a 'Patent Woven Wire Mattress' (£3. 15s.), a 'Horse hair Mattress' (£5) and a ' Feather Bolster' (£1.5s.), all of the 'best'. Besides the furniture, the agents were also to dispatch a treadle-operated sewing machine with all the accessories, including a 'liberal supply' of spare needles which could not be obtained in Pretoria. This, and subsequent orders of groceries and household necessities from Durban, including tins of salmon, sardines and lobsters, reels of cotton and Pears soap, are a measure of the meagreness of the stocks of the local stores, at least by the standards of a middle-class English housewife who insisted on 'none but the best article'.[48]

In September 1885, just nine months after her wedding and while her new house was still under construction, Bertha Marks gave birth, at Nellmapius's home in Pretoria, to her first child, a son they named Louis. Bertha was 23, Sammy 41. In accordance with Jewish tradition Sammy had to arrange for his son's circumcision. As there were only a handful of Jews in the Transvaal at the time and no Jewish clergymen, he sent to Kimberley, the nearest Jewish congregation, for a *mohel* or circumciser. The Reverend Meyer Mendelssohn (father of the great South African bibliographer, Sidney Mendelssohn) came up to Pretoria at Marks's expense to perform the rite. On his return to Kimberley the congregation docked his pay for the period of his absence in the Transvaal. Marks was indignant: he wrote a furious letter, pointing out that although he had been unable to enjoy any of the benefits of membership of the Kimberley congregation for the past four years because of his move to the Transvaal, he had nevertheless continued to pay his annual subscription of £10. 'The least therefore I could expect from you as a congregation was the free use of the services of Mr. Mendelssohn. . . . if you persist in this resolve, which I consider most ungenerous,' he warned, 'I shall have no alternative but to ask you to [remove?] my name from your books, and further to reimburse me the £40 which I have paid you under the belief that I was entitled to the ministrations of the Reverend Gentleman . . .' – a threat not to be taken lightly by an impecunious infant Hebrew congregation.[49]

By the time the house at Zwartkoppies was finally completed in 1886, it had cost Marks 'thousands'. The style was 'neither Gothic nor Tudor but more of Colney Hatch or Newgate', his neighbour Harry Struben of The Willows farm reported. 'He drew the plan I am told on a plank with a piece of charcoal. There is any quantity of it[,] that is one satisfaction and makes a prominent land mark. His little Hebrew wife is quiet and pleasant when you get to know her. . . .'[50]

While in England at the end of 1884 to be married to Bertha, Marks had dusted off a project he had originally suggested some four years previously when Lewis and Marks first entered the Transvaal: the construction of a railway line from Kimberley to Pretoria. For at least a decade, the Boers had dreamed of a railway connection with the coast, an ambition bound up with their desire to reduce the dependence of their land-locked Republic on the neighbouring British colonies. President Burgers's scheme for a line from Delagoa Bay to Pretoria in the mid-1870s had got as far as placing orders for rails, but lack of finance had left these rusting in the Bay. The project was revived after the war of independence by Paul Kruger, who negotiated an arrangement with some Dutch speculators, but these struggled to secure financial backing for what seemed a quixotic scheme. A lengthy railway line crossing fever-ridden terrain, climbing an escarpment and then passing through an undeveloped and lightly populated countryside to an obscure and insignificant destination seemed unlikely to generate the volume of rail traffic and revenue to warrant the heavy investment that would be necessary.

Marks grasped the opportunity to revive his own scheme for a railway from Kimberley to Pretoria. Its advantages seemed obvious: there were no construction difficulties as the terrain was flat and healthy, and there would be a guaranteed income from the coal Marks would send to Kimberley from his Vaal River colliery. This was the scheme's great attraction for Marks; it would make it possible at last to market his coal profitably, and as a bonus, it would allow him to sell Hatherley spirits in Kimberley.

While in England Marks approached a number of leading manufacturers of heavy equipment – principally Robey and Company of Lincoln from whom he had ordered machinery since his Kimberley years – with a proposal that they finance and construct a railway line from Kimberley to the Transvaal. His idea was that they undertake the scheme themselves and only approach the financial world once the railway was properly under way and there was something tangible to show investors.[51]

Marks's next hurdle was to sell the scheme to the Boer leadership when he returned to Africa. Predictably it was well received by those who favoured closer ties between the Boers of Transvaal and the Afrikaners of the Cape: most notably the Transvaal wing of the Afrikaner Bond, led by S. J. du Toit, the influential Superintendent of Education, and Piet Joubert, Paul Kruger's great rival for the presidency. Kruger and his Hollander advisers, on the other hand, were less enthusiastic: a rail connection through British territory financed by British capital was the converse of their cherished dream of an independent rail link, financed by Continental capital, with a port outside British control. In addition, Boer conservatives were unhappy at the prospect of a competitor with their transport-riding business.[52]

To win over the Volksraad and the Executive, Marks enlisted the support of Hugo Nellmapius, lobbyist and concession-hunter extraordinary. Nellmapius was offered a tenth of the profits or £10,000 of shares in the projected railway company if he succeeded in obtaining the concession. Marks also requested his partner's and the syndicate's consent to the use of 'a little "grease" if this was required. Lewis objected strenuously, not so much on moral as on pragmatic grounds, for official corruption was, after all, one of the inescapable facts of life in Kruger's Republic. With money so tight he was not prepared to lay out hard cash merely on speculation. 'You may promise to give those concerned something if you get the Concession . . . but I will not give a single penny on the prospect of attaining this End.'[53]

Lewis's caution was warranted, for, despite Nellmapius's whisperings, Kruger held up proper consideration of the Lewis and Marks application for months, hoping meantime to resuscitate the Delagoa Bay railway project by offering more attractive terms to the Dutch concessionaires. The best he could suggest, meanwhile, was that Marks's railway syndicate invest instead in a £100,000 loan to the hard-pressed Republic.[54]

Marks, for his part, was prepared at least to consider the proposal, for, as Nellmapius needlessly explained, 'it would be of enormous importance to you, if you could manage to help the Govt.' Besides, the collateral security was more than satisfactory: the pick of government farms throughout the country. Lewis, however, was less taken with the idea. Marks should explain to Kruger, he wrote, that the syndicate consisted not of financiers, but of manufacturers, who were interested only in railway construction in the Republic. Financiers proper were 'dead against the Transvaal' for 'the more speculative . . . have been so unsuccessful with their gold ventures that they will not now embark anything more for the present not at all events until they see some better results from that country.'[55]

At this point, in 1885, Lewis might have said the same of his own partnership and its ventures. These were hard times for Lewis and Marks: the diamond trade was in a deep recession; the Vaal River coal-mining operation was at a standstill; and the distillery at Pretoria, Marks's chief concern, was struggling for survival. Knowlegeable observers were very sceptical about the Eerste Fabrieken's prospects. While acknowledging that the business was well managed by Marks and Stokes, and that turnover was steadily increasing – by 1885 it had reached about £10,000 per annum – the local manager of the Standard Bank felt that with its very large capital base of £50,000, the distillery would never be in a position to pay a dividend.[56]

But Marks, a perennial optimist, remained hopeful, if very guardedly so. 'As regards what the future of the business is likely to be,' he had written in May 1885, 'the country is so unsettled that one cannot say; still if there are no wars I can safely tell you it will improve.' In November he wrote: 'Meantime if people won't drink, we can't make them – we make the drinks and bye and bye [sic] when the money pours into the Company by an influx to the Gold Fields we shall be unable to pour out the liquor fast enough – till then the Results will be Poor.'[57]

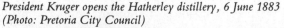

President Kruger opens the Hatherley distillery, 6 June 1883
(Photo: Pretoria City Council)

III

Gold, Gin and Coal, 1885–1895

In early 1884 Fred Struben and his brother Harry, Marks's neighbour at The Willows, began prospecting for gold on the Witwatersrand, an area Marks knew well as he crossed it regularly en route to his properties at the Vaal. Later that year, fossicking to the north of present-day Johannesburg, Fred discovered a rich outcrop at Wilgespruit, which he named the Confidence Reef. Though his confidence was misplaced – the reef lay to the north of the outcrop of the Main Reef series which dipped southwards – Struben's discovery was of historic significance: it drew public attention to the gold-bearing potential of the Witwatersrand region.[1]

While they concentrated on Wilgespruit, the brothers also took out options to lease portions of a further seven farms on the Witwatersrand at rentals ranging from £75 to £300 per annum for 21 years, payable in advance. In August 1885 Harry Struben offered Wilgespruit plus the options to his neighbour at a very substantial premium: £1,000 in commission per option, in a combination of cash and scrip, plus Wilgespruit for £7,500. The total sum involved was £22,500.

Marks was very tempted to take up these options on behalf of his partnership alone but Lewis and Marks were in such straitened circumstances, business was so sluggish at the distillery and the diamond market was so flat, that it seemed they would have to invite other investors to contribute. As H. W. P. Steeds, Marks's secretary of the time, wrote to Isaac Lewis: 'Mr. Marks desires me to say if his firm were not quite so hard up, he should not be inclined to let any of the Kimberley gentlemen have as much as a "smell".'

Marks approached an old associate from his Kimberley days, Julius Wernher, one of the dominant figures in the diamond industry. Wernher, however, felt that Marks was 'too sanguine'. Worse still, Marks's own partners, particularly Isaac Lewis's younger brother Barnet, were equally sceptical about the prospects of the Witwatersrand: 'not only did I not receive any encouragement', he reminded Isaac years later, 'but I was ridiculed and voted an absolute madman and the man who laughed most at my madman's escapade was our youngest partner.'

Writing in Yiddish, Marks warned that they were 'losing a big chance', as they would surely see later on. He regretted he could not take up the Struben offer on his own but he had no money free because he was building a suitable home for Bertha at Zwartkoppies and providing for her marriage settlement. Clearing out a drawer in his safe nine years later, he came across 'the offer from Harry Struben to sell the whole of the Witwatersrand (worth today about 50 millions Stg.) for £22,500. I fear that a very deep sigh escaped me,' he wrote to Isaac Lewis, 'when I remember how cold water was thrown on my recommendations and my excellent friend Mr. Barnet puffed at his cigar having already settled it in his own mind that I would live out an existence in a big asylum "on her majesty's pleasure". So much for all that. We shall never see that chance again.'[2]

Marks's partners' scepticism, which effectively cost them the Witwatersrand, is perhaps understandable. They no doubt suspected a recurrence of the 'gold fever' he had caught when he first arrived in the Transvaal in May 1882. Nearly all the Lydenburg district, he had told them then, was 'full of gold'; so was the stretch of territory between Pretoria and Potchefstroom. Marks was not the only one to believe this. The search for gold in the eastern Transvaal in the early eighties was one of the few sources of excitement in an otherwise sleepy Republic in the years immediately after the restoration of its independence. The conviction that there were payable deposits of gold awaiting discovery somewhere in this geologically promising region drew a steady stream of prospectors and their camp-followers – traders, tavern-keepers and trollops – to the eastern Transvaal.[3]

While Marks was preoccupied with the problems of the distillery, he nevertheless kept an ear open for reports of discoveries, though he treated these with a degree of caution – 'I think you may safely follow the Irishman's example', he wrote, 'and divide in half and take a large percentage from the half remaining.' In early 1884 he took an uncomfortable trip through the area, first by post-cart to the town of Lydenburg, then onwards on horseback, 'as travelling there in a conveyance is almost an impossibility, the roads when there are any, being very stony. . . .' Marks was favourably impressed with the gold fields of the eastern Transvaal: 'I think it is only a matter of time,' he wrote, 'and they will turn out trumps.'[4]

Marks's confident prediction was fulfilled over a year later in the Kaap valley, 'a grand mountainous amphitheatre', close to Swaziland, at the southern edge of the area Marks had visited. A rapid succession of minor discoveries around the rim of this large valley drew scores of gold-seekers, many of them from Natal, who gathered at the newly founded township of Barberton before fanning out into the surrounding hills and mountains. Among these was Edwin Bray, a Yorkshireman who had discovered, and then 'wretchedly managed', a lead mine in the western Transvaal in the 1870s. Prospecting in the hills six miles to the north-east of Barberton, he discovered a reef of gold – the Sheba – so rich that it yielded eight ounces to the ton at the first crushing. A stampede followed, with others rushing to peg off all the ground surrounding Bray's 'Golden Quarry', in the hope that this would be as rich.[5]

Like many diggers in the world of nineteenth-century gold-mining, few of these early arrivals had the capital needed to develop their mining claims, or any intention of doing so. They relied instead on selling out at a handsome profit to the capitalists they hoped would be attracted by the discoveries. Marks was one of the closest to hand. In November 1885 he was visited in Pretoria by Henry Heller, a Natalian trading at De Kaap. Heller represented a seven-man syndicate so hard up that they were unable to afford any tools and lived exclusively on mealie pap. They were anxious to persuade Marks to invest in claims they had pegged off close to Bray's discovery. Heller was a persuasive salesman; the 'glowing account' he gave of the claims greatly excited Marks who immediately wrote to his partner that 'if they are only half as good as he describes . . . we could land a grand coup'. Despite being very busy at the distillery, he decided to go at once to the gold-fields to verify Heller's claims.[6]

Marks's fortnight there, he wrote afterwards, was 'the hardest I ever spent in South Africa'. His hosts, short of supplies, fed him a monotonous diet of mealie pap. He scrambled about their property, set on the steep slopes of a mountain, collecting ore samples 'promiscuously' to prevent them cheating him. He tramped energetically about the neighbourhood and soon identified its chief drawback as a gold-field: there was very little fuel for the batteries that would be needed to crush the ore, for the area was only lightly wooded while the nearest coal-fields were a long way off. Furthermore, the creek that ran nearby was a mere trickle.

True to form Marks rapidly devised a practical solution: the ore could be trammed from the mines on the mountainside to the Kaap River some miles distant where there was sufficient water to drive the batteries. With the assistance of two white and two black men, and a 35-yard length of rope, he measured the route the tram-line would take, and decided that it would have to be about 5^1/$_2$ miles long. It would serve, he hoped, not only the claims he had been offered, now grandly titled the Oriental block, but also Bray's Sheba company and the other neighbouring properties.

On his return to Pretoria in late December 1885, Marks wrote off at once to his partners that there was 'a very big thing to be made' of the gold-fields; 'if you will not consider me too sanguine, my private opinion is it is much larger, likelier, in fact better in every respect than Griqualand West.' If Barnet and Isaac were reluctant to come in, he would do so on his own for 'it would be insanity on my part to let such a chance slip'.[7]

Within a few weeks of his return from Barberton, Marks was on his way to Cape Town, chasing his dream of a railway from Kimberley to the Transvaal. After stalling Marks's application for months, Kruger had at last relented. The breakthrough on this front had come in late 1885 when Kruger found that despite the added inducements he had offered, the Dutch railway concessionaires were still unable to interest European investors in the proposed line from the east coast to Pretoria.

In September 1885 the government had written to Marks, inviting a concrete proposal. After lengthy discussions with the President 'and a great many arguments', Marks had submitted an application which, as he privately conceded to Lewis, was for far more than the partners could reasonably expect. The government was to guarantee a 7 per cent annual return on the capital invested in constructing the railway from Kimberley to Pretoria. Once completed, Lewis and Marks would have a 30-year concession to operate the line as well as first option on all other railway lines built in the Transvaal during this period. To make the scheme more palatable to Kruger, Marks applied at the same time for the right to continue the Kimberley line to Delagoa Bay after it reached Pretoria, though he hastened to add that there should be no binding contractual obligation to do so.[8]

Though still very unenthusiastic about the prospect of a rail connection with the Cape, Kruger accepted Marks's scheme in principle in January 1886. Given an admission by the Dutch concessionaires that there was little prospect of their pulling off the preferred Delagoa Bay scheme, given too the parlous state of the Transvaal economy, any railway was better than none; and at least the Marks scheme offered some possibility, however limited, of the eventual construction of the east coast line. But there was one major precondition. Kruger insisted that before he finally agreed to a Kimberley–Pretoria rail connection, the Cape government should first consent by way of a quid pro quo to a customs union with the Transvaal. Extraordinarily, but not altogether surprisingly, given the rather casual character of Boer government and the undeveloped nature of the Transvaal state, negotiation of this arrangement was left to a private individual: to Sammy Marks assisted by Chief Justice Kotze, who was going down to the Cape on holiday.[9]

Marks met Thomas Upington, the Cape premier, and his ministers in January 1886 and 'urged them in strongest terms at my command to seize the opportunity offered' of gaining control of the Transvaal's rail links with the coast and of bringing the two territories into a closer, more cooperative economic relationship. His trump card, or so he thought, was the threat of an alternative rail route from Delagoa Bay, but this made little impression, presumably because the Cape politicians were fully aware that the eastern line was not viable under existing circumstances. Marks was fobbed off with 'trifling' objections – 'infinitesimally small matters' – by complacent, parochial politicians who saw little purpose in the Cape, the dominant force in the economy of the sub-continent, making any serious concessions to its bankrupt neighbour. As he recalled years later: 'I was everywhere received with kindness but nevertheless felt that the impression I left was that I was very stupid indeed.'[10]

In their defence, the Cape politicians might well have shared the scepticism of other well-placed observers about the viability of Marks's Kimberley–Pretoria scheme and wondered whether it was worth seriously considering at all. As a senior official of the Standard Bank wrote at the time: 'The Railway Scheme of Marks is an insane project. . . . A line of rail to run from Pretoria to Kimberley a distance of 350 miles and passing through only one town of any importance and receiving no feeders on the road must come to grief. . . .'[11]

Despite his disappointment, Marks was not quite ready to abandon all hope of building a trunk-line to the coast. With the Kimberley route ruled out of contention, at least for the foreseeable future, the alternative Delagoa Bay route now became more attractive. The obstacle here was the Dutch syndicate which had struggled so unsuccessfully since 1884 to raise the necessary capital. In April 1886 Lewis and Marks, and Robey and Company, the English machinery manufacturers, applied to the government for a railway concession very similar to the Dutch syndicate's. At the same time they appear to have supported a campaign by General Piet Joubert inside and outside the Volksraad for the cancellation of the unpopular Dutch concession; throughout the session, the ubiquitous Nellmapius disbursed small amounts of cash on their behalf to unnamed recipients. All to no avail however, for Kruger, a master of political close combat, was able to ward off the attacks on his favourite Dutch railway concessionaires, who survived to build and operate the eastern line in the 1890s.[12]

With the discovery of gold on the Witwatersrand later the same year, the economic wheel of fortune went full circle. When the Cape came begging cap in hand for a customs union, Kruger was no longer interested, nor was he prepared to consider a rapid railway connection with the Colony. Marks's railway scheme, so lightly dismissed by the Cape earlier in 1886, would probably have ensured that the Cape railway reached the Transvaal much sooner than it eventually did, and that the Cape enjoyed a long-term dominance of the lucrative transit traffic from the coast to the Rand. It would certainly have made a profound impression on Marks's and Lewis's fortunes! Instead Marks's bold scheme foundered, because of Kruger's insistence on a linkage between the railway and customs issues; because of the shortsightedness and complacency of the Cape politicians; and, above all, because of the petty feuding and parochial jealousies between the colonies and republics.

Marks had more success – at least at first – with his other great hope of 1885–6, the new gold-field near Barberton. For once Marks's enthusiasm, underpinned by the remarkable results at Bray's Golden Quarry, was irresistible and his partners set about rounding up financial backing for both the Oriental mine and the steam tramway to carry ore down the mountain to the Kaap River. While French capital fought shy, Kimberley capital, Julius Wernher's and Alfred Beit's firm in particular, was more receptive. So was the English firm of Robey and Company who manufactured both mining machinery and steam engines. Marks persuaded Kruger to grant a tramway concession on terms that were 'exceptionally advantageous' ('buitengewoon voordeelig'), and steam locomotives, rails and sleepers were ordered from England. The Oriental and Sheba companies were signed up as the principal customers of the projected tramway.[13]

Spurred by Marks's injection of capital and by a flood of dividends from the Sheba mine, the Kaap gold-fields boomed during 1886. A spate of companies was floated with little more to recommend them than their names. The King Solomon, the Wheel of Fortune, the Twice Rejected, the Hidden Treasure and the Lost Ten Tribes, amongst many others, were launched with hopelessly inadequate working capital, producing more paper than gold during their short careers. Throughout 1886 their scrip was hectically traded on the stock exchange at Barberton and their share prices were driven up to absurd levels.[14] Underpinning this bull market was the confident expectation that the crucial ore-transport problem would be rapidly resolved through the construction of Marks's steam tramway from the mines on the mountainside to the stamp batteries at the Kaap River. In early 1887 the public learnt that its faith was misplaced: the tramway company revealed in February that Marks's original estimates were wildly inaccurate. When he had measured the distance from the mines to the river with his rope, he had failed to take full account of the steepness of the terrain, probably because his only previous experience with laying out a mine tramway had been at Kimberley where the gradient was hardly a problem. It now appeared that the length of line required was closer to 11 miles than to 5½, which meant that the company's capital of £25,000 was only half that actually required.[15]

Facing a hostile general meeting of shareholders, Marks was disarmingly frank about what the *Barberton Herald* called a 'brilliant example of miscalculation and unpardonable bungling'. 'A great mistake' had been made and the tramway project would have to be replanned and recapitalised. Unsurprisingly, this proved difficult to arrange. The Standard Bank refused an application for a loan, a Natal syndicate flirted with the idea, then shied away, while Lewis and Marks themselves hesitated about committing further resources to a floundering venture.[16]

The tramway debacle sapped public confidence in the Kaap gold-fields. Increasingly unfavourable comparisons were made with the Rand and many drifted away to that new Eldorado, discovered the year before. While there was no Golden Quarry on the Rand, no body of ore as rich as that at the Sheba mine, the banket of the Witwatersrand was far more reliable, more continuous and uniform in value, than the patchy quartz reefs of De Kaap. Moreover, there were none of the difficulties of terrain at the Rand that bedevilled mining operations at even the richest mines of De Kaap.[17]

Without a tramway down the mountain to the river, the Sheba mine was forced to rely on wagon transport, which was both expensive and unreliable, to move its ore to its mill. While the Sheba found this punitively expensive, lesser mines, like Marks's Oriental, found the costs positively prohibitive. As a result mining at De Kaap was practically at a halt by early 1888, excepting at the Sheba, and even there output and profits were far from satisfactory.[18]

Frustrated by the failure of their mine to live up to its great potential, the London board of the Sheba sent its chairman, B. B. Trench, to South Africa in mid-1888 to investigate. While passing through Pretoria en route to Barberton he was approached by Lewis and Marks, who proposed that he join them in resuscitating the tramway project. Trench hedged. It seems that privately he doubted whether the scheme could ever be successfully completed and, even if it could, whether it was the best solution for the Sheba's problems. After examining the Sheba mine he decided that it was preferable to go it alone and build an aerial tramway or wire-ropeway to carry the Sheba's ore down to the river. As this could follow a more direct route down the mountainside it could be erected and operated at a fraction of the cost of a steam tramway.[19]

Returning to Pretoria he applied to the government for the necessary concession and immediately ran into serious opposition. The promoters of the steam tramway scheme feared that Trench's plan would make it even more difficult than before to raise the funds needed to complete their line: the Sheba was by far the largest potential customer and without it the line might not be economically viable. Consequently Lewis and Marks insisted in public that the Sheba was still bound by the contract it had signed two years previously to transport all its ore over the tramway line once it was built, and that they would hold the Sheba to this.[20]

Behind the scenes Marks and Edward Lippert, the controversial dynamite concessionaire who was the co-promoter of the tramway scheme, lobbied the government in an effort to hold up Trench's application while they worked on a plan to save the tramway. Much to Trench's disgust, which he tactlessly expressed in public, the government agreed to postpone any decision till the following year.[21] The delay gave 'the Pretoria clique' the breathing-space they needed to resuscitate the tramway scheme. This was achieved by amalgamating the principal mining concerns in the vicinity of the Sheba with the tramway company, and refloating the strengthened and enlarged company on the English capital market. The amalgamated company was named the Oriental and Sheba; the confusion this might have caused in investors' minds with the rich Sheba company was perhaps deliberate. In 1890, five years after the tramway scheme was first mooted by Marks, it was at last completed by the consolidated company, but without the crucial support of the 'true' Sheba and much too late to reverse the inexorable decline of the Kaap gold-fields.[22]

The gold-fields of the eastern Transvaal were thus another disappointment to Marks. Instead of the 'grand coup' he had confidently anticipated in late 1885, he had had years of headache with little to compensate for this financially. The cost to his reputation as a successful entrepreneur, at a time when others like Rhodes and Beit were building theirs apace, must also have been considerable. The well-publicised initial failure of the stream tramway project and the controversy surrounding the Sheba's application for an aerial tramway drew much unfavourable public comment. More important, De Kaap distracted Lewis and Marks's attention and tied up a large part of its limited resources at the very time that others were investing heavily on the Rand and ignoring Barberton.

Though Lewis and Marks had missed out in 1881 and again in 1885 on magnificent opportunities to acquire large slices of the Witwatersrand at laughable prices, there were still opportunities in 1886, when the Main Reef was discovered, and in the years immediately following, to make the strategic purchases of mining ground that would have assured the firm a leading position in the gold-mining industry. While the firm did invest substantial sums in the Witwatersrand in its first decade, these investments were, however, very limited in scope when compared with the orgy of spending by the likes of Wernher and Beit, J. B. Robinson, Barney Barnato and Cecil John Rhodes. Furthermore, where Lewis and Marks bought important Rand mining properties and shareholdings, they generally failed to hold on to these until they came good. As Marks ruefully reflected years later about the 'lost' opportunities on the Rand, 'Providence has dealt very bountifully with us and it is our own fault if we failed to take full advantage of the good things thrown in our way by her, especially when we see how rich some of the properties we had in our hands have turned out.'[23]

How can this failure to take full advantage of the Witwatersrand bonanza be explained? Miscalculation clearly played a part, as Marks himself conceded. Then again, the Kaap gold-fields diverted Marks's attention and a significant portion of the firm's resources at the very time when the best bargains were there for the taking on the Rand. But the largest part of the explanation, however, must lie in Marks's conscious decision to concentrate his efforts on his firm's distilling and coal-mining activities. Given the great impetus the discovery of gold on the Witwatersrand provided to these activities – the surge in demand for coal and gin that followed the establishment of the gold-mining industry and Johannesburg – Marks's choice, however questionable in hindsight, made good business sense at the time.

The Rand was the Vaal River colliery's great opportunity. Virtually overnight a great inland market, no more than 35 miles distant, sprang up for its coal. But first Marks had to solve the problem which had bedevilled the colliery from its inception and had forced its closure in the early 1880s: the absence of cheap and reliable transportation for its coal. While Johannesburg was much closer than Kimberley, the problem was no less severe than before. Indeed, in some ways, it was worse. The quantum leap in population at a site deep in the interior, far from any port or railway line, placed impossible demands on the existing means of transport. From the start the Boer transport-riders struggled to keep up with the accelerating demand for their services. By Johannesburg's second and third winters, with grazing at a premium, it was clear that the growth of the mining industry itself was threatened by the total inadequacy of the transport system and that the industry might, literally, be forced to plod along at the pace of the ox. The problem was particularly acute in the case of coal, which, because of its bulk, required the ongoing services of scores of wagons. There was a real possibility that the gold mines might be forced to close during the winter months because of a shortage of coal.[24]

The solution, it seemed to Marks, was a railway line between the Vaal and Johannesburg. To circumvent the Dutch syndicate's railway concession, he chose to call his line a steam tramway rather than a railway, a nice legal distinction of little practical value. In late 1887 Marks approached farmers along the route between the river and the Rand about a right of way across their properties. With a sheaf of agreements in hand, he approached the government, not for a tramway concession, but for the right to buy or rent all strips of government land that straddled the proposed line, and to establish stations in Johannesburg and elsewhere.

Dr W. J. Leyds, the young Hollander who had recently been appointed State Attorney of the Transvaal, objected. Marks, he argued indignantly, was usurping the government's prerogative in these matters; he would have to make formal application for a concession. Besides, a Vaal–Johannesburg line was politically ill-advised at this time as it would skew the railway development of the country in a southwards direction; it would encourage an early connection with the trunk-line from the Cape at the expense of the as yet unbuilt eastern line from Delagoa Bay, the Republic's future independent lifeline to the outside world. In its usual dilatory fashion, the government took months to respond directly to Marks's application. After repeated enquiries by the firm, the state at last replied that a formal request would have to be made for a concession. Nothing came of the application Lewis and Marks then submitted: Leyds's objections clearly prevailed, not the last time he would frustrate Marks's imaginative designs.[25]

The problem of transport became even more urgent at the end of the eighties. The discovery of coal immediately to the east of Johannesburg, first at Boksburg, and then at Brakpan, threatened to place Lewis and Marks's Vaal River colliery at a permanent competitive disadvantage unless some means could be found for transporting its coal more cheaply than by ox-wagon.

By this time the colliery was producing about 200 tons of coal per week for the Rand market. Transport was both costly and laborious. The coal was first bagged in 224-pound sacks, then loaded into wagons. Each of these could carry only four tons, which meant that at least 50 wagons were needed per week the year round. In the summer months the wagons travelled in the cool of the early morning and evening, resting at midday; during winter the few wagons that were available travelled from the Vaal to Johannesburg at night, outspanning at sunrise to allow the oxen the whole day to forage on the bare veld. The cost of transporting coal by these means was 30s. per ton; an expert commissioned by Marks estimated that this could be cut to little more than 5s. if a rail connection was built.[26] Since the state was reluctant to allow this, Marks looked into the possibility of using steam traction engines to haul wagonloads of coal along the road between the Vaal River and the Rand. But nothing came of this idea for the 'road locomotives' of the age were unwieldly and the distance prohibitive.[27]

Early in the next decade the Transvaal was forced to reconsider its opposition to a rail link with the south. When the Delagoa Bay line project appeared to be foundering because of a shortage of capital, the new premier of the Cape, Cecil John Rhodes, stepped into the breach and offered to find the necessary funds if the Transvaal simultaneously agreed to allow a rail connection with the Colony. As he could see little alternative, Kruger reluctantly accepted.

Marks played a small part in these dealings. When Rhodes visited the Transvaal in 1890, before the deal was struck, he travelled by Cape cart to the Vaal River with Sammy Marks and James Sivewright, his railway minister, to inspect the best site for a railway bridge. At the river-bank Rhodes asked Marks how he was to persuade his tight-fisted fellow colonists to advance money to a foreign country for railway construction. How could he demonstrate the utility of such a loan? Like a conjuror producing a rabbit from his hat, Marks immediately reached into his side pocket and drew out a schedule containing the ammunition Rhodes would need. For months past he had stationed men day and night at this river crossing and at the drifts higher up and lower down the river to count the number of ox-wagons and the tonnage of goods crossing into the Transvaal. The schedule gave the name of each transport rider, the articles carried, the place where the wagon had loaded, and the name of the consignee in Johannesburg, compelling evidence of the mounting volume of traffic into the Transvaal which Rhodes and Sivewright could use to persuade their reluctant countrymen to risk a loan for a rival railway line.[28]

The construction of the main line from the south right through the centre of Lewis and Marks's Vaal River property solved the transport problem which had plagued Marks's colliery since its foundation a decade earlier, wholly transforming its prospects. Not only did the railway ensure easier access to the Rand market, but it also itself provided a major new outlet for Vaal River coal. At the beginning of the 1890s the Cape railway system depended largely on coal imported from Wales, drawing only a small proportion of its requirements from local sources, the coal-fields of the Eastern Cape. But as the new trunk-line neared the Vaal, the Cape authorities began to take limited quantities from Marks's colliery at the river. To encourage transport-riders to work the gap between the railhead at Kroonstad and Johannesburg, the railway authorities agreed to purchase coal loaded at the Vaal coal-fields by wagoners returning to Kroonstad from the Rand.[29]

The Cape railways found that the coal was both cheap and burned well in the fireboxes of its engines. Furthermore, unlike the expensive imported Welsh coal and the poorer-quality Eastern Cape coal, it was conveniently available at the point of consumption, for the railway's route lay across Marks's coal property. Once the main line was completed, trucks returning empty from the Witwatersrand could load up with coal for the Cape railways at little extra expense. There was no need to build and operate a lengthy and expensive branch-line to the collieries as in the case of the remote Eastern Cape coal-fields. The cost saving could be very significant once competing trunk-lines from Durban and Delagoa Bay were completed for both of these ran close to major coal-fields and would be supplied with cheap fuel.[30]

These considerations appealed to the Cape railway authorities and in particular to James Sivewright, the Scot who was Commissioner of Crown Lands and Public Works in the Rhodes ministry and political master of the Cape Government Railways. Marks and Sivewright, an expert on telegraphy turned political fixer, had struck up an instant rapport when the Cape minister visited Pretoria to negotiate the extension of the Cape line; and after enjoying Marks's hospitality, Sivewright had affectionately dubbed his host Lord Hatherley. In 1892, the year the southern line at last reached Johannesburg, Marks and Sivewright discussed the possibility of a more formal arrangement between the Cape Government Railways and the colliery. Marks, of course, wanted a long-term contract which would protect the colliery against unpredictable and damaging fluctuations in demand for its coal and enable it to expand without running the risk of wasted investment in underutilised capacity. Sivewright wanted security of supply. If the Cape was to compete effectively with its rivals for the rapidly expanding transit trade to the Rand it needed an assured supply of cheap coal of adequate quality which could be readily expanded as rail traffic grew. A contract with Marks's colliery seemed the best way to guarantee this.[31]

The Cape parliament, or at least its Eastern Cape members, saw matters very differently. Why should a 'foreign' colliery, particularly one situated beyond the customs union in the Transvaal, be favoured at the expense of the Indwe and Cyphergat mines of the Cape? Indwe coal, after all, was in no way inferior to Vaal River coal. Why encourage the development of a 'foreign' industry instead of a local? Allegations were also made that Sivewright, very much a man-on-the-make both politically and financially, had a personal financial interest in the colliery, a charge he strenuously – and truthfully – denied again and again, though he conveniently failed to mention that he had other business dealings with Lewis and Marks.[32]

Ignoring the objections and insinuations, Sivewright negotiated a one-year contract with Lewis and Marks for 1893. The colliery was to supply 7,000 tons of coal per month at 11s. per ton, and the railways could call for a further 6,000 tons per month at 10s. 6d. per ton if extra supplies were needed. Sivewright, who had 'beaten down' Lewis and Marks from 15s. per ton, felt that it was 'a most admirable contract'.[33] His enraged opponents did not agree. Marks was summonsed to Cape Town – 'into the camp of the Philistines' – to defend the contract before a select committee of the Cape parliament. After a rough handling at the hands of members of the committee, he wrote to Isaac Lewis: 'Regarding the Cape Government and Parliament I must tell you in a very few words that with the exception of three or four, they are the biggest lot of damn'd scoundrels and hounds I ever met with, and in business or politics our people here are not a match to them. I believe they would sell their best friend or friends for less than a £10 note, and during the three or four days I was in Cape Town I learned all that, and regarding bribery their price is below £25 per head.'[34]

As Marks correctly suspected, those opposing the use of his coal were hardly disinterested parties: the most vociferous parliamentary critic of the contract, for example, had a stake in one of the neglected Cape collieries. Nevertheless, their opposition was sufficient to prevent the signing of a secure, long-term contract with the Coal Association. With much difficulty, and after bearing a fusillade of insults from politicians whose 'eloquence' was 'hurled against' his firm 'annually for daring to supply their Railways with Coal', Marks eventually won a new contract which gave him a little more security than the original one. The Cape railway would take between 100,000 and 190,000 tons in 1895, but with the option of extending this to three years.[35]

Marks recognised that if these obligations were to be met and parliamentary criticism and the financial penalties in the contract avoided, production would have to be not only maintained but expanded. The chief difficulties in maintaining an adequate level of production at the Vaal River colliery was the general scarcity of labour on the Witwatersrand and in the neighbouring districts during the 1890s. While the labour supply, particularly from Mozambique, grew apace, it fell chronically short of the needs of the rapidly expanding mining industry. Compounding the problem was the high turnover of labour. Blacks coming to work on the mines in the 1890s stayed for a far shorter period than is the case today. Workers would leave after two or three months' service, which meant that at the Vaal River colliery, for example, the entire black workforce, close to 1,000 strong in the mid-nineties, had to be replaced some six times per year.[36]

One possible solution which had been excluded by the mid-nineties was captive labour. In December 1891 Lewis and Marks had asked the government whether it would be willing to supply a few hundred convicts to the Vaal River colliery. De Beers at Kimberley had made successful use of this type of labour for some years, and the firm believed it could do so too, for the mine was isolated, which limited the possibility of contact with the outside world and escape. The prisoners would be housed in a compound supervised by government officials – shades of Marks's proposal a decade before at Kimberley.

The press had welcomed the idea: the Transvaal's prison population, currently a burden on the state (and on the taxpayer), would be turned instead into a productive asset, while the costs of coal production would be cut by as much as half. White labour, however, was less enthusiastic about the prospect of working alongside convict labourers. The government was receptive at first and drew up regulations for the deployment of convict labour in the mining industry. When it came to implementing these, however, it belatedly discovered that there were insufficient prisoners to meet the labour requirements both of the Vaal River colliery and the other mines which had taken an interest in the scheme, and of the state itself. Who would construct public roads and buildings if all the convicts were down the mine?[37]

Like the rest of the mining industry, Marks cast his net very widely for free labour. Approaches were made to the Cape authorities for colonial labour; influential whites in Swaziland were asked to act as recruiters; and, when labour was particularly scarce in the wake of the Jameson Raid and mines were threatened with closure, serious consideration was given to the recruitment of Indian labour in Natal.[38] A source closer to hand was the Vaal River property itself. The black tenant farmers were expected to send their sons to work at the colliery for limited periods of time and, when labour was particularly scarce, workmen were withdrawn from other divisions of the estate and sent down the mine. 'Tell Kok [the estate manager] he must get 50 boys, even if he has to go to Hell for them!' Marks ordered during one such crisis.[39]

With labour in such short supply Marks was determined to extract the maximum benefit from the available workforce. Marks was his own time and motion expert, paying frequent visits to the colliery to check the efficiency of its operations. After one such underground inspection in 1893 he sent his brother Ellia, the mine manager, a list of suggestions to improve the productivity of his workmen. 'I must tell you that I found a good many Kaffirs underground sitting on their behinds. It was dark and I suppose they cannot generally be seen, but if a stranger goes down the mine and puts out his candle, at every turn and corner you will find 2 or 3 of these coloured gentlemen so employed. All they require is a prayer book and a missionary and the business will be complete.'

The white miner-overseers needed to be pushed harder: 'You must make your men understand fully for what they are paid and what the kaffirs are there for

. . . they should give you more for your money than you are now getting, and if they cannot get work out of the boys you should dispense with their services without delay.' The white miners were to be given extra responsibilities: 'They should not grumble at this,' he wrote. 'They do a very small amount of manual labour, and it is not hard work for them to keep their eyes open underground.'[40]

Like his counterparts on the gold mines of the Witwatersrand, Marks was also very concerned with the high rate of absenteeism on Mondays. After a weekend of bingeing, many of the workers were too inebriated either to report for duty or to function effectively if they did. Ironically, Marks, the managing director of a distillery that concentrated largely on the black mine-worker market, seriously considered prohibiting the sale of liquor to his own mine-workers.[41] The working week (and year) at the colliery was long and arduous. To meet the Cape contract the men worked from 6 in the morning to 6 in the evening, Monday to Saturday. They even worked on Christmas and Boxing Day – Marks instructed his brother 'to give all the men some beer and the boys meat' after work – but were given a three-day holiday at the end of the year. Wages in 1894 were between £3 and £4 per month for black workers, and £4 to £7 per week for white.[42]

While the success of the colliery was Marks's first concern, he was anxious at the same time to develop the full potential of the property. Right from the start the Vaal River estate was primarily a coal-mining concern. The Association had acquired its vast holdings along the Vaal in the early 1880s, not because of the agricultural potential of the land, but because of the suspected presence of immense coal measures beneath the surface of these farms. Coal was clearly king; any other operations would always have to play second fiddle.

While Marks shared this basic set of priorities with his partners and was just as aware of the centrality of coal-mining in the company's scheme of things, he nevertheless very rapidly came to attach a growing importance to the non-mining dimension of the estate's work. He was increasingly anxious to make full use of all of its assets, not just of its coal. On occasion this brought him into conflict with his fellow directors, who were far more concerned with maximising their short-term and medium-term returns from coal-mining than with venturing capital on risky agricultural and industrial projects which offered low returns at the very best in the immediate future.

Surveying the estate in the early nineties, Marks was acutely aware of its possibilities. It seemed uniquely endowed with raw materials and natural advantages: it had fuel in abundance; it had acres of fertile and flat land; it had building stone and lime and clay; it had a lengthy river frontage; and it lay on the doorstep of the Rand, the great inland market. Marks's creative imagination played with a variety of ways of combining and exploiting these assets.

He was painfully conscious that the Vaal River coal mine had a very high discard rate compared with other collieries: as much as 30 per cent of all the coal hauled from underground had to be rejected to satisfy the Cape railways, who were very demanding customers. The money spent on extracting and hauling this was literally thrown away, a situation Marks, who hated waste, found intolerable. Why not put the smouldering heaps of 'seconds' to profitable use?

Why not import a steam-mill, he repeatedly suggested to Lewis, to attract the business of the grain farmers of the surrounding districts? 'It is shameful to think that we should be building mountains of nut coal, for which we cannot possibly find a market and which is simply consuming itself while we, at the same time, allow thousands of bags of grain to pass our Estate annually to be ground at Johannesburg at 3/- per bag.' The mill would pay for itself in eighteen months; its fuel costs would obviously be negligible. Marks's idea was not properly followed up till the establishment of the Vereeniging Milling Company, later Vereeniging Consolidated Mills, during the First World War.[43]

While travelling by train to Paris during one of his rare visits to Europe, Marks happened to notice that the engine was burning briquettes made out of compressed coal dust. Why not import the necessary machinery to make these at the Vaal, he asked? If the local coal dust did not contain enough tar, they could mix in either grass or lime, both of which were in plentiful supply on the estate. 'Of course this is only a suggestion of mine,' he added; 'I do not profess to be a practical man.' Then again, why not use the waste coal for power generation, and to pump water to Johannesburg?[44]

The key to much of Marks's thinking about the future of the Vaal River property was its proximity to the Witwatersrand, one of its greatest advantages. Marks felt it was ideally placed to offer a range of vital services to the mushrooming conurbation and its mining industry. Writing in 1892, six years after the foundation of Johannesburg and while the city was recovering from a major slump, he predicted a massive expansion in gold production within the next three years, and, with it, a doubling of the city's population. This would create a great demand, he reasoned, for the utilities his Vaal River property was in an excellent position to provide: water and electric power. Given a doubling of the population and a rapid expansion of mining operations, Johannesburg's existing water supply drawn from the springs and spruits close to town would be 'totally insufficient' in the near future. Under the circumstances, Marks believed, 'The only reliable source to fall back upon is the *Vaal River*.' Its water could be pumped easily and cheaply from the Vaal to Johannesburg, using power provided by burning the colliery's waste coal.

The waste coal could also be used to generate electricity for transmission to Johannesburg and the mines. 'Now in the present age of Electricity,' Marks enthused, 'when so many improvements have been, and are still being made to transmit Electric power over large areas, I do not see that the day is so very far distant when we shall make another bound forward . . . [and] we will find batteries and drilling machines on the Rand being worked by this Electrical transmission from the Vaal River . . . to Johannesburg' – a very potent vision in an age when electricity was not yet a commonplace, and when many, like Marks, were enthralled by electricity, and awed by its potentialities. The cost of the combined scheme? At least one and a half million pounds, Marks guessed.

Marks recognised that the scale, ambition and sheer novelty of the proposal would most likely intimidate his associates. 'These figures will probably throw cold water on the foregoing,' he wrote to one, 'but if you will only take into consideration the enormous revenue accruing to such a scheme, the idea will not look so mad after all.' 'You know I am always looking ahead,' he wrote to another, 'so much so, that I frequently am told I am too much before the times. . . . The idea is not to be condemned as impossible . . . although I may not live to see it, it must come.'[45]

On a less ambitious scale, the property's abundant water supplies could also be used for beer-making. In 1893 Marks thought of asking Anders Ohlsson of the Cape brewery of that name to set up a similar business at Vereeniging to capture the Rand beer market. Technical tests of the local water were not encouraging, though. A year later Marks asked Ohlsson's northern rivals, the South African United Breweries, for a share in their flourishing business, threatening to set up a competing brewery at Hatherley. The threat had the desired effect: Lewis and Marks were sold 12,500 shares in the renamed South African Breweries on condition that they stayed out of the beer-making business.[46]

The Association's landholdings were vast. It held 129,000 acres, equivalent to 201 square miles of land, much of this with a frontage on the Vaal River. How best to put this to use? Marks wondered. Since the early 1880s part of the land had been worked by tenants, black and white, but this was not an altogether satisfactory arrangement, and Marks felt that the Association's valuable acreage was being underutilised. Suitable white tenants, with a market-oriented and progressive approach to farming, were hard to come by. Even the less progressive were hard to catch: 'A Dutchman who understands a little farming will not come to us to hire ground, but will sponge on a friend of his who will give him a strip for friendship's sake or for a political move; he can work on it for a couple of years for nothing. The amount of farming work he does is not very much. Therefore he would not hire ground from us.' At the same time he felt a certain ambivalence about recruiting further black tenants, good farmers as they might be, because of the social implications of black tenancy. 'I am not in favour of the Company receiving rent from the Kaffirs, as soon as the Kaffir pays us a rental he will consider himself his own master, and this will not do, on the other hand I am not in favour of his being dispensed with.'[47]

The difficulty of finding suitable tenants and the consequent underutilisation of the Association's arable land led Marks to consider whether the Association should not itself engage in farming. Rather than relying exclusively on rent and a share of others' crops, it could invest capital in company farming, based on mechanisation. Marks, a pioneer in the application of steam power in diamond-mining at Kimberley, suggested to his fellow shareholders in the Coal Association that they acquire a steam plough, the Victorian forerunner of the modern tractor. The Vaal River property seemed well suited to steam-ploughing: its large farms were relatively level, and coal and water, the essential elements for steam generation, were readily available and inexpensive.

Marks anticipated, correctly, that his co-owners would resist, and that management would object 'that they are not Farmers and have no wish to plant mealies'. After years of cajoling, Lewis eventually capitulated. In 1894 the Association spent close to £7,000 on a steam plough and its accessories. These were supplied by Fowlers of Leeds, the leading English manufacturers of steam ploughs. Fowlers sent with their chief expert on the practical application of steam-ploughing, one W. A. McLaren, who had successfully introduced their steam plough in Germany, Argentina, New Zealand and Australia. South Africa was his nemesis.[48]

One of the steam plough's first tasks was to prepare ground for the planting of trees at Maccauvlei, a farm across the river from present-day Vereeniging. At the beginning of the nineties Maccauvlei was 'a confused jumble of sand hills . . . [a] desertlike farm', apparently incapable of supporting even a single family. During the decade it became the arena for one of Marks's major ambitions (and enthusiasms), the creation of a great commercial plantation which could supply a sizeable portion of the future timber needs of the Witwatersrand.

Marks persuaded his reluctant fellow directors that a small annual investment of £500 or £600 would begin yielding handsome profits in as little as five years. Marks appointed a young German, Otto Brandmuller, with wide experience as a forester and nurseryman. When Brandmuller arrived by coach at Vereeniging in 1893, he asked to be directed to Maccauvlei. He was told that 'when you reach the place where the frogs croak the loudest you will know you have arrived'. The thatched house he was given had been built by 'Kwaai Augus' Pistorius, the original Voortrekker occupant of the farm; inscribed on its front door, in English, was the motto 'Women will ever be deceivers'; outside stood three flourishing oak trees Pistorius had grown from acorns he had brought from Natal. These were to be the nucleus of the great Maccauvlei forest, the first commercial forestry venture on the Highveld. [49]

By late 1895 there was a block of 120,000 oak trees, with a further half a million saplings awaiting replanting. Visiting the plantation in November, a month before the Jameson Raid, Marks excitedly reported that the trees were already laden with acorns. 'No doubt, if you told some English Country Gentleman or Land Owner this, he would not credit it, for in England, an oak will not bear acorns for ten or fifteen years; nevertheless what I state is fact.' As he gazed at the oaks, it occurred to him that though they were still very immature, they could already be turned to profit. Cape farmers fed acorns to their horses, mules and poultry; why not Free State farmers and Transvalers too, he thought, as he calculated the value of his acorn crop.[50]

Then there was the Vaal River property's industrial potential. Marks was aware as early as the 1880s that there were valuable deposits of clay immediately beneath the coal seams.[51] With cheap fuel at hand, he was eager to use this to manufacture firebricks, pipes and pottery. But as always in the early industrial Transvaal it was difficult to find suitable workmen. When Isaac Lewis passed through Cape Town in 1892, Marks sent him off to the local brickfields to recruit artisans: 'The reason I ask you to take this trouble in Cape Town is that it is getting a little out of fashion to employ men who smoke their pipes in the day and get the horrors through drink. . . . If you cannot succeed in getting white men for your business I would not think twice about it, but send up some good malays. They will suit our purposes just as well, will have more respect, and will do more work for less money.'[52]

Lewis was evidently unsuccessful in finding the right people. Production of firebricks began in 1893 without adequate equipment and expertise, and soon encountered consumer resistance because of the poor quality of the product. In addition, Marks also had to contend with costs of production, particularly labour costs, which were far higher than in England, and a daily output that was far lower. New machinery was ordered from England, and an expert imported, but matters failed to improve. The expert bluntly informed Marks that the machine was 'rubbish', which failed to endear him to his employer. But even Marks was eventually forced to concede that he had made a mistake. After a careful examination of the brick plant he wrote to the manufacturers that 'I can only say: "what a waste of money" but of course I cannot deny that you carried out your instructions, and I also remember your saying that if anyone orders a pig from you, you do not send them an ox.'[53]

Marks's industrial ambitions at the Vaal went well beyond the relative simplicity of brickmaking, however. In the early nineties he revived an idea he had first conceived in 1881 soon after acquiring the Vaal River farms: the creation of an iron industry on the Highveld. While the idea might have seemed quixotic in the early eighties when the Transvaal was an impoverished backwater without a significant internal market for industrial goods, it had begun to look more realistic a decade later. The future of the gold-mining industry – with the railways, the largest potential customer for iron products – appeared increasingly assured in the early nineties. Production was expanding rapidly and the mines were beginning to develop the deep levels to the south of the outcrop. It seemed the right time for a scheme as bold and as grand as the establishment of a domestic iron industry.[54]

In August 1892 Marks wrote to his father-in-law, Tobias Guttmann, in Sheffield, asking him to make detailed enquiries locally about the practicalities of iron-making. How much did the machinery cost? What buildings were needed? How many men were required? Would they be prepared to come out from England, and what wages would they expect? Specifications were to be drawn up, 'complete . . . to the last nail'. What Marks had in mind was the establishment at the Vaal River of a 'large' iron works, capable of producing as much as a hundred tons of iron a day. He believed that all the necessary raw materials were available on the farms or nearby: fireclay for refractory bricks to line the furnaces; limestone, iron-ore and coking coal for smelting together into pig iron. The iron-ore was on a farm Marks took under offer, some 12 miles across country from the coal mine and 22 miles by river. Marks hoped eventually to float the iron-ore in small boats to the furnace he would build on the property. Paul Kruger was encouraging but Marks's partners, it seems, were less taken with the idea. Despite Marks's enthusiastic recommendation and his belief that European investors could easily be attracted, the firm did little to pursue the scheme.[55]

Marks expected that the establishment of industries on the property, coupled with the expansion of the colliery and the extension of the main line from the south through the property, would draw large numbers of people to the locality; he was eager to create a township to cater for this influx. The Association had first applied for permission to establish a township, on the Transvaal side of its property, in 1882, a few months after coal-mining began. Pretoria agreed in principle, stipulating that the township was to be called Vereeniging, the Dutch equivalent of 'Association'. But the grant was not taken up: the closure of the coal mine and the severe economic recession of the mid-eighties froze all development plans.[56]

Like much else, the township scheme was rescued by the discovery of gold on the Witwatersrand. The plans were dusted off, and a formal agreement was signed with the state in 1889. This contract ensured that Vereeniging would become a company town though not quite in the North American mould. While the Association would sell township erven on a freehold basis, it reserved the right to all minerals and precious stones or metals that might be discovered within the boundaries of the township. It also held the sole right to provide a number of important public services. It alone could supply water and lighting to the township; it alone could run horse-drawn trams and a telephone service. These prerogatives, together with the Association's status as the major local employer and as the dominant local landowner, gave the company a hold over the town it would retain for decades.[57]

The first auction of Vereeniging erven was held in Johannesburg in 1892 and was timed to coincide with the arrival of the railway from the south. The town was laid out, at least in the auctioneer's plan, on a grid pattern, then the standard South African urban design, with numbered streets intersecting numbered avenues at right angles, and with rectangular and uniform erven, each measuring 200 by 100 feet. In deference to Boer sentiment, 1,000 morgen was set aside as commonage or townland for grazing the community's livestock; and sites were reserved for the major church denominations.[58]

In a display of religious even-handedness, Kruger, who for all his fundamentalism was no bigot, insisted that twelve erven be set aside in the new township for places of worship. When Marks objected that this seemed an excessive number, Kruger explained that he needed at least twelve to ensure equal treatment for the Catholics, the Jews, the Presbyterians, the Wesleyans, the Anglicans and the Dutch Reformed.[59]

The results of the auction were disappointing. Vereeniging was one of a wave of township promotions at this time, some of them very dubious, and suffered in consequence. The public, bitten so often before, were understandably wary of investing in a site so far from the centre of things at Johannesburg. While it can be assumed that Marks was disappointed at the apparent still-birth of a township which was essentially his conception, it is also clear he was by no means despondent. The way forward, he felt, was to hire a gardener from the Cape, who could plant trees and create an attractive public garden at this dry and dusty site which would encourage others to take up erven and build. Without this the township would remain a figment of the surveyor's and promoters' imagination. 'At the present time we cannot expect strangers to come to the property.'[60]

For all Marks's efforts at 'improving' the Vaal River property, for all his dreams of converting Vereeniging into a South African Sheffield, the area retained much of its primal charm. In the early 1890s a herd of a few hundred springbok still roamed the estate. Shooting these was 'seldom allowed' and was a privilege restricted to very important visitors. A four-day hunt on Marks's Vaal River estate was one of the highpoints of a journey through southern Africa in 1891 by Lord Randolph Churchill, father of the future prime minister. Mounted on their ponies, the Churchill party – 'four guns' – chased the buck across the veld during the day, then in the evenings retired to their 'rough and ready' camp where dinner was 'skilfully' prepared by a French chef, presumably hired by their attentive host. The 'bag' gives some sense of the richness of the wildlife that continued to survive on Marks's incipient industrial park (as well as of the qualities of the Churchill party as shots): 'four duck, fifty partridge, four hares, 250 quail, eight koran [korhaan], eleven snipe, one dikkop, one wild turkey, one blue crane, and two springbok.'[61]

Like the Vaal River coal estate, the Hatherley distillery prospered after the discovery of gold on the Witwatersrand. What had been a struggling operation, growing only very slowly in a recessionary economic environment, was transformed within a matter of years into a flourishing concern, catering to a rapidly expanding market. The congregation of tens of thousands of black mine-workers on the Rand created a huge demand for the cheap liquor the distillery produced. Production and sales soared: by 1893 the distillery was selling close to 300,000 gallons of liquor per annum; by 1895, close to 400,000. Profits rose more than proportionately: in 1893 these were close to £50,000; by 1895, they had doubled to close to £100,000. The distillery, converted at the end of 1892 into De Eerste Fabrieken Hatherley Distillery Ltd., a limited liability company registered in the Transvaal, declared annual dividends of between 16 and 20 per cent in the mid-nineties after a decade of passing its dividends.[62]

Success just as much as struggle brought its tensions between the partners. Rapid expansion created its own problems, including a shortage of storage space and a shortage of working capital. Marks, as the managing director, was compelled to spend heavily to provide for the distillery's expanded requirements, particularly for the storage of grain and of the much expanded liquor stock. Isaac Lewis, always intensely conscious of costs, always cautious, was very critical of this expenditure, which he felt was much higher than it ought to be. Marks was quite exasperated by this: 'even were I gifted with more patience . . . even were I to use every possible argument to convince you that money is not being thrown away but is being utilised for the proper extension of our business and works, you would not believe it. We cannot put our spirits in sacks neither can we store our grain on the housetops . . . I am not egotistical, but I flatter myself that few in the country or out of it can teach me to control this place at less cost, and if I am spending money, it is in a good cause, and I shall always be strongly opposed to a penny wise and a pound foolish policy to suit the whims of some people, for which afterwards the Company must pay the piper.'[63]

Marks spent also on experiments with new products; he wanted to broaden the distillery's range beyond cheap gin and brandy and so lessen its dependence on the lower depths of the liquor market. The distillery began producing whisky in the early nineties, using local barley grown from seed Marks distributed to the Boer farmers. But, as Marks was forced to admit, the results were 'not . . . so brilliant as I could have desired'. Still he persisted, hoping that the quality could be improved through skilful blending and lengthy maturation: 'you must not forget', he wrote to his impatient partner, 'that even the whisky that comes out of Scotland was not made in a day and I have no doubt that it took them many years before they could bring their production up to its present standard.'[64]

Marks also experimented with something he called 'spirits of wine'. Sending a sample to Mrs Nellmapius he wrote: 'Perhaps the latter will surprise you, but my reason is that I have made a discovery. Mrs. Marks uses it for her curling tongs and I believe it has the desired effect.'[65] He experimented, too, with liqueur made of oranges supplied by the Boer farmers. Ever mindful of the importance of retaining Boer goodwill, he saw this product serving a double purpose: 'we must support the Farmers in the State, and we must take from them large quantities of oranges . . . with a large business in the article, there is no reason why we should not keep in with the Rulers of the State, and at the same time show a profit on the transaction.'[66]

Expansion and experiment meant extra staff but Marks struggled to find suitable people. Sobriety in particular was essential given the temptations the distillery offered. As Marks wrote to Eerste Fabrieken's agent in Johannesburg: 'In engaging men I would like you to be a little more careful than you have been of late. I do not want you to send me old soldiers and "retired" government officials. You must always look at your man and see how much gin you can tap from his nose. We can make gin here. We don't require to import it.'[67]

Marks ran Eerste Fabrieken from an office at Hatherley and from another in Church Square in the centre of the Boer capital. During the late 1880s and 1890s the South African head office of Lewis and Marks was in Pretoria rather than in Johannesburg. This set it apart from most other Uitlander firms with major mining interests and reflects the distinctive character of its business. Unlike the others, its Witwatersrand gold-mining interests were limited; instead its major involvement was with the colliery on the Vaal River which could be served equally well from Pretoria and Johannesburg, and with the distillery at Hatherley eleven miles outside the capital. Since the distillery and the other activities at Hatherley were so dependent on government support, it made good sense to be headquartered in Pretoria with the Boer legislators and civil servants close at hand.

The Pretoria offices in the 1890s were in a modest building on the east side of an increasingly august Church Square. Besides Lewis and Marks the building also housed a firm of attorneys, Stegman and Esselen, whom Sammy Marks often consulted, and the office of the Selati Railway, a company that defended a dubious concession to build a railroad in the eastern Transvaal by distributing 'spiders' – light carriages – amongst members of the Volksraad. Church Square, the Standard Bank had reported in 1890, was 'the centre of all the financial institutions in Pretoria'. Around the Square lay the Bank of Africa, the Natal Bank, the Standard Bank, the Netherlands Bank, and the National Bank, the South African Republic's proud creation in which Lewis and Marks held a small stake. Despite their share in this indigenous bank, Lewis and Marks kept their account at the Standard for Marks had greater faith in this British-owned bank – South Africa's premier bank until the take-over of the National by Barclays in the 1920s – than in the local bank even though at times he resented the Standard's stringent lending practices: 'if one requires accommodation from the Standard Bank they make you mortgage to them your property, your soul and even the souls of your future generations.'

Dominating Church Square and overshadowing Marks's modest office building were two monuments to the growing prosperity and pretensions of the South African Republic. These were the grand new law courts on the north side of the square, closest to Lewis and Marks, and the imposing government building on the south side of the square which housed the Volksraad chambers. Marks was thus just a short stroll from those on whose support his enterprises depended. Marks conducted much of his business in the street. Always informal, he often met people outside his office to discuss money, politics and the rest. As George Falcke, his nephew and long-time confidential secretary recalls, Sammy would take up 'his familiar attitude just outside the window of his office, his two elbows wedged in the extremities of the window sill, his body leaning, and his one heel against the wall. He would hail people from all parts of Church Square and often assemble a large crowd in this manner.'[68]

The Lewis and Marks office staff in Pretoria was small. Marks ran his burgeoning business with a handful of assistants, involving himself directly in all aspects of it, however minor. At the same time he attempted to minimise bureaucracy. Employees were instructed that the business 'shall not be conducted in the same manner as in the Home Government Offices, and red paperism should be avoided as much as possible.' Sammy's right-hand man in Pretoria was Hugh Crawford, eight years younger than his employer and a devout Presbyterian with extensive experience in banking both in Scotland and in South Africa. After serving as branch manager of the Standard Bank in Kimberley he had left in 1888 to go out on his own. Within a very short space of time he had lost everything through disastrous share dealings and was deeply in debt. Lewis and Marks, in need of capable managers, had come to his rescue. They gave Crawford a position in their Pretoria office at £1,000 per annum plus a small share of the profits. As Isaac Lewis later recalled: 'I took him on, when he came back from Kimberley without boots on his feet. . . . I put him on his feet again and . . . made a rich man of him.' In the words of his former employers at the bank, Crawford was a 'highly respectable man'. He was totally reliable and honest, and since his personal financial disaster, 'very careful' about money. This made him a useful foil to Marks: his reluctance to spend money – his employers' as well as his own – helped to keep a rein on Marks's tendency to spend freely. Crawford was no 'yes man' – he made his opposition quite plain when Marks speculated heavily in land in the mid-1890s, and he objected as well to the large sums of money that Marks disbursed to charity. Crawford 'went for me,' Marks reported to London after one of their disagreements; 'I must confess that he is quite right.'[69]

1895 was Sammy Marks's *annus mirabilis*. In the decade since his move from Kimberley to the Transvaal the firm's assets and his personal fortune had grown steadily rather than spectacularly. As he reminded his partner: 'we have been going on slowly and steadily for so many years, and although we do not figure in the list of millionaires, we have always managed to hold our own and to augment our assets little by little.' This changed dramatically with the 'Kaffir Boom', the great surge in South African mining shares, which began in late 1894, and accelerated in early 1895. British and Continental investors woke up to the attractions of the mines of the Witwatersrand, and poured money into these and other Transvaal ventures.

Eerste Fabrieken, with its soaring sales, attracted the attention of Sir Edgar Vincent, the young and adventurous English financier, who directed the affairs of the Imperial Ottoman Bank (and diverted a large part of its funds – and those of its clients at Constantinople – into the 'Kaffir' market, the market in South African mining shares). Vincent visited South Africa in 1894 and formed a very favourable impression of the prospects of the Hatherley distillery. He bought a large block of shares and encouraged his friends in the European banking community to follow suit, assuring them that there was no better investment in South Africa. During 1895 Vincent helped Isaac Lewis to make a market in Eerste Fabrieken shares in London and Paris, and the price bounded ahead.[70]

The effect on Marks's fortunes was electrifying. His personal income between January and June 1894 had amounted to an unimpressive £6,215, of which just under half was his share of the Lewis and Marks partnership's profits. In the corresponding period in 1895 his earnings rocketed to close to £100,000, most of which came from his one-third share in the profits of the partnership. In addition he registered a capital gain of just under £80,000 from selling part of his personal holdings of Eerste Fabrieken shares. In the second half of 1895, when the 'Kaffir boom' reached its dizzying climax, Marks earned well over £190,000, almost doubling his income of the first half of the year, and he also received £114,520 from the sale of the remainder of his Eerste Fabrieken shares. In a single year Marks's personal income had risen to close to £300,000 while the firm's profits had soared to well over £800,000. In the space of eighteen months, from 30 June 1894 to 31 December 1895, the book value of Marks's net assets had almost quadrupled, from £170,676 to £669,789.[71]

Marks and the firm were more liquid than they had ever been before; the question now was how best to spend or reinvest their profits. In the first instance, Isaac Lewis, the firm's financial expert, placed just short of £700,000 in foreign government stock, a favourite investment of the age. Marks approved of this in principle though he felt that their South American bonds should be replaced by Russian, French, German, English or Yankee bonds, for in the 1890s as today, Latin American governments were unreliable, and 'every now and again you read in the newspaper that some row has taken place'.[72]

Marks was more critical of Lewis's investment in private ventures abroad. Marks cabled his partner to confine speculation to the Transvaal – 'it is no use worrying your life out', he admonished Lewis, 'to make £5 and lose £6 in things about which your knowledge is limited. . . . I am still of opinion that plenty of money can be made in this country without going to America and elsewhere for it.'[73] In this belief Marks channelled a large part of the proceeds from the sale of the distillery shares into landed property, particularly in the western Transvaal. Lewis and Marks, like other Uitlander speculators at this time, looked more to the mineral potential of the land they bought than to the agricultural. This was the age when investors searched for a second Rand, a second golden bonanza to equal the Witwatersrand, a quest which reached northwards across the Transvaal into neighbouring Rhodesia.

Marks's attention was drawn by reports of gold reefs in Lichtenburg, a remote western district of the Transvaal inhabited by a scattering of impoverished Boer farmers. Like many of his contemporaries, Marks went on a speculative spree, based only on a vague report from a farmer, unsubstantiated by any reliable professional opinion or by personal observation. He did not visit the district before buying, nor did he send his geologist until the major investment had already been made.

Isaac Lewis was at first as keen as Marks on speculative investment in land, but as the Transvaal boom ran out of steam in late 1895, he became increasingly anxious and tried to call a halt. Marks, caught up in a speculative frenzy, was quite indignant. Reporting that he had already spent no less than £170,000, he wrote:

My opinion is that as soon as business becomes more settled and brisk we shall be doubly repaid for this outlay, and will have plenty to handle.

My reason for writing this is because you have already cabled three times that we must not buy anything whatsoever. We are fully alive to the fact that buying is one thing and selling another, but there is an old saying that 'well bought is half sold'.

When Lewis continued cabling, Marks snapped: 'I know perfectly well what I am doing, and whenever you are dissatisfied with any purchase I may make, debit my account with same, as long as I have money to pay for it. You on the one hand keep cabling me not to buy, and Mr. Crawford on the other hand keeps persuading me not to buy and this does not tend to improve the state of my liver.'[74]

One consequence of Marks's spending spree was that it drew him into a close business relationship with certain key members of the Boer elite. By 1895 Boer society was by no means as egalitarian as later mythologisers and nationalist ideologues would maintain. It was increasingly stratified, with growing opportunities for accumulating wealth through speculation and the perks of office for some, and increasing difficulties for many others. The well-connected and successful minority were eager to deal with Uitlander speculators like Marks, and to share in the largesse they were dispensing so freely.

During the mining boom in early 1895, Piet Joubert, Commandant-General of the Republic, and a very active speculator in land and mining shares, tried, with little success, to dump certain dubious mining claims in the Klerksdorp gold-fields on Lewis and Marks. Later in the year he sold Marks a 'gold farm' on yet another of the putative gold-fields of the Transvaal, this one some three miles south of Pietersburg. The price was £12,500 plus shares in a company that was to be floated to exploit the reef.

A week after the deal was struck, Joubert called Marks to his sick-bed and confessed he had since discovered that the farm was substantially smaller than originally promised. Would Marks insist on a reduction in price? Wary of displeasing a powerful official, Marks replied that he would still pay the asking price. To Marks's surprise, Joubert was visibly disappointed with this response. The reason soon became apparent: 'after beating about the bush', 'Slim Piet' – as Joubert was popularly known – admitted that he was bluffing and that the farm was substantially larger than the original figure, not smaller; he made it quite obvious, however, that unlike Marks, he expected the price to be adjusted to match the new size, even though the deal had already been struck. 'I did not promise anything,' Marks reported to Lewis, 'but should he ask for extra payment, I shall give him same, as although he has no right to extra payment, I consider it bad policy to fall out with such people over £5,000 or £6,000.' In the event, 'Slim Piet' settled for an extra £3,000.[75]

Koos de la Rey, one of the leading Boer notables of the western Transvaal, dealt more straightforwardly with Marks. A former native commissioner and commandant of the Lichtenburg district and its current member of the Volksraad, he was a natural choice as Lewis and Marks's local representative once they had established a strong presence in the area. De la Rey became Marks's farm superintendent and rent-collector in the Lichtenburg district, entrusted with a broad measure of discretion in setting terms for the tenants. He reported to Marks on the agricultural potential of farms in the district and advised him about ways of conserving the herds of springbok on his properties. In keeping with the new conservationist ethic that was gaining ground in the Transvaal, Marks banned shooting on his farms and appointed local farmers, nominated by De la Rey, as gamekeepers to prevent poaching. De la Rey, a calm, dignified and modest man, became a close personal friend, perhaps the most prized and cherished of Marks's Boer friends.[76]

Besides spending heavily in the western Transvaal in 1895, Marks also bought property in the eastern Transvaal, where coal deposits had recently been uncovered which more than matched the quality of his Vaal River coalbeds. These purchases were linked with the completing of the railway line from Delagoa Bay to the Rand in the same year. Marks anticipated that the larger part of the goods traffic from the coast to the Rand, which currently used the Cape line, would switch to the shorter Delagoa Bay route once it was fully operational. Consequently he was eager to pick up whatever business opportunities were on offer at Delagoa Bay. 'If you can see any other rights at Delagoa Bay standing out,' he wrote to Lewis in London in late 1894, 'I strongly recommend you to secure them even though they may cost a few thousand pounds. Delagoa Bay is as the Transvaal was 10 years ago and there is a great future before it. In the Transvaal, at the time I speak of, people were frightened to invest one shilling where they would now put in a thousand or two. So 'twill be with Delagoa Bay, which is the natural harbour for the Transvaal or northern territories, the Bay being only 430 miles or thereabouts from Pretoria as against 660 from the nearest Cape Port.'[77]

The chief difficulty at Delagoa Bay, and hence the chief opportunity, was the absence of adequate infrastructure. Delagoa Bay was supremely ill-equipped for its new role as the preferred entrepôt of the Transvaal: its landing and storage facilities were no better than rudimentary. There were no berths deep enough for even the smallest of ocean-going vessels. These were forced to anchor in the river, then transfer their passengers and cargoes to barges and lighters which would land them at two rickety piers when the tide was sufficiently high – a clumsy procedure which caused maddening delays and added considerably to costs. Once the goods were finally ashore there was still the problem of finding adequate wharf-side storage space. These problems could only worsen as the volume of imports mounted.[78]

There was clearly money to be made by providing an improved landing and storage service, as Leon Cohen, a dubious Portuguese Jewish resident of Delagoa Bay, recognised. Cohen – a man the local bank manager later described as 'thoroughly unscrupulous . . . with very slight means' – applied for a concession to construct and operate a pier and landing wharf at Delagoa Bay which he then offered to Lewis and Marks. Persuaded that this was 'a business likely to come in as a trump card', Marks encouraged Lewis to strike a deal with Cohen.[79] Despite Cohen's reputed influence with the Portuguese administration, it was no easy matter to win Lisbon's ratification of the concession. Heel-dragging by Portugal's 'erratic' government was to dog this ambitious project for years to come. The delay was doubly frustrating because it held up a related Marks scheme: the development of an export-oriented coal industry in the eastern Transvaal. Marks envisaged the pier serving not only the import traffic bound for the Rand but also an export trade via Delagoa Bay.[80]

In the early 1890s Delagoa Bay's export trade was virtually non-existent, consisting only of very small and occasional shipments of hides and wax. But, as Marks recognised, the opening of the railway line to the Transvaal in 1895 and the increased sea traffic to Delagoa Bay represented a fine opportunity to rectify this situation. The coal deposits of the eastern Transvaal were none too distant from the railway line; coal could be railed to Delagoa Bay and used for bunkers for shipping. There was also the possibility of exports further afield, to Aden, the major coaling station on the sea route from England via Suez to India. Delagoa Bay, after all, was closer than Wales! With the approval of the Kruger government, Marks took over coal interests in the eastern Transvaal belonging to a group of Boer speculators and formed the Transvaal Consolidated Coal Company in August 1895 to exploit the expected export trade through Delagoa Bay.[81]

The pier and the wharf were not the only speculations by Lewis and Marks at Delagoa Bay. Marks and his business associates were confident that the growth of the town would match the growth of the port, and that there would soon be a considerable demand for both residential and commercial space. In mid-1895 Lewis and Marks, Barney Barnato and his Johannesburg Consolidated Investment Company, and the ubiquitous Jimmy Sivewright set up the Delagoa

Bay Lands Syndicate to acquire a portfolio of properties assembled by a local speculator, Dr Oskar Somershields, a Swedish physician whom Marks had met years before in Kimberley.[82]

In August 1895, soon after the land syndicate was formed, Marks and Sivewright travelled to Delagoa Bay along the newly opened railway line to inspect their investments and to explore further possibilities for doing business. Two days were spent looking around, during which they had an interview with the Governor of Lourenço Marques, 'a very nice gentleman . . . [who] knows enough of the English language to carry on a conversation'.

Marks was very taken with Delagoa Bay and its prospects as a deep water port: 'I am convinced that this is the finest harbour in South Africa, reaching 30 miles across, with a depth at the centre of 75 feet at low tide. When the tide is in, the largest vessels can approach to within two hundred yards of the beach.' He was undaunted by its reputation for unhealthiness. Visiting in winter, the best season of the year at Delagoa Bay, he could write: 'In regard to sickness at Delagoa Bay I am of opinion that this is greatly exaggerated and can assure you that if my business called me there tomorrow I could settle down there without hesitation. The swamps certainly are very unpleasant, but with a comparatively small expenditure the place could be made healthier than Cape Town as it is very favourably situated.'

Marks was very keen to increase his firm's stake in Delagoa Bay. The best way to do this, he wrote to Lewis after the visit, was to arrange with Barney Barnato, Edgar Vincent of Ottoman Bank and others for a £1,500,000 loan to the bankrupt Portuguese government on the clear understanding that the money would all be spent on developing Delagoa Bay. Like Joseph Conrad's Nostromo Marks dreamed of transforming a neglected colonial backwater into a modern port-city. The loan would be spent on building a pier which could handle as much as 3,000 tons of goods a day; on additional rolling stock to move this volume of traffic to the Transvaal border at Komatipoort; on filling in the swamps to make the town healthier; on erecting 'respectable' public buildings and installing electric lighting in the town; and on laying out proper thoroughfares – 'at present there are only two streets where one can walk without sinking up to one's knees into the sand'.[83]

In December 1895, at the end of a frantic and remarkable year, which had seen Sammy's modest wealth converted into a fortune, the Marks family left for a holiday in Cape Town. For weeks before, Marks, a man 51 years of age, had felt 'very unwell'. This was presumably the cumulative effect of months of frenetic activity. He now hoped that a 'change' at the sea would 'set [him] up'.[84] But instead of simply resting, he busied himself looking at property. His fortnight stay in Cape Town was very much a busman's holiday. Marks went on his last shopping spree of a free-spending year, this time on his own account rather than the firm's. Stimulated by the gold and diamond discoveries in the interior, Cape Town had grown exponentially since Marks arrived as a young man in 1868. The city now offered many attractive investment possibilities, particularly in property, to a Pretoria businessman flush with cash and seeking, quite sensibly, to spread his investments beyond the Transvaal. Marks bought more land in the

Gardens, the expanding residential area above the city; a holiday home, later renamed Hatherley House, and Beach Road plots in Muizenberg, then entering its heyday as the premier South African seaside resort; 21 lots at the far end of Sea Point, a fast-growing dormitory suburb of Cape Town recently connected to the city by railway line; and a strategically placed property, close to the Cape Houses of Parliament. Suitably impressed by all this free-spending, the City Club, to which the social elite of the town belonged, elected him to its ranks, a singular 'honour', then as now, for a member of Marks's faith.[85]

After a fortnight 'taking things rather easily', Marks and his family returned to Pretoria, arriving home on Sunday 22 December. The following Sunday, Dr Jameson and his armed band crossed the western border of the Transvaal.[86]

Lewis and Marks's offices on the east side of Church Square, Pretoria (Photo: Pretoria City Council)

IV

The Transvaal from Within,
1896–1899

The Jameson Raid – the dramatic and disastrous dénouement of an ill-conceived plot by Uitlander mining magnates and civic leaders to overthrow the Boer government – came as a surprise to Sammy Marks as it did too to Cecil John Rhodes in Cape Town and his fellow conspirators in Johannesburg. They had planned a rising for the turn of the year which was to be followed, not preceded, by an armed intervention across the border. But the impetuous Dr Jameson reversed the order and 'upset . . . [Rhodes's] apple-cart'.[1]

Marks, who had taken little active part in Uitlander politics in the decade since the discovery of the Witwatersrand, had no advance knowledge of the plot. He and the other magnates with known Krugerite leanings were kept in the dark by the conspirators. But after his return from Cape Town he was soon aware that trouble was brewing; the Uitlander manifesto of 26 December calling for radical reform and the announcement of a mass meeting to press Uitlander claims would have confirmed his fears. In the days before the raid, Marks worked hard to calm a threatening situation. He spoke to leading men on both sides, including Colonel Frank Rhodes, Cecil's older brother and deputy in Johannesburg, whom he apparently warned of the dangers of precipitate action, and Piet Joubert, the Commandant-General, who assured him that there would be no bloodshed as the Uitlanders' legitimate grievances would be redressed. He also organised a deputation to Kruger of High Court judges who urged the President to redress the Uitlanders' grievances in order to preserve the independence of the Republic.[2]

Marks's role during the eleven dramatic days between Jameson's entry into the Transvaal on 29 December 1895 and the collapse of the belated rebellion it triggered in Johannesburg, is obscure. All that is recorded is that on the morning of the 30th, before it was generally known in Johannesburg that Jameson had crossed the border, Marks paid a call on John Hays Hammond, an American mining engineer employed by Rhodes's Gold Fields company, and himself deeply implicated in the conspiracy, and sounded him out about the level of Johannesburg's military preparedness. Hammond, well aware that the city was woefully underprepared – the plotters had smuggled in fewer than 1,500 rifles and had no artillery – was craftily evasive.

'Well, Hammond, it looks as though we were going to have bloodshed.'

'I shouldn't be surprised.'

'They say you've got in 30,000 rifles.'

'I don't know how many we've got, but I don't think it's as many as that.'

'And how about artillery? Is it true you've got thirty guns?'

'Oh, no! That's an exaggeration, I'm sure.'

When Marks left the office, Hammond had him followed. Marks caught a special train to Pretoria and there, Hammond later learnt, reported to the President that Johannesburg had at least 30,000 rifles and 30 guns. This disinformation, unwittingly transmitted by Marks, contributed to the government's overestimation of the rebels' strength, which made it more conciliatory towards Johannesburg than it might have otherwise been, given the level of provocation.[3]

After Johannesburg's tame but sensible surrender and the arrest of its leaders, Marks tried to heal the rift between Boer and Uitlander, as well as between Pretoria and London, which was suspected, quite correctly, by the Boers of some degree of complicity in the conspiracy.[4] Marks was a great believer in the efficacy of the face-to-face encounter. As he once wrote: 'I think always that so much more can be got by an interview with a man, than by writing.' Accordingly he now conceived the idea that Paul Kruger should go in person to London to sort out his differences with Joseph Chamberlain, the British Colonial Secretary. On Friday 17 January, Marks cabled Isaac Lewis in London, requesting that he immediately organise a deputation of 'Prominent South Africans' to the Colonial Secretary to urge the British government to invite Kruger to England.

Two days later, on the Sunday, Marks went down to Viljoensdrift station, on the Free State side of his Vaal River property, to confer with his old acquaintance Jimmy Sivewright. Because of Sivewright's friendship with Kruger, the Cape government had sent him to Pretoria to mend the interstate fences damaged by the part played by Rhodes, the premier of the Cape, in the conspiracy. Closeted with Sivewright in his railway carriage, Marks won his friend's support for the proposal that Kruger be invited to Britain. The two worked out the wording of a message which Sivewright would cable directly to Chamberlain, also to Sir Hercules Robinson, the British High Commissioner in South Africa, through Sir Gordon Sprigg, the new premier of the Cape. They agreed too that Jimmy would rally Cape support for an invitation once he returned to Cape Town in a few days' time.[5]

Marks's cable, sent on the previous Friday afternoon, reached Lewis only on the Monday morning, and he decided that it would be wiser to act alone rather than organise a deputation. As Chamberlain was out of town, Lewis had to wait till Wednesday for an interview. Handed Marks's cable, the Colonial Secretary responded very positively, leading Lewis to believe that if Kruger could be brought to England, 'a great deal of good and a lasting settlement would be arranged, as whilst they [Britain] will not have any nonsense they will act fair in every respect. . . . ' With Chamberlain's approval, Lewis drafted a reply to Marks, which was vetted by the Colonial Office: an invitation would be issued to Kruger if Marks would obtain an assurance it would be accepted, thus sparing Britain the embarrassment and the humiliation of a possible refusal by the President. The Transvaal was also to understand that if the President came to London to negotiate with Chamberlain, there could be no discussion of Article 4 of the London Convention, which gave Britain the right to veto any foreign treaty negotiated by the Transvaal, and in this way restricted the Republic's independence.[6]

On receiving the cable, Marks hurried off to Kruger, who expressed his willingness to go to London and a wish that the invitation be issued by the Queen. Relaying this back to London through his partner, Marks urged that Chamberlain 'act promptly as Foreigners ['Hollanders', in the rough draft of the cable] intriguing and must be forestalled' – a reference to Kruger's Dutch advisers, whom Marks suspected of working against a rapid settlement with Britain and of 'doing their utmost to retard the progress of this country in order to further their own ends'. To keep the cable from their eyes, Marks had it sent from Viljoensdrift on the Free State bank of the Vaal for he believed that the Dutch clerks in the telegraph office in Pretoria 'minutely' examined every cable that was handed in.[7]

With Marks's assurance that Kruger would accept, Chamberlain issued a formal invitation on 27 January on behalf of the British government; the Queen was unavailable to do so because of a bereavement. Marks had, it seemed, pulled off a great diplomatic coup – the bringing together of the principal political adversaries on the sub-continent.[8]

So confident were Marks and his confederates that the meeting would actually take place that they turned to debating the composition of the negotiating team that would accompany the President to London, and to jockeying for places. Marks felt that the party should be 'purely Transvaal' in character and reflect the contrasting outlooks of the Boer population: it should include a representative of the older, more conservative burghers, and a senior official – preferably Judge Kotze, the widely respected Chief Justice – representing the educated and more progressive Boers.[9] Jimmy Sivewright, on the other hand, felt that he should be included in the party: 'To me of course it would be a great compliment if Kruger were to ask that I too should accompany him. I know it would help him immensely if I went and I rely upon you . . . to work towards that end as I have striven and am striving to carry out your views.' What he failed to mention was that it would also have been a great boost to his renascent political career.[10]

Lewis, in turn, felt that it would enhance the firm's status if his partner were to accompany the President: 'In the event of the President coming here, I hope you will arrange to come along with him, and that you will have some authority and be consulted, so as to get some recognised standing, otherwise it would be terrible to think, after doing all the work, you are not even recognised when the time comes, and probably other people reap the benefit of our labours. It is no question of money in any shape or way, but it is simply a question to be recognised and be consulted, being the largest interested in the country and working for the good of it generally.'[11]

But all of this was premature; all three were much too sanguine about the success of their manoeuvre. Though Kruger had signalled through Marks his willingness to accept a British invitation, this, as it turned out, was not quite the same as actually accepting an invitation. For weeks after, Britain and the Transvaal haggled about the terms of the invitation. Kruger, who saw the meeting as an opportunity to renegotiate the Republic's formal relationship with Britain and to free it of its residual dependence on that country, held out for the inclusion on the agenda of Article 4 of the London Convention – Britain's right of veto over the Transvaal's international treaties. Conversely, Chamberlain, who was determined to uphold Britain's threatened paramountcy in South Africa, was equally adamant that Article 4 should be excluded. It would seem that when persuading Kruger to indicate his willingness to go to Britain, Marks had played down the significance of Chamberlain's insistence that Article 4 was not negotiable, and had led the President to believe that this could indeed be placed on the agenda. The negotiations eventually dissolved into mutual recrimination. Marks's good intentions had come to naught; rather than easing tensions, his initiative had, if anything, made things worse. 'The whole matter ended in a fiasco,' he later ruefully recalled, 'and our efforts met with not the slightest show of appreciation.'[12]

Marks's strictly domestic efforts to defuse the crisis were, however, more successful. Throughout the aftershock of the Raid he acted as a moderating influence on Kruger, opposing the hardliners' calls for retribution against the Uitlander rebels. As he wrote in mid-crisis:

I have to watch in high quarters to see that no advantage is taken of the present state of affairs, and that the Government is not impelled to act rashly, as they are not always able to discern who are intriguers and who not.

This causes me a great deal of worry and trouble, but up to the present, as is acknowledged by a great many people, I have managed things well. I may yet blunder as no man is infallible, but shall continue to advise the Government to the best of my ability, for our interests in this country are so great, and will be increased that it is perhaps worth my while to lose a few weeks or even months in working for them, even if we do not derive any direct results therefrom.[13]

Marks counselled that the detained Uitlander leaders be treated leniently; he did his 'utmost to induce the Powers that be not to continue the trial against them, but to dismiss them all'. In the event, the ringleaders were sentenced to death, but then reprieved, and the pawns fined and released. Marks also acted as an intermediary between the discredited mining industry and the government. When the managers of Rhodes's disgraced Gold Fields company hesitated to approach the government directly about the difficulties they faced in keeping their mining operations going, they asked Marks to intercede on their behalf, which he did both willingly and successfully.[14]

At the same time Marks nudged the Transvaal towards reform. He suggested in private that overseas and local confidence in the government could be restored through nothing more radical than the pensioning off of the older, less competent senior officials, particularly the Hollanders, and the replacement of his *bête noire* Leyds as State Secretary by the 'pure Africander', Chief Justice Kotze. To muster English support for the idea, he asked Lewis to plant a letter he drafted, in *The Times* or the *Daily Telegraph*; suitably altered, it was to be attributed to an anonymous London-based correspondent, purportedly intimately acquainted with the Transvaal.[15]

Looking back on the Jameson Raid a year on, Marks recognised that it had been a great political disaster: 'It is a thousand pities that all the good work done within the past twelve years towards bringing the two predominant white races in South Africa together should have been upset by a few unprincipled people within the short space of a few months.'[16] The Jameson Raid ended a decade of relative peace and progress for the Transvaal and initiated seven lean years of political strife and economic slump. The Raid was also a milestone for Sammy Marks and his firm: after a decade of improvement and expansion, it heralded a time of severe difficulty and setback.

Once the immediate excitement died down, Marks left with his wife and children for a long anticipated and much delayed vacation in England. Bertha and Sammy planned to visit their oldest son Louis whom they had sent to school in England a short while before. But although the primary purpose of the visit was private and familial, Marks took with him his public cares. In April 1896, while in London, Marks had an interview with Joseph Chamberlain at the Colonial Office which was sufficiently disconcerting to send him post-haste to the Transvaal Agent in the Strand with a request that he cable Kruger about the danger of the current situation. An unconfirmed story told by George Falcke who became Marks's private secretary some years later, has it that Chamberlain said to Marks 'that he had only to press a button, give an order, and so many men-of-war would be on their way to the Cape'. Marks, Falcke claims, 'quietly reminded Mr. Chamberlain that over one thousand miles of land separated the Cape from the Transvaal', a prescient warning the hawkish Colonial Secretary might have done well to heed three and a half years later.[17]

Marks also spent some of his European vacation on his pet project – the establishment of an iron works in the Transvaal to smelt the native ores. Drawings and estimates were commissioned which suggested, rather optimistically as later events were to prove, that a small iron works with two blast furnaces could be erected in the Transvaal for a modest sum.[18]

While Marks was vacationing in England, he received word in July 1896 of a development back home that struck a body blow at all he had accomplished in the Transvaal since his arrival a decade and a half before. The combined forces of the mining industry, concerned about the loss of productivity through drunkenness amongst its black workers, and of the churches and temperance movement had pressured the Volksraad into legislating a total ban on the sale of liquor to blacks, the principal customers of the Hatherley distillery. Marks was completely caught off-balance by the sudden ban. Had he anticipated anything of the sort, he would have cancelled his trip to England. His opponents had taken advantage of his absence – his first trip to Europe in twelve years – to push through legislation he might just have parried, or at least delayed, had he been present.

Marks's first intimation of what was afoot was a cabled report in the *Daily Telegraph*. He left England in such a hurry that there was no time to inspect his son's school as he had planned to do. He hoped to return to the Transvaal in time to persuade his friends in the First Volksraad, the superior chamber, to veto the bill the lower chamber or Second Volksraad had passed when it came before them for ratification.[19] Instead Marks arrived back in Pretoria on 7 August, the day the bill came before the upper chamber, too late to reverse the situation. Had he come a fortnight sooner, one of the leaders of the mining industry crowed, things might well have gone very differently.[20]

At 8.30 on the morning of his return, Marks delivered a letter in person to Kruger and the Executive Council. In it he itemised his services to the state since his arrival in the Transvaal at the beginning of the 1880s, reminded the President of the solemn promise he had made at that time to lend his protection to Marks's enterprises, and warned that the proposed legislation would ruin the Eerste Fabrieken. After the letter was read to the Council, Marks was called in:

I used every argument I could think of against confirmation . . . but it was evident to me from the very outset that all I could say or do would be of little avail. The Executive Council felt it was powerless to prevent the passage of the bill through the First Volksraad later that day. Our opponents had arranged everything so carefully and had spent money so lavishly that every newspaper, minister (and you know what influence ministers have in this country) and 10 members of the Volksraad have been bought over. The remainder who voted for prohibition did so to please their friends.

The Johannesburg people have now seen clearly that they can do more with gold than with lead and set aside their guns and resolved to resort to the former to gain their ends, and this mode of procedure proved very effective and the more so as the legislators of the country are in anything but a flourishing condition financially.[21]

As he later joked to a nephew: 'I have not given the Members of the Volksraad hell, as I daresay some of them will get that after they have passed away. . . .'[22]

Marks found there was virtually no opposition to the passage of the law, excepting from people in the liquor business, and from his clients in the Volksraad (and they only half-heartedly). Even he himself secretly sympathised with the prohibitionists, though they were striking both at his pocket and at his prestige: 'I may mention that even our friends were in favour of total prohibition, and would have voted for the measure had they not been actuated by motives of friendship towards ourselves, and I cannot help thinking that, had I not been so closely connected with the Factory I myself would have worked energetically for the passing of the law.'[23]

Marks acknowledged, at least privately, that his opponents had a strong case:

almost everybody was in favour of confirmation, and I cannot altogether blame the people, for I have found out during the few hours I have been here that between 4–6000 people are engaged in selling spirits of the very lowest quality imported from Delagoa Bay and elsewhere and that Canteen Keepers, in their greed for gain, mix the vilest ingredients with our spirit in order to increase its bulk; whilst so much illicit traffic has been going on in the business that the illicit traffic in Kimberley was as nothing compared with it and I need not remind you of the outrageous trade carried on in Kimberley. We naturally get the credit or rather the discredit of producing this spirit.[24]

Whatever his private reservations, Marks was determined to put up the best fight he could. While he might have shared the sentiments of his fellow white colonists, self-interest dictated that he fight the ban with all the means at his disposal, for its likely effects, if it were not speedily rescinded, were disastrous.

The immediate consequences were devastating: Fabrieken share prices fell precipitously. Sir Edgar Vincent, the international banker, had marketed the shares in 1895 as blue chips in the making; the Fabrieken, he had told his wealthy friends, held a cast-iron concession in a rapidly expanding market. Now this guarantee was simply blown away. By an enactment of the Volksraad the distillery was stripped of its key market, the black consumer. In London Isaac Lewis was 'pretty well beseiged [sic]' by angry shareholders.[25]

While Lewis and Marks were cushioned against the fall, having sold off most of their shareholding in Eerste Fabrieken during the previous year's boom, their reputation suffered serious damage. As Marks acknowledged, the firm was closely identified in investors' minds with the distillery; they now incurred the wrath of those who had seen their investment in Eerste Fabrieken plummet in value within a year of purchase. This made it very difficult for Lewis and Marks to raise capital in Europe for the rest of the decade.

In 1897, the first year the ban was enforced, sales and profits collapsed along with the share price. Many of the distillery's retail customers were stripped of their licences because they had specialised in the black trade, while others, anxious about the future, allowed their stocks to run down rather than re-ordering. Sales fell from close to 300,000 gallons the previous year to little more than 60,000 gallons in 1897; the previous year's profit of close to £70,000 was converted into a loss of £46,000, the first since the company had been restructured five years before.[26] Marks needed all his resourcefulness and resilience to meet the crisis. If the distillery was to be saved from sliding into bankruptcy, he would have to rethink its production and marketing strategy, devise means of reducing or eliminating damaging competition, and persuade the Volksraad to rescind its ban.

The day after the First Volksraad endorsed the ban, Paul Kruger, an acknowledged opponent of prohibition, advised Marks to launch a countrywide campaign to have it repealed. Lewis and Marks should arrange for the circulation of petitions calling for the withdrawal of the ban at the following year's Volksraad session. Kruger's personal contribution would be to work for the unseating of the distillery's enemies in the Volksraad at the next election.[27] Secrecy was vital if the campaign was to succeed. The local agents of the Fabrieken were instructed to arrange petitions in their respective areas, but to do so with the utmost circumspection. 'It is advisable', the distillery wrote to its Johannesburg agent, Samuel Heymann, Marks's kinsman, 'that you draw up your own petitions as the wording of the petitions should be different to ours for fear of it being detected from whence they originated.' F. M. Joseph at

Klerksdorp was given more explicit instructions: he was authorised to spend twenty to forty pounds 'in procuring signatures'; petitions were to be in Dutch and addressed to the Second Volksraad; they were to be left in every canteen and hotel, and an agent was to be engaged to travel the district canvassing for country signatures; above all, 'it must be understood that you are to hold yourself aloof and let some one else act for you.'[28]

The mining industry had fully expected something of the sort, and launched its own 'crusade' against any attempt to repeal prohibition. Public opinion was mobilised in defence of a ban, which, the industry argued, had already improved the productivity of its workforce. Petitions were distributed countrywide and churchmen encouraged to see that their congregants signed. The mining industry's campaign was more effective than the distillery's, as even Marks's campaign manager was soon forced to admit: 'I am afraid that the future of the trade is as dark as ever,' he wrote in early 1897, 'owing to almost ⅔ of the Country . . . standing up in arms against the excessive drink traffic.' Those members of the Volksraad who supported the distillery rather than those who opposed it were in real danger of losing their seats.[29]

The movement for repeal was resoundingly defeated when the Volksraad reconvened in 1897. Marks now had to consider alternative strategies. One possibility was to strike a deal with the mining industry, a course of action Sir Edgar Vincent and Isaac Lewis particularly favoured. Why not arrange a partial lifting of the ban on the sale of liquor to blacks, with the supply of spirits to workers tightly controlled by mine managements, and Eerste Fabrieken as the sole source? The mining industry was tempted by the idea. Prohibition had not been a great success in practice. As in America decades later, it had stimulated massive evasion, organised by criminal syndicates, contemptuous of the feeble attempts of the state at enforcement. An 'entente' with the Fabrieken which would allow black mine-workers to consume a 'rational quantity' of good quality spirits, would undercut the 'bootleggers' and their poisonous concoctions. It might even improve the overall supply of labour to the mines. Blacks, the industry's leaders argued, were accustomed to a certain amount of drink, and resented any attempt to cut off their supply completely. Remove this grievance and the flow of labour might increase.

The deal foundered because the mining industry did not trust Marks – a mistrust he heartily reciprocated – and because the industry reckoned it was too risky. Once the mine-owners reversed their stance and argued for the partial lifting of the ban, there could be no going back; the principle on which the present law was based would have been compromised. Rather stand by prohibition and work for stricter enforcement.[30]

A further alternative was to do a deal with the government. After its defeat in the Volksraad in 1897, the Fabrieken wrote to Kruger, arguing that prohibition represented a partial abrogation of the liquor concession granted originally to Nellmapius in 1881. By passing a law banning the sale of liquor to blacks, the Transvaal state had unilaterally stripped the distillery of its lawful rights. The factory should be fully compensated for this: the state could either extend the concession for a further fifteen years, or pay the distillery a lump sum by way of compensation; alternatively, it could allow the Fabrieken to import material duty-free for a period of years.

The state rejected this claim. It was unwilling to concede any legal liability and was confident that it had a strong case. Marks was understandably reluctant to press the matter: it would be very 'impolitic' to take the government, upon which the firm depended so heavily, to court; besides, there was a very good chance the distillery would lose the action. If the state would not compensate, perhaps it would expropriate? Expropriation and the creation of a state liquor monopoly 'would be the best solution of the difficulty for everyone concerned,' Isaac Lewis argued. 'From our point of view also this would be the best way out of the matter as one gets sick and tired of continually quarrelling and fighting with everyone.' Marks resisted the suggestion; he was far more attached to the distillery than his partner, for he had, after all, invested close on two decades of effort in the business. Money was scarce, he argued, and the state was therefore not in a position to consider expropriation. The firm should rather sit tight for a few years. Matters were bound to improve.[31]

Marks looked to the state to do something as well about the smuggling of cheap foreign alcohol into the Transvaal via Delagoa Bay. Since the opening of the railway line from the east coast in 1895, German potato spirits had flooded into the Transvaal from the neighbouring Portuguese colony. This masqueraded as the product of Mozambique in order to take advantage of a treaty of commerce between the South African Republic and Portugal which allowed the duty-free import into the Transvaal of goods produced in Mozambique. An embattled Eerste Fabrieken, fighting for a shrinking market, could ill afford this underhand competition. Marks sent an agent to Mozambique to investigate. Despite an attempt by a Portuguese official to dupe the agent, he discovered irrefutable evidence of massive evasion of both the Transvaal's and Mozambique's customs regulations. There was a huge discrepancy between the total productive capacity of all the distilleries in the Portuguese colony and the amount of liquor that was going forward duty-free to the Transvaal because it was supposedly produced in Mozambique.

The agent found that German potato spirit was smuggled ashore from the monthly steamship from Hamburg, past the less than vigilant Portuguese customs authorities. It was then certificated as the product of Mozambique, and as such, forwarded duty-free to Johannesburg. There it would go to five wholesalers who held distilling licences; they would dilute the alcohol with water to reduce the strength, add colouring and flavouring, bottle it, attach false labels and capsules, and sell the product as regular whisky, gin, brandy or whatever. The adulterated liquor was often unfit for human consumption. Marks said it would be used elsewhere in the world 'strictly as fuel or to mix paints'. It was sold to black consumers by syndicates of illicit liquor dealers through an army of runners and touts who bore the brunt of such limited police action as there was against the illicit trade. Profits were as high as 500 per cent. The landed cost at Delagoa Bay of the smuggled German potato spirit was a mere 1s. 10d. per gallon, less than a third of the production costs of alcohol distilled at Hatherley.[32]

Despite all the information Marks presented, Kruger failed to act to stem the tide of illicit imports. Even though there was indisputable evidence of smuggling on a giant scale, even though the state lost heavily through the evasion of customs duties, and even though the smuggling undercut a local industry which provided a market for local farm produce, the government was reluctant to take any action against the importation of foreign liquor disguised as the product of Mozambique. It was 'impolitic to . . . quarrel with the Portuguese' over the liquor traffic: Delagoa Bay was the closest port to the Transvaal and the only one outside British control; free access to it depended on retaining Portuguese goodwill, and there were influential individuals in Lisbon who had a stake in the liquor traffic.[33] Strategic considerations of this sort naturally outweighed the difficulties of a local distillery, or even the problems the mining industry experienced with an inebriated workforce. Under the circumstances, Marks resigned himself to the unchecked continuation of the illicit flow of foreign liquor into the Transvaal at least until the Republic's treaty with Portugal expired in 1902. He consoled himself and Lewis with the thought that the distillery's concession would still have ten years to run after that, during which they would hopefully make up all the lost ground.[34]

Meanwhile Marks reconsidered the entire nature of Eerste Fabrieken's business. One option he briefly flirted with when the ban on liquor sales to blacks was first announced was beer-making, a business he felt was bound to be profitable. The obstacle here was a verbal restraint-of-trade agreement he had made with the Castle Brewery of Johannesburg in return for a large allocation of shares, but this could possibly be renegotiated. 'I promised I would not put up a brewery but did not say for always, and it was only a verbal conversation.' Perhaps the Castle people could now be persuaded to merge their interests with Eerste Fabrieken?[35]

A further option was the manufacture of mineral waters. At Marks's request, the firm's London office searched for an expert, prepared to work for a percentage of the profits, but nothing much came of this idea either.[36] The third and most serious option was to reposition the distillery in the local liquor market; that is, to shift production and sales away from the embattled lower end of the market to its apparently more secure upper end. Though the Eerste Fabrieken had been obliged to concentrate on the 'native trade' almost from the start, Marks had continued to hope for a breakthrough into the 'white' market – hence his heavy investment in the early nineties in the lengthy and costly maturation of whisky. When prohibition arrived in 1896, what had previously seemed a desirable departure became a life-saving necessity: 'We must now set about manufacturing a better class of spirit and cater for the white trade,' Marks insisted. But there were two major obstacles to moving upmarket: the quality of Hatherley's spirits and the white public's negative perception of the distillery. Hatherley's gin and brandy, its staple products, were widely believed to be 'poisonous'; Kruger told Marks that he fielded complaints about this 'with the recommendation not to touch Fabrieken Spirit as then they need have no fear of being poisoned'. Hatherley's whisky stocks, which Marks hoped would be its future salvation, were equally troublesome. The whisky was not only too light in colour but had a questionable taste. Marks quarrelled about this with the new distillery manager who insisted that his predecessor's whisky had a 'vile flavour' and was quite undrinkable: 'Mr. Marks clings to his opinion and will probably do so until the last drop of this stuff has evaporated or leaked from the casks, he will hear nothing against it, and religiously drinks it himself.'[37]

For all his apparent obduracy, Marks was prepared to seek expensive solutions to these problems. He told Lewis he was willing to pay as much as £3,000 a year for a master blender to improve the quality of the factory's spirits. At his request, the firm recruited R. van Eibergen Santhagens, a Dutch distiller, who immediately raised the standards of its brandy and gin. Marks also ordered 9,000 gallons of real Scotch for blending with his Highveld whisky. The results of his efforts were pleasing: at a tasting in late 1898, local judges thought 'very highly' of the whisky which they adjudged 'as good as any imported whisky'. Marks was relieved that 'there is no necessity to pitch it into the Pienaar's River'. [38]

The image problem – the unfavourable public perception of the distillery and its products – was solved by concealing the origins of the spirits. Marks noted that the German distilleries were able to sell 'the greatest rubbish' to Transvaal customers simply because their bottles were 'nicely got up'. He thought it a good idea to follow suit and repackage the distillery's products – to give them 'a better and neater appearance'. Cases were ordered from Europe, as were capsules to cover the cork bottle-stoppers, and specially printed labels. The 'fancy names' to be used on these were all 'assumed . . . no such firms are in existence'. The company's name, Eerste Fabrieken, was not to appear anywhere. If it did, the labels 'would be of no use to us as we cannot dispose of any of our products under the company's name, owing to the prejudice that exists against our liquors'. (The Argus printing works almost blew the gaff by placing its own name in a prominent position on wrapping paper it prepared for the factory, and by using the Irish spelling – whiskey – rather than the Scottish.)[39]

Marks's stratagem, which was perfectly legal in the absence of any local trade descriptions law, worked. Eerste Fabrieken sales gradually improved as its 'Martinette Cognac', its 'McPherson's Whisky' and its 'H. Gilbert and Company Dry Gin' began to penetrate an unsuspecting white market. In 1898 its sales, which had fallen to a low of 63,191 gallons the previous year, recovered to a more respectable 153,594 gallons, though this was still less than half the 1895 figures.[40]

The personal price Marks paid for achieving this turnaround was a heavy one. 'The Fabrieken is claiming nearly all my time and is giving me great anxiety,' he wrote in 1898. 'This concern has given me so much worry during the past two years that I have hardly been able to go away for a single day.' Though Lewis and Marks had greatly diluted its direct stake in the Fabrieken during the 1895 stock-market boom, it was nevertheless closely identified in investors' minds with the distillery. Since the partnership's reputation rode on the factory's recovery, Marks had been obliged to devote most of his time to this concern, often, he felt, at the expense of the partners' other interests.[41]

For all his efforts, and for all the improvement in the Eerste Fabrieken's performance, the distillery remained a dead-weight around the partnership's neck. European investors refused to forgive Lewis and Marks for the collapse in the value of their shareholdings in 1896, and this bedevilled efforts to raise capital for the partners' other ventures. The distillery, Marks wrote in 1899, 'has done so much to damage our name'. Lewis agreed: 'Whilst in Paris I satisfied myself that our greatest trouble has been and still is . . . the failure of the Fabrieken, as these shares have been placed in such good hands and taken up by people who looked upon it as an absolute investment and not as a mining share, that they feel very sore about it now and I am afraid it has done us more harm and cost us more than the value of the Fabrieken three times over.'

Besides the distillery, Marks also established and ran a number of smaller industrial ventures at Eerste Fabrieken. All were limited in scale; all drew on locally available raw materials; all faced stiff foreign competition; all had political overtones, whether established to please local interest groups or reliant on government protection for survival; and all were bothersome and marginal at best.

A year and a half before the Raid and two years before prohibition, Marks had given a great deal of thought to expanding the Eerste Fabrieken complex. The logical ancillary, he felt, to what was then a flourishing distillery was a glass works, a project he had first considered soon after Lewis and Marks's arrival in the Transvaal at the start of the eighties. The capital investment need not be large. There was sand and lead within a few miles of Hatherley; the complex would soon be linked by rail to Johannesburg; and there were major customers close at hand, the distillery itself and the Castle Brewery of Johannesburg, which might even be persuaded to put up part of the capital and share the risk. The small operation Marks contemplated would not only turn a profit but would also win goodwill by fulfilling a promise made to Kruger long ago when he extended the life of the liquor concession.[42]

This combination of low business risk and of possible political gain won Lewis's approval of the scheme. Construction of the factory was much delayed though and it eventually cost upwards of £25,000, far more than was originally anticipated. But before it was even completed and operational, Marks was already dreaming of expansion and of diversifying the product line. Why not invest in additional plant to turn out household glassware, not the expensive lines, but cheap tumblers, sugar basins and the like? He was convinced that there was a large local market waiting for inexpensive locally made 'second class table ware'.[43] Lewis, lacking, as always, Marks's entrepreneurial zeal, and alarmed no doubt by the cost overrun, was less convinced. He felt that they ought to see how bottle-making went before buying any further machinery. 'I am getting a little tired of new industries,' he wrote late in 1896, 'and certainly don't feel disposed at the present juncture to start or take up anything new. Our aim should be to see that our present industries are economically and well managed and beginning to pay as we cannot always be sending money from this side. Some of them should now be self-supporting and we ought to begin to see a return from somewhere.'[44]

The glass factory was officially opened by President Kruger on 28 November 1896. As in the case of the parent factory over a decade before, Marks invited the Executive and the Volksraad, who spent 'a very merry day' at Hatherley. The band of the Volunteers played 'some very nice musical selections'; Kruger spoke and was presented with a glass walking-stick; and in the afternoon, all enjoyed a 'sumptuous luncheon'.[45]

After the christening came the predictable teething pains, as severe as any encountered in Marks's previous ventures. The factory was badly designed and poorly constructed, and within six weeks Marks was forced to shut down the furnace. Besides the loss of production, this meant heavy additional expenditure on rebuilding. The new factory also experienced severe quality control problems: the Castle Brewery complained the bottles were not of a uniform size, which made stacking very awkward, and that a large number had burst.[46]

Competition from cheap foreign imports was yet another problem, but Marks fought back aggressively. To secure the business of the Castle Brewery, the major customer for bottles in Johannesburg, the factory at first sold it bottles at a price below production cost. When it seemed that the brewery might nevertheless look elsewhere – imported English bottles were still 5s. per gross cheaper – Marks warned Lewis, who was on the board of South African Breweries, the controlling company, that unless they used the local product, he would 'start to work and see that a heavy duty is imposed on imported malt which will cost them more than 5/-'. He was quite prepared to use his political influence to redress his competitive disadvantage.[47]

To cap it all, Marks was faced with a militant workforce, well aware of the relative strength of its position because of the scarcity value of its skills in the Transvaal. Soon after the factory went into production there were complaints that the imported workmen were 'combining together to extort outrageous wages' and were producing far fewer bottles than they would have in Europe. The rate of production was a continuing source of conflict between management and workers, who felt that the targets they were set were unreasonably high. When a strike threatened, supposedly placing the factory's contracts in jeopardy, Marks's manager resolved to have the men arrested if they struck, 'for the sooner we put down our foot the better'. Even if the men did not come out, he was keen to use the first opportunity to 'clear every jack of them from the Factory for a lower set of men I have never before met and the only way to deal with them is to get rid of them'. Marks shared this view and planned to replace the entire skilled workforce with men from abroad 'who are not connected with the Union'.[48]

Labour militancy aside, management was also concerned about cases of absenteeism and drunkenness. On one memorable occasion most of the skilled workmen went absent from work and 'on the "spree" for a week'.[49] Despite these difficulties, Marks's glass factory slowly prospered. After cutting its costs of production and steadily reducing its losses, it seemed to be heading for profit at last in 1899, its books full of orders for pint and quart beer bottles for the breweries, and soda water and lemonade bottles for the mineral water merchants.[50]

Marks was very conscious of the paradox that while the Transvaal was a
republic of farmers, it was nevertheless heavily dependent on imports of
foodstuffs, much of this highly priced, to feed the burgeoning urban population.
Part of the problem, Marks realised, was the difficulty of marketing local
produce. Transvaal farmers produced substantial quantities of fruit, but much
of this was left to rot because there were no facilities for preserving or processing
fruit on anything larger than a domestic scale. After consulting an expert from
the Cape fruit-growing area of Paarl, Marks spent £7,500 on erecting and
equipping a jam factory at Hatherley, which began operations in January 1895.
The Boer farmers responded with a will. Marks, eager to please and encourage
his suppliers, took everything he was offered, including fruit so badly damaged
after long and rough wagon journeys that it was unusable. Within a year the
company had built up a stock of 170,000 lb of goods, its wide range of products
including quince, orange and lemon marmalade, apricot, plum, tomato and fig
jam.

The difficulty lay in selling the stuff. Despite Marks's insistence that his jam
was 'splendid' and despite the gold medal it won at the Witwatersrand
Agricultural Show, the consumers preferred the imported product. Price was
one consideration, at least at first: because the cost of skilled labour was so high
in the Transvaal, foreign jams were substantially cheaper to start with than local
jams. To negate this price advantage, Marks demanded and was granted tariff
protection, but even with this, the jam factory continued to struggle,
presumably because of the powerful contemporary prejudice amongst consumers against locally made goods.

By 1898 Isaac Lewis was keen to shut down this unprofitable operation, but
Marks, who as the man on the spot had a keener sense than his London-based
partner of what it took to do business in the Transvaal, insisted it carry on: the
jam factory was the equivalent in republican politics of the loss leader in modern
retailing. While Marks admitted that the factory was a commercial failure, he
felt that closure, which would deprive Kruger's Boers of a market for their fruit,
would be politically unwise: 'There are several little matters in which we require
the aid of the Government. . . . I think it will be better to keep faith with the
Government and to keep the concern going for another 12 months.'[51]

The jam factory, then, with the distillery and the glass works, was more of a
burden than a source of strength for the house of Lewis and Marks in the last
years of the decade, more a relentless drain on resources than a fountain of profit.
Troubled by all this, Sammy looked eastwards once again, as he had in the
mid-1880s, to the gold-fields near Barberton for a substitute cornucopia. 'The
Sheba has always been a favourite of mine,' he wrote in 1897, 'and I have always
considered it one of the best properties in the Transvaal.' At the beginning of
the decade Sammy and Isaac had looked enviously at the Sheba mine and its
Golden Quarry. Sammy's rival company – the Oriental and Sheba – was a pale
shadow of its namesake; Sammy's much-delayed tramway, without the support
of the Sheba mine, an instant failure. But through the judicious purchase of
claims and their resale to the Sheba company, Lewis and Marks became

practically the largest shareholders in the Sheba mine by the last years of the decade and in this way came to share in its prosperity.

Despite its slack management, controlled as it was at long range by a board of directors in London, the Sheba mine thrived during much of the 1890s. With its managers picking the eyes of the mine – mining rich ores but neglecting those of lower grade – its gold output hovered around an impressive 7,000 oz per month and on one occasion even soared to a magnificent 8,000 oz, when Sammy rewarded the management with a case of champagne. The Sheba mine, which produced about two-thirds of the gold mined in the Barberton area, yielded approximately £2,000,000 of the metal in the ten years before the South African War and paid its shareholders, including Lewis and Marks, dividends to match. But there was always something precarious about its prosperity. Unlike the mines of the Rand, whose gold reefs had a high degree of predictability with values holding up well at depth, Sheba's geology was more complicated, its veins of gold far less reliable. By late 1898 its ore grades were falling precipitously and damaging rumours soon began circulating that after more than a decade of spectacular results the legendary Golden Quarry was at last worked out. The market in Sheba shares collapsed and with it one of Lewis and Marks's most prized and largest investments. The Sheba was not to pay a further dividend until 1912. Once again, Lewis and Marks had backed the wrong horse.[52]

The sudden collapse of the Sheba in 1898–9 meant that despite Sammy's efforts to broaden the base of the firm, and to establish a strong presence in gold-mining, coal-mining remained the mainstay of the house of Lewis and Marks. The Vaal River estate with its lucrative Cape coal contract fared better than the Eerste Fabrieken during the post-Raid depression, though it too had its share of disappointments. The most important new departure during these difficult times was the conversion of the Coal Association, a private partnership since its formation in 1880, into a listed public company. Since the early nineties Lewis had been eager to convert the firm's substantial holding in the Association into a more marketable form. He was doubly keen to do so when the market in South African mining shares soared in 1895. Here was a splendid opportunity to create paper which he could trade at great profit on the London and Paris exchanges. Marks resisted the idea, as he had since it was first mooted, suggesting that rather than floating the Association and diluting the firm's share in it, they should instead buy out the remaining outside partners and develop it even more vigorously on their own: 'to tell you the truth I do not wish to part with this property and am convinced that if I devote 12 or 18 months to it, it will yield us £30,000 per year, and not for one or two years, but permanently.' Marks opposed flotation because of the immense attraction the Vaal River property held for him and his unbounded faith in its potential. For this reason he was reluctant to concede even one iota of control to outsiders. He saw the property as a family patrimony, a legacy he hoped to pass on intact to his descendants and to Lewis's: 'I am averse to taking any more partners into the Concern, as I think we already have too many. . . . I wish all the worry and work this is costing me to be in the interests of myself and my friends[;] in fact I am desirous of keeping the estate for Lewis and Marks's children, it will always yield them 6% on a capital of £500,000.'[53]

This prospect was far more alluring than a quick killing on the stock exchange. Marks had never taken much interest in the stock market. By his own admission he was profoundly ignorant of its inner mysteries, and was therefore normally content to leave this side of the business to Lewis in London. Marks had none of his partner's passion for playing the market, a compulsion to which Lewis once bashfully admitted: 'But there is a drawback with me – as long as I am in London or at the Cape I can never be away from speculating.' Unlike Lewis, Marks did not see the essential nature of the firm's business as the creation of assets for marketing at the first good opportunity on the Paris Bourse and the London Stock Exchange.[54]

Marks managed to hold off Lewis for a while, but finally yielded to his partner's pressure in 1897. Annoyed at losing out on a golden opportunity in 1895, Lewis saw to it that the company was floated at last when the share market showed signs of revival in 1897. The South African and Orange Free State Coal and Mineral Mining Association became the Vereeniging Estates, Limited, with an issued capital of £730,000. The timing of the flotation was less fortunate than Eerste Fabrieken's a few years before. The market in 1897 had little appetite for South African shares, and Lewis and Marks were left holding most of the stock. Given his reluctance to let go of the Vaal River estates, Marks might well have been secretly pleased! [55]

Whatever the status of the Vaal River property, Marks was as determined as ever to make full use of all of its resources, its fertile lands, its abundant water, its clay, lime and stone, and not just its coal. When the rinderpest swept through the northern Transvaal in late 1896, decimating herds and bringing famine in its wake, Marks saw an opportunity to recruit tenants for the Vaal River farms. Agents were sent to the Zoutpansberg district to induce a couple of hundred black families to come south to the estates. By arrangement with the authorities, these were to be transported to the Vaal free of charge on wagons the government had sent northwards with emergency food supplies. Once at the estates, housing was to be provided, ground broken by the company's steam plough (a seemingly powerful inducement to peasant farmers who had lost most of their draught animals) and jobs offered on the company's mines.

Marks expected to reap considerable rewards – 'You may rely upon my arranging matters in such a way', he assured his partner, 'that the kaffirs will not live at our expense.' He estimated that the company's half-share in the crops of the new arrivals would amount to as much as 3,000 bags of grain per year, thus doubling the yield from the 250 black families already living on the estates. He also intended to insist that each family provide one 'able-bodied' male per week for service on the mines: this would ensure that the company's collieries always had a reliable supply of labour. Marks was disappointed with the initial response. Not a single family took up the offer of free transport southwards. Waxing biblical, as he often did, he complained that 'I am willing to assist in a good cause, but have no wish to encourage a lot of good-for-nothing lazy rascals. In Genesis it is stated "In the sweat of thy brow shalt thou earn thy bread." '

Despite the failure of these efforts, the Vaal River farms rapidly filled up with black tenants in the last few years of the decade. Black settlers arrived from other white-owned farms or were recruited by Marks from Basutoland. (Sammy had a particularly high regard for the Basotho – they were 'excellent agriculturalists . . . [and] industrious,' he wrote in 1903, 'the only class in South Africa from whom we are likely to obtain adequate returns resulting from agriculture. . . .') By the eve of the South African War there was a concentration of black tenant farmers on Marks's Vaal River farms on a scale which attracted the attention of envious Boer neighbours at the time, and of those social historians since who have explored the energetic black response to the opportunities that the mineral revolution and the consequent growth of markets offered enterprising agriculturists. A list Sammy Marks sent Isaac Lewis in September 1899 shows that no fewer than 352 tenants, their 398 wives and 1,680 other dependants occupied the sixteen Transvaal and Free State farms of the Vereeniging Estates that were under cultivation. Of the 352 tenants only 14 were white and these had no edge over their black neighbours. The sixteen farms produced 31,210 bags – each equalling a muid or 203 lb – of grain, of which the company claimed 18,585, as well as 47,520 bags of oats of which the company took 38,835. Even these impressive figures, Marks reminded his London partner, grossly understated the true output of the Vaal farms – 2,430 people lived off the ripening crop, from the time the mealies were green until Marks's manager arrived to claim the company's half-share after the harvest. Some of these black sharecroppers were champion producers. In 1897 the company prepared a photographic album – itself a unique visual record of sharecropper success on the late-nineteenth-century Highveld – which proudly portrayed some of these star tenants surrounded by herds, flocks and walls of mealie bags: Ephraim who reaped 440 muids in 1897, Jantje who reaped 200.

The vast concentration of black tenants on Marks's Vaal River farms was a flagrant contravention of the squatter laws of both the Republics which, in the case of the Transvaal, theoretically restricted the number of black tenant families to 5 per farm, and in the case of the Free State to 15. Marks seems to have got away with this without much difficulty, despite bitter complaints by nearby Boer farmers that his encouragement of large-scale sharecropping deprived them of black labour, thus forcing them to keep their children out of school to help with their farming. Sammy's success in subverting the squatter law is a measure of his influence within Boer society as well as of the lackadaisical way in which the law was generally enforced by governments dominated by large Boer landowners who themselves benefited from the presence of substantial black tenant communities on their properties.

Marks's success in attracting large numbers of black tenants while his Boer neighbours often struggled to find or keep them, had much to do with the comparative liberality of his treatment of his tenants. Marks made fewer demands on his tenants than many Boer landowners. As the 90-year-old Abraham Mokale, who had spent part of his adolescence on Marks's Vaal River property, recalled in an interview in 1980: 'Mangolwane [Sammy Marks or one of his managers] did not bother anybody. After planting time, you did not have anything to worry about. Yours was just to look after the crop in the field. He would never come and worry you. After harvest he would come and you would give him his share and he would not burden you with anything.'

By contrast, as one of Sammy's farm managers noted in 1899, Boer landowners expected a range of unpaid services from their black tenants in addition to a share of the crop. Younger members of tenant families, for example, were required to work in the landowner's fields and in the homesteads for nothing more than their food and 'scanty wearing apparel'. When Marks's tenants, however, were called to work in his colliery or in his plantation at Maccauvlei they were paid, the manager noted, between 1s. 6d. and 2s. per day. Even these demands, the evidence suggests, Marks's tenants were sometimes able to resist.

Marks's behaviour towards his tenants – both at the Vaal River and on his many other farms – can be gauged from a letter he wrote in 1895 to a chief in the Lydenburg district of the Transvaal. The chief and his people could remain on Marks's land if they paid rent regularly and sent all the young men not engaged in farming to work on his mines if required. He was at pains to emphasise, however, that he did not expect this work for nothing but would pay the princely sum of £1 per month, or more if they worked well. He absolutely forbade the shooting of buck and birds on his farms, and with a nice disregard for the racial etiquette of the Boer Transvaal, gave the chief the right to bind with raw hide thongs – *riemen* – any white or black caught shooting or chopping wood without permission, and to deliver him to Marks's local agent. No white, excepting the veld-cornet – the minor government official in charge of the ward – and Marks's agent, had the right to demand anything of the chief; if any whites mistreated the chief or his people, the chief could send a messenger to Sammy Marks in Pretoria and he would come himself to investigate. He warned, though, that the chief should not behave provocatively towards whites and should not come to Marks and tell lies. This, Marks concluded his letter, was how he treated his many tenants on his Vaal River property; he would like to treat the chief's people in exactly the same way. But while Sammy's conduct at the Vaal River and elsewhere differed in a significant degree from that of many of his Boer neighbours, his relatively 'benign' behaviour – recalled so many decades later by the aged Abraham Mokale – concealed, as we shall see later, racial attitudes of some ferocity, little different from those of his white contemporaries in the Transvaal.[56]

One alternative to tenant-farming was direct farming by the company, based on the steam plough Marks had introduced in the early nineties. The results of steam-ploughing, however, were disappointing for the machine was cumbersome and liable to break down, and within a few years of starting, Lewis was calling for the abandonment of the experiment. While he objected to the steam plough on grounds of costs, the estate's Boer neighbours objected on less rational grounds. They sneered at 'a fearsome looking . . . detested novelty. . . . These superstitious farmers thought it sacrilegious to employ an infernal machine that hauled an eight-furrow plough through 16 inches deep of ground in any weather.' To allay Boer hostility towards the steam plough and to foster the image of the firm as progressive farmers, Marks invited Kruger and his colleagues to a demonstration of steam-ploughing at the Vaal River in December 1896. But, for all the success of the outing, Kruger failed to take up a suggestion that the government purchase two or more steam ploughs for the benefit of those burghers who had lost their plough-teams to the rinderpest.

By 1899 even Marks was disillusioned with the steam plough, or at least with the man in charge of the operation. McLaren had performed well below expectations, Marks wrote, and should be dismissed; if at all possible, the steam plough should be leased out rather than operated by the company itself. Nothing came of this. After a brief nibble the prospective lessees backed away, leaving Marks's Vereeniging company with its white elephant.[57]

Marks also attempted in the 1890s to make profitable use of the estate's abundant water supply. Marks had recognised early in the decade that Johannesburg's existing water supply would be 'totally insufficient' in a relatively short space of time and that the only long-term solution was to pump water from the Vaal, the nearest major river to Johannesburg. In the mid-nineties he had taken the idea to the Corner House, the leading firm on the Rand, but no business had resulted; cheaper schemes, drawing on underground sources closer to hand, still seemed more attractive. The idea lay dormant till 1898, when Johannesburg once again faced a crippling drought. This time there was a very real danger that the mines would be forced to close down, at least temporarily, with all the dire consequences that would have for profits. With shut-down looming, Marks offered a solution: the Vaal.

After exploratory discussions with the likely customers, the mining men of the Rand, and with Paul Kruger, who promised his personal support, Marks applied to the government for permission to supply Johannesburg with water drawn from the Vaal in the vicinity of Vereeniging. The scheme would cost, he estimated, some £500,000 or £600,000, and would solve the city's problems. True to his promise, the President endorsed the application, discounting in the process a string of rival applications including one from the Chamber of Mines, as well as objections raised by his own burghers and the Free State government who feared that the Marks proposal would dangerously lower the level of the Vaal River to the serious disadvantage of local farmers.

With the support of the Executive Council wrapped up, all that remained was to secure the Volksraad's endorsement of the scheme. Here Marks anticipated 'a little trouble', though with the help of Frikkie Eloff (Paul Kruger's private secretary, son-in-law and fixer) and the judicious expenditure of £7,500 he expected to carry the day. Before he embarked on this 'campaign', however, he needed to tie up the support of the leading mining houses, both as investors and as the major consumers of water on the Witwatersrand. The scheme could not hope to succeed, he explained to his partner, without the backing of Wernher Beit in particular, the firm which controlled half the mines on the Witwatersrand. This proved more difficult to arrange than he had expected. Wernher Beit had a stake in a rival water supply scheme and consequently were reluctant to commit themselves to Marks's scheme. Rather than refusing outright though, they chose to stall, forcing Marks in his turn to stall an increasingly impatient government. After a series of postponements and extensions, Marks finally had to withdraw. Sammy's scheme was successfully revived many years later but this time as a public rather than a private initiative. Borrowing Marks's bold conception, the Rand Water Board, formed in 1903, eventually solved the water difficulties of the Witwatersrand by damming the Vaal River and pumping its water from Vereeniging to Johannesburg.[58]

There was very little progress, too, with Marks's great ambition of transforming Vereeniging into a major centre of industry. The brick works with its unsatisfactory equipment had also to contend with the effects of a severe commercial recession in its primary market, the Witwatersrand, while the iron works moved no closer to materialisation despite the plans and estimates Marks had had prepared when he vacationed in England in 1896. On his return to Africa, Marks had discussed the venture with his friend Jimmy Sivewright, the sounding board for so many of his ideas at this time, who suggested that Barney Barnato be brought in to lend his money and reputation to the scheme. The proposed vehicle was a long-dormant concession granted by Kruger to Nellmapius, the great concession hunter, in 1882. After Nellmapius went insolvent this had been picked up for a song by John Henderson, another of the speculators who descended on the Transvaal in its free-wheeling days. Like others of its kind, the terms of the iron concession were extremely generous, for while it placed the concessionaire under no real obligation to implement his grand promise of founding iron and steel works, it guaranteed him effective protection against both foreign and domestic competition if he did so, as well as a preferent right to supply the government with its requirements of iron.

The chief difficulty was that the concession was due to expire in a few years' time. Without delay Marks, the consummate lobbyist, set to work to persuade the members of the Volksraad and the government to renew the concession for a further 21 years. With the predictable exception of Marks's *bête noire,* W. J. Leyds, the State Secretary, almost all were amenable. Isaac Lewis, however, was not, and promptly knocked the scheme on its head. Sceptical, it seems, from the start about the chances of success of such an ambitious industrial venture in a business environment as hazardous as that in the South African Republic, Lewis was frightened off when Henderson spoke of an asking price of £45,000 for his concession. Faced with his partner's veto, Marks was once again forced to pigeon-hole his favourite project. [59]

Looking back in May 1899 on a decade of expansion at the Vaal River, Isaac Lewis wrote:

I am convinced we shall never make much money out of agriculture. We have wasted enough time and money in carrying on these industrial operations whilst other people have been going in for mining, and they have had and still have the best of us all round. We must try now to give our attention more to mining things, especially to those we already have. I quite agree that the tree plantation should be kept on but all the other things to my mind should be given out to other people to work, with a share in the profits, but as before stated I am quite content with what you do in all these matters.[60]

Lewis's gloomy verdict on a decade of heavy investment at Vereeniging was equally applicable to the industrial experiments at Eerste Fabrieken. While it does admittedly reflect his essentially short-term view on investment and the differing time-horizons of the partners, it nevertheless contains a kernel of truth. By 1899 the firm had been outstripped by houses with which it had originally been on level terms, but which, unlike Lewis and Marks, had concentrated, highly successfully, on gold-mining. Lewis and Marks were now overshadowed by Rand heavyweights like the Corner House and the Gold Fields company, as well as by Barnato Brothers and by J. B. Robinson. Without a substantial stake in Rand gold-mining, they were condemned to the second rank of mining and financial houses. Their experience would seem to demonstrate that in an undeveloped economy like the Transvaal's, on the furthest fringes of the industrial world, extractive industry like gold-mining, serving the needs of metropolitan economies, was likely to be far more profitable than secondary industries focused on supplying small local markets.

While acknowledging his courage and vision, it must be admitted that Sammy Marks was a premature industrialist. Industry in the Transvaal in the 1890s was hamstrung by the smallness of local markets which prevented it from achieving the economies of scale it needed to compete effectively with cheaper imports. Far from the established centres of manufacturing, Transvaal industry had to grapple moreover with the very high costs of importing machinery, and the severe difficulties involved in keeping these in proper running order a long way away from the suppliers. Then again, its remoteness led to the Transvaal suffering a severe skills famine in the 1890s, which meant that expert advice or assistance was seldom readily available, and when it was, it was very expensive. All the more credit, perhaps, to Marks for attempting such a Sisyphean task as the establishing of secondary industry in Kruger's Transvaal.

Collecting the company's half-share of the maize crop from prosperous black tenants of Lewis and Marks's Vaal River farms, 1897 (Photo: Vaal Teknorama)

V

Courting Kruger:
Sammy Marks and the President

In August 1895, just four months before Cecil Rhodes attempted to topple Paul Kruger and his government, Sammy Marks had offered – in complete contrast – to erect a marble statue of the President. Sammy Marks was the king of lobbyists. He knew that his pioneering industrial ventures had one crucial feature in common: they all depended, to a lesser or greater degree, on state support. In view of this he worked very hard at courting officialdom. As Marks was to learn, Boer government was very informal. Much depended on personal relationships between legislators and officials on the one hand and their clients, the public, on the other. Marks, in consequence, invested a great deal of effort and expense in fostering these.

The small change of his relationships with Boer officialdom were cases of liquor from the Hatherley distillery (an enduring South African custom it seems), wedding presents and the occasional spree. 'As your spider [carriage] is here,' Sammy wrote from the distillery to C. J. Joubert, the eminently corruptible Minister of Mines, 'I think it best to send you a couple of cases to mix with water as a preventative against cold.' Besides cases of Hatherley's finest, Marks also organised junketing day-trips to the distillery and to the Vaal River property. Arranging one such trip, he had his guests assemble at Nellmapius's house rather than at the Lewis and Marks office: 'If they leave our Office, the papers may again say I want another Concession.' He also sent wedding presents for officials' daughters. When Vice-President Smit's daughter married, Marks instructed his wife to 'choose a present for £25 to £30 – see that it is a good one, say solid silver'.[1]

The hard currency of Marks's relationship with Boer officialdom were loans on easy terms to hard-pressed functionaries and legislators and their relatives and friends. The schedule of debtors in Marks's balance-sheets reads like an abstract from the Transvaal civil service list, and included such luminaries as Dr Leyds (who owed £50), Judge De Korte, Ewald Esselen, one-time State Attorney of the Transvaal, and J. S. Smit, the government railway commissioner. The loans were readily granted. When the Postmaster-General visited England in 1897, Marks instructed his London office:

Should Mr. van Alphen require a loan of say £500 to £1000 please advance him the money on his good for and should the Firm not wish to advance the money debit my account with it.

Kindly show Mr. van Alphen every attention and everything you may do for him I shall esteem as a personal favour. Mr. van Alphen has a great deal of influence here, and besides is a Director of our Transvaal Consolidated Coal Mines.[2]

Similarly when General N. J. Smit, hero of the battle of Amajuba in the Transvaal's war of independence and Vice-President of the Republic, unwisely granted the incorrigible Hugo Nellmapius an open power of attorney and inevitably found himself in 'a very big mess', owing no less than £7,000, Marks agreed to help, possibly at Paul Kruger's request. As Sammy explained to Isaac: 'we have to render a little assistance to General Smit. Well of course we could do better with our money, but under the circumstances we could not refuse.'[2]

The largest of Marks's loans was to C. J. Joubert, Oom Krisjan, the absentee head of the mines department, who kept his job for many years despite his manifest incompetence because of the political clout he wielded as a leading layman in the Nederduitsch Hervormde Kerk, one of the major church denominations. In 1888 Marks loaned Joubert £2,000, which was never repaid. Four years later, Marks joined a consortium of Rand capitalists who saved the Minister of Mines the ignominy of sequestration by the Netherlands Bank; in return, a greatly relieved Joubert promised 'to devote the whole of his time to the interests of Gold Fields where he trusts that his efforts on their behalf will prove his gratitude'. By 1896 Joubert's debt to Marks had soared over the £5,000 mark; he failed to pay interest on this for the rest of the decade.[3]

Marks was not overly concerned with the payment of interest on his loans to officialdom or with the repayment of the principal sums. When Isaac Lewis grumbled about the amounts outstanding in the partnership's books, Marks explained that these were soft loans for political purposes: 'I note what you write nearly every week . . . but when I inform you that this money is in nearly every case advanced to influential officials, whom we may require at any moment, I think you will agree with me that it is worth our while to forgo the interest on say £10,000 which would amount to about £800 per annum to keep on good terms with them.'[4]

Naturally Marks paid special attention to the President himself. Kruger's goodwill was crucial for he exercised an extraordinary personal dominance over government in the Transvaal. Kruger imposed his will on the Volksraad by sheer force of personality, and it was said that when he launched into one of his tirades, even his arch-rival General Piet Joubert was scared to look him in the eye. Similarly his wishes held sway in the Executive Council. As Marks reported on an application to the state, 'The members of the Executive are in our favour, but of course everything depends upon the "Old Man".'[5]

Marks was very attentive to Kruger. The President's birthdays were marked with gifts which were chosen with characteristic care and attention to detail. Ordering a set of razors from Sheffield for Kruger, the former cutlery pedlar specified that there was to be a razor for every day of the week, that they were to have ivory handles, and that the President's name was to be stamped on each blade. A big meerschaum pipe for a later birthday had to be mounted in gold with a ferrule engraved with the President's name and date of birth; it was to be sent out in secret, not, Marks hastened to explain, to evade customs duty, but to ensure surprise.[6]

Marks went to particular trouble every year to see that his children whom he had sent to school in England acknowledged the President's birthday. Early on in their stay he sent their tutor the text of a congratulatory cable which was to be addressed to the President 'as from my two boys'. Later efforts were a little more spontaneous though no less patriotic:

May it please your honour,
Many happy returns of your Birthday and I hope God will grant you many more. I trust you Mr President and Madame Kruger are very well. I am first rate. . . . I am improving in my studies and Music and take a great interest in all the sports of my School, so that when I return to my native land I may be a useful citizen and of some service to the State. . . .
  I am, Mr. President,
  Your little friend,
  Montie Marks.

The 'old gentleman was very pleased' with these letters, and passed them on for the proud father's perusal; 'he often speaks to me of you,' Marks wrote to his sons, 'and hopes you will do your best to become a credit to the country in which you were born.'[7]

Marks was as solicitous of Gezina Kruger, Mrs Paul Kruger, as he was of her husband. He sent a large bottle of Hatherley eau-de-Cologne on her birthday, and one of his best cows when Mrs Kruger's suddenly stopped producing milk. (Marks, it seems, kept a close watch on the Kruger herd! On another occasion he took over from Nellmapius one of the President's cows which was in poor condition, and fattened it on green mealies.) Marks was clearly fond of Mrs Kruger, 'the good soul', and gently amused by her innocence of the modern world. When the President opened the railway line at Hatherley, Mrs Kruger told Marks that 'it was the first time she had ever been on the train and . . . it was nearly as comfortable as an oxwagon but she was frightened it would go off the rails'. Whenever they met, Mrs Kruger would ask about the Marks boys who were at school in England. 'The old Lady often enquires after you and wants to know when you will come out to take over your Father's business and give him a rest.'[8]

Marks was equally solicitous of Kruger's extended family. The bonds between the Kruger clan and Marks were strengthened by wedding presents, personal loans and business arrangements. As Sammy assured Frikkie Eloff (the President's son-in-law and fixer) on one such occasion, 'I shall be very pleased to do business with you.' Marks was especially close to Piet Grobler, the President's 'very likeable' and good-humoured great-nephew and protégé who at the tender age of 25 was made a senior civil servant. Marks loaned Grobler £1,700; he fitted out the 'salon' in Grobler's new house, instructing that the curtaining, carpeting and furniture he ordered for Grobler from England 'be pretty decent but nothing out of the way'; he provided Grobler with a good milk-cow (the peripatetic Zwartkoppies herd, it seems, produced political goodwill as much as dairy products); and he accompanied Grobler to England in 1896 and introduced him to the firm's influential friends. Marks was perfectly aware that Grobler had ready access to his great-uncle and that his advice carried considerable weight with the 'Old Man'. On occasion Marks attempted to use this to supplement his own efforts to influence the President.[9]

The most important personal service Marks performed for Kruger was one not unfamiliar to students of the modern American presidency: the transformation by the great man's businessmen friends of his modest financial assets into a small personal fortune. Lewis and Marks were the 'originators' of the deal – in the mid-1890s – which made the President a very wealthy man. With the firm as go-betweens, Kruger sold the farm Geduld on the as yet unproven Far East Rand gold-field to a syndicate which included Lewis and Marks, Edward Lippert, the notorious dynamite concessionaire, and Adolf Goerz, the German financier who created what later became the Union Corporation (now part of Gencor). Geduld had originally cost the President £3,700; he sold it for £107,700.

For Lewis and Marks the deal made as much political sense as it did financial. While Marks certainly believed that the property was a 'good thing', he was not oblivious to the off-balance-sheet gains Geduld offered the firm. 'Things in this country must be managed very adroitly,' Marks had written to Lewis when Kruger had earlier suggested a modification in the terms of the deal which was strictly to his own advantage; 'you cannot push our people but must lead them, and this is one of the reasons that induced me to cable you to accede to the President's request with regard to Geduld.'[10]

Marks's courtship of Kruger was not always as private and discreet. Flush with funds in August 1895 after the firm's stock-market successes, Marks offered the city of Pretoria £10,000 for the erection of a marble statue of the President at a site to be chosen by the great man himself. The government gratefully accepted this 'munificent gift'. Kruger chose Burghers Park and suggested that any balance left unspent be used to lay out a zoological garden in Pretoria. He also indicated that he would rather be immortalised in bronze than in marble.

Marks's gesture, a public demonstration of his loyalty to the Republic and his regard for its leader, was not untypical of the age. Civic statues honouring the 'great man' or, in certain special cases, the 'great woman', were a prominent feature of the public spaces of the Victorian city. Thus Queen Victoria's dumpy form was endlessly replicated in parks and squares throughout her empire. While clearly part of this broader phenomenon, the Kruger statue was distinctive in certain ways. It was a new departure for a Republic which had not previously chosen to honour its leaders in this particular way: the erection of a memorial to a living personage with his full approval had a monarchical flavour to it, out of keeping with the egalitarian ethos of Boer society and with the carefully nurtured image of Kruger as the people's president, dispensing hospitality – coffee and tobacco – to backveld visitors on the presidential stoep. Moreover, unlike its equivalents elsewhere, which were typically funded by public subscription, the Kruger statue was initiated and funded by a single individual, a controversial aspect of the scheme which drew criticism at the time.

True to form, Marks's involvement in the project went well beyond simply stumping up the cash. Though he was no connoisseur and Zwartkoppies contained little of the fine art that adorned the Park Lane mansions of his peers, he helped to select the sculptor, a young and untried Dutch artist who had settled in Pretoria a few years earlier. Anton van Wouw was chosen, despite his inexperience, because he was 'well acquainted with the Old Man' and had 'studied his ways and peculiarities for a period of six years'.

Marks negotiated the terms with the sculptor: Van Wouw would travel to Europe at once to see to the casting of the statue in bronze (marble was jettisoned for fear that it would not resist the extreme temperature variations of the Transvaal). While abroad he would be paid £40 per month plus his travelling costs and those of his wife and child; Marks would meet all the studio costs and would retain the right to supervise the work; once casting was completed, within a period of one and a half years, Van Wouw would return to Pretoria and see to the erection of the statue.

Marks's right of supervision proved troublesome, at least for the artist. Much to Van Wouw's annoyance, he received a stream of enquiries from Isaac Lewis, on behalf of his partner, about the likely date of completion, when work went slower than was originally anticipated. 'These people', Van Wouw wrote to his father, 'have very little idea about art and think that one makes a statue just as easily as one planes a plank.'

Marks, meanwhile, chose a plinth for the statue – imported Scottish granite rather than the local stone some would have preferred. He also persuaded the President that Church Square, right at the centre of the town, would be a more suitable site than Burghers Park: here 'every visitor to our capital would view the statue'. When, in mid-1899, the statue and its accessories, four bas reliefs of major landmarks in Kruger's career, and four Boer sentries to stand guard around the President, were at last complete (and almost all the money spent), Van Wouw returned to South Africa to see to their erection. He arrived in Pretoria in September, just weeks before the outbreak of war. Sammy Marks's tribute to the President was an early casualty of the conflict: the Kruger statue was left in store in a Delagoa Bay warehouse where it remained, half-forgotten, for some years.[11]

Kruger was more than willing to reciprocate Marks's gesture. In 1898 he allowed Marks the extraordinary privilege of private use of the state mint for a day. Marks struck 215 golden tickeys – threepenny pieces normally made of silver – as keepsakes for his relatives and friends, including, naturally, the

President and members of the Volksraad. The gold would probably have come from the Sheba mine, the only major gold mine in which Lewis and Marks had a substantial stake. This famous incident, perhaps the best-known of all Sammy Marks stories, says as much about his special relationship with the Kruger state as it does about the pre-modern informality of that state, with its blurred divide between public property and the personal property of the ruling elite, an indistinctness which a feudal monarch would have recognised.[12]

Marks was a frequent and very welcome visitor to the President's home, an 'unpretentious villa' in Church Street built for Kruger by his old, and grateful, friend Nellmapius. Sammy and the President would sit either in the voorkamer – a large and 'simply furnished' drawing room – or on the 'darkly-shaded verandah' – the stoep – at the front of the house. If they remained outside on the stoep Kruger would sit in his favourite chair – 'a peculiar little structure', placed in a nook to the right of the main entrance to the house – and would work away at his long hooked pipe as they spoke and argued in the local variant of Dutch. (Unlike Marks who abhorred smoking, Kruger shared the Boer addiction to the pipe, from which 'he seemed to derive satisfaction', an amused English guest wrote, 'as much by a kind of blowpipe operation as by sucking'.)[13]

Kruger clearly enjoyed Marks's company – the lively, 'slim' argument, sometimes bordering on the insolent; the cross-fire of argument-clinching illustrations from their favourite text, the Bible; and the banter about Marks's supposed religious wrongheadedness.

'Sam, there is one thing I would very much like to do before I die.'

'What is that, President?'

'I would like to make a Christian of you.'

'No, President . . . if you could do that you would have to banish me from the country, for a converted Jew is no good.'[14]

Marks was allowed an unusual degree of latitude by a man with a deserved reputation for ferocity, who was not known for his tolerance of opposing points of view. (A mutual acquaintance wrote of Kruger that 'there was a fear of facing him. He could be terrible in denunciation.') As others recognised, Marks had a certain licence to say what was normally best left unsaid. When Kruger and President Reitz of the Free State met on the banks of the Vaal in 1892 for the opening of the railway bridge between their states, Marks was called aside by Reitz who asked ' a very big favour' of him. Would he speak to Kruger and warn him not to put too much trust in his Hollander officials, especially Dr Leyds? Marks balked at first: 'Indeed, I replied, you are more fitted than I am to tell him that.' But when Reitz insisted, arguing that the Transvaal President 'would listen . . . a great deal better' to the Pretoria magnate than to himself, Marks at last agreed to broach the sensitive subject of Hollander influence over the Transvaal administration with Kruger.

Soon after breakfast the following morning, Marks went to Kruger's room where he found him enjoying a quiet smoke with Eloff, his private secretary. 'I opened the conversation by apologising for what I was about to say, and asking that I might be excused if he deemed me in the wrong. He replied that as long as I did not insult him I could speak openly.' After some hemming and hawing,

Marks told Kruger that he had spoken to many people in the Transvaal, including the young burghers, and that they all thought that Leyds would eventually get the country into trouble. 'The Old Man was by no means pleased, he jumped out of his chair, knocked his pipe on the table, put his hands one across the other and said: "Rather than dispense with Dr Leyds I would have my arms cut off, he knows all my State Secrets and all my business." '

Marks replied that Leyds was not indispensable; if Leyds were dead Kruger would have to find a replacement and there was bound to be someone suitable in the Transvaal, the Cape or the Free State; 'think of him as dead and get another in his place.'

'He has served me for a long time,' Kruger retorted, 'I cannot treat him in that manner.'

Then pension him off, Marks pleaded, give him a large present, 'at all events, do not allow everybody to say behind your back that Leyds will cause the ruination of your country.'

But Kruger would not be moved. Marks apologised once again, then as his last shot, warned that while he hoped he would be proved wrong, he could not help feeling that unless Kruger acted as he advised, the Transvaal would lose its independence within ten years.

This thoroughly annoyed Kruger: 'I am sorry to hear you, who I depend upon so much, say this,' he barked at his Cassandra.

Marks left the room with Kruger's private secretary; once outside, Eloff turned to him and said: 'Mr. Marks if I was not ashamed to do so, I would kiss you for it because there is not one of us, not even I who have slept in the same wagon with the Old Man, and eaten out of the same plate, who would have dared to speak to him as you have done.'[15]

While still at the river, Marks was able to offer the President an unusual service. Troubled, like Marks, by 'rheumatics' – and no doubt by annoying, unsolicited advice! – Kruger was in 'a grumpy mood'. Marks, who prided himself on his knowledge of 'medicine', persuaded the President to sit in an improvised bath of hot water in which about a bushel of eucalyptus leaves had soaked, while Marks laved his patient's feet with the brew.[16]

Kruger was not always forbearing with Marks, who on occasion overstepped the limits of the President's tolerance, provoking outbursts of genuine or manufactured anger. When in July 1898 Marks threatened to close his eastern Transvaal coal-mining operation because of inadequate support from the Netherlands railway company, 'the Old Man worked himself up into a rage and said that if I stopped the mine he would confiscate our property. I informed him that this would greatly satisfy me. . . . ' Again, at the height of the political crisis in 1899, Marks 'went down to see the Old Man . . . and he refused to discuss anything but politics. When I touched upon business he told me that was all I cared for. I retorted that business was all I could talk about seeing that I was debarred by the laws of the land from taking part in politics. At this he nearly jumped at my throat and said that I ought to know that Jewish disabilities would be removed.'

Marks's Jewishness was an important element in his relation with Kruger. Despite the President's occasional provocative jests – legend has it that he opened the Park Synagogue in Johannesburg in 1892 'in the name of our Lord Jesus Christ' – despite his conviction of the overwhelming superiority of his own brand of Calvinist Christianity, and despite his deeply harboured and publicly expressed hopes for the eventual conversion of the Jews, the President was no religious bigot. Flat-earther and Calvinist fundamentalist though he might have been, he was remarkably liberal in his attitude towards Catholics and Jews. Kruger's tolerance was not necessarily shared by all his burghers. *Land en Volk*, an opposition newspaper, lambasted the President for surrounding himself with 'a commando' of Hollanders and 'foreign' Jews 'who encircle him like vultures', concessionaires like Sammy Marks, Alois Hugo Nellmapius and Edward Lippert, the notorious dynamite king. General Joubert, one-time business associate of Sammy Marks and leader of the Boer opposition to Kruger, articulated the hostility of many when he promised, during his campaign for the presidency in 1892–3, to 'do all in his power to counteract the Hebraic influence that is making itself felt in the land'.

The *Grondwet* or constitution of the South African Republic embodied these prejudices: Jews and Catholics – all non-Protestants – were debarred from holding military or civil office, and from membership of the Volksraad. Egged on by Marks and other Jewish friends, Kruger sought to remove these disabilities in 1899 but his efforts were obstructed by the obstinate bigotry of the Volksraad and then overtaken by the political crisis of late 1899. Kruger, it seems, was a philosemite who felt an affinity with Marks and his co-religionists. The Jews were the Chosen People; so were the Boers. The Jews were the people of the Book, something Sammy played on in his conversations with Kruger; so were the Boers. But there was obviously more to it than religious sentiment. Kruger, it appears, saw Jews like Sammy Marks as agents of economic growth and as useful neutrals who could be trusted because they stood outside the rancorous quarrel between Boer and Brit and who could therefore be entrusted on occasion with delicate assignments.[17]

Besides his personal services for Kruger and other Boer officials, Marks performed a variety of services for the state as such, some minor, but some quite major and, at least potentially, very profitable for the firm. (Marks clearly espoused Cecil John Rhodes's credo of patriotism plus ten per cent.) Marks lent his active support when the Boers campaigned against their black neighbours. It has already been mentioned that Marks imported dynamite for use against the Pedi in the early 1880s. Again, in 1894, when the Boers fought Chief Malaboch, and Uitlanders were commandeered for service, Marks, 50 years old and untrained, sent a doctor as his substitute, together with an assistant and all the equipment necessary for a field ambulance.[18]

Perhaps the most profitable of the services Marks offered the state was one his remote ancestors, the *Hofjuden* or Court Jews of early modern times, had traditionally performed for the crowned heads of Europe: the provision of ready cash. At various points in the 1880s and 1890s Paul Kruger's financially inept government found itself short of funds to meet either its running or its capital expenses. At such times Marks was more than willing to serve as a financial broker between the state and his firm's banker friends. Without venturing its own limited funds, Lewis and Marks stood to earn a sizeable commission, the gratitude of the government, and the prestige that went with successful brokerage on behalf of a state, and all this without any serious financial risk to the firm.

Shortly after his very first visit to the Transvaal in 1881, Marks tried to interest French financiers in a £150,000 loan to the government, but they could not be persuaded to lend money to what was still a pauper republic. Four years later, Marks proposed to Lewis that their railway construction syndicate take up a £100,000 state loan at 6 per cent interest; Kruger, desperately short of funds, was prepared to offer the firm a commission of no less than £10,000. Lewis vetoed the idea on the grounds that the syndicate's members were manufacturers not financiers; besides, financiers were 'dead against the Transvaal'.[19]

The discovery of the Witwatersrand the next year radically altered investor perceptions, as well as the scale of the Transvaal's financial needs. By 1892 Kruger was looking for a vastly greater sum to finance the last stages of his cherished railway line from Delagoa Bay to Pretoria. Eager to avoid any compromising dependence on financiers with strong British connections, he turned to local capitalists known to be sympathetic to the Republic. After trying unsuccessfully to raise £600,000 through J. B. Robinson, Kruger spoke to Marks, who in turn approached the Standard Bank of which he was a valued customer. When the Standard refused to cooperate, Kruger took up an offer, with Marks's encouragement, of £2,500,000 from the London Rothschilds.

Despite the magnitude of this loan it was insufficient to complete the proposed railway system. Consequently, Marks approached the Standard once more, in late 1892, this time for £400,000, but was again rebuffed. The bank, it seems, feared that the government and the railway company were overextending themselves. Marks turned instead to the Standard's local rival, the newly established National Bank. The National was more willing than the Standard, and loaned the railways £350,000; Lewis and Marks's commission, the Standard enviously estimated, was over £40,000.[20]

In the half-decade between the Jameson Raid and the South African War, the government was more in need than ever of extra funding. The Raid had shown just how unprepared the Republic was for war, and to rectify this large sums had to be found for forts and guns. At the same time drought and a virulent cattle disease, the rinderpest, ravaged the countryside, obliging Kruger to spend heavily on mules and mealies for his destitute burghers. Political opponents complained of immense waste in the administering of this relief, as they did of his lavish spending on a rapidly growing civil service.

The severe commercial and industrial recession of the late 1890s complicated the task of finding the funds. Tumbling imports meant that government income, heavily dependent on customs duties, fell well below expectations, forcing Kruger to consider outside sources of funding. The problem, as ever, was one of avoiding dependence on hostile financiers who might demand far-reaching concessions to the Uitlander population and the mining industry as the price of their support.

Marks was very keen to oblige. Weeks after the Raid, he and the President arranged a 25-year loan of £300,000 at 4 per cent interest per annum, but this facility was never used. Later in the year Marks approached Leyds, the State Secretary, about raising a public loan, but was roundly rebuffed by his old antagonist. 'His answer was emphatically no,' as in terms of its charter, the National Bank had the preferent right to negotiate loans for the government.[21]

When the Transvaal's finances took a turn for the worse in mid-1897, with its treasury emptying at an alarming rate, Marks was ready once again to negotiate a long-term credit facility for the state, this time for as much as £1,000,000. The government, in the absence of Leyds who was visiting Europe, settled instead for a short-term accommodation of £200,000, half from J. B. Robinson, half from Marks's firm. 'Rather than disturb their own investments', Lewis and Marks asked the Standard Bank for a special overdraft to cover their commitment. This they were granted at 4 per cent interest per annum; they promptly loaned it onwards to the government at 6 per cent. While Kruger clearly felt this was a reasonable commission, his political opponents did not; nor did the Standard Bank, when it discovered that its customers were charging the state 6 per cent for money that could have been borrowed directly from the bank at 5 per cent. Further proof, the bank felt, of the financial incompetence of the Boer government.[22]

The following year, 1898, Kruger went hunting for the colossal sum of £6,000,000 to finance railway expansion and public works, though he was prepared to settle for a lot less. Amongst those he approached were Lewis and Marks, who in their turn sounded out their French friends. But these failed to bite because the European financial market was in one of its periodic crises and was in no mood to lend the unreformed Republic vast sums of money. Marks then made overtures to his old friends at the Standard Bank, but they were still peeved about the 2 per cent commission the firm had charged the year before. Why, should Lewis and Marks be allowed, they argued, to profit once again from the bank's money? Finally, as a last resort, Marks contacted J. B. Robinson, who in turn spoke to the other major gold-mining firms. But these were very reluctant to help the Republic without major concessions in return by the government, something Kruger could not easily accept.[23]

Under the circumstances Marks was unable to pull off what would have been a giant coup for his firm, a deal which would not only have been very profitable for Lewis and Marks but which could possibly have raised it out the second rank of South African mining and financial houses into the premier league. Ironically, its failure to secure the loan was due, at least in part, to its second-rank standing: the firm's capacity to mobilise funds on behalf of the Kruger government was clearly limited by the relative weakness of its ties to European financial capital and by its restricted clout with local financial institutions.

Not all of Marks's dealings with the government were as profitable and painless as raising state loans. Witness his abortive venture into the arms trade in the early 1890s. The firm contracted with Piet Joubert, the Commandant-

General, to import 2,000 Martini-Henry rifles from Belgium. When many of these were found to be defective, the government refused to pay up; Lewis and Marks had to meet the costs of the repairs, and had to wait months for payment. 'It is no use my trying to explain what is wrong with them,' Marks belatedly admitted to his partner, 'as we do not understand the business.'[24]

Marks also served on occasion as a willing instrument of Kruger's ambitions in the region. The Delagoa Bay pier project was at least in part a scheme to consolidate Transvaal influence over a port which was so vital to its strategic interests. Marks clearly acted in consultation with Paul Kruger and the Transvaal government, as he also did with regard to nearby Swaziland.[25] During the last decades of the nineteenth century the Swazi kingdom was the hapless victim of massive white commercial and political penetration. Its feeble king, Mbandzeni, granted concession after concession to Boer and British fortune-hunters who swarmed through his territory in search of gold and grazing land. After his death in 1889 his kingdom became a pawn in the southern African struggle between British imperialism and Boer sub-imperialism. The expansionist Boers were anxious to assert control over their eastern neighbour and to gain a corridor to the sea, while the British were more than willing to sacrifice the Swazis to curb Boer ambition elsewhere in the region.[26]

Lewis and Marks played a small but not insignificant part in the Boer and capitalist expropriation of Swaziland and in the diplomatic game that accompanied it. The most far-reaching and promising of the concessions belonged to a London-based company – the Umbandine Swazieland [sic] Concessions Syndicate. Besides a monopoly of liquor and tobacco importation, printing and banking, it held the remarkable right to all Swazi land and minerals that had not yet been allotted to other concessionaires, or were abandoned or forfeited by these in the future. In 1894 Lewis and Marks took the concessions on offer with a view to selling them to the Transvaal government. When Marks discussed this with Kruger, the President hinted that the government might be interested if Marks would first do the state a service: certain English concessionaires in Swaziland were holding out against transfer of control over the kingdom to the Transvaal. Could Marks visit the territory and persuade some of them to accept a Boer take-over?[27]

At the end of July 1894 Marks paid a secret visit to Swaziland, where he conferred with leading members of the local English community. He persuaded them to rally support for transfer to the Transvaal, agreeing to cover their costs if they needed to spend 'a few pounds here and there for presents'. At the same time he paid his respects to the Swazi queen regent and her son, the boy-king Ngwane: 'to get into their huts we had to crawl on our hands and knees. I gave a present to the queen of two tablecloths and to the king her son a boy of about 17 years old a nice overcoat, we drank some of the beer they make, "Guala" they call it. . . . '

Marks was very taken with Swaziland which he had never visited before: 'to tell you the truth,' he reported to Jimmy Sivewright, 'I am rather sweet on the Country: I think there is some good to be derived by getting better acquainted with it.' But he was less impressed with the inhabitants: 'the Swazie race are an awful lot for begging for money, drink, matches, candles, in fact anything and everything; the men make the women do all the work whilst they walk about all day with their Assegais, Shields and Battle axes. . . . ' Worse still, they showed no inclination to volunteer their services to white employers. How was the great tin-mining industry which Marks foresaw for Swaziland, to be viable without their cheap labour?[28]

In December 1894 Britain at last agreed to a Boer take-over of Swaziland. The following year Marks offered the Umbandine Syndicate's concessions to the state for £100,000, but despite Kruger's earlier hint, the government declined the offer. Marks was convinced Leyds was responsible. Not only was he hostile to the firm, but he also had concessionaire friends who stood to lose if Marks's offer was accepted.[29]

After Leyds's resignation as State Secretary in 1898 the Transvaal showed renewed interest in the wide-ranging, quasi-governmental concessions of the Umbandine Syndicate, now renamed the Swaziland Corporation. Marks was approached unofficially by Smuts, the new State Attorney, and by his friend Piet Grobler, the Under-Secretary of State responsible for Swazi affairs, and later by Kruger himself. Marks told the President that the price had risen since he had made his original offer. Kruger allowed that he might just consider a slightly higher price as the state 'now had more money'. Nothing had been finalised by the time war broke out in late 1899.[30]

Given the range of services, public and private, Sammy performed for the Boer state and its ruling elite, and his widely advertised investment in the agricultural and industrial development of the Republic, it is no surprise that he and his firm were viewed very favourably by the President. Sammy Marks was Paul Kruger's tame mining capitalist – the very antithesis of the traitorous Randlords who plotted the overthrow of the President in 1895–6. Lewis and Marks was held up as a model of loyalty and enterprise by Kruger. As the President told an Uitlander audience at the opening in 1895 of the first agricultural show on the Witwatersrand, ' whatever that firm – Lewis and Marks – undertook, he knew they would carry through.' On other occasions Kruger exhorted his fellow countrymen to adopt Sammy Marks's 'pattern . . . [of] industry, thrift and enterprise'.[31]

Marks's intimacy with Kruger and the Boer elite set him apart from much of the rest of the mining industry, as did the priority he gave to secondary industry over mining. As we have seen, Marks was also directly at odds with the mining industry over the liquor question. Yet, for all that, his relationship with the Randlords was not wholly adversarial. Marks needed the mining industry – the gold mines bought his coal, and he hoped they would buy the water he planned to pipe from the Vaal. They, in turn, found him a useful ally on occasion, precisely because of his influence at 'court'. When in 1895 the industry faced the threat of the creation of a state-supported cyanide monopoly similar to the notorious dynamite monopoly, Lionel Phillips, the chairman of the Chamber of Mines, came to Pretoria and asked Sammy Marks to intercede with the government on the industry's behalf. As Sammy later laconically reported, he managed 'by dint of hard work to get the [prospective cyanide] concessions thrown out'. Again, when Rhodes's Gold Fields company needed to mend its tattered relationship with Pretoria after the Jameson Raid, it approached Sammy Marks.

In the right company and at the right moment, Marks, who had well-concealed doubts about the competence of an aging President, was not wholly uncritical of Kruger. When it was politic to do so, he privately indicated to the mining industry that he was sympathetic to their many grievances against the Boer administration. In 1896 and 1897, when the industry was trapped in a deep post-Raid recession, Marks combined with other members of the industry to propel the President towards reform. As Marks told an English friend, he 'worked incessantly . . . to this end, and . . . repeatedly interviewed the President on the subject'. As a result of his efforts, Marks crowed, the government decided to appoint a commission of inquiry into the condition of the mining industry. But little came of the extensive deliberations of this commission.

While Marks was privately critical of Kruger, he was equally critical, in other company, of the mining industry. Marks was secretly scathing about the severe shortcomings of an industry which he privately held as much responsible for the economic depression of the late-1890s as the government. He felt that the Witwatersrand gold industry had brought its troubles upon itself through 'mismanagement and wilful squandering of money'. Mine managements were not keeping working costs under proper control. As a result, very few of the mines were able to pay dividends. The dividends of the few that did were largely fictitious; they were more often the fruits of share-dealings than of actual gold-mining, a practice Marks cynically dismissed as 'robbing Piet to pay Paul'. These and other abuses were of such gross proportions that it would be years before the industry was truly profitable.[32]

All of this was said in the strictest confidence. As he told an English friend: 'You know the old saying "The bigger the truth, the bigger the libel" and if it became known that I am writing to you as I am, I would have far more names to add to my list of friends than I already have here for you know well enough that no one likes to hear the truth said of him.' In public Marks held his tongue. He had no more wish to offend the powerful mining industry than he had to offend the government. Marks, who was most amiable by nature and who believed strongly in conciliation and the avoidance of conflict, maintained cordial personal relations with his fellow mining magnates whatever his private feelings about them. Thus, despite his sense, dating from his Kimberley days, that Barney Barnato and his nephews, the Joels, were not to be trusted, and that Barney was dangerously manipulative, Sammy was willing to do business with them. Despite Sammy's secret view that Barney Barnato was 'as dangerous as a stick is for a snake' and that the members of his firm were 'false to the core', Barnato Bros became the closest ally of Lewis and Marks within the mining industry. Lewis and Marks were granted participations in Barney Barnato's major ventures, including the the South African Breweries and the Johannesburg Consolidated Investment Company, and the two firms invested jointly in Delagoa Bay.[33]

Like many others in the mining industry Marks was deeply angered by the wayward and self-seeking behavior of the obnoxious J. B. Robinson but he chose to avoid confrontation. Similarly, he tiptoed around the Corner House – the firm of Wernher Beit represented in Johannesburg by H. Eckstein and Co. – though he was convinced that this mighty firm, as dominant in the mining industry of the 1890s as Anglo American were to become in the late twentieth century, were secretly hostile to Lewis and Marks. As Marks wrote in characteristically cautious terms to his partner at the end of the decade, 'The Corner House are at the present moment the absolute masters of the position. . . . It behoves us therefore, as I have before advised you, to be guarded in our expression of feeling against these people even in our own dining rooms.'

Marks's suspicions about the chronic hostility of the Corner House were in fact justified. Julius Wernher, founder with Alfred Beit of the Corner House, and an old business associate of Sammy's from their Kimberley days, was privately dismissive of Marks's firm – 'L. and M. have no following and nobody ever makes anything out of them', he had written in 1892. Lionel Phillips, the young and arrogant heir apparent to the Corner House, was even more contemptuous. Instructing his Johannesburg junior, Percy FitzPatrick, to ignore Sammy's extraordinary advice in 1897, at the time of the commission of inquiry into the mining industry, 'to attack that Government here upon corruption and trickery', Phillips wrote, harshly: 'We cannot forget that Marks has vowed vengeance against the mining industry over the liquor law, and that he has consistently abused the authorities behind their backs and cringed to them in person, and that he has tried to induce others to expose the failures, the incompetence, and the iniquities perpetrated, while he posed as their friend.' FitzPatrick himself was understandably amused when he heard, a short while later, that Sammy Marks – President Kruger's favourite capitalist – momentarily despairing of the pace of reform in the Transvaal, had muttered the disloyal thought that he would give £100,000 to have the British flag fluttering over his money. 'Sammy is an inscrutable', FitzPatrick jested.[34]

Finally, there was the greatest of the Randlords, the man Marks once mockingly referred to as 'the great Cecil'. Marks was not a subscriber to the Rhodes cult of personality, at least during the lifetime of the 'colossus'. Sammy had the tongue-in-cheek scepticism of one who had known the great man in his more humble days, long before he became a living legend. Marks spoke cynically of seeing the 'big man' on a visit to Pretoria with 'so many apostles fluttering around' him. But Rhodes, more than any other magnate, needed careful cultivation, particularly in the early 1890s, before his fall from grace. As premier of the Cape Colony and as the political master of the Cape railways, Rhodes had held the key to the coal contract on which the fortunes of Sammy's Vaal River coal-field depended. Marks remained on good terms with the fallen hero after the Jameson Raid and his ignominious loss of office. Rhodes, Marks well knew, was still a force to be reckoned with on the Witwatersrand and in the region as a whole.

Rhodes, in turn, seems to have enjoyed his lengthy but infrequent conversations with Marks. As Isaac Lewis reported to his partner soon after

Marks had paid a brief visit to England: 'He [Rhodes] asked me particularly to tell you that he is very sorry he did not see you as he would have very much liked a chat with you on general matters.' Sammy, whose interests, like the Great Cecil's, extended well beyond mining and money, gave the colonial statesman the benefit of his views on subjects of mutual concern ranging from the future of Swaziland and Delagoa Bay to the possibilities of establishing a fruit industry in the Western Cape.

After Rhodes's early death, in 1902, Marks made all the required noises about 'our lamented and esteemed friend Rhodes'. He ordered a portrait of the great man, and later a bust from the studio of Thackeray Edwards in Cape Town. Edwards sent instructions 'that when it is necessary to wash the bust you should only use Hudson's Extract of Soap with water' – surely an unnecessary instruction to one as expert in applying soft soap to political egos as Sammy Marks.[35]

As his simultaneous friendship with Paul Kruger and his principal antagonist Cecil Rhodes attests, Sammy Marks was unhampered by any compelling political convictions during the deeply polarised late 1890s. He was the classic outsider, the Russian Jewish immigrant, who was unswayed by either the call to the blood of British imperialism after the Raid or of its opposite, Boer republicanism. As far as Sammy Marks was concerned, both Kruger and Rhodes, both Boer and Brit, were critical to the continuance of his business ventures. Both were powerful. Both, therefore, were to be courted. And where better than at Zwartkoppies, Marks's inviting country estate close to Pretoria?

The opening of the railway bridge over the Vaal in 1892, with presidents Reitz and Kruger on the left and Marks third from right (Photo: Sammy Marks Museum)

VI

A Country House on the Highveld: Zwartkoppies in the 1890s

As a grandmaster in the art of lobbying, Sammy Marks was acutely aware of the political value of hospitality. His influential Boer friends – and many others – were regularly entertained at his country home twelve miles east of Pretoria. The guest book at Zwartkoppies reads like a roll-call of Pretoria's elite and of the distinguished visitors who came to the capital. Sammy Marks's country estate was a popular stop-over on any grand tour of southern Africa. Lord Randolph Churchill visited in 1891 en route to the Mashonaland gold-fields, while H. M. Stanley stayed at Zwartkoppies in November 1897. His host found 'the Great African Traveller . . . a very interesting person'. Marks greatly enjoyed entertaining visitors and freely issued invitations to his home. 'My invitation to your friends still holds good,' he wrote to the prominent English politician John Morley in 1896, 'and should friends of yours contemplate visiting this country, either on business or pleasure bent, they will always receive a hearty welcome from me.' But at the same time Marks jokingly complained that he was overrun with visitors – 'I am constantly being assailed by people who come to me with letters of introduction from my numerous friends and as these people usually come out here on Sunday, I have not much time for private correspondence.' [1]

Marks was nothing if not even-handed in his hospitality. According to a well-informed contemporary, Paul Kruger was a 'frequent' guest at Zwartkoppies. The Marks papers record at least two visits by 'the Old Man', one of these, in March 1886, a working breakfast with Sammy before the President set out on an official tour of the backveld. Rhodes came to stay while on a visit to Pretoria in the early 1890s as premier of the Cape. The visit had unforeseen consequences for the economy of the Western Cape. Marks and his guest discussed the plight of the Cape wine industry which had been devastated by the spread of the dreaded phylloxera, an insect pest that ravaged the vineyards. Marks took Rhodes for a stroll through his orchard and proudly showed him his flourishing fruit trees. Pointing to one laden with peaches, he told Rhodes that if these peaches could be placed on the London market, they would fetch 1s. a piece. Why not persuade the stricken Cape wine farmers, he suggested, to turn their attention to growing fruit for export to England? In his early years in South Africa he had smoused in the Western Cape and knew the area well. It was eminently suited, he felt, for fruit-growing.

Rhodes said nothing at the time but that evening at dinner asked his host how he would go about implementing his idea. Marks suggested Rhodes buy land, hire an American or European expert, and set up a fruit-farming operation which would serve as a model for the surrounding farmers. To avoid a surge in price once it was known that Rhodes was in the market for farming land, Marks suggested a bluff: Rhodes should tell an agent that he was seeking to purchase a single farm but that he wanted options over a number to ensure that he had a good choice. Once the agent brought him the options, which under the circumstances would no doubt be competitively priced, he should buy the lot. The next day Marks recommended an agent he had himself used. He heard nothing further from Rhodes on the subject but somewhile later read that Rhodes was buying up tracts of land in the Western Cape. In 1898 H. E. V. Pickstone, the pioneer of the Cape fruit industry, established the Rhodes Fruit Farms on these properties.[2]

Marks was particularly proud of his fruit, and overnight guests (and Marks's children) could expect an early morning visit from their host (or father) bearing Zwartkoppies' finest. When the eminent jurist James Rose Innes came to Pretoria in February 1896, soon after the Jameson Raid, to observe the trial of the Reformers, he spent a night at Zwartkoppies. As he wrote to his wife in Cape Town afterwards, he was collected on a Tuesday afternoon in Pretoria by Marks and driven 'in a landau and four spanking horses' to the farm. The future Chief Justice of the Union found that Marks had 'a large house, very well appointed, several bath rooms, billiard rooms [sic], and long and airy passages. I had a splendid bedroom and was very comfortable; indeed, they were kindness itself. On a cabinet in my room were three photos: Sivewright in Court dress in the middle, flanked on either side by Rhodes and Kruger; and under the protection of the trio I slept well!!' When Rose Innes awoke, Marks came in with a huge bunch of grapes and proceeded to hold forth on what Rose Innes later learnt was Marks's favourite topic – 'the preeminent excellence of Transvaal fruit'. Interrupting the flow, Rose Innes pointed to the photographs of what he called in his autobiography 'Sammy's political trinity', and asked: 'Cecil Rhodes seems down and out, do you think we shall hear of him again?' Marks put down the grapes 'and with a rapt look, as if contemplating an eternal verity, he said, "My dear sir, how can you keep down a man with two millions?" ' (The photographs were not the only evidence at Zwartkoppies of Marks's studied political ecumenism and conspicuous neutrality: he had a roll specially inserted in a large music box so that it could play the anthems of the South African Republic and of the Orange Free State as well as 'God Save the Queen'.)[3]

Marks was immensely hospitable and Sundays at Zwartkoppies were intensely sociable. Marks, who was gregarious to a fault, invited scores of guests. Sometimes as many as 40 people would sit down to Sunday lunch, which would start at 1 o'clock and run on past 4. Marks, according to his nephew and long-time confidential secretary George Falcke, was 'an expert carver . . . [who]

demolished a turkey in record time', a very genial and attentive host who 'was full of chaff and anecdote and often relapsed into reminiscences'. Despite his detestation of smoking he kept a large stock of cigars for his guests. (In July 1902 he had over 4,000 in his inventory.) When he could no longer bear the smoke he would put on his pith helmet and lead his guests into the garden, past the croquet lawn and the tennis court, and conduct them around the estate, proudly pointing out with a walking-stick what he had done to improve the property and what he still intended doing.[4]

But Zwartkoppies was more than simply an outlet for Marks's generous and gregarious instincts, more too than simply an arena for cementing useful political connections. Zwartkoppies was a major focus for Marks's abounding creative energies as well as a source of great personal delight and pleasure. It was the physical embodiment of his social aspirations and a crucial means of realising these. Throughout the 1890s and beyond Marks spent a small fortune in transforming Zwartkoppies into the Highveld equivalent of an English country estate. Like others who had made their money in South Africa, and indeed like many other upwardly mobile Victorians, Marks was eager to emulate the lifestyle of the English upper-classes he so admired and to acquire the trappings of gentility. The transformation of Zwartkoppies was a vital element of this social strategy.

Marks's Zwartkoppies reflects a Victorian passion for improvement, for modernity, at least of the material kind, and for the taming of nature. During the nineties the house was successively enlarged to accommodate the expanding needs of a growing family, which by 1897 consisted of six children: four boys and two girls. Alterations to the original structure were designed by De Zwaan, one of the Dutch architects who had been drawn to the Transvaal by its new wealth and who were remaking its capital. The alterations were executed by John Johnston Kirkness, the Scottish building contractor, who built a large part of Republican Pretoria. The most impressive of the additions was a splendid and spacious billiard room, status symbol supreme in affluent Victorian homes. Here Bertha Marks and their visitors played billiards while Sammy, no sportsman, looked on. A miniature cue was ordered for the children. Marks also added a new stable, a 'splendid place', which, he said, 'looks quite like a mansion', with room for fourteen horses and at least five carriages. This housed the Basuto ponies, Daisy, Poppins and the rest, which his wife Bertha and their children rode, and the carriage and 'spiders' which Sammy ordered from America. 'I only require the very best make and quality,' he so characteristically wrote to the carriage-makers, the Milburn Manufacturing Company of St Louis, Missouri, when requesting their catalogue. By 1896 Marks had acquired no fewer than eight spiders and carriages.[5]

Marks added a range of modern conveniences and amenities to Zwartkoppies, including a telephone, a swimming pool, and tennis court, the surface of which, Marks said, was 'like the floor of the Kafir huts'. He bought an orchestron, a 'graphaphone' (Alexander Graham Bell's answer to Thomas Alva Edison's phonograph) and a 'splendid' piano, for the Marks family, like other Victorian middle-class families, took shared pleasure in domestic music-making. Marks also installed electricity. This was generated by a turbine powered by water running down a two-and-a-half-mile furrow 'with tremendous force' from a dam Marks built for this purpose on the Pienaars River. Marks found electric lighting 'a vast improvement . . . we play billiards now in the evening, but it is turned out at ten o'clock'.[6]

. Marks reclaimed and 'greened' Zwartkoppies, creating a civilised landscape in what his secretary described as a wilderness. Over a period of years thousands of loads of rocks and stones were dynamited and removed and thousands of trees were planted, mainly exotic varieties, for this was the first great age of pine in South Africa. Extensive orchards and vineyards were also established, and Marks annually sent boxes of fruit from these to his children after they left home for school in England. Marks also added a maze, a croquet lawn, a grand avenue lined with evergreen trees, a cricket cum football field for the Marks boys, and a park in which he sat on summer evenings, enjoying the cool breezes from the hills. Nor was farming neglected. When he had first come to Zwartkoppies in the early 1880s, the farm was so swampy in parts that his horse had sunk up to the saddle. However, after drainage and reclamation, eighteen acres were planted with cereals, and these regularly yielded two profitable crops per annum. Even at home, Marks was the methodical and conscientious commercial farmer, carefully costing his farming operations.[7]

But nature resisted Marks's efforts at landscaping. In August 1896 a destructive veld fire 'wrought sad havoc' at Zwartkoppies, destroying between 20,000 and 30,000 trees. Marks was furious with his forester, who only the week before had assured him that his trees were quite safe against fire but had in actual fact failed to clear the grass around the plantation: 'Mr. Baikie can be stamped with a double L, for he is a liar and he is lazy,' Marks wrote, seeking a suitable replacement, stipulating only that he had 'a strong objection to Germans, Irishmen and Italians'. Undeterred, Marks replanted, continuing his civilising mission. But something of the older, more primitive Zwartkoppies was left intact, and in fact encouraged and protected. With Paul Kruger and other members of the Transvaal gentry, Marks shared in the emerging enthusiasm for conservation, which was to save a small part of South Africa's once abundant wildlife from extinction. Marks noted with delight the increasing number of blesbuck and guinea-fowl on his estate: 'I allow no shooting on my farm and the consequence is that when these birds are fired on elsewhere they make straight for my farm.'[8]

The impression all of this made on visitors – especially those accustomed to the ugliness of Johannesburg and the austerity of backveld life in the Transvaal – was profound. As a Johannesburg journalist wrote at the end of the 1890s, 'Swartkopjes (i.e., "black-hills") is a dream of comfort and luxuriousness. He [Marks] has transformed a barren tract of land into a veritable paradise, and all within a few years.'[9]

Besides investing heavily, emotionally as much as financially, in the creation of a country estate on the Highveld, Marks also spent heavily on something less tangible but nevertheless part of the same drive towards respectability and gentility: the education of his children. Years before he married, Marks had expressed his preference for a large family. Four boys and two girls were the 'proper number'. In the event, he and Bertha had eight: five boys and three girls. The first seven were born in Pretoria at the homes of friends rather than at remote Zwartkoppies where medical care was at least two hours away. Louis, the oldest, was born at Nellmapius's house in 1885, the year after his parents married, when Sammy was 41. Montague, nicknamed Montie, was born in 1888 at the home of Bishop Bousfield, the Anglican Bishop of Pretoria and a friend of Sammy's. Gertrude Miriam, the first daughter, named after Marks's late mother Miriam and nicknamed Girlie, was born in 1889 at the home of her uncle Ellia. Leonora Josephine, who died in infancy, was born in 1890 at the home of Piet Joubert; Joseph Mordechai, named after Sammy's father and known as Joe, was born in 1892; and Theodore, nicknamed Teddy, in 1894.[10]

Fanny Beatrice, 'Tootles' at first but later 'Dolly', was born in 1897 in Pretoria, at the home of Dr Kay, the family doctor. 'My wife presented me', the excited father wrote, 'with a handsome dividend in the shape of a little daughter.' Fanny was a 'very small' baby and a cause of much concern. 'I regret to say that my little daughter is giving us a great deal of anxiety,' Marks wrote of her at five weeks. 'She is very delicate, does not seem to grow much and this morning was so poorly that I had to send for the Doctor, whose opinion did not tend to reassure me.' Three weeks later, though, he was able to report to Fanny's older brothers in England that 'The baby is improving greatly and will soon be able to type you a letter on the new machine.' The 'very delicate' baby of 1897, nicknamed Dolly because of her birth-size, is today Mrs Dolly Maisels, a vigorous nonagenarian, who is Sammy Marks's only surviving child.[11]

Phillip Marks, the laatlammetjie, was born in Muizenberg six months after the outbreak of the South African War, when Sammy was in his mid-fifties. His father saw him for the first time when he was 18 months old, when Bertha and the younger children returned to wartime Zwartkoppies. Phil's later life was predictably unsettled after its unsettled start: he was, among other things, a whisky salesman in South America and a stage comedian.[12]

Marks enjoyed the company of children and had a special rapport with them, something which was no doubt facilitated by the pocketfuls of sweets he regularly dispensed. He enjoyed talking to children and often at the end of a strenuous day, his long-time secretary remembers, could be seen in 'deep conversation with a little child, scarcely higher than his knee'. All the more reason for the profound regret he felt in his later years for missing a large part of the childhood of his own offspring. When they were small he was frequently absent from home on business; when they were older they were sent to school in England and were away from home for many years.[13]

Like other children of their social class, they were initially educated at home by a governess. First Miss Kretschmer and later a sucession of English governesses, Miss Reid, Miss Lorimer and Miss Loxton, taught the elementary skills, as well as German, French and music, in a small schoolroom at Zwartkoppies. The boys left for boarding-school when they were 8, but the girls remained with the governess till they were 12.[14]

Marks shared the benign zealotry of other Russian Jewish immigrant parents about the education of their children, particularly of their sons, and was determined that they should receive the best schooling his money could buy. This meant sending his boys to school in England for Marks, like other wealthy Jewish parents in the Transvaal, felt that the local alternatives were unacceptable. There were no suitable state schools, for an Anglophobic Boer government refused to subsidise English-medium education, while the synagogue-linked Jewish private school established in Johannesburg in the 1890s was a frail institution which held little attraction for those parents who could afford something better. Boarding-schools elsewhere in South Africa were little more appealing. Marks was sceptical of their disciplinary standards. Writing to an educationist in England about a nephew who had been to Grey College in Bloemfontein, Marks warned: 'I daresay you will find him rather troublesome at times, but you must remember that he has been educated for the most part in South Africa where the masters are altogether too lenient with the pupils and the latter act much as they please.'[15]

Local schooling failed to provide a proper moral education and meant mixing with the socially undesirable: 'I am certain that, although you may consider it a sweeping assertion[,] nearly 75 per cent of the children who are educated in the Transvaal are devoid of two qualities essential in a well-regulated society, namely gratitude and straightforwardness, and I should not like my children to mix with others who may be deficient in these two respects. I pity children of strangers when I see them contracting bad habits and I should certainly be failing in my duty as father if I did not place my own children among good and straightforward companions.' Such companions were to be found in the English public school. Marks's decision to send Louis 'home' was more than a negative decision forced on him by the lack of acceptable local options. It reflects a positive desire, shared by other upwardly mobile Victorians of humble or alien origin, to place their sons in the English upper-middle-class mainstream by making English gentlemen of them.[16]

Louis Marks, Sammy's first-born and the repository of his hopes and ambitions, was sent to England in 1894 at the age of 8. He was enrolled at Tivoli House, a small Jewish preparatory school in Gravesend, run by the Reverend M. Berkowitz. The intention, it seems, was to prepare Louis for entry to a good public school but at the same time to provide him with 'a good grounding in Judaism'. Sammy was very anxious about the boy, and ambivalent about the difficult decision to send him so far from home. His first letter to Berkowitz after Louis's arrival at the school was typical of many that were to follow:

Although he is very young, almost too young to leave home, I consider it better for him that he should for certain reasons be placed at school, although I am most anxious that the little fellow should not be over taxed for his age. I want more particularly that if you can grant him any indulgence, to do so. I mean that I would prefer your placing the boy at your own table with your wife and children, and that you should treat him entirely as one of your own family. If you at any time allow your children to attend any amusements, I shall be obliged by your allowing my son to accompany them, of course debiting his proportion of expenses to me.

I would also like him to take riding exercises every day or alternate days, time and weather permitting. He should ride a quiet pony and only the same animal from time to time. The person you place in charge must be thoroughly trustworthy and of good behavior as I have no desire that the lad should acquire bad behavior . . . whatever you may consider good for the boy, which means an outlay of a little money you may depend I will not begrudge.[17]

Sammy was anxious for news of his son's activities. Writing soon after the 8-year-old's arrival at the school, Marks asked Louis for 'full details' of his activities, including the games he played. He was eager to know about his son's prowess at cricket 'and if you think you will be able to represent South Africa at some future time'. He followed this, though, with a typical caution: 'I trust you do not neglect your lessons for the sake of play as although I am always pleased to hear of all your games I am also anxious to hear of your studies. . . .' This was not merely fatherly chaff, but an expression of Sammy's priorities. His passionate belief that study was far more important than play, a repeated theme in his letters to his children over the years, was part of his *shtetl* heritage. It was somewhat at odds, though, with the playing-fields ethic of the English public schools, to which he hoped to send his children.[18]

Sammy was as concerned about Louis's treatment at Tivoli House as he was about the quality of the schooling. Various members of the Lewis family were asked to make the trip to Gravesend to check on the school:

I hope you keep an eye on Louis and see that he is treated well, and well looked after [as] regards clothing, food etc. and that he is brought up as a gentleman.

I think the best way to find this out would be to take him away from school for a day or two, if you have not already done so, and ask him what he gets for breakfast, lunch etc.[19]

The answers were apparently satisfactory, for a year and a half after Louis arrived in Gravesend, he was joined by his younger brother Montie. But for all the reassurances, both from the Lewis family and from Berkowitz, Marks continued to agonise at long range. As he wrote to Berkowitz:

If you will, for one moment, place yourself in my position and realise what it is to have one's children educated at a distance of 7–8000 miles away from one's home, you will comprehend that I spend some very anxious moments on account of my boys. Every parent is naturally anxious that his children should be brought up and educated to a position above his own level, I spare no expense in the training of my boys and have never yet disputed one item in any one account you have sent me but I sometimes wonder whether I am not too indulgent and whether my boys are not perhaps being spoiled by having a little too much. There is, I fear, great danger in allowing boys of their age too many privileges. They may get it into their heads that they are better than their comrades, or, it may be pointed out to them too often that their father in Africa is very rich. . . . I have your assurance that my boys are being brought up as gentlemen and place reliance in your assurances.[20]

Berkowitz was asked to prepare Louis for the admission examination to public school, the social escalator in late-nineteenth-century England which carried the scions of the newly rich into the upper classes. Marks was keen that his son should go to Eton, but when this proved impossible, accepted Harrow as the next best. Louis Marks was in good company in this respect for Harrow had been the second choice of young Winston Churchill, too, a few years before. [21]

After over a year's preparation, Louis wrote and passed the entrance examination to his father's delight. Marks had great expectations of Harrow: it would make a gentleman of his son, and would lay the academic foundations for his future entry into a profession, preferably electrical engineering which had captured Marks's imagination. Electricity stood on the frontier of science in the late nineteenth century and fascinated Marks and many of his Victorian contemporaries, including a German Jewish refugee in England with a similar sounding name – Karl Marx. Electrical engineering seemed the ideal vocation for the son of a father deeply interested in technology and imbued with a Victorian love of material progress. [22]

But while Harrow was greatly promising, it was hazardous too, as father warned son:

Now my boy, you are going to a strange public school where you will meet all kinds of boys and will see a good many things to which you have not been accustomed and which you have been taught are wrong although to a schoolboy they may appear to be manly. You must make up your mind from the outset to become a gentleman and to be honest straightforward and truthful.

You may also meet Jewish boys who are ashamed to call themselves Jews. You must never be ashamed of your religion; you have no reason to be. You will find Jews amongst the greatest men in every profession and every calling in life of which we have every reason to be proud. If you hear anybody speak ill of your religion you have simply to say that differences of opinion will always exist in religion as in other matters and everyone cannot be of one religion, England is a free country and everybody has the right to worship God in his own way. . . .

Within the past four months you have become a man according to our religion and you now have to become a man in a worldly sense.

. . . I hope you will . . . throw in your lot with the other boys and be contented with the same treatment as they get. [23]

To make doubly sure that Louis did not forget his roots Marks requested that his son study Hebrew at Harrow. [24]

Marks's old anxieties were carried over into the new environment: he wanted Berkowitz to visit Louis regularly at Harrow, and he wanted Sankey, Louis's new housemaster, to report fortnightly or monthly. Harrow, sadly, was a disappointment. Despite favourable reports while he had been at preparatory school, Louis, a mediocre pupil at the very best, was unable to cope with the academic demands of the school. Marks's dream that his son would be prepared for eventual entry into one of the professions gradually faded. Marks had to settle for a commercial training for his son in Switzerland and Germany after he left Harrow. But despite this disappointment, Marks's younger sons followed their older brother, years later, to English public schools: Joe to Clifton in Bristol, which had a Jewish house; Teddy to Tunbridge Wells; and Phil, the youngest, to Charterhouse. A public school education still held the alluring, all-important promise of full acceptance and integration into English society.[25]

Sammy Marks's deep ambivalence – his raging Anglophilia, epitomised by his desire to create an English country house on the Highveld and to turn his sons into English 'gentlemen', and his concurrent and well-rewarded loyalty to the Boers and to Kruger in particular – was unproblematic as long as Britain and the Transvaal were at peace. Once the two sides drew their swords in 1899, however, Marks was trapped between his rival allegiances. The eternal trimmer, he spent the next few years cautiously navigating the narrow and dangerous channel between the two.

Victorian domestic status symbol supreme – the billiard room at Zwartkoppies (Photo: Berndt Zibol)

VII

Between the Lines,
1899–1902

Marks paid one of his rare visits to Europe in early 1899 to consult his partner. Passing through Cape Town in April on his way home, he added to his portfolio of Cape properties. In the years since the Jameson Raid had destabilised the region he had quietly built up his stake at the Cape as a hedge against the uncertain future of the Transvaal. In 1896 he had added to his strategically placed property close to the Cape Houses of Parliament. This had cost him £23,000. A year later he had taken a quarter share at Sivewright's invitation in a syndicate which planned to develop a four-mile stretch of coastal land beyond Woodstock. This township was to be named Milnerton in honour of the new High Commisioner, Sir Alfred Milner. Marks's share had cost him £5,000. Now Marks spent a further £21,000, on a site stretching between Queen Victoria and Keerom streets and occupied by a stable. This had once been 'the worst neighbourhood in Cape Town', but it now looked very promising. Enriched by the railway and customs revenue generated by the Transvaal trade, the Cape government had taken a lively interest in the area. Marks's property adjoined a piece of ground the government had bought for the high court and there were already three other government buildings in the immediate vicinity. Marks clearly hoped to benefit from any further growth in government and from the consequent demand for additional office space.[1]

Sentiment played less part in Marks's decision to invest at the Cape than it did for some of his fellow mining magnates. Unlike Cecil Rhodes and Abe Bailey, for example, Marks was not particularly fond of the city. 'Cape Town is the dullest place in South Africa,' he had written in 1897. 'Cape Town always was rather a dirty town and just the sort of place a plague would get a hold on,' he noted a few years later when the city was struck by the bubonic plague. Unlike J. B. Robinson and others who had made their fortunes in the Transvaal, Marks had no intention of taking up residence at the Cape: he far preferred Zwartkoppies.[2]

Marks invested in Cape property because it seemed to offer a secure investment, a sound return on capital and the promise of capital growth. The Cape property market was riding a boom in the 1890s, driven by immigration and rapid population growth, railway expansion and economic development to the north. Marks hoped to capitalise on this and at the same time to reduce his exposure to political risk. His precautionary investment in Cape property after the Raid meant that by 1899 he had close to £60,000 in real estate well away from the turbulent Transvaal, and was a major Cape property-owner.

During his brief stop-over in Cape Town in April, Marks found some time for recreation between property dealings. He visited the Turkish baths in what he called 'Rolling [Roeland] Street' and was much impressed. He commissioned John Parker, a young local architect, to prepare a drawing of these so that could have one installed at Zwartkoppies. Marks, who was 'generally troubled with rheumatics' in the Transvaal winter, hoped that a Turkish bath would help.[3]

When he returned to the Transvaal later in the month, it was seething with political discord. Spurred on by Milner in Cape Town, who was anxious to curb the threat he believed Kruger's Transvaal posed to British supremacy in South Africa, Uitlander agitators campaigned furiously for the immediate redress of their grievances, chief amongst which was the Republic's restrictive franchise which effectively excluded them from the political mainstream. Kruger, for his part, was determined to resist these pressures, which he felt threatened the hard-won independence of his Republic.

Like many others, Marks was very hopeful that the Bloemfontein summit between Milner and Kruger in late May 1899 would achieve a 'lasting settlement' and avert 'bloodshed'. As his efforts to bring Kruger and Chamberlain together after the Jameson Raid testify, Marks attached great value to personal encounters of this kind: face-to-face discussion had always eased the severe tensions within his own partnership; why should it not succeed now on the broader stage? Despite Kruger's assurances to Marks before he left for Bloemfontein that he would 'do everything in his power to arrive at an amicable settlement', providing there was no tampering with the independence of the Republic, the conference was a dismal and damaging failure, with both the President and the High Commissioner talking past each other to their impassioned followers outside the conference room. Greatly alarmed, Marks and Lewis felt compelled to set aside their shared conviction 'that business people should not meddle in politics on either side', and to join with those working for peace.

Days after the Bloemfontein fiasco, on 13 June, Lewis cabled Marks that the great Rothschilds banking house wanted him to approach Kruger secretly on their behalf to offer their services as intermediaries between the Transvaal and British governments. Lewis felt that this 'opened a door for the President to enable him to secure without any loss of dignity, peace and prosperity for the country'. But Kruger thought otherwise. He was convinced that the Roths-childs, who earlier that year had attached onerous conditions to a loan requested by the Transvaal, were working 'hand in hand' with Chamberlain and Cecil Rhodes to defraud the Republic of its independence. 'This impression it seems impossible to remove,' Marks reported after relaying the Rothschilds' offer to Kruger. 'I have argued with the Old Man on the subject and have been assisted in this by the State Attorney [Jan Smuts], but the Old Man always comes back to the one point, that England will never be satisfied until she has the Transvaal, and this idea has such a hold on the Old Man that no argument I may adduce seems to shake it.'[4]

Kruger's peremptory rejection of the offer, and of a repeat offer by the Rothschilds a few weeks later, was a sore disappointment to the partners. As Lewis wrote to Marks: 'I must draw your attention even more strongly to the great loss it must be to our friends on the other side to alienate the sympathy of a firm so all-powerful. . . . There is not the slightest doubt as to the enormous influence they hold, and that they should have volunteered their services to assist in bringing about a peaceful solution seemed to me a wonderful step to have gained. I am the more surprised therefore and disappointed that their intervention should in the end have been so badly received. . . .'[5]

While Lewis lobbied in London, Marks canvassed in Cape Town and Bloemfontein. A few days after his frustrating interview with Kruger, he sent a secret message with George Falcke, his confidential secretary, to Abraham Fischer, President Steyn's chief lieutenant and a highly regarded diplomatist. Marks and a group of friends, all 'well-wishers of this country' and all anxious about the 'very critical' political situation, believed that if the Republic was to be rescued from its present difficulties, 'we must have some powerful assistance'. Who better under the circumstances than Fischer and Steyn? Who were better placed than these trusted allies of the Transvaal to persuade Kruger to offer more liberal franchise terms than he had at Bloemfontein?[6]

Marks sent a similar message care of the Standard Bank in Cape Town to 'Onze Jan' Hofmeyr, leader of the Cape Afrikaners: he should come at once to Pretoria with his Free State counterparts and point out to the Kruger government 'not only the danger they are putting themselves into, but also a way to retreat gracefully'. Hofmeyr's presence, together with Steyn's and Fischer's, would have a powerful moral effect on the 'old Burghers', Kruger's conservative supporters, whose resistance to reform was a major obstacle to a peaceful settlement.[7]

While awaiting their arrival, Marks redoubled his efforts to persuade Kruger to meet Milner's demands, convinced as he was that these were not unreasonable and that the Boers could be brought to accept them. His hopes were raised by an hour-long interview on 24 June with the President, who appeared 'much calmer' than at their previous meeting. True to form, Kruger first read Marks a history lesson, rehearsing the full record of British perfidy towards the Boers from 1830 to the present. Marks countered in kind with a lesson drawn from Scriptures. Making 'free use of the Bible', he drew a cautionary parallel between the fate of his own people and the present predicament of Kruger's *volk*: 'As long as they [the Hebrews] followed in the ways of God and obeyed the laws of the world, they were left in peace, but as soon as they set these laws in defiance, they were driven out of the country, and to this day they have remained a scattered nation.' Kruger had no answer to this rather unorthodox reading of the Bible; instead he simply reaffirmed that 'he would not give up his country without a struggle'.

Marks then turned to the arithmetic of a South African war. Even with the support of the Cape Dutch, the Transvaal and Free State could only put 40,000 men into the field; was this sufficient to do battle and to protect 2,000 miles of frontier? Again Kruger could not disagree, but simply insisted 'that God had been with them up to the present and would not forsake them now'.

After all this preliminary skirmishing, Kruger at last revealed, in strictest confidence, that he was in fact preparing to make a major concession to the British on the franchise question, and that he was also willing to consider Milner's other demands: 'as long as these matters did not interfere with the independence of the country he would endeavour to persuade the burghers of the country to concede them, but he is determined not to concede on one point that interferes with the independence of the country.' Marks was greatly reassured by this. As he wrote soon after to his partner, he felt sure that if Kruger kept his promise, 'Milner will be satisfied' and a peaceful settlement would be speedily arranged. Marks still believed that Milner was acting in good faith and genuinely wished to avoid conflict: he had no sense of the High Commissioner's intransigence, of his steely determination to break Kruger's Republic once and for all, even if this meant war.[8]

Marks was more perceptive about the intentions of Joseph Chamberlain, Milner's political master at Whitehall, whom he had met in London after the Jameson Raid. Writing on 9 July 1899, days after the Volksraad had voted in secret session for franchise reform after impassioned speeches by Hofmeyr and Fischer, Marks noted: 'Although everyone is very sanguine, and it is generally admitted here that things look much brighter, I cannot help thinking that the horizon is not quite clear. I believe that Chamberlain and party do not care so much whether the franchise is granted as they would make believe. They want something more and have yet a card to play, and I shall not be in the least surprised if before very long that card is placed upon the table.'[9]

Chamberlain played that trump in the House of Commons on the 28th of the month, plunging South Africa once again into crisis. In a vitriolic speech, immediately cabled to Pretoria, the Colonial Secretary raised the ante dramatically. After launching a bitter attack on Kruger's Transvaal, he claimed that Britain had a right to intervene in the domestic affairs of the Republic. This, together with a provocative request a few days later for an unprecedented joint Anglo–Boer inquiry into the franchise law, constituted a frontal assault on the cherished independence of the Transvaal.[10]

Marks's instinct, more pragmatic than principled, more sensible than heroic, was to encourage the Boers to accept the inevitable and yield to British pressure: after all, 'England has shown that she means business and our people must realise that they cannot do much against a power like Great Britain.' Understandably, his old friend Paul Kruger saw things otherwise. Yielding meant denying the guiding principle of a lifetime, the preservation of the independence of the Republic.[11]

Marks swung into action once more. An old hand at lobbying the Volksraad, he 'worked very hard' at swaying its members, but this proved an up-hill struggle: 'I am sick and tired of talking with the Members of the Volksraad, although I have determined not to relax my efforts. Of all the 28 members of the First Volksraad, although they are almost without exception desirous of seeing a peaceful settlement arrived at, and are willing even to grant the 5 years franchise, there is not one who has the moral courage to stand up in the Raadzaal and openly declare himself to that effect, for fear that the President will taunt them with disloyalty to the country and its independence. General Joubert is no exception.'[12]

Marks had hoped that the Commandant-General – Kruger's old political rival, who held more liberal views on the franchise question – would act as a rallying point for those more willing to compromise, but Joubert, brave warrior as he was, shied away from a direct confrontation with the President. 'I have had conversations with him and sometimes in the presence of Beckett [a prominent Pretoria merchant]. The general has appeared to be convinced and Beckett and myself have more than once been led to believe that the General would go down to the Volksraad next day and brave the Old Man, but once in the Volksraad he is dumb and when asked why he does not speak out his opinions says that he can not speak for fear of being declared a traitor to and an enemy of the country.'[13]

Marks blamed the 'Hollander clique', the Dutch officials Kruger had imported to man his civil service, for the President's stubbornness. Fearful of losing their well-paid jobs if the system of government was overhauled, they were encouraging Kruger, Marks believed, to hold out against all demands for reform. Dr Leyds in particular, formerly the State Secretary, now the Republic's roving ambassador in Europe, was the 'evil councillor' whose 'pernicious advice', cabled to Pretoria, was hardening Kruger's heart. During the weeks that followed, Marks attempted to counter this 'baneful influence', but found it increasingly difficult, and dangerous, to do so as the political atmosphere grew ever more emotionally charged and explosive. 'One has to be very careful in one's actions at the present moment,' he warned his partner in late August; '. . . nearly everyone is looked upon with suspicion and mistrust.' Increasingly, anyone who spoke out was likely to be branded as 'Engelschgezind and a traitor to the country'.[14]

Nevertheless, Marks, braver than Joubert, was still prepared to tackle the Old Man directly. Kruger became 'very angry' with Marks when he tried to persuade the President that he should not attach too much value to promises of support by foreign powers: that treaties with these were worth very little as Britain was clearly 'mistress' of southern Africa. Kruger also roundly denounced Marks's partner; Isaac Lewis was 'no friend of his', for he refused to subscribe to a fund established by the Republic's English sympathisers to put the Boer case before the British public.[15]

Despite the rising animosity and the preparations for war, the arrival of British reinforcements and the mass exodus of Uitlander refugees, Marks still believed in early September 1899 that the peace would be kept. 'We are still here and I do not think there will be war,' he reassured his son Montie at school in England. 'There is a great deal of talk but people are getting too civilized to kill each other for trifles.'[16] All were preoccupied with the political crisis and business was at a standstill. As Marks complained, 'in the present unsettled state of affairs and with each day bringing fresh complications I cannot sit down and work with a clear head.' The only reprieve from the excitement and hysteria was at Zwartkoppies 'where all is quiet and peaceful and not disturbed by constant rumours'. Here, Marks wrote to his partner's wife, 'I watch the trees and plants grow and expand and when away from the worry of business I enjoy a quiet walk in my own grounds where everything is so peaceful.'[17]

At work Marks, a cautious and conscientious manager, took steps to protect the firm's interests in case of trouble, even though he still believed that sense would prevail. His first concern was to see that operations continued even if the worst occurred. Rumours of war had greatly unsettled the workmen at the collieries and at the Fabrieken, and many of these had joined the great Uitlander exodus to the coast on packed passenger and goods trains. To stem the tide Marks approached the governments of the Transvaal and Free State for written assurances of his workmen's safety in case of hostilities, and these were posted up prominently at his mines and factories. To protect the works against overzealous burghers or 'loafers . . . of all nationalities' who might be tempted to loot, Marks arranged for the posting of guards and obtained official authority to use force if this was necessary. Marks also laid in emergency stocks to guarantee his men an adequate supply of food at reasonable prices should war be declared; they were also assured of their wages even if war prevented their working. These guarantees were sufficiently persuasive to keep at least a rump of the workforce at their posts; production continued, though at a reduced rate.[18]

For all his contingency arrangements, Marks had not yet given up hope. In mid-September he promised to underwrite a last-ditch attempt to persuade the Transvaal government to be more conciliatory. He was approached by a group of Volksraad members, who planned to send a secret deputation to Bloemfontein to urge the Free State authorities to lean on their allies before it was too late. Marks agreed to meet the costs of a special train to carry the delegation post-haste to Bloemfontein. A quarter of an hour before the train was to leave Pretoria, word reached the station platform that Kruger disapproved of their mission; duly intimidated, the delegation dispersed.[19]

By late September, even peaceful Zwartkoppies was caught up in the excitement: 'Even my little Teddie, when I come home in the evening asks me if there is going to be a war and if the Queen is going to kill the poor farmers.' Even Marks, the incurable optimist, could no longer convince himself, as he had till now, that 'alles zal recht kom'. In the final week of September he at last arranged for his pregnant wife and their small children to leave for their holiday home in Muizenberg. 'The packing is tremendous,' he wrote to one of the older children in England; 'I do not think a regiment of soldiers would require more than our dear little lot.' Marks's parting instructions to his wife were that she was not to take in any fellow refugees: 'The house at Muizenberg is for you and for your children only. . . .' There was no question, however, of his leaving with them for the safety of the coast, for he saw it as his duty to stay on in the Transvaal to guard the firm's interests.[20]

Signs of war's rapid approach were now everywhere. Describing the 'simply deplorable' state of affairs at Pretoria in one of his last letters before the Boers sent their fateful ultimatum on 9 October 1899, Marks wrote: on 9 October 1899 'When I tell you that from the Judges to the policemen and from the Bankers downwards, as well as youngsters of about 12 to old men of 60 or older, everyone is going about dressed up in a bandoleer full of cartridges with a "Mauser" over his shoulder, you will hardly believe that we are living in the nineteenth Century. It reminds me of the time when I was a youngster at home, reading from the old books about the Jews when they were wandering from place to place. . . . Race hatred in 1881 [at the time of the Transvaal War] is nothing to what it is now.'[21]

Marks's efforts, like those of the friends of the Republic in the Cape and the Free State, had failed to halt the slide towards war. Faced with a determination to bring matters to a head whatever the cost, and with an equal determination to resist at all costs, common sense and goodwill were left impotent. All that could be hoped for now was that the war would be mercifully brief: 'It will be a terrible struggle and we are all hoping it will soon be over.'[22]

During the first months of the war, Marks did his duty as a loyal burgher, offering both material aid as well as advice to the Boers. He raised no strong objections when the Boer authorities commandeered close to £9,000 of raw gold from the Sheba mine; he put the two ponts the Vereeniging Estates company operated on the Vaal River at the disposal of the Commandant-General; and he provided a wagon and mule team for use as a field ambulance and fitted out Dr Liknaitzky who took it to the front. (Liknaitzky promptly lost everything in a clash with the British in the Free State and returned home.) Marks also sold the Boer commissariat a thousand bags of Vereeniging Estates' mealies, at 20s. a bag, for the commandos on the western and Natal fronts, and 580 bales of fodder from the Irene estate which had been taken over from Nellmapius. The Boers were debited £638 for the forage but only paid £478 after subtracting a quarter for spoilage. Marks supplied Hatherley whisky and brandy to the commandos and contributed to a fund organised by a Pretoria newspaper to provide the men at the front with extra tobacco. He also offered his unsold jam to the commandos but he had no better luck than before the war; despite an urgent need for supplies, the Boers, like Uitlander shoppers before the war, found Marks's jam eminently resistible.[23]

While loyally supporting the Boer war effort Marks was very sympathetic to the plight of the British prisoners of war who were brought to Pretoria and imprisoned in a camp at the racecourse. He paid for books for the POWs and sent grapes from the vineyards at Zwartkoppies to the camp hospital, thoughtful gestures which were much appreciated by the prisoners. In addition, £1,000 was channelled through his firm by the International Red Cross Society for prisoner comforts and 'necessaries'. Tobacco was high on the list of these; in January 1900 Marks's office received a desperate request from Corporal Todd of the 18th Hussars for tobacco and cigarettes and the wooden pipes promised on a previous visit to the racecourse camp. 'We have some tobacco to go on with, but the cigarette smokers have completely run out.' Meanwhile, Captain

Vaughan, wounded and captured during the fierce fighting at General Cronjé's laager at Paardeberg, was desperate for news of his friends. Would Marks please obtain the British casualty lists for the battle? 'It is a terrible trial of patience to be here.'[24]

There is no indication in the Marks papers whether Marks was able to meet the request and supply the information. The Transvaal was effectively isolated by a British blockade. Little news filtered through and it was difficult to communicate with the outside world. Ingenious as ever, Marks occasionally found ways of doing this. Letters to his children in England were posted via his nephew Phil Levy who was at school in Holland. Other letters were sent by hand. The few replies that slipped through the blockade, which came through an intermediary in Delagoa Bay, were usually much delayed.[25]

Marks was understandably reticent in these letters. As he explained to Jimmy Sivewright in a letter which was sent out in May with an acquaintance who left for Europe via Delagoa Bay: 'I will not say anything about the present state of affairs in South Africa, because whatever a man says he is sure to displease somebody. Therefore I have made up my mind just to *think only* and to think very quietly too.' He warned his nephew in Holland to be equally circumspect when writing to Pretoria: 'You must not write about the war at present as no one is allowed to write any nonsense about it here. All letters are opened and read by the authorities before despatch and delivery.'[26]

Marks largely confined himself to innocuous detail about his daily life. Work was very much at a standstill, he reported: 'In fact offices are not wanted here just now as there is no business doing. All that we have got to do is to keep the doors open and lend money!!' Zwartkoppies, without Bertha and the children, was quiet and lonely. John Murray, an elderly Scot who was Marks's long-time friend and gentleman companion, kept him company at home; his brother Ellia, who managed Vereeniging Estates before and during the war, visited Zwartkoppies when his heavy responsibilities at the coal mine allowed. (The mine was seriously shortstaffed because numbers of its British employees had fled the Republic while many of its Boer staff had gone to the front.) Ironically, the first summer of the war was a golden one at the deserted Zwartkoppies. With ample rain Zwartkoppies looked 'splendid' and there was an abundance of fruit which Marks regularly took into town for 'sick, wounded and poor burghers'.[27]

Marks was able to keep in touch to a limited degree with the events of his sons' lives. He learnt in April, for example, that Montie, at Berkowitz's preparatory school in Gravesend, was learning to ride a bicycle. Overprotective as ever, he anxiously warned: 'Be careful until you learn perfectly. . . . Do not get any broken bones in the attempt, and do not make any experiments until you are complete master of your machine.' He was very gratified to hear that Montie, a more assiduous pupil than his older brother Louis, had passed his examinations: 'I hope you will show us in the future that all the money I have spent in your education has not been spent in vain.' He urged him to prepare carefully for the entrance exam to Harrow, his brother's public school: 'I shall be very disappointed if you fail.'[28]

It was often easier to correspond with his children in England than with his wife in Cape Town. It appears to have taken some days before Marks discovered that he had again become a father. Because of the war Marks missed the birth of his fifth and final son. Phillip Marks was born at the family's Muizenberg holiday home on 27 March 1900. Bertha had not seen her husband since the early months of her pregnancy and Sammy was not to see the child until he was 18 months old. For the meantime photographs Bertha sent of the children had to suffice.[29]

Because of Marks's reticence and the paucity of correspondence during these early months of the conflict, one catches only occasional glimpses of him through the fog of war. He was spotted in Delagoa Bay in November 1899 by the Standard Bank. He had arrived with a party of influential Transvalers, including the Postmaster-General and the Chief Justice, who had come, the bank suspected, to make secret arrangements for supplying the Republic with food and medicine as well as badly needed saddlery for its commandos. The local branch of the Standard Bank subsequently received a request from Lewis and Marks to insure and ship to Germany gold to the value of £10,000 per month and to allow Lewis and Marks to draw against this shipment. The bank was very tempted by the prospect of an arrangement of this sort with 'such old and valued customers', as it would allow the bank to profit from the surplus reserves it held at Delagoa Bay. But it reluctantly declined for it suspected that the gold was in fact the property of the Transvaal government and feared that the bank would become entangled in a scheme to breach the British blockade.[30]

Marks's liquor business was hamstrung by the wartime extension of the pre-war prohibition on the sale of spirits to blacks, to whites as well. Hatherley's gin, brandy and whisky could only be lawfully purchased for medicinal purposes. At Christmas-time 1899 Marks was forced to apply for a permit to hand out his customary gifts of liquor to his clients and associates. In April 1900 he was peremptorily informed that the British staff at the Eerste Fabrieken would have to leave the Transvaal within eight days. Marks complained that this would cause irreparable damage to the business.[31]

After the Boers' initial military successes, the sheer weight of the British forces began to tell. Lord Roberts's army advanced into the Free State and by March 1900 had captured Bloemfontein. As the likelihood of a British invasion of the Transvaal grew, the government began to debate whether it should destroy the gold mines in such an eventuality. Hardliners like F. W. Reitz, the State Secretary, urged the dynamiting of the mines as an act of reprisal against the Randlords, whom they held responsible in large measure for the war. Others, possibly including Kruger himself, proposed that the threat of destruction be used to force intervention by the European powers in the war, if only in defence of their countrymen's investments. Others again were loth to damage private property; besides, the act seemed pointless and would certainly harm the Boers' reputation.

Marks, one of the few mining men who remained in the Transvaal after the outbreak of war, caught wind of these intentions when in early March newspapers close to the government carried suggestions that the mines be destroyed together with all Uitlander property. Sensing the seriousness of the threat, Marks decided to do all he could to dissuade the Boers from such a course. He went to the President immediately and was assured that Kruger would not allow any destruction of property.

Marks also buttonholed his old business associate Piet Joubert, who assured him that as long as he was Commandant-General he would not agree to the destruction of property. Marks was only partly reassured by this, especially when he heard fresh rumours of preparations for the dynamiting of the mines. Consequently he decided to approach the commanders in the field directly and get them to bring their considerable influence to bear on the civilian leaders in Pretoria. Marks sent Johan Rissik, a close friend of Louis Botha's, who was Boer commander on the Natal front, to see the General about the threat to the mines and at the same time 'to persuade Louis Botha to lay down his arms'. He sent a similar message to his close friend Lucas Meyer, another of the senior field commanders, who had recently spent three weeks recuperating from illness at Zwartkoppies. Finally, he contacted Koos de la Rey, his old Lichtenburg friend, who had already emerged as the most capable Boer general on the western front. All three declared they would not allow the destruction of mine property, but had no intention of laying down arms.

Marks made further approaches to Kruger and the Executive Council. On one such occasion he clashed with the hawkish State Secretary who jibed that '*Marks is bang hy zal zyn geld verloor*'. When Reitz remarked 'that if the English took the country they ought to find it like Sodom and Gomorrah', Marks retorted 'that surely there were more than five good people left in the country'. The President smiled and said that 'he would not allow the country to be destroyed.' Worried by these mixed signals, Marks saw Botha and Meyer when they passed through Pretoria en route to the Free State from the Natal front. Botha, by then the most indispensable of the Boer commanders, told Marks he would resign if the mines were destroyed. Botha's promise held good. His instructions ensured that the mines went unscathed even when the retreating Boer forces passed through Johannesburg a few months later.[32]

In mid-May 1900 Marks joined a small deputation, all confidants of the President, who approached Kruger with a proposal which offered an honourable way out of a struggle that had become hopeless. Rather than making a humiliating formal surrender, the Transvaal should lay down its arms 'under protest' – it should unilaterally declare the war at an end, an ingenious if somewhat unusual procedure under the circumstances. While the authorship of the idea is not clear, it does bear the hallmarks of Marks's brand of unconventional, lateral thinking. Kruger, anxious to avoid further loss of life and destruction of property, was receptive to the idea, but it was effectively quashed by President Steyn of the Orange Free State, whose determination to continue the struggle was much greater at this point than his northern colleague's.[33]

The British advance rolled on relentlessly through the Free State, and by the last week of May had reached the outskirts of Marks's property at the Vaal River. The Vereeniging coal mines had for some time past been a source of concern for the imperial army's planning staff. The momentum of the advance depended on a steady stream of supplies passing up the railway line from the coast, but as the distance from the ports increased this became increasingly difficult to maintain. One of the chief problems as the lines of communications stretched was that at least one train out of every eight had to be set aside to carry coal northwards to meet the needs of the military railway itself. If the Vereeniging collieries could be captured intact, this problem could be overcome. Coal could then move southwards down the line in empty trucks, freeing no less than one-eighth of the north-bound trucks for military supplies.[34]

Fortunately for the British commissariat, the battle for Vereeniging was little more than a skirmish. The Boer rearguard, lying on the slag heap of the Central mine on the north bank of the river, traded shots with the British advance guard at the Cornelia mine on the south bank. When the Boers slipped away from their positions, mine officials at the Central telephoned the 'all-clear' to the British at the mine office across the river. As the Boers withdrew from Vereeniging, they blew up the railway bridge and set fire to the railway station, but left the all-important coal mines intact.[35]

They took with them, however, a large part of the estate's livestock. On a Friday evening a short while before the Boers retreated across the Vaal, Kruger had sent for Marks and asked him to sell the horses of the Vereeniging Estates to the army. When Marks protested that these were unsuitable for military service as they were either young animals or breeding horses, the President threatened to commandeer the herd. Given Hobson's choice, Marks 'voluntarily' surrendered 116 horses for which he was promised £20 a piece; payment was never made. Similar worthless receipts were issued for several thousand pounds' worth of horned cattle taken for slaughtering purposes, and for large quantities of mealies and kaffircorn.[36]

The British forces advanced rapidly after the capture of Vereeniging. Johannesburg and its mines were taken intact on 31 May 1900, thanks to General Botha's respect for private property. Two days before, Paul Kruger and his closest colleagues had slipped quietly out of Pretoria by coach to avoid unfavourable attention and had caught the train at Eerste Fabrieken for Machadodorp in the eastern Transvaal. It is more than likely that Marks was at Eerste Fabrieken station to see off his old friend the President on the first stage of what was to become a long journey into exile. This would have been the last time they met, the last, sad encounter in an extraordinary relationship that stretched back to Marks's first exploratory visit to the Transvaal two decades before.

On 5 June 1900, Pretoria, deserted by its President, fell without a fight despite its ring of forts. The disheartened commandos had already retreated eastwards along the Delagoa Bay line, on their way passing through Hatherley. On the same day the Boer generals held a council of war in Marks's office at the factory to consider whether or not to continue what to many of the fighting men seemed a lost cause. Marks was present, at least at the start, and pointed out, discouragingly, that foreign intervention, a last desperate hope of the Boers, was most improbable. Even the normally resolute Botha was despondent, and seemed willing to give up the struggle. Had a vote been taken at this point, it might well have gone in favour of surrender. Instead, the council of war decided to postpone a decision till it reconvened in a few days' time.[37]

While the generals conferred at Hatherley, the war passed through Marks's front yard at nearby Zwartkoppies. On the same day the defeatist council of war met at the factory, Marks played reluctant host to thousands of burghers who milled around the farm and helped themselves to food, forage, whisky and cigars. Marks chatted to some he knew and attempted to persuade them to lay down their arms, warning them of the consequences if they did not. One of the burghers was so annoyed at this that he suggested to a friend they take Marks away and shoot him; instead his friend chose Marks's advice and deserted his commando at the first opportunity.

The English came the next day, 6 June. First to arrive at Zwartkoppies was a bewildered army padre, searching for his missing flock. No more than 200 yards away, forty Boers lay in ambush in a large hole Marks had quarried for the foundation stones of his house. Marks quietly warned off the chaplain. 'I dared not point my finger to them,' he later wrote, 'as these good people were no doubt looking at us.' The chaplain, a 'sensible' fellow, beat a hasty retreat; so did the small parties of scouts who followed later that day, though not before enjoying Marks's non-partisan hospitality. 'As you may imagine all those who came certainly did not go away empty-handed, as they were all very hungry. Some of them liked whisky and bread and butter, and the Australians again were more fond of milk and bread and butter, but they were nevertheless all satisfied.'

The scouts who came the following day were less easily dissuaded, dismissing Marks's warning about the Boer ambush: it was their business, after all, to locate the enemy's position. After the (by now) customary bread, butter and whisky, they set off from the house in search of the foe, only to return soon after, 'quicker than they went'. Luckily, they all escaped unhurt.

Early on the morning of the 8th Marks crossed the front-line with Annie Botha, the Boer commander's English-speaking wife, to persuade her husband to lay down arms. Just when Marks thought he had succeeded, with the aid of a very emotional Mrs Botha, a telegram arrived announcing a great Boer victory in the Free State: 2,000 British prisoners had been taken and the battlefield was covered in enemy dead. After the telegram was read out aloud, Louis Botha turned to Marks, and asked: 'What must I do now?'

'All that I could answer him', Marks recalled later, 'was "If you believe this telegram then I have nothing to say." He then put the question to me "Do you disbelieve it then?" And I told him that I certainly did.'

Botha evidently did not. He asked Marks to leave at once, and then took farewell of his wife, urging her to return to town immediately as there would soon be fighting. Heartened by the news of De Wet's spectacular victory at Rooiwal, which gave them fresh hope, the Boer council of war confirmed their leader's decision to fight on. Marks, meanwhile, had driven back to Zwart-koppies with Mrs Botha. After she had breakfasted, he sent her off to Pretoria in a cart with his driver. She had not been gone for more than 25 minutes when the shelling began. A Long Tom round fell close to the cart, and had it not been

for a British officer helping her to find cover, she might have been killed by her
husband's artillery.

Two days later Marks himself set off for town. Crossing the small spruit at
The Willows, he came across Lord Roberts, the British Commander-in-Chief,
breakfasting with his staff; Marks was promptly introduced to the great man by
his aide-de-camp.[38] Roberts, who had believed that the Boers would surrender
once he had captured their capital, was now preparing once again for battle. One
of the last set-piece actions of the war, the Battle of Diamond Hill – Donkerhoek
to the Boers – was fought in the hills and poorts immediately to the east of
Zwartkoppies on 11 and 12 June 1900. The farm lay in the centre of the British
line, but fortunately for its owner, Lord Roberts chose to launch his attack from
the flanks, well away from the Marks property. Sitting at ringside, Marks had
'a very exciting time' with shells passing overhead 'on their way to
Pienaarspoort and back to Koedoespoort'. The battle itself was indecisive, with
the Boers disengaging during the night of the 12th, after suffering only light
losses, and moving off eastwards to continue their retreat. The sound
performance of Botha's army, coming after a long and demoralising retreat, did,
however, have 'an inspiriting effect', Jan Smuts recalled later, 'which could
scarcely have been improved by a real victory'.[39]

Though Zwartkoppies was on the edge of the battlefield, damage to the
property was slight. Ian Hamilton's 6th Division and Reginald Pole-Carew's
11th uprooted all the wooden fencing posts, 6,800 in total, cut down over 500
of the gum, wattle and pine trees so lovingly nurtured by Marks, tore out twelve
tons of wild thorn and syringa trees, dismantled the summer house and chopped
up the garden seats, besides filching 300 muids of potatoes. When Marks
complained to Lord Roberts, who was all too aware that his poorly fed soldiers,
campaigning during a Highveld winter, were both hungry and cold, 'Bobs'
preferred to turn a Nelsonian eye; Marks was told that 'it was no use bothering,
as the Troops had to have firewood'.

Privately, Marks accepted his petty losses philosophically. 'My property was
not damaged,' he wrote to his son Louis at Harrow, 'but I have not a wooden
fencing pole standing on my property, these forming excellent firewood for Mr.
Thomas Atkins. However I must not grumble as the poor fellows have had very
rough times and had to get fuel for cooking their food. They were good enough
to leave a quantity of empty tins as a momento of their passage which however
do not tend to embellish the place. A good many of my cattle have been
requisitioned and no doubt some of my poles helped to cook them for
Tommy.'[40] The distillery at nearby Hatherley escaped just as lightly as
Zwartkoppies: a detachment of Highlanders, escorting a construction train
marooned for several hours at the factory siding, liberated 72 bottles of whisky;
Pte Fitzgerald was sent to the guard room in Pretoria in a state of 'alcoholic
insensibility' and was sentenced to 28 days without hard labour.[41]

Soon after, Marks took an oath of neutrality like many other prominent
burghers. His transfer of allegiances was eased by a sense that the war, which he
had thought a grave error from the start, was as good as over and that British
rule was now an accomplished reality. It was also smoothed by his peculiar

status within Transvaal society. Though a long-term resident of the country and a naturalised burgher, with close ties to the ruling elite, he had nevertheless always remained an outsider, an Uitlander, albeit far more acceptable to the Boers than most. Together with the Becketts, the Bourkes, and the Johnstones, Marks was a member of the English business community of pre-war Pretoria. Despite the Lithuanian origins of the partners, Lewis and Marks was very much an English firm, with two of the three partners based permanently in London and with its affairs conducted in English, for even though they were both Yiddish-speaking, Isaac and Sammy nevertheless wrote to each other in their adopted rather than their mother tongue. Like other successful Russian-born Jews in the Transvaal, Marks had identified culturally and socially with English society rather than Boer. His wife was English, his children were taught by an English governess, and they were sent to England to be educated as English gentlemen. Given this admiration for the English and for Englishness, at least of the upper-class variety, and given his sense from the very beginning that the war had been a fatal mistake on the part of the Boers and that their defeat was inevitable, a transfer of loyalty was painlessly accomplished.

The months immediately after Diamond Hill were the most hopeful of the war for Marks. With the disintegration of the main Boer army, peace seemed assured as soon as the Boer leaders could be persuaded to see reason, as they surely must. Once there was peace, the country would be taken in hand by progressive and benevolent men who would do all they could to see it prosper and to reconcile the two white 'races'.[42]

Marks felt far less isolated than he had since the start of the war the year before. After the long silence imposed by the British blockade of the Republic, Marks could once again correspond with his family and with his partner in England, though the first batch of letters was much delayed in the mail. Letters posted in June and July in England only arrived in Pretoria in mid-October, but after this slow start the mails became more regular.[43]

Although his wife and children remained at the coast, Marks was reunited with some of his closest associates. Dr Kay, the family's physician, who had escaped from the Transvaal on the eve of the war, returned with Roberts's army to Pretoria, where he saw Marks often. George Falcke, Marks's nephew and confidential secretary, who had joined the Uitlander exodus the previous September, returned to the Transvaal in August; so too did his Pretoria manager, Hugh Crawford. The fact that his nephew and office manager were allowed to return when the great majority of refugees were not, suggests the influence that Marks had very rapidly acquired with the military, many of whom became regular guests at Zwartkoppies.[44]

Marks once more entertained on his pre-war scale. 'We have lots of people out on Sundays, mostly officers who ride out from town.' Then there were 'a nice lot of Canadians' stationed at Hatherley. 'I have the officers up to dine with me very often,' Marks wrote to his older daughter Girlie. Their replacements, officers of a Scottish regiment, reciprocated Marks's hospitality by inviting him to dine with them on St Andrew's night, an invitation he was happy to accept. All these visitors were entertained liberally. In December Marks sent an order to London for a hundred cases of claret, 'same as last', ten cases of 'good' Port and five of 'good' Cognac.[45]

Besides thirsty regimental officers, Marks also hosted higher-ranking guests. 'I had the pleasure of entertaining in my house some of the most distinguished British generals,' Marks wrote to his oldest son Louis in September. 'Even now I am constantly visited by distinguished officers whom it is a great pleasure to meet and converse with.' He saw a 'great deal' of General Pole-Carew, who commanded the 11th Division during Roberts's great advance and who billeted with him for three weeks at Zwartkoppies. Pole-Carew asked for Bertha Marks's address and promised to call on her when he went home. An officer and a gentleman, he kept his word.[46]

The social highpoint of Marks's war was a visit by the Commander-in-Chief himself in early October. Since their alfresco meeting at The Willows in June 1900, Marks and Lord Roberts had had dealings on a number of occasions. In July, the Field Marshal had presided at the official opening of a military hospital in the Palace of Justice building on Church Square; Lewis and Marks and other Pretoria firms, anxious to demonstrate their goodwill to the conquerors, had furnished the wards at their own expense. In August the firm had requested additional protection for its coal mines at Vereeniging, but while Roberts was sympathetic, he could not spare the troops. However, in September when Marks asked the Commander-in-Chief to allow his Jewish soldiers to attend synagogue on the approaching High Festivals, Roberts 'gave his consent with pleasure and without the slightest hesitation'.[47]

Arrangements for Roberts's visit to Zwartkoppies on 1 October were made with military precision. The Military Governor of Pretoria sent Marks detailed instructions, with a personal request from the Field Marshal that 'the hours given are punctually adhered to'. Lord Roberts and his wife and two daughters, who were visiting South Africa despite Queen Victoria's disapproval of such camp-followers, were to take the train from Pretoria to Eerste Fabrieken at 6 a.m.; they were to be met at the station by a carriage and four horses, and were to be taken directly to Zwartkoppies for breakfast; at 8 a.m. they would leave for Diamond Hill, site of the recent battle; Lord Roberts and one of his daughters would ride, the other would travel with her mother in Marks's carriage; they would return for lunch at Zwartkoppies at 1 o'clock, and would take the train back to town at 2.[48] The principal object of the visit was to pay the family's respects at the grave of the Earl of Airlie, killed in action at Diamond Hill while commanding the 12th Lancers. The Roberts family were the first of a stream of aristocratic pilgrims to the site, to whom Marks played eager host. At Lord Roberts's request, he also later made arrangements for the purchase and prettifying of the ground around the grave.[49]

While Roberts was at Zwartkoppies, Marks, who was bubbling as usual with bright ideas, took the opportunity to press the case for state support of agriculture in the Transvaal. He hoped that when the Field Marshal returned to England in the near future, he would encourage the British government to underwrite agricultural improvement in the new colony, particularly in the form of a comprehensive irrigation scheme, long a dream of Marks's. The government should also establish a school of mines in the Transvaal. Part of the funding could come from the money collected before the war by the Uitlander community to establish an English-medium education system. (The Boers had persistently refused to subsidise schooling in anything but Dutch.) The school could be the start of something much larger. Its chemists could help to transform Transvaal agriculture by analysis of the soils of the different regions to determine their agricultural potential, while in the course of time, its curriculum could be expanded to make it more than a school of mines. Marks seems to have envisaged the creation of a college of science and technology.[50]

A few days after the Roberts visit, Marks undertook a larger service for his august guest with a view to hastening the end of the war. On 6 October, Marks addressed an impassioned plea to his Lichtenburg agent, Koos de la Rey, now the principal Boer commander in the western Transvaal:

My dear old friend

Once more I am sending a messenger to you and hope he will meet with as favourable a reception as the last.

I wish you to read this letter and to consider its contents in the calm manner you used to listen to me when I spoke to you in my room.

You will remember that I have repeatedly pointed out to you the futility of this country struggling against a mighty power like Great Britain, a country having at her command almost unlimited means and vast numbers of men.

. . . During yesterday and today I have met British generals who have been right through the country as far as Komatipoort, and the picture they paint of the sufferings of the old Burghers, women and children throughout the country and the ruin caused to them, are most harrowing and would move you, brave men as you are, to tears.

The longer the war lasts, the worse will be the sufferings of the inhabitants of this country while you cannot possibly prevail and I counsel you in the interests of humanity to submit without delay to the inevitable.

Now my dear Koos I wish you to read this letter, not as a Fighting General, but as a father, a husband and a Christian. You will no doubt wonder how Sam Marks can counsel you as a Christian, my reason for doing so is because during the whole course of the war the President has been quoting scripture profusely although his actions show that he has not lived up to the spirit of Christianity. Every religion teaches us humanity. If the President had been serious in his professions of sacrificing everything for the independence of the country, would he have transferred his farms into the names of his children and taken the money he had in the Banks and divided it among them. The only answer that can be given to this question is no, emphatically no.

Think, I beg of you, of the number of women who have become widows, and the number of children who have been rendered fatherless and destitute as a result of the war, and that number is daily being added to. Who is to provide for these women and children? . . .

You expressed yourself to the effect that you would do all in your power to avert war but, if hostilities broke out, you would conduct yourself as a man. That you have fought like a man even your enemies are forced to admit. You can do no possible good by prolonging the struggle whereas you can save your people much misery by yourself submitting and advising others to do likewise. . . . The President himself has deserted the cause notwithstanding his professions and convictions and is now, with his principal officials, in Delagoa Bay. He has . . . transferred his property to his children and divided his money among them, and some of the money has actually been found in jars secreted in the walls of their dwellings.[51]

There is no record of De la Rey's response, if any. His future actions, though, his vigorous prosecution of the war in the western Transvaal, indicate that he wholly discounted the letter.

At the end of October Marks drafted a similar appeal to Louis Botha, Commandant-General of the Transvaal. Again he appealed to friendship to win a patient hearing, though from the tone of the letter it is plain that he was on less intimate terms with Botha than with De la Rey. The arguments he presented for surrender were very similar: continued struggle was futile for there was no hope of a favourable military outcome. After allowing for heavy casualties and subtracting the large number of Boers who were POWs or had taken an oath of neutrality, Marks 'computed' that there could not be many more than 10,000 men still in the field. 'Now my dear Louis I ask you and my other friends if 10,000 men can possibly hope to prevail against a mighty Power like England, backed by her Colonies and Dependencies, which has at her command almost unlimited funds and almost numberless men.' Prolonging the struggle would only increase the general misery.

It is not necessary for me to point to the number of widows and orphans as a result of the war and to tell you that the number is rapidly increasing, and what will be the end?

It is all very well for our brave leaders and men in the field to talk about fighting to the bitter end, but you must not forget the thousands of prisoners who are exiled from their country and have been for months. The longer the war lasts the greater will be the destruction wrought and the consequences will be that, when the prisoners are brought back to the country after the war they will have no house to receive them. Do you not think as a man, a General, a husband and father, you should determine to make the best of things and prevail upon others to do the same.

To these arguments, he added a third he had not made to De la Rey: there was now absolutely no hope of foreign intervention on behalf of the Boers; the evidence of large-scale corruption placed before a British commission of inquiry into Kruger's pre-war concessions policy had ensured 'that not a single European Power will, or dare, lift a finger to assist us.' To hammer the point home, Marks attached a page extract of the evidence before the commission, detailing the bribes accepted by Leyds and an impressive list of Boer luminaries from the dynamite concessionaires. Marks presumably hoped that this pointed reminder of the venality of the pre-war order would help to call in question Botha's resolve to fight on.

Marks asked Botha not to keep the letter to himself, but to read it to President Steyn of the Free State, Reitz, the State Secretary, and others: 'I wish the letter to obtain as much publicity as possible among our leading men because I know I have enemies among those who are aiding you in your struggle and I should not like anybody to say or think that old Marks is going to make a lot of money out of the British government and that is why he is writing to our General.'[52]

Marks had thought of asking Annie Botha, who had gone with him to her husband in June, to deliver the letter, but was told by some of the General's close friends that Botha had instructed his wife not to interfere in politics in any way. Marks's second choice was Mrs Joubert, widow of Botha's predecessor as Commandant-General, and a highly respected *volksmoeder* (or 'mother of the nation'). As her escort he chose the Reverend H. S. Bosman, a Dutch Reformed Church minister in Pretoria and perhaps the most prominent *predikant* in the Transvaal. Bosman agreed to go to Botha if publicly requested to do so by leading local citizens. Marks organised the required petition, which was signed by senior members of the former government and other Transvaal notables who had taken the oath of neutrality, and obtained permits for the party, which was to include Mrs Joubert's daughter-in-law, Mrs Abram Malan, and a driver from Zwartkoppies. While Marks was making the necessary arrangements, Bosman was having second thoughts. After it became public knowledge that he might form part of a peace delegation, he was bombarded with appeals, including one from his *kerkraad* – his parish council – not to go. Fearing schism within his congregation, Bosman withdrew.[53]

Mrs Joubert and her daughter-in-law set off alone for Botha's camp near Warmbaths in a spider provided by Marks. Their peace mission in November 1900, like similar attempts at this stage of the war, was a failure. The *bittereinders* were only at the start of their guerilla campaign and were still far from the acute war-weariness of later months. While at Botha's laager, the elderly Mrs Joubert fell seriously ill, which infuriated her son-in-law, Commandant Abe Malan, who had until recently led a commando of Cape colonials, Free Staters and Transvalers known popularly as the Wild Horsemen. The decimation of this dashing unit through death, disease and desertion had left him in a very angry mood, and he now fired off a vitriolic letter to Marks, accusing him of misusing a 'poor old widow'. By sending Mrs Joubert on such a dubious mission, Marks had jeopardised her unblemished reputation amongst her people. All those Boers who had come before to persuade the *bittereinders* to surrender were regarded as traitors, and where possible, court-martialled and punished. 'To a similar danger you exposed General Joubert's widow.' Not only had Marks risked her reputation, but her health as well. 'If she had succumbed you had better have left the country before you sent her as her loving people would never forgive you.'

Malan also roundly denounced the signatories of the petition Marks had organised. They were the very people who were instrumental in bringing about the war, and who had since surrendered and turned traitor. He and his fellow *bittereinders* rejected as insulting any attempt at negotiation through these people; if the British wanted to parley, let them do so directly. 'We would respect and sooner consider any communication from our enemies direct. I again say we are desirous of peace but not peace at any price. If we are to lose our independence, which is still a matter of doubt, yet we are not prepared to sacrifice our honour as well by coming as dogs to sue for peace.'[54]

Marks was deeply hurt by Malan's reply, which was the only one he received despite a promise that Botha would also respond. He read and reread the letter, and after long hours of reflection, decided to draft a response for the record; he was not sure that he would actually send it. In the letter he defended his decision

to send Mrs Joubert: he had the highest respect for her, and would never have
contemplated asking her to do anything that would antagonise her people. 'I feel
and she feels that our people have struggled nobly and have won the respect of
the entire world for their bravery, but that they have been grievously misled and
can gain nothing by further resistance.' Had he foreseen that Mrs Joubert would
fall ill, something he greatly regretted, he would have taken the letter to Botha
himself. 'I have the courage of my convictions and am not afraid of meeting the
Burgers whom I have always found reasonable. I did not decide to go in the first
instance because I concluded that Mrs Joubert's words would carry more weight
than mine.' As for Malan's intemperate attack on the signatories of the petition,
Marks warned him against judging over-hastily. 'You wrong some of these
people who, from the very first were opposed to the war. . . . You are a young
man yet and should not condemn anyone lightly.'[55]

Marks's sense of urgency about the ending of the war had a very personal
edge. Alarming reports had reached him from England in August 1900 about his
second oldest son, Montie. Isaac Lewis had written that the 12-year-old had lost
a great deal of weight and was 'very delicate and . . . anything but right'. Acting
as a surrogate parent in the absence of Sammy in Pretoria and Bertha in Cape
Town, Lewis had taken the boy to see a specialist in London. The doctor had
been reassuring and Montie had returned to his Jewish preparatory school in
Gravesend. In September Marks received a cable from England that Montie had
taken a turn for the worse. The sympathetic military authorities in Pretoria
allowed the anxious (and influential) father the special privilege of using the
telegraph, normally reserved for official signals, to contact Bertha in Cape
Town. She set off at once for England while her husband, trapped in the
Transvaal by the war and torn between duty to his partners and duty to his
family, looked on helplessly. Marks felt that he had to remain in the Transvaal
to safeguard the partnership's interests; if he left the Transvaal, he might well not
be allowed to return. By October Marks feared the worst. 'The news I get of
Montie is very unsatisfactory, and I am sorely afraid he will not survive this
wretched illness. I cannot write any more now being too much upset. . . . '
Again, 'I cannot help thinking that I shall never see my boy again but hope and
pray that I may be mistaken.'

Montie died on 12 December 1900. 'Although not altogether unexpected,'
Marks later told his junior partner Barnet Lewis, 'the news caused me a great
shock.' At once he sent a short note to Bertha: 'I need not tell you how terribly
grieved I am. I hope you will bear up bravely under the circumstances and
remember that we have other children whom we must look after.' Five days
later, after receiving a cable from Isaac Lewis that Bertha was indeed 'bearing up
bravely', he wrote again: 'It is terribly hard to lose one's children but we must
submit to the inevitable. . . . We are not the only people who have lost a dear
child; many parents in England and in this country are in the same sad position
as ourselves.' He wrote in the same stoical vein to Louis, his oldest son: 'Our loss
is very sad and has upset me very much, but it was God's will that Montie should
be taken from us and we must submit to it. . . . I hope that you will take care
of yourself and see that while you take exercise and pleasure you do not

overexcite yourself and above all devote yourself to your studies and prove a blessing to your mother and myself.' Understandably, the loss of Montie had heightened his old anxieties about his children's well-being. The tragedy also intensified his longings for his family. 'You cannot be more anxious to see me than I am to see you all,' he wrote to Louis a month after Montie's death, ' but I cannot leave here now and do not know when I should be able to get back if I did leave. It is very lonely at Zwartkopje without Mother and the children.'[56]

In his loneliness and grief Marks struck out at his partners, Barnet and Isaac Lewis. (Perhaps unconsciously he blamed them for his enforced absence from Montie's sickbed. It was duty to the partnership that had, after all, becalmed him in the Transvaal.) Writing to thank Joe Lewis, Isaac's younger brother who was not a member of the partnership, for visiting Bertha in Gravesend before Montie's death, he noted bitterly that 'The journey was apparently too far for your brothers or perhaps important business kept them and Sarah [Lewis, Isaac's wife] away from Gravesend.'[57]

The failure of Marks's peace initiative of October–November 1900, which he insisted was his own inspiration rather than a British ploy, and the associated unpleasantness, was a chastening experience for Marks. In the months that followed he made no further attempts at independent mediation but contented himself, if barely so, with leading the quiet life that martial law imposed on civilians in the wartime Transvaal.

Conducting business under martial law was stressful and frustrating. As Marks reported to Lewis: 'Business is attended here with all sorts of drawbacks, harassing in themselves, but which are necessary under martial law. I must admit that we receive every consideration, but nevertheless business is very much hampered.' Movement was severely restricted, seriously inhibiting business activity. While Marks enjoyed a limited measure of favour in this respect, because of his influential connections and his usefulness to the military authorities, he nevertheless found the wartime travel restrictions most irksome and obstructive: 'Under present circumstances the Authorities are perfectly justified in taking strick [sic] measures but business is out of the question while the restrictions are so severe.'

Unlike most civilians Marks was allowed to travel in and out of Pretoria freely, at least to and from Zwartkoppies. During the week he went into town almost every day, carrying a pass issued by his friend General Maxwell, the Military Governor of Pretoria, which permitted him to make the twelve-mile roundtrip but not to deviate from the route. (The pass issued in September 1900 describes Marks with military economy of expression: 'Age 55. Height 5ft 5in. Eyes Grey. Colour of Hair: face grey; head grey.') Travelling into Pretoria from Zwartkoppies, Marks would stop at the military posts en route to chat to the soldiers, whom he usually brought small gifts of fruit from his orchards. He took his own suplies to town: he disliked the wartime food at the Pretoria Club, preferring packed cold lunches from Zwartkoppies; he also brought forage for his horses because this was both scarce and expensive in town. He hurried home early in the afternoon because of the curfew, leaving Pretoria at 3.30 so that he could pass the blockhouses before 5 p.m.; at each post he gave the soldiers the latest war news.

Travelling further afield was much more difficult. It was virtually impossible to move through the countryside because of the state of war, which meant that Marks was unable to visit his scattered properties. Non-military train travel was discouraged by the authorities, but even if a civilian could occasionally do so there were, as Marks discovered, attendant difficulties. There was a severe shortage of hotel accommodation in Johannesburg. On one visit Marks found that he could not get a hotel bed and had to be content with 'a shake down' on the floor of a hotel reading-room. 'As you know I am not a stranger in this country,' he wrote to his son Louis, 'and yet I have to put up with that sort of thing.'[58]

When Marks travelled to Vereeniging at the end of 1900 to inspect the colliery, the train was twenty minutes late and consequently only arrived at Vereeniging station at 6.20 in the evening, shortly after the curfew. When Marks asked the officer in charge if he could go on to his brother Ellia's nearby home, the officer insisted that he remain on the platform. 'Remonstrance was useless': when Ellia explained that Sammy was his brother, the officer said he knew very well who Sammy Marks was but that he still would have to spend the night on the platform. What Marks felt was so unreasonable about this refusal to bend the rules slightly was that he had arrived in the early evening, not in the middle of the night.[59]

War conditions also created severe staffing difficulties. Fresh recruits were simply unavailable. Marks found that he could not dismiss an unsatisfactory employee at Vereeniging Estates for example, 'for the simple reason that it is next to impossible to get him replaced'. Obtaining permission from the military authorities to bring someone up from the coast was a painfully slow and uncertain business.[60] Then again Marks feared that wartime military censorship interfered with the confidentiality of business communication, especially with his partner. He complained that often the censors were not regular soldiers but volunteers, men who in civvy street were brokers and clerks in the City of London and 'keen on business', men who were on the prowl for useful titbits of business intelligence. This meant, Marks warned Lewis, that 'while this state of affairs lasts, I cannot write you all I should like'.[61]

The result of these restrictions on the conduct of business was that Marks, a man of immense energy who was normally extremely active, discovered that he had far more leisure time than he desired. He found the enforced idleness deeply frustrating. He occupied his empty hours supervising the redecoration and replanting of Zwartkoppies. He built an oven outside the kitchen for baking bread; he sent Bertha orders for carpets which were to be sent out from England; he had a painter come out from Pretoria to redecorate some of the rooms; and he converted a spare room into a music room, with panels painted on the wall that looked like satin. He saw to it that the gardener put the flower beds in order and supervised the construction of a dam and the planting of oak trees and vines.[62]

Marks sent grapes to the military hospital in Pretoria for the patients, who greatly enjoyed these. He also made white wine, claret and vinegar from those grapes he saved from 200 marauding Australian troopers who invaded his vineyard at Zwartkoppies, planning to fill their horses' nosebags. 'I just arrived on the scene to stop their little game although I gave them some,' he wrote to his son Joe in England. Eternal vigilance was essential: 'My grapes are in constant danger of being demolished so I have to keep my own patrols going,' he wrote to his oldest son Louis. In an atmosphere of siege nothing was exempt from suspicion. The authorities sent a detective to investigate Marks's home-made wine-making and only approved it on condition that none of the 1901 Zwartkoppies vintage was offered for sale.[63]

For all the restrictions on his daily life Marks was more fortunate than most for he had a champion right at the heart of the military government, a guide through the labyrinth of martial law. This was Major-General John Maxwell, the Military Governor of Pretoria, who was responsible for civil administration throughout the Transvaal excepting the Witwatersrand. The General was a man of great charm and good humour, 'full of tact [and] very courteous'. Marks and he had taken to each other instantly and had very quickly established a mutually beneficial working relationship which was cemented by Marks's hospitality. Writing to his 'old friend' years after the war, Maxwell spoke nostalgically of riding over on Sundays for dinner at 'hospitable Schwartzkoppies'. His wife week-ended at Zwartkoppies when she joined her husband in the Transvaal and had taken a sympathetic interest in Montie Marks's illness. She had very kindly reassured her anxious host that, as a child, she had recovered from the same malady. Marks often called at the General's office with suggestions and requests, and was always well received. 'The governor always gives me a patient hearing,' he reported to Lewis, 'and is always most courteous.' Maxwell, in turn, found Marks a useful advisor; with his intimate knowledge of local affairs, he could always be tapped for information about local personalities and issues.[64]

On a number of occasions Maxwell shielded Marks against the malice and suspicion of lesser officials. When the district commissioner's office at Vereeniging insinuated early in 1901 that Lewis and Marks had made some sort of underhand deal with the Boers to leave their property untouched, Maxwell sprang at once to their defence. A long letter 'enlightening' the errant officials about Sammy Marks drew the abashed response that 'I . . . had no idea they had been useful to you'. On another occasion Marks was hauled off to a Pretoria police station after a heated exchange in Church Street with a Corporal Macdonald who insisted that Marks outspan his cart at once, even though his stables were just around the corner, as one of the mules seemed lame. At the station Marks was severely 'dressed down' by the officer in charge. After Sammy complained, Maxwell ordered the Commissioner of Police to make a full inquiry into his subordinates' apparent lack of civility towards his friend.[65]

Maxwell also made representations on Marks's behalf to the upper echelons. Through the Military Governor, Marks had indirect access to Roberts's successor as Commander-in-Chief, for Maxwell had served with Kitchener in the Sudan and was a member of his inner circle. Though Kitchener had fewer dealings with local civilians, he too found Marks useful: 'I well know how much you helped both me and the troops,' he wrote to Marks some years later. Not least of the 'help' was the 'gift', at Kitchener's explicit request, of the bronze sentries which Marks had commissioned for the Kruger statue; Kitchener set up two of these trophies in the grounds of his country estate in England after the war. Marks also presented the Commander-in-Chief with pheasants shot on Isaac Lewis's country estate in Kent, which, despite their hazardous wartime journey, arrived in Pretoria in perfect condition.[66]

While Marks bonded rapidly and easily with the new masters of the Transvaal, he nevertheless retained important links with the old. Throughout the guerilla war, Marks and the *bittereinders* appear to have had a vague and unspoken understanding, an undefined and precarious relationship, which lent Marks a limited but crucial degree of personal immunity, for all his conspicuous collaboration with the conquerors. It seems that Marks's sympathy towards the Republic before the war still stood him in good stead, as did his personal ties with a significant number of the *bittereinders*. 'I do not think there is a single Commando', he wrote rebutting the accusation of disloyalty made against him by the assistant district commissioner at Vereeniging, 'that does not contain several farmers who are under some obligation to us either for money advanced, permission to live on farms rent free, or some other privilege, otherwise we would have to chronicle further losses.'[67]

Similarly, he must have earned considerable goodwill for the compassion he showed the *bittereinders*' wives and children. Clearing his actions with the Military Governor, he wrote: 'It is a matter of frequent occurance [sic] that the wives of burghers actually on commando come to me for food and sustenance. They are often in a starving condition and bring with them little children in a similar state. Ordinary humanity has made me feed them, and I do not for a moment think that you will consider that I am doing wrong.'[68]

Furthermore, Marks also kept open a personal line of communication of a tenuous sort with the Boer government-in-exile, with British knowledge and approval. Marks corresponded, if only very occasionally and cautiously, and very largely about private matters, with his young friend Piet Grobler, who had accompanied his great-uncle, President Kruger, into European exile. He also corresponded with A. D. W. Wolmarans, once a leader of the Kruger faction in the Volksraad, now a member of a Boer mission seeking foreign intervention, quite futilely, on behalf of the Republics. Marks kept a watching brief on their business affairs. He saw that their houses in Pretoria remained in good repair and that their rents were regularly collected. He ensured that their relatives were well looked after and supplied with food, and, through his influence with the Military Governor, he helped to arrange Mrs Wolmarans's departure for Europe to join her husband.[69]

All of these considerations guaranteed Marks's personal safety and the inviolacy of his fixed property throughout the war: no attempt was ever made to damage Zwartkoppies or the mines at Vereeniging. But they were no protection for his moveable possessions. As he himself recognised, these were a tempting target for Boer commandos on the run and desperately short of supplies, particularly of horses. Just after 11 o'clock on the night of 26 February 1901, thirty Boers slipped into Zwartkoppies. While Marks slept, they picked the locks on the stable door and drove off all the animals: four imported carriage horses, two salted Basuto ponies, and two horses in safekeeping for Boer notables. Nothing else was damaged or taken during their brief visit. The next day Marks fired a rocket at Piet Grobler in the Hague: the burghers had taken his horses on the eve of Amajuba Day 'when other thoughts should have engrossed their minds. I do not think I have merited this treatment,' he continued; 'I am a rich burgher no doubt but nobody likes to have things taken away from him by force. . . . The loss of the horses does not worry me much but I am astounded at the utter want of gratitude displayed.' He made light of the incident, though, in a reassuring letter to his wife in England: he would now be forced to travel about with mules; if these were taken, he would have to resort to the bicycle.[70]

Eight nights later the Boers came on a cattle raid, but 'decamped at a great rate', empty-handed, when they came under fire from a detachment of mounted police, posted meantime to Zwartkoppies. After this the farm was left alone for a while, but Marks was under no illusion that the reprieve was permanent. The enemy were still everywhere. While the mounted police played cricket at Hatherley, the Boers watched the game from a nearby hill. Marks was certain that they looked too, 'with a longing eye', at his cattle.[71]

The blow, when it came, fell on the Vereeniging Estates. For the first half-year of the guerilla campaign, Marks's Vaal River properties had led a charmed existence. Though the Boers had been very active locally, attacking British patrols and destroying farm property, they had left the estate and its employees alone. The workmen operating the steam ploughs on a farm miles away from the nearest garrison were told on a number of occasions that they were free to plough and sow; on another, the oxen hauling water for the steam ploughs were driven off, but swiftly returned with an apology when the Boers found they bore the Estates' brand.[72]

This immunity ended in March 1901. On the 16th, the Boers took 49 donkeys and, less than a month later, 480 horses and mules. Deeply indignant, Marks told Wolmarans that despite this undeserved treatment, which he would not quickly forget, he would continue to do whatever he could, within the limits of the law, for the burghers. Early in July, at harvest time, the Boers took 25 more animals, and fired the crops still on the ground. The Boer raids were a measure of the increasing difficulty the commandos were experiencing in sustaining their war of mobility. Horses and mules were in short supply, and so was forage as the British burnt the veld. As a bitterly cold winter set in, Marks's hopes began to rise once more of an early end to the war.[73]

By early October 1901 the war had receded from Marks's district. 'It is so quiet around Zwartkopje,' he wrote, 'that sometimes it is difficult to realise that a war is going on in the country.' An impression Milner confirmed in November: reporting on the state of the war, he confidently asserted that the central region of the Transvaal had been cleared, completely and permanently, of the enemy. Under the circumstances, Marks decided that it was at last safe to bring his family home. Passage was booked from England and permission obtained for their return to the Transvaal, significantly without much difficulty at a time when the issue of permits was still restricted. Marks arranged to travel down to Cape Town to meet the boat.[74]

Just days before Marks was due to leave, and after months of quiet, the Boers returned to Zwartkoppies. At midnight on Saturday 7 December, Boer raiders stole into the farm and began driving off the cattle penned in the kraal, a short distance from the main house where Marks was entertaining two British army officers. Awoken by the noise, Oom Dantje Haumann, the estate manager, opened the window of his cottage and pleaded with the raiders to leave the herd, reminding them 'that Mr. Marks had done a great deal for our people'. When this failed, he went into the farmyard and rang the big bell, hoping that this would scare off the marauders. Undeterred, they took all 106 head, worth close to £2,000 as many were salted against lung-sickness and the rinderpest.

Early the next morning Marks sent Geelbooi, a black employee who knew all his master's cattle and who had himself lost a cow and an ox in the raid, to follow the trail and recover what he could. With the approval of Marks's English guests, one of whom, Lieutenant Martin, was secretary to the Military Governor, Geelbooi was given a pass in English and Dutch, and told that he 'could go into the Boer laager as they would not hurt me'. Geelbooi had second thoughts about this when he reached the Boer encampment, and rather than walking in and demanding the return of Marks's cattle, beat a hasty and sensible retreat. On the way home he was intercepted by Jack, a black scout, who reported the matter to his English superior. No friend of 'handsome Sam', he in turn reported it to the Provost-Marshal in Pretoria, hoping, he said, that at last 'we may get at this old devil'.

Geelbooi's pass created a stir at army headquarters: Marks stood accused of the grave offence of 'communicating with the enemy'. Once again his champion, General Maxwell, rode to the rescue. He argued that although Marks might be technically at fault, he had intended nothing more treasonous than to recover his cattle: hence his own secretary's approval of the pass. Maxwell discussed the matter with the Commander-in-Chief, and with Kitchener's approval the charge was effectively spiked.[75]

Though he was angered by the raid which he felt was most undeserved, he chose to ignore its warning message that the countryside was still too unsafe for his family, and set off for Cape Town to collect them. It would seem that his understandable eagerness to be reunited with Bertha and the children after more than two years of separation overcame his natural caution. The break at the Cape after so 'many weary months' of isolation in the Transvaal did Marks 'a great deal of good', as did the reunion with his family and their return home. 'I am very pleased indeed to have them back at Zwartkopje,' he wrote to one of the older boys who remained behind at school in England. 'I find the children all grown much taller and also naughtier and shall have to be very strict with them until they become disciplined again.'[76]

One month after they returned home, the unlearnt lesson of the December cattle raid was driven home in a very alarming and unpleasant fashion. Whatever the High Commissioner might believe, the central Transvaal countryside remained a very dangerous place. Late one Tuesday night in February 1902, while Marks was away on business in Johannesburg, 35 armed 'gentlemen' rode up to Zwartkoppies, called Bertha out of bed and demanded food and clothing at gunpoint. Remaining till 4 in the morning, they took 'every stitch' of Marks's clothing, including all his underlinen and boots, leaving only an old pair of clogs which he wore around the farm in wet weather. They pulled all the blankets off the beds, emptied the pantry, and snaffled the cigars. They broke into the stables and took a little pony Marks had just bought for his daughter Girlie, plus the mules he had been forced to use since the disappearance of his horses in an earlier raid.

Marks was terribly upset. Writing to order a replacement wardrobe, he took out all his anger and indignation on his unfortunate partner: 'Now perhaps this will give you some idea of the life we have to live here. Just imagine yourself in my place and think how you would like it!!' What made matters worse was that the raiding party had included people he knew, one of them a youngster whose education he had paid for before the war. 'Now this is my thanks.'[77]

Bertha, understandably, wanted to leave Zwartkoppies for the greater safety of Johannesburg, but her husband persuaded her to stay, a decision he must have regretted when a few weeks later the Boers came calling again on a night when Marks was away on business. 'This time they cleared out everything . . . except toothpicks,' he quipped. 'I expect they did not want these as Lord Kitchener does not give them much time to use such articles.' The raiders 'did not leave me so much as a shoe lace, and I am sadly in want of something to cover my nakedness.' His partner did not take such a flippant view: 'I . . . was very much surprised to see that you are still occupying Zwartkoppies. From your last experience I should have thought you would have locked the doors and left the place to take care of itself for however severe the loss may be it is better to suffer that than to run the risks as you are doing.'[78]

One reason for Marks's more cheerful response to this Boer raid than to the previous one was that the war was at last, and quite unmistakably, drawing to an end. Despite the occasional flurry, Boer resistance was now at a very low ebb. By early April 1902 the *bittereinder* leaders were seriously considering ending their struggle. After a preliminary meeting in Klerksdorp, representatives of the Free State and Transvaal governments went by train to Pretoria to negotiate with Kitchener. On Monday 14 April, General De la Rey, Assistant Commandant-General of the Republican forces, sent for his old friend and confidant, Sammy Marks, whom he had last seen when the British had captured Pretoria in June 1900. After months of isolation from the outside world De la Rey wanted to know whether there was any hopeful news from Europe. 'I took up a little tobacco that was lying on the table,' Marks wrote shortly after, 'and told him that he must not expect as much assistance from Europe as the value represented by that tobacco.'

De la Rey then asked Marks what he thought should be done. 'I told him that before the war started I was against it, as he knew, and that my opinion was that no time should be lost in bringing it to an end in the best possible way, that when a man falls into the mud, it is useless for him to try and find out how he got there, he must look ahead and see to get out of it. He then asked how they were to get out of it, explaining that the country was ruined, that in some cases the very foundations of the houses had been blown out with dynamite, and that there was nothing for them to return to.'

Marks replied that if it was a question of money, De la Rey could rest assured that Britain would deal generously with the Boers and repair the damage done by her troops. De la Rey laughed when Marks estimated the damage at five million pounds; even eighty would be an underestimate. 'He told me that if I had seen, as he had, between 40,000 and 50,000 sheep driven together and maxims turned on them so that not one came out alive, and had seen horses driven together in a kraal around which men were stationed with guns and ordered to fire, I might realise the extent of the damage.' Marks could only lamely reply that such was war, that the Franco–Prussian conflict had been equally destructive, and turn the discussion away from this raw topic.

What did De la Rey think was the best way of settling the matter? Independence, De la Rey replied, the only acceptable solution was one that allowed the Republics to retain their independence; if this was conceded, they would grant equal rights to all-comers, and would even waive their claims to financial compensation. Too late, said Marks. But why not ask instead for a united South Africa? The Transvaal must have its independence first, De la Rey countered; the rest would come in time. His only alternative if they were not allowed their independence was to return to his burghers and fight until they were all either killed or caught. They had been fighting all this time for their independence; he could not ask them now to lay down their arms without having anything to offer them.

Now was the time to make peace, Marks urged; very likely, there would not be another such opportunity. If the fate of the Cape rebels – those Cape Afrikaners (and British subjects) who had joined the Republican forces at the risk of execution for treason – was the obstacle, then De la Rey could be sure that if peace was made at once, the new King would grant a general amnesty at his coronation. That might be so, De la Rey conceded, 'but their flag they must have'. Exasperated, Marks exclaimed that 'if that were the case, I was at a loss to understand why he had come in at all.' At this point Marks and De la Rey were joined by the other Boer leaders, and once again Marks urged that now was the time for peace. His parting words were that if they decided otherwise, they should fight on in the same civilised fashion as they had till now 'and not allow any cruelties or outrages to be perpetrated'. He told them he had heard British generals and soldiers praise the fair way they fought.[79]

The part this discussion played in persuading the Boer leaders, and De la Rey in particular, can only be guessed at. Presumably it was only one of a number of similarly agonised discussions the Boers conducted. The upshot of these was a decision to call together a representative assembly of the Boers still in the field to consider whether to continue the war or not. After consultation with Kitchener the Boer leaders settled on Vereeniging as the site for the conference, which was to convene on 15 May. Vereeniging was chosen, it can be assumed, because of its geographical convenience. It was a convenient meeting-point for the representatives of the commandos of the eastern and western Transvaal as well as the Free State, and was only a short distance from Pretoria by rail should the Boers wish to confer with Kitchener.

Marks went down to Vereeniging the week before the conference, ostensibly to assist with the practical arrangements. The tents to house the delegates and the large marquee for the meetings were pitched on open ground to the west of the township, some 200 yards from the estate company's bricksheds. Water and light were laid on by the company. Marks's ulterior motive in going down early was to buttonhole the delegates as they arrived: 'if there is any chance', he wrote to Lewis in London, 'of my assisting to convince some of my old burgher friends that it is now time to do something to put an end to the present state of affairs, I will be there and do my level best. You may rest assured', he told his apprehensive partner, 'I have not taken this step of my own accord, nor on my own responsibility.' The hand of Maxwell or of Marks's other high-ranking British friends can surely be detected.[80]

The conference began officially on 15 May 1902 with reports from the delegates about the military situation in their respective districts. It was soon obvious that the delegates were divided into three groups: those, chiefly from the Free State, who would settle for nothing short of independence and were prepared to fight on indefinitely until the bitter end; those, chiefly from the eastern Transvaal where the Boer war effort was on the point of collapse, who believed that the bitter end had in fact arrived and that the Boers should make the best terms they possibly could; and those, including De la Rey and his relatively successful western Transvalers, who were both ready and able to fight on, but were willing to be persuaded otherwise. The casting vote lay effectively with this last group; the decisive voice within this group was De la Rey's.

The day after the 'very stormy' opening session Marks was called to meet Jan Smuts, De la Rey's military protégé who had led a daring raid into the Cape Colony a few months before and who had now been recalled to act as legal adviser to the Transvaal government at the conference. Marks asked the young Boer general, who was eight days short of his thirty-second birthday, whether he had come to Vereeniging to assist in making peace or whether he was still for fighting on. Smuts replied: 'if I was still for fighting I would not have been here.' Marks then took Smuts through all the points he had made to De la Rey in Pretoria the month before, 'with perhaps a little more added to it'. Smuts agreed with these and promised to do all he could for peace. He was afraid of one thing though, that 'some of the young firey [sic] Boers, and especially some of the Free Staters, would be very stobborn [sic] and difficult to win over'. What if they refused to accept a peace agreement and 'stuck out against it'? To prevent this happening, the Boers needed more time to meet. 'You know as well as I do,' Smuts told Marks, 'that the Boers cannot be driven, but if they are allowed time to quarrel amongst themselves, and think things over, something may come out of it.' Marks saw that Smuts's request for extra time for consultation was passed on immediately to Kitchener. As a result, the Boers were granted extra time for their consultations.

A while later Marks had a further appointment with Smuts, and this time they were joined by General De la Rey for well over an hour's discussion. 'The three of us took a little walk together and talked everything over and over again.' As they strolled along, Marks posed a question to his two companions: 'Has not the time now arrived to make peace. . . . If it is not done now, it never will be done. It is needless to point out that there will not be another chance given.'

'Could the British be trusted to keep the promises they were now making to the Boers?' De la Rey wondered. 'Can we believe them?' Smuts asked. Lord Milner, Marks responded, was a man of his word – 'take my word for it, I will guarantee that he will perform every thing that he promises. If you like I will back my guarantee with fifty or a hundred thousand pounds. . . . believe me after the war is over, Lord Milner will be one of the best friends you have in South Africa.'

Before parting, Marks, the Jewish outsider, once a loyal burgher and now a loyal British subject, confessed to his old friends 'that although my sympathy was with them, I could not feel in the matter the same way as they. I could not feel that I had lost the country in the same way as they did, although I am living in it. And as I had not been in the Veld as they had been for nearly three years, I could not feel exactly as they did.' We can 'quite understand that', Smuts and De la Rey, the two great *bittereinders,* generously responded.[81]

Smuts and De la Rey returned to their discussions with the delegates. The outcome of these was a decision to send representatives of the Free State and Transvaal governments to negotiate with Kitchener and Milner in Pretoria. Smuts played a crucial role at these talks, keeping them afloat when they threatened to break down. The leaders returned to Vereeniging to persuade the representatives of the commandos to accept the terms of surrender they had negotiated. In a dramatic debate on 31 May, when peace hung in the balance, it was a call by the revered General De la Rey to lay down arms that carried the day. The conference voted overwhelmingly to end the struggle. De la Rey, Botha, De Wet and the other leaders went the same evening to Pretoria to sign what was to become known as the Treaty of Vereeniging.[82]

Marks's role in the process of peace-making had been essentially supportive. He had helped to strengthen a growing conviction on the part of General De la Rey that the time had come to make terms with the enemy; he had also helped to reassure the General that the enemy could be trusted to keep their word. Given De la Rey's pre-eminence in the military struggle – the region he commanded, the western Transvaal, was one of the very few where it was seriously possible to talk of fighting on – and given De la Rey's great influence with the delegates at Vereeniging, Marks's efforts to persuade him of the necessity of peace assume a considerable importance.

Days after the peace, Marks sent his personal assessment of the events of the past weeks to Lewis. The leaders he had counselled had played a vital role: 'I can tell you as far as I can gather, if it had not been for De la Rey, Botha and Smuts, the late State Attorney, the present trouble would very likely still have been going on.' Of his own role since the generals first came in from the veld in April, he wrote:

a person is always satisfied when his work is not thrown away. I do congratulate myself on that little business. I do not think there was anybody in Johannesburg or Pretoria who could, or would have done it. You must not forget that these people are extremely suspicious and jealous of everybody, and of that kind with whom you must be careful of every word you say, and of every move you make. However, my safety and influence lay in the fact that I did not in any way change my behavior towards my old burgher friends after the British came and whenever the Military Authorities would allow me I assisted them as far as I could. And in this work I must place on record how much I was indebted to General Maxwell, who was Governor of Pretoria. He is one of the most sensible and courteous gentlemen I have met, and it is not too much to say that during the last few weeks I have been reaping the fruits of the many little acts of kindness I was enabled to perform during his term of Governorship.[83]

The departure from Zwartkoppies on 1 October 1900 of Marks's most distinguished wartime visitor, Lord Roberts, his wife and daughters (Photo: Marks Museum)

VIII

Keeping the Peace,
1902–1908

The peace treaty was signed in Pretoria late on Saturday evening, 31 May 1902. Lord Milner spent the next day at Zwartkoppies with Marks, who thought him 'a very nice gentleman'. For the first time in two years Marks felt completely at ease; peace brought release from the severe stresses he had endured throughout the guerilla struggle. For all his stoicism and surface calm, Marks had felt deeply anxious underneath:

From that day [the Battle of Diamond Hill] on until . . . Sunday morning we were always in mortal terror and fright that some of the Burghers should come and do something outrageous. I do not allude to our Burghers, but to two other classes, namely, the burghers who joined from the Cape Colony, and are called rebels, and the Foreigners, especially the Hollanders, as they were well aware that I did not have too much love for them. Although I never told anybody about it, every night when I went to rest in my house, I used to put my clothes very nicely together, so that I could dress myself very quickly in case anything should have happened, and you can imagine how nice and comfortable I used to feel.[1]

'First thing' on the Monday morning, the Boer leaders sent for Marks and asked him to accompany them to Vereeniging, where they were to rejoin the other delegates. On the train down they made it quite clear to Marks that they felt 'a certain amount of responsibility rested upon me to see that the farmers were well treated by the English. . . . They also expected me to see that laws are not made which will interfere with their freedom.' Marks assured them once again that the British would keep their word.

When they arrived at Vereeniging, Marks 'was pulled into the Camp amongst the crowd, and there I had to reiterate over and over again the same thing. They are very hard to convince that Great Britain will keep her promises.' In order to allay this profound distrust Marks felt it was 'absolutely necessary' that Britain go beyond the £3 million promised to the Boers at the conference table. While this was very generous under the circumstances – Britain, after all, was compensating those who had started the war – nevertheless, far more was needed to rehabilitate 'these poor people' and to consolidate the peace. Why not a great public fund, launched by the Lord Mayor of London and supported by the Rothschilds and the people of Britain and of Johannesburg, he suggested to Lewis. This 'would have a very excellent effect on the burghers and their children'; it would do much to prove 'to these poor people that the people of Great Britain are not the wicked creatures they have been represented, not only by the Foreign Press but even in the House of Commons. . . . It would show them that Great Britain was always honourable and just, and did not take advantage of the weak.' Johannesburg's contribution would help to reduce the Boers' hostility towards a city they held responsible for the war.[2]

As the demobilised burghers poured in from the veld, Marks dealt with a stream of requests for assistance that left him no time 'even to get my meals properly'. As he complained to his partner: 'All the Dutch people are in, and as you know they have no patience and no consideration whatever for anybody and especially for those they consider as their enemies. Therefore I am kept extremely busy one way and another endeavouring to fulfill the promises I made.'[3]

For all his irritation at their importunate behaviour, Marks was touched by the plight of the returning *bittereinders* and by the youthfulness of so many of them. 'Although you are very young yet,' he wrote to his eldest son Louis, 'you can believe me that these poor people require assistance very badly. I wish you could only have seen the little boys who have been fighting. Some of them are about two years younger than yourself, and some of them have been very brave. I suppose they thought because their grandfathers and fathers fought they must also fight.'[4]

Besides the small amounts he disbursed to lesser applicants, Marks also made more substantial loans to the Boer generals, including Christiaan de Wet of the Free State (£3,500 in two instalments) and Lucas Meyer of the Transvaal. Money was set aside too for Louis Botha in case he requested it. Conscious of his partner's cautiousness with money, Marks justified his spending in terms of the future advantages this might bring the firm: 'You will no doubt be thinking . . . that I have been rather liberal in assisting certain people in money matters. But you know when you want those people to do certain things for you, you must assist them.' £10,000 was the limit, he assured Lewis.[5]

Marks helped to rehabilitate General De la Rey, who before the war had been a wealthy landowner, but who was now in urgent need of funds to rebuild and restock his devastated properties and to provide for his children's future. In desperation De la Rey took his title-deeds to a bank in Pretoria and negotiated to mortgage his properties. As he later reminisced:

They were very decent to me, but the interest and the charges were very heavy and they advised me to consult my lawyer before concluding the agreement with them.

I was walking down the steps from the bank to look for a lawyer when I met Ou Marks. . . . You know the 'old Jew' has got very sharp eyes, and after we had greeted each other he stopped me from going further, and said, 'Koos, what were you doing in there?'

'I had some business with the bank.'

'What is that under your arm, that big envelope?' And before I could answer he said to me: 'These are your documents.'

I told him then that I had been to the bank because I must have money for the education of my children. I think he had been going into the bank himself, but he turned round, caught me by the arm and said, 'Come to my office, I want to see you.' I went to his office in the corner of the Square, and to his own little room at the back. He got up and locked the door. Then he was quite angry with me and said: 'Are you a fool, or are you mad? You will just tie yourself up and be ruined.'

'But I must have the money for my children's education.'

Then Marks turned to me as if he were going to bite me. In a few years, he said, I should be ruined and everything taken. Why did I not go to my own friends and get their help, even their advice. I answered that my friends could do nothing: they had to look after themselves.

'Am I not one of your friends?' he said, 'here give it to me,' and he pulled the papers out of my hand, and asked how much I wanted. To me it was a big sum because I had to provide for many things, and I told him what it was (something like £2,000 or £3,000). After looking at the papers he said: 'Here, you are not to go to any of these banks or lending companies. I will let you have the money on your own promissory note without any security; you keep your titles'; and he named an interest much less than the bank had named. That is what the 'old Jew' did for me. He is the best friend I have ever had, and he saved us all.[6]

Marks reciprocated these warm feelings. 'De la Rey . . . is a very sensitive man. He thinks a lot and speaks very little. I thought I knew him pretty well, but during the conversations I have had with him since the 10th of May last I have been quite astonished to find out how many good qualities he has got, and which I did not think he possessed.'[7]

In the weeks after Vereeniging Marks worked hard at reconciling the generals and their followers to the new state of things. 'Perhaps you may say', he wrote to his partner,

that it is neither your business nor mine to trouble ourselves further in the matter, and that there are many cleverer people whose business it is to see to it, and who get well paid for doing the work. But as I have told you before, it is not to our interest nor to the interest of South Africa that after the arms and ammunition have been laid down, things should be allowed to go as they like. I think it is the business of everyone who has got the welfare of the country at heart, and who wishes that the people who are to live in this country, may do so peacefully and harmoniously, to see that the future settlement should be such a one as will preclude any chance whatever of giving the enemies of Great Britain . . . an opportunity of causing further trouble and disturbance in South Africa. . . . I say let us see to it that everything is properly settled now, and try to satisfy everybody even to the lowest Dutchman who lives in the bush-veld.[8]

On 4 June, days after the peace Marks had a 'very gratifying' discussion with Louis Botha at his office. When, early in the discussion, the General turned the conversation to the wrongs of recent history – 'old sores' – Marks immediately stopped him and told him: 'we must forget everything that has happened and wipe off the slate . . . we must try and start afresh and assist those people who went blindfolded into the mud.' To Marks's delight, Botha agreed wholeheartedly, and gave him his solemn word that in the future he would do everything in his power to bring Boer and Brit together.[9]

Botha planned meanwhile to visit Europe with his fellow generals, De Wet and De la Rey. The ostensible purpose of the tour was to raise funds for Boer widows and orphans, the unstated purpose to meet the Boer leaders in exile and to win their endorsement of the new leadership. Marks disapproved of the visit. He felt that the Boer leaders would fall in with critics of British policy in South Africa, who would 'make any amount of noise and praise them up to the skies' but give them very little money. Still, he had no way of preventing the trip which had been agreed to at the Vereeniging conference. The best he could do was to limit the potential damage.

The tour had to be piloted into safe waters: the generals had to be persuaded to travel to Europe on a British boat, to land first in England rather than on the Continent, to meet the right people once there, and to avoid provocative behaviour that might offend British sensibilities. Above all, it was imperative that the generals' visit to Europe should not become an anti-British demonstration. Marks asked Lewis to meet the generals at Southampton docks and take them under his wing. 'I do not want these men to go to Europe and meet a lot of foreigners, nor to meet some of our Englishmen who would not scruple to make mischief for these people to write or preach.' Lewis was 'to make the Generals understand as they have now got to live under the British Flag they must honour and respect it. I have spoken enough on this subject to them here but when they get across the water they may forget, and I want you to remind them.'

Next, the generals had to be persuaded, and this Marks did from his sickbed. After returning from Vereeniging in an open truck – because the guardsvan, the only covered carriage on the train, was packed with returning women and children refugees – Marks, now a man of 58, had developed a severe eye inflammation. He was confined to bed for a fortnight in a darkened room in the home of the family's physician, Dr Kay, in Pretoria. De la Rey and Botha were asked to visit the invalid. Seated around the bed where Marks lay with his eyes bandaged, they discussed the impending tour. Marks suggested that if they knew no one in England, he could cable Lewis to meet them on arrival and 'make them comfortable'. Botha and De la Rey were 'highly pleased and satisfied'. Midway through their visit, Hugh Crawford, the manager at Marks's Pretoria office, came in and asked if he could speak privately to his employer for a few minutes. Once the generals were out of the room, Crawford read a letter which had just arrived from De Jongh of Lewis and Marks's Johannesburg office.

De Jongh had been to see Milner, presumably at Marks's behest, to discuss the generals' tour. They had agreed it was of great political importance that the generals receive some official recognition from the government while in England, and that, if possible, they be introduced to King Edward. 'I am convinced from what I have heard of the King's personal charm of manner and total absence of anything like hauteur', De Jongh wrote, 'that much good from a meeting of this kind would result for the future.' Would Marks ascertain whether the generals would be willing to fall in with something of the sort? Would Marks and the generals meet Milner on Monday?

Listening to the letter, Marks recognised immediately that he would need to disguise the origins of the suggestion. Accepting a proposal of this sort if it came from Lord Milner might well be politically awkward and embarrassing for the Boer leaders. Bluff seemed necessary. Calling the generals back into the room, Marks told them that Crawford had brought a cable from Lewis in London, enquiring whether they would like to meet Joseph Chamberlain and other high-ranking individuals, perhaps even the King. Botha and De la Rey were a bit hesitant at first, but finally agreed that as soon as they arrived in England they would write to Chamberlain to ask for an interview. Continuing the charade, Marks asked them to return later that afternoon; in the meantime, he told them, he expected further cables from Lewis. When they came back at 6, Marks told them there had been no further messages from London, but that Milner would like to meet them on Monday, to which they readily agreed. When Milner came to Pretoria, he stopped by at Dr Kay's house, 'not on business, but just to see how I was'. In 'casual' conversation Milner expressed the hope that Marks's friends 'would not catch that disease known as Swollen Head' when they got to England.[10]

Marks relied on Lewis to see this did not happen. In Marks's scenario for the visit, Lewis would receive the generals at Southampton, taking along Bertha Marks – then visiting England – to meet Mrs De la Rey, 'a very nice homely sensible person', make them as 'comfortable' as possible in London and invite them to weekend at Bedgebury, his country estate. Lewis would act as the generals' mentor throughout their stay; he would discourage them from visiting Germany, Holland and France and from associating with 'the enemies of Great Britain and other mischief makers'; and he would 'make them understand that England does not promise anything but she does it'.

Marks's sickbed diplomacy was frustrated by his partner's inertia. Though Marks had asked Lewis to make a special effort and to set aside his work if necessary, he did nothing of the sort. Lewis was recuperating at a sanatorium in Switzerland and was most reluctant to cut short his stay, though he did wire instructions to his London office to book the generals into Horrex's Hotel in the Strand. By the time Lewis returned to England, the generals had already left for the Continent.

Lewis was quite unrepentant about his failure to act on his partner's urgent request. 'As it happens I am rather glad I was not here to receive them, as I am sure that I could have done nothing with them, considering they had the best invitations and the finest reception which anyone could possibly wish for. Still they were stupid enough to treat everything lightly . . . I feel very sorry for them and the country generally as they have lost a great chance and opportunity.' Without the 'benefit' of Lewis's advice the generals made a series of what Marks thought were egregious blunders. They no sooner arrived in England than they left for Holland; they snubbed Chamberlain when he invited them to the naval review; and they put 'preposterous' demands to the British government. 'I expect that the old saying "Give them rope enough and they will hang themselves" will just suit them,' Marks noted in exasperation.[11]

The Transvaal to which the generals soon returned was one in the throes of a grand – if ultimately futile and illusory – experiment in social and political engineering. The High Commisioner and Governor of the Transvaal, Alfred Milner, a man of matchless arrogance, limitless confidence and self-righteousness, hoped to chain the conquered Republic to the British empire through a thoroughgoing reconstruction of its economic and social life. The Transvaal was to be recast as a loyal British colony by means of a tide of English immigration funded by a resurgent mining industry, stimulated in turn by efficient and honest government of the sort the Boers had conspicuously failed to provide before the war.

Sammy Marks, who had not escaped the tidal wave of jingoism that swept British South Africa during the war, had a profound admiration for Milner, whom he saw as indispensable if political stability was to be restored and British rule preserved in South Africa. When it was rumoured shortly before the end of the war that Milner would be sent home, Marks had written:

Well if this is done, it will be one of the greatest mistakes that the British Government ever made in South Africa, at least during the last 21 years since Paul Kruger got his country back. . . . If Lord Milner is taken away from South Africa, mark my words, within the next 15 years we will have another revolution here. Never mind how it will come about, come it will, and that, notwithstanding all that the English may do to nurse the Dutch, or all that they may give them, and in the next war I make bold to say that at least 3/4ths of the loyal British subjects in South Africa will join the Boers. Now this is perhaps saying a great deal, but mark my words, it will be so.

If Lord Milner is removed, no matter how able the statesman who succeeds him, it will take that statesman a very long time before he learns all the slimness of the Africander, and by that time the mischief will be done.[12]

A few months after the war Marks complained that Milner was not being given the full power and authority he needed to grapple with the country's great problems. As Marks wrote to a friend in Britain, Milner should be given full discretion to spend between five and ten million pounds without consulting anyone, and should be allowed, indeed made, to stay for the next five years.[13]

Marks's letter was passed on to Joseph Chamberlain. The Colonial Secretary was so incensed by its contents that he chose, contrary to his usual practice in cases of this sort, to respond at length, reading Marks a lesson in constitutional law – and in imperial arrogance and condescension – while at the same time explaining and defining his relationship with Lord Milner. Recalling his pre-war meetings with Marks, Chamberlain wrote: 'although I do not know him well, I recognize that he is both shrewd and energetic, and that he has an exceptional knowledge of South Africa. But this makes it all the more discouraging that he should understand so little of what is going on and should urge a policy which even the simplest of our home politicians would know to be impossible.' Marks's fear that Lord Milner was not being granted sufficient authority was quite unfounded, Chamberlain insisted, while Marks's call for Milner's appointment for at least five years was misdirected:

Now as a matter of fact Lord Milner has more power, and has been more strenuously supported from home, than any Governor at any period of our history. After all, the Home Government, unless it is to be a mere puppet, must have its own opinions, and occasionally express and even insist upon them. But I have so much confidence in Lord Milner's wisdom and discretion, that I have given him a free hand in all minor matters, and in every important case I accept his views unless the very strongest reasons prevent me from doing so. It is my firm conviction that the best thing for South Africa would be that the High Commissioner should remain in office say as long as Lord Cromer has done in Egypt: but this does not rest with me – it rests with Lord Milner himself and hitherto he has warned me again and again, that he will not be ready to stay in South Africa for more than a limited time. I cannot, as Mr. Marks appears to think, 'make' him stay. . . .

Marks's suggestion that Milner be given free rein to spend as he pleased was plainly unconstitutional. 'I cannot admit that anyone, even Lord Milner, can be allowed to spend five or ten millions, or even five or ten thousands, without consulting the Secretary of State who has the responsibility of defending the expenditure to the House of Commons. It is necessary that I should know and approve of what is going on, but subject to this, Lord Milner's recommendations have great weight with me and in the matter of expenditure I do not think he has even [sic] been refused anything for which he has asked.' [14]

Marks's high regard for Milner survived all the difficulties and disappointments of the years that followed, all the sobering realities of Milner's governorship of the Transvaal. In all Marks's years in South Africa, he wrote at the end of Milner's term of office, Britain had only twice had 'sound and able representatives' in South Africa – Sir Bartle Frere, the aggressive High Commissioner whom he had met in Kimberley in the 1870s and for whom he had conceived an enduring esteem, and Lord Milner. Milner 'richly' deserved all the praise showered on him at his farewell: 'He has had endless worry and anxiety since Lord Kitchener left, he has done lots of excellent work and it is but right that this should meet with recognition by us. There are grumblers here but these can be found all the world over. . . .' [15]

Milner in turn regarded Marks with a certain fondness tempered with cynicism and upper-class condescension. After returning to England, Milner wrote: 'I *do* want Sammy to come over here, and go to Windsor like the rest of his tribe. It really would be the proper crown to his career and I should like him to have that triumph, for he is not a bad little fellow and the best "Vicar of Bray" I ever remember' .(Milner's snide and snobbish reference was to King Edward VII's notorious friendships with Jewish financiers like Sir Ernest Cassel and the Sassoons.) [16]

Marks was in broad sympathy with Milnerism, the pacification and anglicisation of the Transvaal and its comprehensive reconstruction along modern lines. He had been swept along by the currents of chauvinist passion that flowed so strongly during the war, and had emerged at the end 'a great Jingo' whose views on the dangers of a Boer revival were indistinguishable from those of any Milnerite. Milner's close attention to the needs of the mining industry and the importance he attached to the modernisation of farming inevitably appealed to Marks as a colliery-owner and a progressive farmer. He was an ardent

supporter of the government's new agricultural department and a keen advocate
of the importation of Chinese labour, the remedy Milner adopted for the severe
post-war labour shortage that threatened the success of Milnerism.[17]

While Marks admired Milner and approved of Milnerism, he was annoyed by
Milner's young men. He clearly found the Kindergarten – the coterie of young
Oxonian enthusiasts which the High Commissioner gathered around himself –
and the style of administration they imposed, a trial of his patience and
composure. Their insistence on proper bureaucratic form was particularly
irksome after the cosy rough-and-readiness of Krugerite administration. Marks
had flourished in an environment where officials could be persuaded to overlook
procedure; Milner's young men could not. 'The new service', he complained in
mid-1902, 'is full of young men just out from England, and every one is more
anxious than his neighbour to shew how clever he is. Consequently if it is only
a farthings worth of business, they make as much noise about it as if it were a
million pounds worth. It is therefore useless to expect anything like reasonable
treatment at their hands.'[18] Two further years of punctilious administration by
Milner's young men only strengthened this perception. In late 1904 he wrote:
'the young Officials in our Government here are trying their level best to give
the public trouble in every possible way, and are always on the look out for
mistakes in documents and will kick up a row even if they should come across
an undotted "i" or an unstroked "t".'[19]

Ultimately Marks came to terms with the new style of administration.
Reflecting some years later on the metamorphosis in government after the
British conquest, Marks told Lewis, who hoped to postpone their company
meetings, 'I wish you would begin to realize that this country is now under the
British flag and that the laws have to be complied with. There is no going to
interview the Registrar of Companies and other officials, as might have been
done in days of old, and asking them to grant us time beyond the period
prescribed by law in which to hold our meetings because this is the wish of Lewis
and Marks London. The law is there and must be complied with. . . .'[20]

For all these reservations, Marks nevertheless continued to court government
officials as he had before the war, 'to humour them up to a point and nurse
them'. Thus, when Sir Hamilton Goold-Adams, the Lieutenant-Governor of
the Orange River Colony, went 'home' on leave, Marks expected Lewis to pay
him a call and invite him for a day's shooting at Lewis's country estate. 'You will
find him a very nice man, and I find it is always best to be friendly with such
people, and to shew them a little attention, they like it.'[21]

Marks also worked at persuading his old friends to accept the new order,
making a number of attempts to bring the Boer leaders together with the new
masters of the country. When Joseph Chamberlain toured South Africa early in
1903, Marks encouraged Botha and De la Rey to take a Boer deputation to
Bloemfontein in order to meet the Colonial Secretary. On the basis of 'a very
nice and satisfactory talk' with Chamberlain in Pretoria, Marks had come to the
conclusion that the Colonial Secretary was more willing to compromise on Boer
demands than he had been prepared to admit at earlier interviews with the Boer
leaders. But Botha and De la Rey should see 'that our burghers who will meet

Mr. Chamberlain will not press upon him or ask too much from him. As you know an Englishman does not like it too well to be constantly told what he should do.' If necessary, Marks would meet the costs of the deputation. The suggestion, like so many others Marks made, was not taken up.[22]

Marks also attempted to bring De la Rey and Milner together. He made overtures to the Boer general on the High Commissioner's behalf and tried to persuade him, it seems, to drop his strong reservations about Milner.[23]

Lord Milner left South Africa in early 1905. As a parting token his secretary sent Marks a photograph of the great man; in return, Marks placed twelve boxes of fruit aboard ship for Milner to enjoy on the voyage home. The unevenness of this exchange and its indirectness epitomise their relationship during Milner's years in the Transvaal; Marks had admired the High Commissioner from afar, for Milner's aloof and austere manner had not invited or encouraged any intimacy.[24]

His successsor was to be more approachable, though. The Earl of Selborne, who was affable and cordial by nature, welcomed Marks's advances. Marks had first encountered the future High Commissioner on his visit to London in 1896. Then Under-Secretary of State for the Colonies, Selborne had sat behind Chamberlain when Marks and Piet Grobler were interviewed at the Colonial Office. Marks was quite taken with Selborne, who 'appeared to have a frank, honest, open countenance'. Four years later, when the war seemed to be at an end, and arrangements were being made for the administration of the conquered territories, Marks suggested that Lewis whisper in influential ears that Selborne would be the best possible choice as administrator of the Transvaal and Orange River colonies.[25]

Before Lord and Lady Selborne sailed for South Africa in 1905, Marks sent advice through a well-connected friend: 'he [Selborne] should always be very careful to treat the Boers very kindly but strictly, he must be very friendly with them, be as much as possible accessible to them and not let them feel that he is accustomed to move in a higher sphere. If he will do this, there is a strong probability that he will gain their confidence and possibly later on their co-operation.' Marks also included advice for Lady Selborne. 'Here as in other parts of the world woman's influence will carry great weight, even in the realm of politics.' To assist her husband's task of reconciliation, she should establish an orphanage for Boer children.[26]

Whether on the advice of Marks, or others, or through personal inclination, the new Governor chose a conciliatory course. From the start he was more accessible than his predecessor and made a deliberate effort to court the locals, both Boer and Brit. Meeting Marks again, he 'cordially invited' him 'to have a chat'.[27] Marks and Selborne spent a long weekend together on the Vereeniging property in August 1905. Saturday was spent shooting on one of the farms, a privilege the company reserved for the important few. On Sunday they visited the Maccauvlei plantation, for Selborne shared Marks's enthusiasm for silviculture. On Monday they inspected Vereeniging, but, according to an onlooker, Selborne seemed less than impressed with the township, which was still largely unbuilt.[28]

During the weekend Marks 'had ample opportunity for discussing several matters' with the Governor. As he had with Lord Roberts a few years before, Marks grasped the chance to press his favourite schemes. Selborne listened attentively. When Marks suggested that the government grant a bonus to encourage farmers to plant trees suitable for railway sleepers, he took careful note. 'Now I never neglect a good suggestion,' he subsequently wrote, 'and therefore I followed yours up.' Patrick Duncan (Colonial Secretary of the Transvaal), the agricultural department and the government's railway committee were all instructed to report. After detailed consideration and a visit by Duncan to the Vaal River plantation, the idea was finally dropped. The money, it was felt, would be better spent on state forestry schemes.[29]

Selborne's charm and attentiveness won Marks completely. As he wrote to General De la Rey soon after the Vereeniging weekend, 'although as you know I thought a lot of Lord Milner, I have come to the conclusion that Lord Selborne is a better man.' [30]

During the weekend there was much discussion apparently of the need for reconciliation between Boer and Brit. At the request of Selborne, who was anxious to woo his reluctant Afrikaner subjects, Marks suggested to his old friend De la Rey that he accompany the Governor for part of a tour he planned of the western districts of the Transvaal. Given the tragic recent history of the country and De la Rey's pre-eminence within the resurgent Afrikaner political movement, this was a highly sensitive invitation. Selborne counted upon Marks's tact and discretion to avoid any embarrassment, either to the government or to De la Rey: 'It would give me much pleasure to have the opportunity of getting to know General Delarey better, but I do not want either to ask him to do something which he is not prepared to do or put him in the position of having to refuse a suggestion which however indirectly might seem to emanate from myself. . . . Perhaps neither of us would be the worse for getting to know each other better.'[31] Marks, a great believer in the value of personal encounters of this kind, was eager to oblige. 'Now my dear Koos,' he wrote, 'take it from me that it is essentially necessary that you should meet and speak openly.' After a show of reluctance, De la Rey agreed.[32]

This was the first of a number of services Marks performed for the High Commissioner. Selborne drew on Marks for information about industrial and agricultural matters and clearly valued his advice. He tried to persuade him to serve on a government commission investigating the establishment of a land bank for the Transvaal, but Marks, whose hands were already full simply coping with the affairs of a firm passing through hard times, managed to dodge this.[33] Selborne was more successful in tapping Marks's generosity than his time. He was effusively grateful for a promise of £1,000 for a personal project on which he had 'set his heart', the provision of accommodation for young Transvalers who wished to study at the government's new experimental farms. 'I thank you; again I thank you and mean it,' he wrote.[34]

Marks, in turn, took business problems to Selborne, who attempted to be helpful whenever he could. When it was rumoured that the Natal collieries were to be allowed into Vereeniging Estates' traditional market, Marks took the matter directly to Selborne, who presided over the committee that set the all-important railway rates on the carriage of coal. When a scheme to settle blacks from Bechuanaland on Marks's farms in the Marico district was held up by the Commissioner of Native Affairs, Marks went over his head to Selborne; the Governor suggested a way of circumventing his own official.

Again, when Marks went hunting for railway coal contracts, he spoke to Selborne, whose response was an enigmatic smile. This smile sparked a minor flare-up within the firm. Lewis's cynical response – 'I don't wonder at the smile for I have been fed with this medicine for a very long time' – angered Marks. 'You . . . rubbed me up a little about that smile!!' he complained. 'All that I want is that when you do dictate your letters that you should take into consideration that I am, I think, seven years older than you, and that I am not yet 95, or in my second childhood.'[35]

The Marks–Selborne friendship was oiled by invitations to Government House in Pretoria, which were much appreciated by Bertha Marks, and by gifts of fruit about which the Governor was highly enthusiastic. 'I can honestly say that I do not think I have ever tasted better fruit than yours,' he wrote thanking Marks for one such gift. When Lady Selborne enquired on another occasion about the kind of grape Marks had given her, he sent her cuttings of hanepoot for planting in her garden at Government House. At Marks's invitation the Selbornes visited Zwartkoppies on 7 February 1906. Describing what he felt had been 'a very nice day', Marks wrote to Colonel Hamilton, a wartime friend, that the weather had been perfect, not too hot, and that 'everything was looking its best'. The grass was green after the recent rains and the trees were loaded with fruit. The visitors had seen the improvements and additions Marks had made to Zwartkoppies since Hamilton's wartime calls. Marks had built a new dam to expand the farm's water supply and had acquired a 'fleet' of rowing boats which had been specially ordered from England: 'although I am not a Navy man I have three fine boats on my lake and nine beautiful English Swans. That will tell you we are getting a little civilized, but there was plenty of room!!' Marks was particularly keen to show Selborne – like himself, a gentleman farmer with a passion for agricultural improvement – the orange trees at his nearby Pienaarspoort farm. Shortly before the war he had planted these on an experimental basis and had found that they thrived locally; he now proposed the government distribute orange trees amongst the farmers of the Transvaal.[36]

Selborne also helped Marks to engineer his greatest social coup: a shooting party in August 1907 for the visiting Crown Prince of Portugal on Marks's estate at the Vaal. The royal party included the Portuguese Minister of Colonies and the Governor-General of Mozambique as well as Lord Selborne and General Smuts representing the Transvaal government, all gentlemen whom Marks was eager to woo. It excluded Sir Hamilton Goold-Adams, who felt it was inappropriate for the Lieutenant-Governor of the Orange River Colony to accept an invitation to a shoot in the closed season, but who nevertheless instructed his officials to turn a blind eye to this breach of the regulations.

The day was a 'great success'. Marks, who never carried a gun, watched as the prince shot at buck in comfort, from a spider at a distance of about 300 yards, before a splendid lunch at a luxurious camp Marks had set up on the farm Schaapplaats on the Vereeniging Estates property. Congratulating Marks afterwards, Selborne said that the arrangements had been 'perfect' and that the prince had 'thoroughly' enjoyed himself. Marks, who found the prince 'a very nice, staightforward, gentlemanly, young fellow', arranged, at his request, to have two of the buck-heads cured and mounted at the museum in Pretoria and sent on to him. Bertha missed out on Sammy's encounter with royalty. For reasons of health, she was wintering in Durban. 'What swells we are getting mixing so much with Royalty,' she wrote half-teasingly, half-enviously to her husband, the one-time pedlar. 'He [the Crown Prince] is to be here on August 24. You might as you are so pally with him, tell him your wife is at the Marine [Hotel] so that he may honour me with a word. It seems a pity that I am to miss the chance of bowing to His Highness.' She encouraged her husband, no dancer, to attend the state reception at Government House. 'You ought to go to the Ball at the Selbornes. You need not dance. But I am sure you would spend a pleasant hour chatting with your chums Lord Selborne and His Royal Highness to say nothing of Lady S.' The Crown Prince never received the buck-heads; he was assassinated a few month's after his visit to Vereeniging Estates.[37]

Marks's enthusiasm for Lord Selborne was unbounded. When it seemed Selborne might be replaced after the Liberals came into power in England in 1905, Marks asked Sivewright – now living in retirement in Scotland – to canvass his influential friends on the High Commissioner's behalf. 'I have already told you more than once and I can only repeat it that the British Government could not send out a better man to represent them here, and to bring all the Races into accord as quietly and nicely as Lord Selborne is doing, and according to my way of thinking it would be an absolute crime to remove him at present, or even to suggest such a thing.'[38]

This enthusiasm for Selborne, however, disguised a quiet shift in Marks's political position. While he had supported Milnerism immediately after the war and while he greatly admired Milner's successor, Marks's political allegiances had begun to mutate secretly as a resurgent Afrikanerdom, mobilised by his old friends, the Boer generals, moved closer to power in the mid-1900s. The reasons are not made explicit in his correspondence. It can be presumed, though, that these were partly sentimental but largely pragmatic. Unlike most of his fellow mining magnates, who staunchly resisted the rise of Afrikaner power, Marks had close personal ties with the Boer leaders – intimate ties which predated and survived the war and which would have made him more sympathetic than most to the Afrikaner cause once he had shaken off his wartime jingoist fever. Marks also seems to have believed that the Afrikaners were somehow the natural rulers of the country. Asked, in 1904, for his views about the future of the Transvaal by his wartime friend, Colonel Hubert Hamilton, Marks wrote: 'Well the present Dutchman, his father and his grandfather were born in the country and were its pioneers and half civilized it, and I think his children, grand children and great grand children will have to be the rulers of the country. I am not now speaking as a Dutchman or as an Africander but I tell you what I can see is going to happen.'[39]

Marks, the supreme pragmatist, an opportunist with finely tuned political antennae, seems to have sensed well before less sensitive observers the seismic shift which was soon to occur in the Transvaal Colony: the substitution of Het Volkism – of Afrikaner power – for Milnerism. Marks's network of friendships with both leading and less prominent Boers meant that he was better placed than most other magnates, including his partner Isaac Lewis, to observe what was happening on the ground.

Marks's metamorphosis was gradual and was concealed even from his partner at first. Isaac Lewis had long been opposed to Marks or the firm taking an active part in politics. Indeed, they had largely avoided doing so, restricting their involvement to a secret subscription in 1905 of £1,000, in the company of other mining houses, to the Transvaal Progressive Association, the political organi- sation formed to further imperial and capitalist interests in the Transvaal. But Lewis changed mind when, in 1906, the recently elected Liberal government in England, eager to reduce imperial commitments in South Africa and to conciliate the Boers, promised to grant responsible government – self- government – to the Transvaal. As the elections approached for the first parliament of the Transvaal Colony, it seemed to Lewis that it might be in the interests of his firm to secure parliamentary representation:

our interests there are very large and they never required greater safeguarding than they do now and will continue to require in the near future when the new parliament holds sway there . . . there must be a means whereby we can have someone to watch and protect our interests also. The change in the political conditions in South Africa during recent years is such that we must make our voice heard and felt in the inner-most Councils where decisions are often come to which are of material interest to us, and I think it can but add a powerful weight to your own power and efforts if we can have someone who could make himself a factor to be reckoned with in the new Assembly.'[40]

Other firms, large and small, were scrambling for places in parliament. Ought not Lewis and Marks to have its bloc of representatives to protect its extensive interests and to 'secure a voice in the management of the country's affairs'? The obvious candidates were J. N. de Jongh, chairman of Vereeniging Estates and currently president of the Chamber of Mines, a highly respected figure, described by no less than Lord Selborne as 'the best man I have met in Johannesburg to talk with'; Sir Edwin Dunning, managing director of African and European, Lewis and Marks's land company; Isaac Lewis's son Henry who was doing a stint in the firm's Johannesburg office; and of course, Marks himself. One of these should stand for Vereeniging, which Lewis urged should be declared a separate electoral division. He clearly felt that the firm was entitled to its own pocket borough, a notion which arose out of his view, not entirely mistaken, that Transvaal politics was a matter of spoils and special interests. Lewis took it for granted that his firm's representatives would line up in parliament with the group most closely identified with the mining industry – 'if we ally ourselves with any party there is only one with which we can identify ourselves that is the English Progressive.' He himself spoke to Sir George

Farrar, the mining magnate who led the Transvaal Progressive Association, and Farrar promised to support any candidate Lewis and Marks nominated.[41]

Marks took up the idea that Vereeniging form an independent electoral division with his friend Lord Selborne. But he was unenthusiastic about the rest of the proposal and found all sorts of excuses for inaction, much to Lewis's annoyance. Marks argued that politics was time-consuming and expensive, and that overt involvement in politics in the Transvaal inevitably meant making enemies, something Marks instinctively avoided wherever possible: 'in this country it is not as it is in Europe, because here if you do not agree with anybody in Politics he is your enemy.' Placing an employee in parliament would be a costly exercise. The firm would still have to meet his salary 'and moreover it would be necessary for him to be able to spend a little money'. Besides, it was more than likely that 'we should derive very little benefit from him'.[42]

The true reason for Marks's reluctance only emerged after much prodding: his political sympathies had shifted in a direction diametrically opposed to his partner's. 'For myself, personally, I do not wish to join any party. The Party which I would join, if any, would be Het Volk, but as my business does not allow me to do so, I can stand and look on and laugh at them all. My ambition is not a politician and meetings, Public and Private, I do not attend like a good many in Johannesburg.' But Marks had not counted on his partner's flexibility or his cynical pragmatism, nor on the strength of his conviction that the firm should be properly represented in parliament, nor indeed on his fatherly pride. To secure a seat for his son Henry as an independent, Isaac was willing to make an electoral arrangement with the Boers' Het Volk party. For the sake of parliamentary representation for the firm he was equally willing to see his partner Sammy take a seat in the legislature as a representative of Het Volk. He urged Marks by cable to take up a seat he had been offered by the Boer party.[43]

Marks cabled a terse reply three days before Christmas: 'Saml. Marks unfit any position. Wish you all compliments of season.' The letter that followed elaborated: 'Regarding myself it is out of the question. Whenever I will take a hand in Politics (and I am afraid I am already too old in the season) I shall want to follow out my own ideas absolutely, and as my ideas do not agree with those of my friends I must leave it alone rather than put myself into a false position.' As for Isaac's son Henry, he would be pulled to pieces on a public platform. 'It is not only education a man wants to attract the public, he wants cheek and confidence.' Lewis gave up: 'under the circumstances, as you have shown such passive resistance to all our efforts, I have decided to take no part in the coming political campaign but to hold aloof. . . .'[44]

Marks's switch of allegiances was covert. He gave little public indication that he now supported Het Volk. When asked to lend his endorsement to the Progressive candidate in Heidelberg, the constituency that included Vereeniging, he was deliberately evasive and gave no indication where his political heart now lay. At the same time he seems to have encouraged Jan Smuts to believe that Het Volk could count on his tacit support in this constituency. With or without this, Het Volk won the constituency, and the 1907 election as a whole. Sammy Marks's old friends, the Boer generals, Botha and Smuts, took office in the

Transvaal just short of five years after the peace conference at Vereeniging. Their change of fortunes was as dramatic as Marks's shift of allegiances. In less than a decade these had come full circle: between 1899 and 1907 Milner's favourite Vicar of Bray had swung from Krugerism through Milnerism to Het Volkism, an impressive feat of political acrobatics.[45]

Marks's greatest social coup – a shooting party for the Crown Prince of Portugal on his Vaal River estate on 19 August 1908 (Photo: Sammy Marks Museum)

IX

Reconstructing the Business,
1902–1908

Alfred Milner's reconstruction of the Transvaal after the South African War had its parallel within Lewis and Marks. In the half-decade after Vereeniging, Sammy Marks faced the task of rebuilding a business which had been largely predicated on the political and economic order that Lord Milner and the war had swept away. More than most Transvaal magnates, Marks had been the beneficiary of Krugerism. His industrial ventures in particular had depended on the South African Republic's controversial blend of state-supported monopoly, tariff protection, and pliable administration. In the post-war period Marks faced a government which was essentially incorruptible and which rejected the pre-war industrial concessions policy outright. The new government reversed the priorities of the old. Kruger had favoured non-mining concerns over the gold-mining industry, which he saw as a threat to the continued independence of the Transvaal. Milner, on the other hand, saw the mining industry as his chief ally in consolidating British control over the Transvaal; its needs, therefore, took precedence over those of manufacturing industry. Marks was obliged to restructure his business to take account of these new realities.

As the war drew to an end, the Transvaal property market came back to life. The prospect of peace and of a prosperous and progressive Transvaal under benign British rule led to a land boom with soaring property prices. In the first two months of 1902 alone, values rocketed by between 50 and 100 per cent. Marks had anticipated the land rush. In August 1901 he asked his partner's authorisation to re-enter the land market for soon there would be bargains aplenty as Boers returning from the war were forced to sell off their farms to raise funds for their immediate needs.[1]

For once, Lewis readily agreed. Despite mounting reservations as prices accelerated, Marks, with the approval of his partner, bought and bought, mainly in the western Transvaal where they focussed their purchasing before the war. By September 1902 he had added 52,000 morgen to their portfolio, had spent in the region of £50,000 and was still buying, aiming to push up the total to £60,000.[2]

While Lewis approved of Marks's farm purchases, he was less enthusiastic about his partner's schemes for redeveloping their extensive portfolio of urban properties. The firm held potentially valuable sites throughout central Pretoria; embarrassingly, these were occupied by what Marks himself described as 'shanties'. As urban renewal began in wartime Pretoria, so pressure was brought to bear on Marks by the authorities to erect more suitable structures. 'It is pointed out here that L & M have the best building sites and yet the most ramshackle buildings in the town.' Marks was warned that unless he did something, the authorities would refuse to renew the trading licences of his tenants. Lewis was unperturbed; the loss of the tiny rental income from these properties was no great threat. As he wrote of Marks's suggestion: 'we must not worry about this at the moment. We must go in for other business which is more profitable at the present moment. The stands will not run away, and we can discuss the question of building later on.'[3]

Marks, who by his own admission was 'very fond of bricks and mortar', in the same way that Lewis was a stocks and shares man, was not prepared to wait, and chose to go it alone and develop some of his personal property. Marks owned a choice site opposite Pretoria's Market Square, occupied by old iron buildings, which brought in a paltry monthly rental of £30. He now proposed to build a row of shops and a theatre, modelled on those he had seen in London. 'The latter is badly wanted here as there is not a decent one in the town,' he wrote. 'The situation is a very good one for a theatre as the position is a very central one for most of the better class of people who live at Sunnyside and Arcadia.'

To raise the £24,000–£28,000 he needed, Marks instructed Lewis to sell off his holdings of the stocks 'of paltry Foreign Governments, which are always more or less risky'. In an age when capital moved freely across international boundaries, Brazilian, Chilean, and Chinese bonds paid for a building in central Pretoria. Construction began in 1902. Nothing came of the theatre project, but the shops, in all their original redbrick and sandstone charm, still stand across Church Street from the State Opera House.[4]

All of these investments were in commercial and office developments; Marks had a dread of residential property. 'When a shop is once let you have very little trouble with it, but in the case of a private house, one tenant comes in, and by and by he goes away leaving the place infested with bugs and other such undesirables, while the paper has been torn off the walls etc. etc. Another tenant comes in and repeats the operation, and all the profits are swallowed up keeping the house in repair.'[5]

At the end of the war Marks also invested heavily at the Cape. The city had boomed during the war because of the presence of the imperial army, and property had fetched 'fabulous prices'. Persuaded that this would last, Marks paid £23,000 to round off the block opposite the Cape parliament he had begun to assemble before the war. By his own admission, he paid at least £7,000 more than the property was worth, so keen was he to complete his block.[6]

Marks commissioned Herbert Baker's firm to redesign his Muizenberg holiday home. The alterations the fashionable architect made were less than modest. The plans show a double-storey house that was a far cry from the simplicity of Rhodes's nearby seaside cottage. Baker provided for three rooms downstairs for the white servants, and one for the blacks; a pantry, a larder and a scullery; a large hall, a dining-room for the adults and a separate one for the children; upstairs rooms for the governess and the lady's maid, plus three for the family, besides a night nursery and a separate day nursery. Bertha Marks was rather startled when she inspected the house in June 1902. She felt it was a great pity Baker had not sent the plans to Pretoria. There were several features which would surely displease her husband, including a porch which 'looks large enough for a Castle and quite out of place'.[7]

Bertha was mistaken, for later that same year Baker was commissioned to design an imposing, seven-storey office building for the site opposite parliament Marks had assembled at such great expense. Before finalising the plans, the architect discussed these with the High Commissioner's office in Johannesburg. As the premises were so well placed, Baker and Marks hoped that the Crown would lease them as the Cape agency of the governments of the Transvaal and Orange River colonies. Milner indicated that he might be interested if the terms were reasonable; given the advantages of having such a tenant, he felt that Marks should be satisfied with £750 per annum.[8]

During these hopeful times Marks also took a close interest in the development of Milnerton, the township across Table Bay in which he had invested before the war. He went by cart to inspect the estate in November 1903 and was much impressed. He came away convinced that within five years there would be many hundreds of houses on the site, for Cape Town was 'pressing itself out' in that direction. The beach in the centre of the property had 'a great future for the simple reason that it is better adapted for sea bathing than Muizenberg'. In view of this, he felt the South African Breweries, in which his firm had a large stake, should buy a site for a hotel; this would ensure that it was first in a very promising field. While Marks thought more of Milnerton than of Muizenberg, he nevertheless gave some consideration to the development of the windy False Bay resort. He showed interest in an ambitious scheme to convert the vlei at Muizenberg into an ornamental lake, suitable for boat racing and swimming contests. Linked to the sea by a tidal channel, it would be flanked by a grand esplanade. The scheme never materialised. It was overtaken by the commercial recession which set in at the Cape once the war-end boom petered out.[9]

Meanwhile Marks continued to add farms to the firm's property portfolio after the great Transvaal land rush of 1902 died down. By 1904 the firm held an 'enormous number of farms', and ranked in the top five of private landowners in the Transvaal. But for all its impressive size, the portfolio failed to produce sufficient income to pay even the quitrent on the properties. 'You will admit', Lewis wrote to Marks, 'this is not business.' The root of the problem lay in the recent war which had devastated the white farming community, while allowing their black tenants to throw off the control farmers had formerly exercised over them, and to accumulate wealth through employment in the imperial war effort

and through seizure of Boer cattle. As Marks wrote to Lewis after a tour of
inspection of their western Transvaal farms:

At the outset I must tell you that we cannot receive any adequate return for the present.
The farmers are impoverished to a degree almost inconceivable, they possess hardly any
cattle and, in the majority of cases, three or four families can only muster about 7 bullocks
between them to enable them to carry on work.

In those parts of the country visited by the troops, all buildings were demolished, and
where the troops did not go, the buildings were rendered useless by the Kaffirs, even
those living on the farms participating in the destruction, who took away every piece of
woodwork, door, windows and roofs. I know of cases where farmers had costly and
comfortable houses which today are total wrecks.

The white tenants were in no position to pay their rents, the black tenants in no
mood to do so:

As to the Natives, they are in many cases affluent, they have plenty of cattle and are
therefore able to plough at their will. They have become quite unmanageable and
absolutely free and appear to have come to the conclusion that, as they live under the
British flag, the whole country and everything in it are at their disposal. I have
determined to do my utmost to remedy this state of affairs and have already approached
the Attorney General. . . . [10]

A way had to be found to turn the farm portfolio to account. In early 1904 Lewis
and Marks decided to place all their farms in an investment company which
could be marketed on the stock exchange. By doing so, the firm would
strengthen its financial position but at the same time retain control over the
assets.

The African and European Investment Company was registered in mid-1904
and held its first board meeting on 6 September. The Lewis and Marks
partnership sold it 716,442 acres (1,119 square miles) of farm land, much of it in
the western Transvaal, the region Marks had long believed was the most
promising in the country. The prospectus claimed that the ground, which had
'been most carefully selected', had 'great mineral prospects' as well as
'agricultural value . . . owing to the abundance of water and the rich quality of
the soil'. In addition, the partnership sold the public company large blocs of
shares in the Vereeniging Estates, the Swazieland Corporation, and in its mining
investments on the east and south Rand, shares which were not otherwise
marketable in an increasingly depressed share market. In return, Lewis and
Marks as the vendors received £1,000,000 in fully paid shares, representing
two-thirds of the nominal capital of the Investment Company. As founders of
the company, they also claimed the right to one quarter of all future dividend
payments once the shareholders had received dividends equal to the face value
of their shares. Founders' rights of this sort were a controversial aspect of
Transvaal flotations at this time. [11]

Besides expanding and restructuring the partnership's property holdings,
Sammy also struggled, less successfully, to reconstruct Lewis and Marks's
industrial interests during this period. The Eerste Fabrieken complex had been
a casualty of the South African War. From the start of the conflict it was badly

affected by the departure of many of its skilled workmen and by the general disruption of business. When the British occupied Pretoria in June 1900, they closed the distillery, the centre-piece of the complex. With business at a standstill and much time on their hands, Lewis and Marks had an opportunity to reconsider the future of their industrial operations. Isaac Lewis was determined that they should abandon once and for all the unprofitable petty industries they had established at Hatherley to please Kruger and the pre-war ruling elite. Writing of the jam factory, Lewis noted: 'I trust . . . that on no account will you authorise restarting manufacturing again, as we have already had quite enough of this class of business and have no intention of resuming same. We must try to direct our efforts and energies in other directions where the chances of profit are more reasonable.' Given the shaky performance of the Eerste Fabrieken in the years between the Jameson Raid and the war, Marks could hardly disagree. After the war he supervised the lengthy and tedious process of selling off the remaining stock of the factories, renting out the premises and liquidating the companies.[12]

Despite these disappointments, Marks had not yet given up on his dream of local industrialisation. Twelve weeks after the Peace of Vereeniging, Marks set out a scheme for the promotion of industry in the Transvaal and sent it to a friend in Britain – William Bailey of the Irish Land Commission, whom Marks had entertained at Zwartkoppies before the war – with the request that he pass it on to their mutual friend, John Morley, one of the leading figures in the Liberal Party. Morley, in turn, was to hand it on to Lord Rosebery, the former Liberal prime minister. There was nothing modest about Marks's scheme: he proposed that the British government ('which is practically Mr. Chamberlain') subsidise the industrialisation of the Transvaal on a massive scale. In order to overcome the reluctance of private individuals to invest in anything other than mining, Whitehall should offer to match, on a pound for pound basis, investments by British and colonial entrepreneurs in establishing factories and in importing the necessary workmen. These should preferably all be British as should be all the machinery. This would be 'of great assistance in bringing about that which we all desire, namely, the peopling of this country with English people'. At the same time it would help British manufacturers secure the South African market against their robust foreign business rivals. German, Belgian, American and even Japanese travellers, he warned, were busily canvassing orders locally. Marks was playing, quite explicitly, on current fears that Britain had begun to lag behind its commercial competitors.

The centre-piece of the state-aided industrial scheme would be an iron foundry. It would cost no more than £500,000 and would be assured of profitability. 'It is no use saying that a business of this kind would not pay,' Marks wrote to a friend in England, 'as I am positive it would.' Marks anticipated that the country would grow rapidly over the next ten years: £25–£27 million would be invested in mining within a 50-mile radius of the Rand as well as large sums on railway construction further afield. As a result, there would be a very large market, at good prices, for the products of the iron foundry. Without the burden of high transport expenses which multiplied the costs of imported iron and steel, the iron foundry would enjoy a handsome profit margin. Once established, the foundry could branch out in various directions. Why not, for example, manufacture the large iron pots that hundreds of thousands of natives used to cook their food? And talking of the large black population, why not establish a factory to manufacture blankets? South Africa exported thousands of bales of wool annually, then imported tens of thousands of blankets, mostly made in Germany from old bags 'and all kinds of rubbish. . . . Here is another industry waiting to be taken in hand.'[13]

Marks's industrial programme, together with his thoughts on the indispensability of Lord Milner, was passed along to the man he thought was the dominant figure in the British government: Joseph Chamberlain, the Colonial Secretary, himself once a leading industrialist and screw manufacturer. It received the same rough treatment as his suggestion that Lord Milner be allowed a free hand in South Africa. Just as Marks was castigated for his apparent ignorance of British constitutional practice, so he was chastised for his naïveté about political economy. Marks's suggestion that 'the Home Government . . . should add to all its other labours the work of starting new industries in South Africa' was patently absurd, or at least so it seemed in an age when state ownership of industry was still anathema, at least in *laissez-faire* England: 'Now, really from a man of Mr. Marks' capacity this is a suggestion which destroys all hope that even the most intelligent colonists will ever be able to understand anything of the principles of colonial administration.' While Chamberlain accepted that the railways in South Africa would be operated by the state, 'to add to this the work of starting factories, which, once begun, would be a precedent for similar work in a hundred different trades, is a policy which no man of the slightest experience either of business or of Government could possibly defend.'

Turning the tables, Chamberlain issued a challenge to Marks and his fellow capitalists.

Why don't the financiers who have made millions in South Africa themselves engage in businesses which, he says, are certain to pay if they were well managed? If the Government were to touch them, all private effort would be discouraged. Accordingly I will have nothing to do with any proposal of the kind. The industrial development of a country must be left to private enterprise. There is no lack either of brains or of money. My business is to secure peace, order, and security, and individual effort must supply the rest. If the present capitalists of South Africa are so helpless that they will not undertake work which lies at their doors and which would give them a good profit, I do not wonder that foreigners come in great numbers to pick up the opportunities which they let fall.

Chamberlain ended with a final swipe at Marks and other impertinent colonials who dared to venture grandiose suggestions for the future development of their country.

Downing Street is doing its best. We are engaged in promoting emigration, agriculture, and indirectly other industrial enterprises. No suggestion from any quarter is neglected, although for one practical proposal we have to wade through a hundred propositions which seem to us to come from a lunatic asylum.

The real fact is that the man on the spot is always parochial and never able to take a broad view of the situation but only to see his own particular interests and to promote his own very often crude ideas.

I have written a long letter contrary to my custom, but that is evidence of the importance I attach to Colonial opinion even when I think it entirely mistaken.[14]

In mid-1903 Marks visited England for the first time since the start of the war. While his first priority was to consult his partner and to see his children at school in England, he also used the opportunity to explore his iron and steel scheme, travelling to Sheffield to consult with the local iron-masters. In London he discussed the project with Leo Weinthal, 'Leo the Liar', editor of a pro-Kruger Pretoria newspaper before the war and now the proprietor of a London weekly, *The African World and Cape to Cairo Express*, devoted to the promotion of Rhodes's great vision of a British Africa. Weinthal introduced Marks to A. de Vere Hunt, a company promoter, who spoke airily of establishing a large iron and steel works in South Africa, and of sending out experts to identify suitable iron-ore deposits. By his own admission, Marks had a weakness for chancers; Nellmapius is only the most obvious example of this.

Isaac Lewis, mindful perhaps of Marks's pre-war opinion that 'Mr. Weinthal is a fool, a liar, and he is deceiptful [sic]', was impressed neither with the promoters, nor with the scheme itself. Writing at a stage when the economic outlook in South Africa was deteriorating, Lewis felt the time was not yet ripe for large industrial projects of this sort, which stood little chance of making a profit. 'Therefore, for the present it would be better to look after the things we have got at work and try to make them as successful and profitable as possible.' Despite this douche of cold water, Marks nevertheless went on dreaming and hoping, convinced that 'in the end an iron and steel Factory here is bound to be a success'.[15]

Meanwhile he had to contend with the effects of a deepening regional economic recession. His Cape properties were particularly hard hit. He very much regretted having committed himself to the costly office project opposite parliament, but he felt that as a contract had been signed and building was already under way, this would have to be completed. With so much of his money tied up in this venture, it became especially important to see that it was fully tenanted when it became ready for occupation. In April 1904 he approached Dr Smartt, the Cape's Commissioner of Crown Lands and Public Works, and offered the government office-space fitted with all modern conveniences – electric light, speaking tubes and electric bells imported from 'the old country'. It was a bad time to approach the Cape government. It had recently suffered a serious budgetary deficit and was therefore anxious to economise wherever possible. After much hesitation the government at last accepted Marks's offer and became the principal tenant of what was soon known as the Marks Building.[16]

Marks was less fortunate with his other Cape properties. Rents had to be reduced to keep tenants who were being enticed away by other landlords; the sale of plots at Milnerton had to be postponed indefinitely; and there were no takers when he placed the Muizenberg house on the market. As his agent reported in February 1906, all was gloom: Capetonians 'were feeling the bad times very much; failures are rampant, rents are being reduced all round; it is very difficult to get the rents in at the proper time, and any amount of places are to be let or for sale. At the present time,' he continued, 'we cannot see any silver lining to the cloud now hanging over this colony. . . . '[17]

The picture was equally gloomy in the coal industry, the mainstay since the early 1890s of Lewis and Marks. Marks's collieries had functioned throughout the war, though at a much reduced level of output. The closure of most of the gold mines, the departure of many of his staff, either on commando or as refugees, and the severe shortage of railway rolling-stock to transport his coal, had forced a severe curtailment of operations. At times the Vereeniging collieries could only work a one-day week. Production in the Transvaal coal industry as a whole plummeted from a pre-war peak of close to two million tons in 1898 to a-quarter of that amount in 1900, recovering only very slowly the following year.[18]

Marks and his fellow coal-owners had great expectations of the coal industry and of the mining industry as a whole at the end of the war. The coming of peace, the return to normality, the replacement of obstructive Boer government by benign and efficient British rule, seemed to guarantee the future prosperity of the gold-mining industry and of the Highveld coal industry which clung to gold's coat-tails. Coal production expanded at a breakneck pace immediately after the war in anticipation of a swift economic recovery. As the gold-mining industry awoke from its wartime hibernation, the colliery-owners stepped up production at their existing mines and opened 'half-a-score' new ventures. Most of these were in the Middelburg district, which tended to yield coal of better quality than the older east Rand and Vaal River coal-fields.[19]

Production expanded as rapidly as it did because of the ease of entry into Highveld coal-mining: entry costs were low especially compared with gold-mining. There was coal-bearing ground in abundance at a fraction of the cost of auriferous ground. Coal seams were thick, shallow and relatively unfaulted, and consequently could be cheaply mined. Development costs too were far lower than in the gold-mining industry. In the first decades of the century a coal mine with a capacity of 3,000 tons per day could be equipped and brought to the production stage for as little as £40,000. A deep-level gold mine might require eight times as much development capital.[20]

The outcome was overproduction as demand failed to keep pace with expanding capacity. Plagued by labour scarcity, the gold-mining industry – together with the railways, the collieries' principal customer – failed to recover at the anticipated rate. In consequence the coal-mining industry found itself facing a yawning gulf between its output and its sales. Prices sagged and profit margins shrank as colliery-owners trampled each other in pursuit of elusive customers. Collieries competed ruthlessly for each other's established clients; price cut followed price cut in quick succession. In early 1905, for example, the Great Eastern, a colliery Lewis and Marks had opened near Springs in the 1890s, sold coal to the Robinson Deep, an old customer, at 7s. 6d. per ton. The

Clydesdale quietly approached the Robinson Deep and offered coal at 7s. 3d. per ton. Hearing of this, Marks's marketing agent swiftly countered with an offer of 7s. per ton; Clydesdale immediately reduced its price to 6s. 11d. Given that working costs had remained unchanged, neither colliery could expect much profit at this price level. As Marks lamented: 'The competition now going on is ruinous to the coal mining industry.'[21]

His private calculations about the likely growth in demand for coal by the gold industry suggested a very gloomy future. In early 1905 altogether 6,000 stamps were in operation; each required the equivalent of 500 tons of coal per annum. If one assumed the number of stamps increased by 50 per cent within the next five years, the demand for coal would still only be 4½ million tons. At a less optimistic figure of 4 million tons, and at a profit margin of 1s. per ton, the total profit from sales to the gold-mining industry would only reach £200,000 per annum. And this would have to be divided between 25 companies. 'You will thus see', he wrote to his partner, 'that coal mining cannot be looked upon as a lucrative investment.'

The crux of the problem, he reiterated, was the imbalance between supply, present and potential, and demand, which was strictly finite: 'while the sources from which supplies are drawn are almost unlimited, the demand is comparatively speaking very small.' There was little possibility, Marks recognised, of relief through increased prices and profit margins. Even though the Randlords owned and operated extensive coal-mining properties, it was in their interests to maintain low coal prices; low energy costs boosted gold-mining profit margins. The Corner House and their ilk saw coal-mining as no more than the handmaiden of gold-mining. 'From the foregoing you will see that there is not a very bright future before coal mines.'[22]

Of the Lewis and Marks collieries, the Great Eastern on the east Rand was the most exposed to the chill winds of competition. Its primary market was the cut-throat Rand gold-mine coal trade in which it competed at a serious disadvantage. Since Lewis and Marks owned no gold mines excepting the Sheba at distant Barberton, the Great Eastern, unlike its rivals which had connections to gold-mining concerns, lacked captive customers on the Rand. Unless they were offered very substantial discounts, gold-mining firms were reluctant to place their coal orders with outside collieries, preferring coal mines in which they had a financial interest. Thus despite Lewis and Marks's pleadings, their old friend Solly Joel would not give them a significant share of Johannesburg Consolidated Investment's coal order. Similarly J. B. Robinson, who had a large stake in the Witbank colliery, would not give the Lewis and Marks collieries orders for his gold mines. When the Great Eastern won contracts, these were usually short-term only. In a buyers' market customers preferred one-month contracts. This meant chronic uncertainty, stop-start production and inflated unit costs of production. At times the colliery worked only three or four shifts a week, on occasion as little as two.[23]

The Vereeniging Estates company fared less disastrously than the Great Eastern but it too struggled, hovering uncertainly for years between profit and loss. As before the war, it was insulated to a degree from the difficulties

experienced by the rest of the Highveld coal industry: during the war and after
it retained the Cape railway contract, which ensured that it had a secure
medium-term customer for a large part of its output. But as the decade advanced
the shelter the Cape contract provided shrank dangerously.

Late in 1901 Lewis and Marks had negotiated for a renewal of the railway
contract. During the negotations Lewis reported a rumour that the Cape was
considering using oil from Borneo in its railway engines. Marks retorted that he
had recently read a magazine article which predicted that in the future train
boilers would use solar energy rather than coal to generate steam. He assured
Lewis that the Cape Government Railways (CGR) would use neither Borneo oil
nor 'sun rays' for some while yet! Lewis and Marks were granted a very
satisfactory three-year renewal of the railway contract. Vereeniging was to
supply 15,000 tons per month at 10s. per ton; the railway had the option of
increasing this to 25,000 tons per month on two months' notice. But when the
contract came up for renewal towards the end of 1904, however, the CGR
would only agree to a disappointing one-year arrangement; it would merely take
10,000 tons per month at 9s. per ton with an option of a further 5,000 tons. It
no longer needed the same volume of coal as its carrying trade to the Transvaal
had fallen off considerably because of the severe regional economic recession and
the competition of Durban and Delagoa Bay. There was a further deterioration
at the end of 1905 when the Cape agreed to take only 65,000 tons at 8s. 2$\frac{1}{2}$d. per
ton over the whole of the following year. By the end of 1907 the contract price
was down to 6s. 6d. per ton, and it was clear to Marks that his old friends at the
Cape were eager to switch from Vereeniging to better-quality Middelburg
coal.[24]

The contraction of the Cape coal order after 1904 led to a frantic search for
additional customers to take up the shortfall. Vereeniging Estates won a portion
of the Central South African Railways contract; it bid unsuccessfully against
Natal competition for the De Beers contract at Kimberley; it joined the desperate
scramble for the gold-mine market; and it even tendered for a small part of the
Natal Government Railways coal supply.[25] Marketing coal in a buyers' market
was an unenviable task. 'You can never expect to make more than from 6d to
1/- per ton profit,' Marks complained to Lewis, 'and you can only do that
through favouritism. By favouritism I mean that you must be good friends with
every Engineer and with every Fireman, and that friendship cannot exist from
smoke through a pipe. In addition to that you must be constantly looking up
every individual director of every Company. You must be directly or indirectly
interested in every business, and you must even be in the swim of Bridge Playing
and Racing as well.' Kickbacks were standard procedure in the Transvaal:
'nothing is done in this country without Commissions presents and bonuses.'[26]

One possible way to boost sales of Highveld coal was through the
development of an export trade, but here too Marks suffered continued
disappointment. Transvaal Consolidated Coal, Lewis and Marks' coal concern
in the eastern Transvaal, teetered on the brink of closure for years, running up
substantial losses. Its failure and eventual liquidation in 1909 were directly
connected with the continuing difficulties Marks experienced after the war in

establishing a coal export trade through Delagoa Bay, the *raison d'être* of this concern.[27]

As the colliery closest to Delagoa Bay, Transvaal Consolidated Coal at Belfast had seemed best placed at the end of the war to capitalise on the anticipated post-war rush of sea-traffic to the port. But first Marks had to solve the problem that had bedevilled his pre-war attempts to establish an export and bunker trade: the absence of adequate harbour infrastructure at Delagoa Bay. Since there were no deep-water quays at the port, coal had to be unloaded from railway trucks, transferred manually in baskets to lighters and barges waiting at a flimsy wooden jetty, then unloaded once again into the ships riding at anchor in the bay. This laborious process cost 7s. 6d. per ton, which effectively eliminated any possibility of competing with a better-equipped Durban.[28]

In 1903 Marks visited Lisbon (where he was most impressed by the electric trams) and secured the rights which had eluded him before the war and which were essential if he were to invest in the building of a deep-water pier. But before he went any further, his scheme was pre-empted by the Portuguese authorities who undertook the construction of their own deep-water pier. Under the circumstances a competing private pier seemed a poor investment.

The harbour improvements at Delagoa Bay did not achieve the results Marks had once so confidently expected. Despite the government pier and the introduction of electric cranes, the port and the coal export trade failed to thrive in the years before the unification of the South African colonies in 1910. Marks blamed this in part on Portuguese mismanagement of the harbour: on poor working systems for handling cargo; on unsatisfactory officials who had no sense of urgency, 'who do not understand their work, and who muddle things up'; and on the interruptions caused by an excessive number of public holidays.[29]

But there were other reasons too, Marks felt, for the Highveld's failure to make inroads into Natal's continued domination after the war of the South African coal export trade. The cost structure of the Natal industry was more favourable: the Natal collieries employed 'indentured coolies' on three-year contracts at 15s. per month while the Transvaal collieries were obliged to pay £2 per month for their black workers. The Natal collieries were less regulated than their Transvaal competitors: they had no racial restrictions on blasting or any requirement about the number of white men down the mine; they were not hampered by safety regulations and inspections of the sort imposed on the mines of the Transvaal since the war.

The Natal collieries were, moreover, supported by a sympathetic government and a state railway which was prepared to carry coal at a loss, if necessary, to foster the industry. By contrast the Transvaal government saw the Highveld coal industry as a milch-cow: railway rates on coal were an important source of revenue which a financially hard-pressed state was reluctant to sacrifice. Unlike that in Natal, the Highveld coal industry was a Cinderella concern. As far as the state was concerned, 'the main industry of the country is the Gold Industry'; the coal industry, Marks reluctantly acknowledged, would have to manage as best as it could with restricted state support.[30]

Besides overproduction, the other major difficulty Marks experienced in the post-war years was the acute scarcity of black labour. As already noted, the crisis of overproduction in the Highveld coal-mining industry was directly related to the disappointingly slow recovery of gold-mining after the war. This in turn was largely the result of the severe post-war labour crisis, a phenomenon Marks put down to the disruption of the rural social order brought about by the substitution of liberal British law for Boer. As Marks explained to a military friend who had served in India: 'Since the war the Kaffir has become quite unmanageable. Many of the Natives on my farms positively refuse to work for themselves or anybody else or even to pay rent for the land they are occupying. The English Law treats the Native as an equal of the White Man and if anybody can appreciate the disastrous effect of such treatment on the mind of the Native I am sure you can in view of your Indian experience.'[31]

Though he strongly supported the importation of Chinese labour, Marks rejected the mining industry's public rationalisation of this scheme (endorsed by the Transvaal Labour Commission of 1903) that sufficient labour was simply not available in the region. Marks believed instead that there were ample local reserves of labour awaiting tapping. 'All that is wanted', he told W. T. Stead, the famed English journalist then visiting South Africa, 'is the introduction of a shipload or two of Yellow boys. Their coming will give the Kaffirs such a fright they will pour into the mines, and we shall have all the labour we want.'[32]

The difficulties experienced through the scarcity of labour were exacerbated by a high rate of wastage through breach of contract. Desertion had been a major problem on the mines before the war; it continued so afterwards, reaching epidemic proportions at Vereeniging and on the Rand. In the second half of 1902, for example, no less than 1,100 black workers deserted from the compound of Marks's Cornelia colliery at the Vaal. This was roughly equivalent to a 100 per cent turnover in the mine's workforce in a six-month period. Many of these workers decamped to other mines, aided and abetted by corrupt compound police (one of whom was caught forging the compound manager's signature on passes) and by officials at rival mines who were hungry for labour and consequently asked few questions. A police raid on a neighbouring mine bagged 51 deserters from Vereeniging Estates' Cornelia colliery; they were tried, sentenced to 14 days' hard labour or a £2 fine, and, after imprisonment, returned to the Cornelia to complete their contracts. The local pass official at Vereeniging expected they would desert again at the first opportunity.[33]

The labour famine jeopardised Vereeniging Estates' relations with its customers. The collieries were often so short of labour that they were unable to produce sufficient coal to meet their contractual obligations to their clients. This was particularly worrisome in a buyers' market where customer dissatisfaction might easily lead to a loss of business to a rival colliery. Marks was especially anxious about fulfilling the terms of the Estates' contract with the Cape railways. To appease this highly valued customer he was forced at the height of the labour famine to divert all the first-class coal Vereeniging produced to the railways and to starve the rest of his clientele of good coal.[34]

The labour famine also pushed up the cost of production. The scarcity of cheap black labour meant that the most economical use could not be made of the mines' expensive white labour. As Marks impressed on Dr Jameson, the Cape premier, Vereeniging Estates could not repeatedly adjust its complement of white workers to match the constant fluctuations in the supply of black labour: 'we had at all times to keep the same establishment of whites as we could not possibly keep on dispensing with men's services when native labour failed us and re-engage others again when the labour supply was more favourable.' As a result, expensive white workers stood idle when black workers were absent.[35]

In the years after the war, Marks considered a variety of strategies to cope with the chronic scarcity of labour and the disruptive irregularity of supply. One of these was the amelioration of conditions in his compounds. Marks was apparently aware that workers tended to avoid, if they could, mines with particularly bad reputations, and that harsh conditions encouraged desertion and labour turnover. He, like the other mine-owners, was also under pressure from a colonial state more concerned about working and living conditions on the mines and about the high levels of mortality amongst the workforce than its *laissez-faire* Boer predecessors.[36]

After an *in loco* inspection at the Vaal River collieries, a fellow director reported to Marks in January 1904 that the compound at the Cornelia mine was in 'a disgraceful condition': sanitary arrangements were totally inadequate and the native hospital woefully cramped, with no more than half the space per patient of the Johannesburg Hospital. Conditions at the Cornelia's sister mine, the Central, were only marginally superior. The workers lived in small huts 'dotted about the veld without any semblance of order or symmetry'; some of these were three times more cramped than the accommodation in the local 'Coolie location'.[37]

Efforts were subsequently made to improve living and working conditions but these were always constrained by a desire to avoid heavy expenditure at marginally profitable and aging mines. A pail system was introduced in place of open cesspits; a 'shower bath' was fitted up at the Cornelia on Marks's instructions; and double-tiered iron bunks were ordered for the compounds. At Marks's suggestion the mine doctor was instructed to make daily inspections of the compounds, while he himself paid monthly visits and enquired through an interpreter about grievances. Improvements were made, too, to the mine hospital: the floor was laid with bricks and a mortuary was added, which doubled as an operating theatre.[38]

Rations were slowly upgraded. Workers were fed on mealies and vegetables, very often pumpkin, grown on the estate, but meat seems to have remained a Christmas treat until close to the end of the decade, when twice-weekly meat rations were introduced in an attempt to defuse grievances. (The company accepted a tender of about 3d. per pound from Marks's nephews, the Falcke brothers, whom he had set up in a concession store at the colliery.)[39]

The effects of these efforts at amelioration, constrained as they were by considerations of cost, were necessarily limited: the compounds remained a harsh and alienating environment and desertion continued apace. Part of the problem was the quality of supervision of the compounds. A prospective compound manager needed few qualifications. Youth and inexperience were no obstacle; Marks was satisfied if he could speak Dutch and the 'Kaffir languages' and 'write a little English'. The result of this casual system of selection was a succession of unsatisfactory compound managers. Worker resentment of their working and living conditions is hinted at in the minute books of the Vereeniging Estates. These speak briefly and tantalisingly of a 'native disturbance' at the Cornelia in late 1904, of a wave of unspecified 'misde-meanours' starting in late 1905 and continuing for years after, of complaints by the workers of poor treatment in 1908, and of the need to effect 'a better feeling among the natives'.[40]

The vagaries of the labour supply led Marks to experiment with an option that represented a radical break with the past. In the early years of the twentieth century Marks and the mining industry at large seriously contemplated a new labour strategy that broke with the practice of labour migration, which had dominated their industry since the start of the mineral revolution at Kimberley in the 1870s. This was labour stabilisation, the creation of a stable workforce who would live permanently with their families on mine property rather than oscillating between a bachelor existence in the mine compound and their family homesteads in the faraway countryside. In 1904, at the height of the labour crisis, Vereeniging Estates arranged to settle black families from the Cape Colony on its property and to provide them with agricultural land. In return, each family was to supply one workman for the coal mines at all times and to pay half of its produce as ground rent. The families were left to build their own huts with timber grown on the estate and Spanish reed which abounded near the river.

Labour stabilisation brought problems of its own. Marks stipulated that the married quarters be established at what he considered a safe distance from the 'bachelor' compound. But the two-mile gap he suggested proved insufficient. To management's chagrin women in the married quarters supplemented their family incomes by brewing beer for the 'bachelors'. Management complained bitterly that through this 'indiscriminate and whole-sale selling of Kaffir Beer and Clarrie', the married quarters were 'weakening rather than strengthening the Labour Supply'. After debating whether they should move the married quarters further away from the compound or closer by to tighten supervision, or, alternatively and more drastically, whether they should abandon the experiment altogether and abolish the married quarters, they settled instead on a purge of the undesirables – defined, as was customary, in ethnic terms – who were supposedly responsible for the illicit brewing. All the trouble had been caused by 'Mxosa, Hottentots and Bastards'; the rest of the 'married natives' were 'orderly and industrious'. Marks and his colleagues resolved that 'the obstreperous married natives be instantly discharged' and that the company's recruiting agents be warned against recruiting any more 'married natives' from these 'tribes'.[41]

Labour stabilisation was never more than a partial remedy for the mines' chronic labour difficulties. Marks's collieries at Vereeniging continued to rely primarily on migrant labour, and strenuous efforts were made to recruit these during the labour famine. While numbers of workers presented themselves voluntarily at the coal mines, most were actively recruited, either through the Witwatersrand Native Labour Association (WNLA), the recruiting arm of the Chamber of Mines, or through independent labour agents. The Vereeniging Estates recruited workers in a wide arc stretching from Mozambique in the east through Basutoland and the Eastern Cape to Kimberley in the west.[42]

The Witwatersrand Native Labour Association supplied Mozambican workers to the colliery at Vereeniging. These were housed in a special 'Shangaan' compound built to Chamber of Mines specifications. In 1906, however, Lewis and Marks decided to make independent arrangements for recruiting labour in Mozambique. The dubious Cohen brothers of Lourenço Marques, who a decade before had sold Marks the abortive Delagoa Bay pier concession, were engaged to supply a thousand Mozambican workers on one-year contracts. Reports soon filtered back that the Cohens, or rather their friends in the Mozambican administration, were using strongarm methods to obtain the labour. The Cohens' 'recruits' were being pressganged from their homes in the Inhambane district by Portuguese officials, acting, it was alleged, under instructions from the Governor-General in Lourenço Marques. They were then marched on board ship at Inhambane with their hands tied behind their backs, leaving their 'womenfolk . . . shrieking and howling at the end of the pier'. Once in Lourenço Marques they were taken under armed escort to the railway station.

After an investigation by the British Consulate-General at Lourenço Marques, Lord Selborne put these charges to Marks who adamantly denied them. Ben Cohen had assured him that the recruits had come of their own free will and that reports to the contrary were malicious rumours spread by WNLA agents. Marks gave his word to the Governor that he would not permit any improprieties. This satisfied Lord Selborne. 'Mr. Marks', he wrote to Lord Elgin at the Colonial Office, 'is a man in whose honour and respectability I have complete confidence.' Soon after Marks prudently cancelled the arrangement with the Cohen brothers and returned to the WNLA fold.[43]

Marks's agents in Basutoland were no less troublesome. They misled recruits by quoting the highest wages possible under the collieries' piece-work system rather than the standard wage. Marks forbade this 'pernicious' practice which antagonised other employers of labour and angered workers, whose wages fell short of the promised levels. Furthermore, Russell Harding, Marks's labour agent at Kimberley, was a disreputable character who had been imprisoned for debt. But he was a highly effective recruiter who continued to forward workers to Vereeniging during the worst of the labour drought, when other agents failed. Vereeniging Estates built Harding a compound in Kimberley and instructed him not to recruit 'Batlapines [sic]', who 'were unsatisfactory and invariably grumbled at their treatment'.[44]

Ironically, Marks's recruiting efforts were least successful closest to home: when his estate manager did the rounds of the black tenants to make up a temporary shortfall in the mining workforce at Vereeniging, he was unable to rout out a single volunteer, even for a fortnight's work.[45]

Mechanisation was another possible solution to the labour problem, if only a limited one, given the current state of mining technology. The coal-mining industry in Britain, Marks's admired model, was slowly substituting mechanical cutting for hand mining. These coal-cutting machines, however, were not only expensive but also unsuited to the mining of thick seams of coal of the sort that were found on the Highveld coal-fields – or so the conventional wisdom of the 1900s had it. Marks, who had a fascination with machines and an exaggerated belief in their efficacy, contested the conventional view. He had been very impressed by mechanical coal-cutters when he saw them in operation at coal mines he visited during his post-Jameson Raid visit to Britain in 1896; he had imported one of these before the war but it had been 'pronounced useless' by successive managers at the Vaal River collieries, who, he felt, had never given it a fair trial. He was concerned about reports in 1904 that the rival Natal coal industry was mechanising on a considerable scale and felt it was essential that the Vereeniging collieries follow the same route. Though the initial expenditure might be heavy, this would be 'infinitesimal' compared with the eventual saving of labour: 'we must keep abreast of the times, and must have labour saving appliances.' Isaac Lewis preferred the conventional wisdom and the advice of a technical expert, and hurriedly vetoed his partner's suggestion on the grounds of cost.[46]

The containment of costs was of critical importance in an industry struggling with the effects of overproduction. In 1907 Isaac Lewis complained to Marks that their collieries still suffered 'continuous loss'. Marks responded: 'I am aware that our Collieries are working at a loss and regret this as much as you possibly can . . . if the coal mines controlled by us belonged to me privately, I should not hesitate to close them down. I do not see how matters can be improved with the keen competition that is going on. . . . *The coal is black and the business in it is black.* I am sorry I can offer no suggestions for improving the situation.' Marks's pessimism and uncharacteristic negativism to the contrary, the next few years were to provide solutions.[47]

Besides its huge and troubled investment in what contemporaries called the 'black diamond industry', Lewis and Marks also had a significant stake in the genuine article. In the post-war period the firm attempted to establish a strong presence in both the diamond and gold industries. Sammy Marks was well aware that Lewis and Marks had been left behind by firms of similar or lesser vintage which had chosen from the start to concentrate on gold or diamond mining. Without a significant stake in either of these, Lewis and Marks was clearly condemned in perpetuity to the second rank of mining houses. In the years after the war Sammy struggled to rectify this. The focus of his gold-mining efforts was the Far East Rand, not the Central Rand where mining on the Witwatersrand had begun in the mid-1880s. Right from those earliest days there had been fears that the great river of gold, the Main Reef series, might soon dry up. Consequently men searched for its continuation both to the south, where it plunged deep into the earth, and to the east and west. As they moved further and further eastwards along the Rand, the outcrop – tell-tale sign of the presence of the Main Reef series – simply disappeared.

Like other speculators Marks and Lewis gambled on the continuation of the reef despite the absence of any surface indications. In the late 1890s they bought Grootvlei and Palmietkuil (shared with the mighty Corner House) but did precious little before the war to verify the presence of the reefs beneath these farms. After the Boer forces retreated from the Rand in mid-1900, there was a flurry of interest in the prospects of the Far East Rand, and Isaac Lewis, the firm's financial expert, hastened to capitalise on this. In early 1901 he formed the East Rand Mining Estates Limited with a nominal capital of no less than £500,000; its purpose, to exploit Grootvlei and Palmietkuil. During the brief post-war upsurge of confidence diamond drilling began on both farms. The diamond drills went through coal beds and through dolomite, until at last the eastwards extension of the Main Reef series – the Van Ryn reef – was intersected, just as Marks had hoped. At Grootvlei the boreholes cut the reef at depths ranging between 2,375 and 4,300 feet. This was very deep by the standards of the age and meant, Marks recognised, that 'enormous' sums of capital would be required to develop the mine and that there would be a very lengthy delay before the mine could begin repaying investors.

In 1905 Marks urged Julius Wernher, an old friend from his Kimberley days, to form a joint company with Lewis and Marks to mine Palmietkuil. As he indicated to Wernher, it was not so much the Corner House's capital he wanted as its high reputation in European financial circles. It seems that as a small, second-rank mining house, with only limited access to European finance capital, Lewis and Marks desperately needed Wernher Beit to lend its name if the firm was to launch successfully a scheme as ambitious and costly as the development of deep-level gold-mining on the Far East Rand. Advised by his Johannesburg officials, who were increasingly shy of risk after the war and who were reluctant to lend the Corner House's reputation to what they saw as a dubious project, Julius Wernher prevaricated. This effectively paralysed a scheme which might have raised Lewis and Marks to the first rank of mining houses. Sammy Marks lost, through Wernher Beit's caution, a chance, once again, as he had in the mid-1880s, to pioneer a major new gold-field. Only a few years after Sammy's failure to interest the Corner House in his venture, the Far East Rand was to become the successor to the Central Rand as the hub of the South African gold-mining industry.[48]

Then there was Sammy's and Isaac's costly attempt to re-establish the firm as a force in the diamond industry. Though the Transvaal was renowned for its gold deposits, the first great discovery of the post-war era was of precious minerals rather than metals. In November 1902 Thomas Cullinan, a Johannesburg building contractor and brickmaker and sometime prospector, bought Elandsfontein, a farm a few miles north-east of Zwartkoppies in the Magaliesberg range, from the Prinsloo clan, who like many other Boer families had been ruined by the war. Cullinan paid £52,000 for a property which he suspected held a great diamond pipe of Kimberley-like proportions. Within months his faith had been vindicated. The Premier, the diamond mine he established on the property, paid a profit of double the purchase price of the farm in its first year of operation. Then, in 1905, it yielded a 3,106 carat giant, the largest diamond ever discovered, a stone which was subsequently presented by Louis Botha to King Edward VII as a token of the Transvaal's new-found loyalty to the Empire, and mounted in the Imperial Sceptre and Imperial State Crown. The 'Cullinan' diamond was only the most dramatic of a steady stream of discoveries at the mine. By the time the gift was made in 1907, the Premier had already produced close to £5,000,000 of diamonds, and had shattered the monopoly of South African diamond production Cecil John Rhodes had so painstakingly (and deviously) constructed two decades before. In the process it stirred a diamond fever akin to that of the early days of Kimberley. As *The African World* noted in 1906: 'The wondrous rise of the Premier has made many a would-be Cullinan persevere and dream of future millions when prospecting and option fees are eking out the very soul of his meagre bank account!'[49]

Dazzled by the Premier's results, Lewis and Marks also caught diamond fever, or at least had a fresh attack of an old illness. Lewis and Marks had taken part in the original rush to Kimberley at the beginning of the 1870s and had made their first fortune on the diamond fields. But with the creation of the De Beers monopoly in the late 1880s, Lewis and Marks's involvement in diamond production and trading at Kimberley had effectively ceased. For the next ten years they had concentrated most of their efforts and resources on the less glamorous pursuit of 'black diamonds' at Vereeniging and on the distilling of 'white mother's ruin' at Hatherley. Marks's dormant interest in diamonds had been, however, first reawakened in 1897, a decade after the great amalgamation at Kimberley, by the chance discovery of diamonds virtually on the doorstep of Zwartkoppies.

On an August morning in 1897 Oscar Schuller, a young and athletic German Uitlander, prospecting the farm Rietfontein a short distance to the east of Zwartkoppies for coal and cinnabar, playfully kicked over an antheap and spotted a 'pretty and bright crystal' lying in the dust. By complete chance Schuller had discovered a new diamond field, the first in the Transvaal. With his wife Bertha, an excited Marks rode over to the farm which was only a 40-minute drive from Zwartkoppies and adjoined his plantation at Pienaarspoort. While her husband inspected the shallow pit Schuller and his associates had sunk into the diamond pipe, Bertha picked up a diamond she spotted on the ground. Marks came away convinced that Schuller had discovered a diamond pipe that would rival Kimberley. The firm of Lewis and Marks agreed to provide the working capital to open up the mine, while Sammy undertook to persuade his Boer friends to grant generous mining rights. Marks arranged tours of the mine for Kruger and members of the Volksraad, and spent liberally on smoothing the passage of the necessary legislation. A total of £5,000 was 'promised to different people for their services in connection with the framing of the new diamond law'. The money was well spent. Lewis and Marks's Boer friends 'worked hard' on their behalf and a 'satisfactory' law was placed on the statute books.[50]

The Schuller mine, however, failed to live up to its initial promise, forcing Marks to scale down his expectations. The quality of the stones found near the surface was 'not so good as we used to find on the surface of the Kimberley mine'; the deeper, blue ground was even more disappointing. Left to disintegrate on the surface during the enforced stoppage of the war years, the blue ground excavated before the war refused to 'weather' satisfactorily. The owners put it about after the war that pilferage of stones, not the poverty of the mine, had cut down its output. It was alleged that after the Battle of Diamond Hill in June 1900, Roberts's Tommies had helped themselves to souvenirs from the floor of the Schuller mine. This, plus thieving by a crooked employee, was held accountable for the mine's disappointing yield. As in the early days at Kimberley, diamond theft provided a handy rationalisation for poor performance.[51]

While Marks's Schuller mine was itself a failure, it did succeed in attracting attention to the mineral prospects of the Pretoria district. Thomas Cullinan's discovery of the Premier mine in 1902 was a direct result of Marks's abortive venture. It was the Schuller mine that drew diamond prospectors like Cullinan to the Pretoria district. In turn, the run-away success of the Premier drew Lewis and Marks into a further spate of diamond speculations, despite their burning their fingers over the Schuller.

In the search for a new Kimberley or at least a second Premier, which they hoped would raise their concern to the first rank of mining houses, Lewis and Marks pursued prospects however remote these were from the existing areas of diamond production. One prospector was sent northwards to the Limpopo River; another, promised a £1,000 reward for a payable discovery, fossicked on African and European farms in the Marico. At one time Marks even considered scouring the river-bed at Vereeniging for diamonds.[52]

One of the chief obstacles in the search for diamonds was the scarcity of energetic and sober prospectors who were prepared to do more than simply supervise the prospecting efforts of African labourers. As Marks complained to Lewis at the height of the post-war diamond boom: 'You can get plenty of prospectors but it is very difficult to get one of the right sort. There is one class who are very nice gentlemen and who will go out and *take charge* of the prospecting. Another kind there is who will go and work themselves but they will take with them a few cases of gin and whiskey. A real good man is very difficult to get.'[53]

For all their eagerness to discover their own diamond mine, Lewis and Marks's major investments were made in diamond-mining operations that others had initiated. In 1903 a diamond pipe was discovered on a farm called Damplaats, 20 miles out of the 'sleeping, slumbering' hamlet of Boshof in the western Free State. The farm, which adjoined a Lewis and Marks property, belonged to the deceased estate of one John Roberts. His widow and children were advised by John Fraser, a shrewd Bloemfontein lawyer and local politician, with whom Marks had dealt since he first took an interest in the Vaal River property in the 1880s.

After a cool response to Marks's first overtures, African and European were allowed a limited participation in the company, the Roberts Victor, formed to exploit the discovery. But the heirs and their solicitor made certain they retained control, claiming half the shares of the new company as vendors of the property and two life directorships on the board. Isaac Lewis was convinced that the mine was a Premier in the making, and that there was therefore a real danger it might be snatched away from his partnership and swallowed up by the predatory heavyweights of the diamond industry, the De Beers and the Barnatos. Consequently he began buying additional shares in the company whenever these were offered on the market, with little regard for price, hoping in this way to secure unassailable control over the mine. Under this buying pressure the price of the company's £1 shares soared to over £14 during the early months of the company's operation.

Though Marks was more sceptical about the mine's prospects than his partner, and suspected that the firm would do better to invest elsewhere, he nevertheless bowed to his partner's insistence that they spend freely in order to hold the Roberts Victor. Lewis, after all, was the firm's financial expert, and share-dealing was his prerogative. At Lewis's urging, Marks parlayed with the widow Roberts and the other heirs about their shares in the company. Marks found her a formidable and well-informed adversary, who kept in daily telegraphic contact with both the mine and the share market in Johannesburg. 'She is a very cautious and a particularly suspicious old woman and does not like to part with her shares for fear of not making sufficient money on them,' Marks reported to his partner.[54]

Despite disquieting reports from the mine itself in late 1906 and early 1907, Lewis continued to pick up shares where he could. Marks warned him that the Roberts Victor was a 'treacherous mine' which would have to be worked very carefully. The rock surrounding the diamond pipe was a soft Ecca shale, prone to collapse into the open workings. To prevent this, the shale eventually had to be cut back in terraces, an expensive and unproductive operation which eroded profit margins. Then again, the original surface indications of the mine proved misleading. As the diamond pipe went deeper, it narrowed significantly; at depth, the Roberts Victor mine was much smaller than it had appeared on the surface. Moreover, the pipe was intersected by floating reef, patches of worthless barren rock.[55]

In May 1907 Marks relayed a message from a senior employee who until then had assiduously fed Lewis's optimism about the mine. He now suggested 'that it would be better if we were out of the concern and had our money back'. To Marks's utter consternation, he discovered the next month that despite his warnings and his urgings that they reduce their investment, Lewis had continued to add to their holdings of Roberts Victors, and this on a massive scale. 'I cannot understand your action,' he bellowed at his partner.[56]

The minor disaster of the Roberts Victor diamond mine was overtaken in the same year by a larger disaster. This was the collapse of the international diamond market because of an economic crisis in America, the leading customer for South African gemstones. By December 1907 Lewis and Marks, and African and European (which was 90 per cent owned by the partnership), were saddled with an investment which had been acquired at prices far above the face value of the shares and had cost them close to £140,000, but which was now worth only a fraction of that sum as the share price hovered uncertainly just above par. In the following year their investment shrank even further as the share price sank lower. No wonder, then, that Marks pronounced an anathema on the mine: 'So far as I am concerned I think it would be better for my health and for everything else as well, if I did not mention the name of this Company again.'[57]

Marks felt similarly about another of the partnership's new ventures: the Imperial Cold Storage Company. While business had been at a standstill for much of the South African War, the war itself had offered certain business opportunities. Britain had sent a vast army to South Africa to subdue the Boers. This army needed to be supplied and fed. One of those who cashed in was David Graaff, a wholesale butcher and former mayor of Cape Town. A few months before the war he had established the South African Supply and Cold Storage Company to import frozen meat from Australasia. This was to make up the local shortfall in supply caused by the decimation of South Africa's herds by the rinderpest epidemic, which had swept the sub-continent in the late nineties. Marks had been offered a participation in the company by his old friend, the ubiquitous Jimmy Sivewright, who was co-promoter with David Graaff of the scheme, but had declined. 'I do not like the gentlemen connected with it nor do I approve of their methods of doing business,' he explained to Lewis. 'As you say, we are not getting younger and we must try and have connections with people who are honourable and whom we do not need to be constantly watching.'

Lewis must have regretted his partner's caution when he read the first annual reports of Graaff's company. Graaff won the crucial contract to supply the British expeditionary force with meat. His profits were astronomical, even in an age accustomed to colossal windfalls from gold and diamond mining: the company earned close to £500,000 between July 1899 and June 1900 on a capital base that was not much larger. In the financial year that followed, its profits soared over the £1,000,000 mark and it was able to pay a dividend of 105 per cent and still top up its reserve fund to £1,000,000.

Profits of this magnitude were bound to attract competition. As Lewis noted, *sotto voce*, when he posted Marks a copy of the 1901 report, 'I cannot help thinking that there ought to be a good business in that direction. . . . ' Lewis and Marks cast round for likely partners. Their old allies, Barnato Brothers and Johannesburg Consolidated Investment, seemed a good choice as they controlled numbers of mines which could be tied up as customers after the war. Then there was Cecil Rhodes's De Beers company, which had recently set up its own cold storage operation in Cape Town; Rhodes's political connections could be very useful. In February 1902 Lewis and Marks, Barnato Brothers–JCI and De Beers established the Imperial Cold Storage and Supply Company, with an initial capitalisation of £500,000, which was subsequently doubled to a full million. De Beers contributed one half, Lewis and Marks a by no means insignificant one tenth. Isaac Lewis was confident this was money well spent: 'I need hardly tell you', he wrote to his partner, 'that this is going to be a very important affair and a very lasting one.'[58]

Soon after its launching, Imperial Cold Storage captured the army contract, depriving Graaff of his major source of revenue. It seems that the British government, which was all too aware of the old company's mega-profits, was keen to introduce fresh blood into the business. But the new company was not to benefit for very long: when the war ended in May 1902, a large part of the imperial army went home. This, coupled with gross mismanagement, led to staggering losses within the first six months of operation. Since both old and new companies were in very bad shape, it seemed to make sense to merge the two, in August 1902, to eliminate costly competition. From the start, though, it was an unhappy marriage, with neither side trusting the other. Marks was soon convinced that David Graaff and Sir James Sivewright were out to despoil the merged company: 'I can only characterise Graaff, the Stainless Knight [Sivewright] . . . and a few of their apostles as a pack of thieves,' he wrote indignantly; 'that crowd have made up their minds to rob the whole concern with capital and all.' Marks was doubly indignant when he belatedly discovered that Graaff had overstated his company's profit figures during the merger negotiations; that he had grossly overvalued the Dock Road premises in Cape Town which he had transferred to Imperial Cold Storage; and that the stock of meat he had handed over to the merged company was both short and stale.[59]

Working with Graaff and Sivewright was wasted effort, Marks felt: 'For . . . all the time one takes in watching these scoundrels and keeping one's hands in one's pockets to prevent them from robbing one, something else can be done.' When the company transferred its head office from Johannnesburg to Cape Town in early 1905, Marks took the opportunity to resign from the board. At the same time he urged Lewis to sell off their holding in Imperial Cold Storage, whatever the loss. But Lewis refused, and at his insistence, Marks returned to the board in 1907. Little had changed in the interim. Marks found that he was simply a 'dummy director', seldom consulted and usually ignored by Graaff's appointees: 'I am never approached unless there is some difficulty to be overcome. I am expected to take responsibility without however being informed of what is transpiring. I cannot see the practical utility of my being merely a dummy Director and if anything goes wrong I shall have to share the opprobrium without being in any way to blame.' But despite his misgivings he remained, very grudgingly, on the board of what was eventually to become one of South Africa's leading companies.[60]

Marks drew some consolation for the disappointments at Roberts Victor and at Imperial Cold Storage from the relative success of the forestry project at the Vaal River which he had begun in the mid-1890s. By the mid-1900s the plantation at Maccauvlei had become one of the great sights of the Highveld, a virtually obligatory stop-over on the itineraries of distinguished visitors to the region. It had also achieved the unofficial status of an experimental station where government forestry experts went for advice and information. After visiting the 3,000-acre forest in 1908, a reporter from the *Transvaal Leader* enthused: 'The plantations are beautifully laid out, with fine, broad roads between, running in all directions for future convenience of hauling the timber when ready for use. In these plantations there are a million English oak trees, as well as hundreds of acres of various kinds of pines, maple, ash, eucalypti, etc., etc. The soil is most suitable; the growth and healthy appearance of every tree can only be realised by personal inspection. Some day these trees should return immense sums to the company. . . .'[61]

Marks and his German forester, Otto Brandmuller, were kindred spirits who spent days together, walking the estate or inspecting it by Cape cart. Besides their common passion for arboriculture, they shared a love of experiment and a capacity for taking infinite pains. With Marks's enthusiastic encouragement, Brandmuller experimented with the growing of apples for export to England, and also of asparagus for the Johannesburg market – he was reputedly the first to grow this commercially in South Africa. Osiers for basket-making and Spanish reed for papermaking were planted along the river-bank. Marks hoped that the reed, which was proof against locusts and drought, the great scourges of Highveld agriculture, would supplant the mealie as the staple crop of the estate and supply the raw materials for a great paper-mill he hoped to establish at Vereeniging if a power station could be built locally to supply cheap electricity. Attempts to introduce alien fauna, presumably to give the plantation something of the character of the European forests Marks and Brandmuller remembered from their youths, were less successful. The animals and birds they introduced were ill adapted to local conditions. Fallow deer imported from Scotland were so tame that they were easily poached by the local black inhabitants; imported pheasants roosted on the ground and were soon destroyed by wild cats.

The chief difficulty with Brandmuller's work was the time it was taking to make the forest a revenue-producer. In the early nineties Marks had forecast, typically over-optimistically, that it would be a source of profit in just five years; a decade and a half later he had to reassure his partner that 'the outlook for Maccauvlei is not so black and it is not necessary to wait for generations to come before revenue can be derived from our plantation if this is desired.'[62]

While the northern Orange Free State and the Transvaal had been the primary focus of the Lewis and Marks partnership since the 1880s, and the Cape the chief area of Marks's private investment beyond the Transvaal, the firm, like other Transvaal mining houses, had also accumulated a range of secondary interests throughout the region. As we have already noted, Marks had invested in Swaziland and at Delagoa Bay in Portuguese East Africa before the South African War. Typically, Sammy had been highly optimistic at the outset about both these investments, but both had disappointed. Delagoa Bay did not become the hinge of a great coal export trade during Marks's lifetime, while the Swaziland Corporation was stripped of its wide-ranging concessions and claims to much of Swaziland by the British government which assumed responsibility for the territory after the South African War. The Nyassa Company was equally promising at the outset and equally disappointing. During the great 1895 stock-market boom Lewis and Marks had acquired a large interest in a recently formed chartered company which controlled, at least on paper, no less than 100,000 square miles of East African bush in the far north of Mozambique. In return for virtually unlimited authority over the local inhabitants, the chartered company, like its Rhodesian equivalent, was meant to administer and develop a huge but remote territory, almost three times greater in extent than Portugal itself. Far from realising its shareholders' dreams, however, the Nyassa Company's territory became little more than a labour reservoir for the labour-hungry Witwatersrand until recruitment was halted in 1913 by the South African authorities.

Besides its unsuccessful investments in Swaziland and southern and northern Mozambique, all dating from the pre-war period, Lewis and Marks also invested in Rhodesia and Bechuanaland in the post-war decade. Once rashly touted as a second Rand in the making, Rhodesian gold-mining was successfully reorganised after the war to take account of its far more modest but none the less considerable potential. This attracted the attention of Lewis and Marks who, together with other Transvaal mining houses, invested heavily – if ultimately not very profitably – in Rhodesian mining. Further south, African and European invested in British Bechuanaland in 1907, acquiring 42 farms, equalling 119,000 morgen or a quarter of a million acres; the company hoped to use these for cattle-ranching to supply not only the Witwatersrand market but European markets as well. Though all these were substantial investments and conse-quently of great importance to Sammy Marks, he had very little to do with their day-to-day management. Rhodesia, Bechuanaland, Swaziland and northern Mozambique were part of Isaac Lewis's fiefdom and were supervised from the London office, not from Johannesburg. Instead Sammy's staff in South Africa were preoccupied with the partnership's core business, its enormous – and highly troubled – interests in the Transvaal and Orange Free State.[63]

The reconstruction of Lewis and Marks's business in the years after the war was accompanied by important staff changes. Hugh Crawford, Marks's right-hand man at the Pretoria office before the war, resigned in 1904 after sixteen years of faithful service. Isaac Lewis angrily refused to pay out his claim to a share in the partnership's profits. Marks insisted that they pay: Crawford was their longest-serving employee; in the 1890s he 'was almost indispensable to us and served us loyally through many years when his share of the profits were very small'. If Lewis still refused, Marks was prepared to pay Crawford out of his own pocket.[64]

The loss of such an old hand was less of a blow to Lewis and Marks than might have been expected. Their Pretoria office had diminished in importance since the war. The closure of the distillery at Hatherley and the replacement of a pliable Boer regime by a less approachable British admininstration had stripped it of its key functions: administrative control over Eerste Fabrieken and the lobbying of Boer officials and legislators. The Pretoria office was progressively overshad-owed by the partnership's Johannesburg office, which was increasingly recognised as the South African head office of Lewis and Marks. This made good sense. Johannesburg, with its politically powerful gold-mining industry, was the *de facto* capital – the commercial capital – of the British Transvaal, whatever the official status of Pretoria. Then again, with the closure of Eerste Fabrieken, most of the partnership's remaining interests had Johannesburg offices. This meant that Marks spent more and more time in Johannesburg, and less and less in Pretoria.

Marks was assisted in Johannesburg by three key employees: Jacobus Nicholas de Jongh, Sir Edwin Harris Dunning and Dr Frederick Henry Hatch. Fourteen years younger than Marks, Jimmy de Jongh was a Cape-educated lawyer whom Sammy recruited in 1896 to represent the partnership in Johannesburg: in the fraught political climate after the Jameson Raid, Marks, ever the diplomat, felt it necessary to employ someone who was bilingual 'and who can work himself in with both English and Dutch'. De Jongh, Marks assured Lewis, 'is straight and would no doubt work loyally in our behalf'.[65]

Marks was not disappointed. Eight years later, when De Jongh's contract came up for renewal, Marks's assessment was still favourable though he had developed certain reservations: 'Jimmy is a very able man and can get through a lot of work if he puts his back into it.' The trouble, at least as far as the puritanical Marks was concerned, was that De Jongh was too fond of the racetrack: 'I should be very pleased if Jimmy could be induced to give up horses. Before he left I threw out a suggestion to him that if he would sell his horses I would buy him a nice present and he took this very nicely. I expect he will be reluctant to do this because he has been brought up as a sportsman and is a keen sportsman in every way. Besides he will urge that being a Steward he is thrown into contact with people which is in the interest of business.' Marks asked Lewis to talk to De Jongh about giving up horse-racing but without hurting his feelings. 'We must take into consideration the fact that not everybody has been brought up as we have and cannot therefore constantly be slaving without any recreation.'

De Jongh's active participation in public life in Johannesburg, often at the expense of his business duties, was more of a problem for Lewis than for Marks, who had a more keenly developed sense of the firm's public responsibilities. 'Jimmy is a general favourite here,' Sammy wrote to Isaac. 'He makes himself useful and does a lot of work for the public. He is a keen and competent lawyer and people here like a man who will relieve them of responsibility. Possibly you may urge that we do not require a man to work for the public, but this is essential in a community like ours. . . . Every big corporation or firm here is bound to take an interest in public matters.'[66]

De Jongh was elected president of the Transvaal Chamber of Mines in 1906. This appointment brought lustre to Lewis and Marks: outside of major public office the presidency of the Chamber of Mines was the most prestigious position in the Transvaal. But public service and prestige had their costs. De Jongh's presidency coincided with the Chinese labour crisis and his official duties consequently ate up two-thirds of his working-time, much to the chagrin of Isaac Lewis who resented paying a high salary to someone who spent so little of his day working for his employers.[67]

The appointments of Sir Edwin Harris Dunning and of Dr Frederick Henry Hatch were linked with the expansion and reconstruction of the business after the war. Dunning, who had had extensive experience at Kimberley and Barberton and on the early Rand, was brought back out of retirement in

England to serve as managing director of African and European. Hatch, one of the great early experts on the geology of the Witwatersrand gold-fields, was appointed as chief consulting engineer to Lewis and Marks with a brief to establish an engineering department for the partnership. Both their appointments were a measure of the increasing bureaucratisation of the business.

The creation of African and European in 1904 had been part of a broader process of restructuring that had begun with the flotation of Vereeniging Estates two years before the war – the institutionalisation of the business. As the business grew larger, as it increasingly went public, so there was a steady shift from the highly personalised management style Marks had originally practised – and greatly preferred – to a more formal and bureaucratic style of management, with formalised procedures for making and executing decisions. This bureaucratisation of the business was perhaps a necessary and inevitable process but it was not one that Sammy Marks, a free-wheeling entrepreneur by nature, found at all congenial.

Bureaucratisation meant that there were many more meetings that Sammy had to attend than in the past when he had managed Lewis and Marks's enterprises virtually single-handed. He increasingly spent his week at board meetings at his Johannesburg office, which after the war had effectively become the partnership's South African headquarters. Marks found attendance at these extremely tiresome. 'Personally I find it rather trying to sit on so many boards,' he complained to his partner, 'and I experience at the moment the greatest difficulty in getting about and seeing our properties. . . . ' Tuesday to Friday was spent in Johannesburg attending meetings 'so that I have very little time to myself and I cannot possibly attend to everything personally as you would wish me to do'. Marks, who was a restless and energetic person, found sitting at board meetings for long periods a great trial. According to George Falcke, he would invent all manner of pretexts to escape the boardroom for a breather.[68]

Marks disliked the formalisation of decision-making that accompanied the bureaucratising of the business. He found it irksome that matters, large and small, had to be submitted for the approval of the board, for he was accustomed to making rapid decisions on his own without over-much consultation. He found the necessity of negotiating his schemes through board meetings very frustrating. As he wrote rather wistfully to his partner a few years after war, explaining why he had been reluctant to act in a particular case: 'I have found for the last few years that if I want anything to be done for the benefit of any of the concerns we are connected with I must not do it directly, but must first lay it before the Consulting Engineers, then have it submitted to the Directors, and then, if they decide to adopt my scheme, it is in order.'[69]

Bureaucratisation seemed only to complicate the onerous task of reconstructing the business in the wake of the South African War. And to make matters worse, it was accompanied by enforced adjustments in Sammy's private life. Marks also deeply resented the drastic rearrangement of his private life necessitated by the reorientation of his business in the decade after the war. He paid what he felt – and what he forcefully reminded his partner – was a heavy personal price for the post-war reconstruction of Lewis and Marks.

X

The Gilded Cage:
Zwartkoppies after the War

The political and economic uncertainties of the decade after the South African War were paralleled in Marks's private life. As in his public life, there was no smooth or easy return to pre-war normality. The 1900s were an unsettled time at Zwartkoppies. Before the war Marks's country house was his haven from the demands of the world. During the war it had been both a solace and a prison. After the war it progressively became, against its owner's wishes, little more than a weekend retreat. Because the centre of gravity of his business had shifted from Pretoria to Johannesburg, Marks was regularly absent from home for most of the week; his business now required that he spend his time in Johannesburg rather than in Pretoria. Consequently Bertha Marks felt increasingly isolated at Zwartkoppies. Sammy was forced eventually to recognise this and, very reluctantly, to reshape his domestic arrangements. At the same time he was struggling with a sense of disappointment over the unintended consequences of his sons' education at English public schools, with a sense of anxiety about his children's commitment to the Jewish faith, and with the infirmities of old age.

Sammy and Bertha Marks's marriage was an essentially solid and enduring one, but it was very much a marriage of its time. Sammy was the Victorian paterfamilias, continually chiding, instructing and exhorting his wife. When, for example, she failed to attend speech day at her son Louis's Harrow in 1901 because of a prior social engagement, he wrote:

I can fully enter in Louis' disappointment and certainly think that of the two events you might have chosen the Speech Day as the fittest and most interesting to attend no matter who the people might be with whom you had arranged to go to the Regatta.

After all your eldest son should be dearer to you than those you had invited to go to Henley. It would have been an encouragement to Louis, and it would have been nice to have shown Girlie, and especially Joe and Ted what an English Public School is like on Speech Day. I shall not write any more on this subject, but later on when we meet, I shall have more to say to you.[1]

While she was on a subsequent trip to England in 1902 to seek medical treatment for their son Teddy, who had had fits and had become deranged, he wrote: 'I do

not need to point out to you the great necessity there is for the utmost care and
attention on your part. Friends and pleasure must all be put on one side, because
the whole object of your trip was to look after Ted.'[2]

Bertha clearly belonged to a lesser sex, given to idle chatter and preoccupied
with trivialities. Replying to a 24-page letter from Bertha (which has not
survived) with all the male condescension a Victorian could muster, he wrote:
'There are certainly some amusing little things in it, but of course being a
woman you must be excused!!' He airily dismissed the 'other things' in a
subsequent letter 'as I think they are all what I would call "women's talk".'[3] His
sense of superiority as a male was reinforced by the large age gap of eighteen
years between the partners. When Bertha fired an unsuitable nurse she had hired
against Sammy's advice, he stood on his dignity as the older spouse: 'I should
like you to bear in mind and mark carefully for future that when I tell you
anything especially as to people's characters, you will allow me to be a better
judge than you are, and it is only natural I should be so when you will consider
the difference in years there is between us.' [4]

Marks, in common with many of his peers, felt that his wife spent too lavishly
and too freely; the alleged extravagance of spouses was one of the domestic
issues of the age. Sammy issued a series of reminders and rebukes to Bertha
about her spending while on holiday in England and on the Continent in 1902:
'it is no doubt needless for me to point out to you that you have spent a lot of
money. . . . I suppose it is my business in this world to instruct Lewis to issue
cheques and drafts.' [5] Less than four weeks later, ' . . . in regard to your buying
so many things I think the only way to stop you buying will be to ask Lewis not
to accept your drafts any more. The things which you bought some time back
are still lying at East London. Do you expect to open a retail shop at
Zwartkoppies, or are you afraid that the manufacturers will cease making more
things?'[6] Joking later with his daughter Girlie about her mother's outlay on
dresses and hats, he wrote: 'Now you will see something of the trouble of a
husband with an extravagant wife, and you must be careful when you grow
up!!'[7]

On another occasion he rebuked Bertha, who was on holiday at the Marine
Hotel in Durban, for spending the grand sum of £80 on insuring her jewellery.
'I wonder if you have any idea of the value of money and if you remember that
I have to work hard for all the money I give you. I shall not say much in writing
but it seems to me the only remedy I have got will be to stop all cheques for
money which I have to work for.' His complaint might seem like needless
carping when one examines the inventory Bertha supplied to the insurers. The
list includes a string of pearls – 70 in all – with a diamond clasp (valued at £500);
a pair of pearl earrings (£100); a tortoise-shell hairpin set with seven pearls
(£12.10); an emerald and diamond brooch (£100); a coronet brooch with five
pearls and sapphires, rubies and diamonds (£30); a medallion with two heads on
ivory set with pearls and diamonds, and a platinum chain (£100); a gold card case
with diamonds and rubies (£75); a gold purse (£8.10); a gold bracelet watch
(£8.10); three gold mounted combs (£12.10); two gold hatpins set with precious
stones (£10); and a variety of rings, including a diamond (£85), a sapphire (£45)

and a ruby (£35). This was not the full extent of Bertha's collection. In 1906, when she was 44 years old, she had sent some of her jewellery to England. The list included a diamond tiara with a diamond chain; a diamond brooch star; a necklace with 36 diamonds, a blue enamelled diamond locket and a diamond hook; a pair of single-stone diamond earrings; a diamond watch; three diamond bracelets; and three diamond rings – a collection which reflected Bertha's position in society as much as her personal taste.[8]

Like any good Victorian or Edwardian wife, Bertha was expected to obey her husband's wishes. Marks issued polite yet firm instructions: 'I hear on good authority that the Marine Hotel is a place frequented by Gamblers, horseracing men and the Military, and I shall be pleased if you will, after you have rested for a bit, move to another place for the few days you are there.'[9]

But while authority within the marriage lay clearly with her husband, Bertha did possess a degree of influence and independent initiative which she might not otherwise have enjoyed, given the usual distribution of power in a middle-class Victorian household. She was one of the very few women in the Transvaal in the 1890s who was allowed to operate her own banking account. She would draw on this for her household and personal expenses and her husband would then settle with the bank at regular intervals. The decision to send their children to be educated abroad and the difficulties Marks experienced in travelling to England because of the war and the demands of his business, meant that of necessity many of the important decisions about the children were taken by Bertha and that she bore the larger part of the burden when problems arose with them. Marks fully acknowledged this and was quite prepared to defer to her judgement about the best course of action, a view consistent with his philosophy that the person on the spot was always best able to judge a situation.[10]

Marks, like other members of the Victorian and Edwardian middle and upper classes, believed that woman's proper sphere was the domestic. Bertha's chief responsibility was to organise and direct the household. This, he readily acknowledged, was no small chore: 'it is a great trouble to manage such a big house,' he wrote; it 'contains quite a labyrinth of rooms, and we are obliged to keep an army of servants.' Before the war the estate had employed a motley assortment of staff, recruited from far and wide. Besides an unspecified number of blacks, who were summonsed to work daily by a bell in front of the stables, Marks had also sent to Durban for ten 'Madras Coolies' for the orchards and for two 'good, steady, reliable and trustworthy Zulu Boys who can be thoroughly depended on for Night Watchmen'. Marks had brought a governess for the children from Europe, while in Cape Town he had sought to hire a suitable Malay couple for Zwartkoppies: the husband was to look after the stables, the wife to do the washing. Similarly, in 1895 Bertha had written off to Cape Town for a suitable parlour maid: 'What I want is a good English parlour maid, one who has been in the Country for some years preferred, also one who has no objection to coloured people, as I have two slightly coloured servants and one coloured boy. . . . Should she object to occupying the same room as the Coloured Girls, I shall provide separate sleeping accommodation for her.'[11]

During the war Marks's thoughts had turned, in common with fellow members of the Anglo–Transvaal elite, to the systematic importation of white female servants from Britain. Besides improving the supply of domestic labour, this would supposedly improve the quality. 'I am sure people, who at present have black girls working in their houses, would be very pleased indeed', he argued, 'to have in their stead, respectable white girls.' His reasoning reflected contemporary anxieties about the presence of black females in white households and resentment of their independence: 'In the first place native girls are not trustworthy and their morals, as a rule, are not of a high standard. In the second place their wants are so few that they are very independent and if their demands are not met, they go away and live in their kraals.'[12]

At the same time, the immigration of female servants would serve a broader political purpose – the entrenchment of British control over the Transvaal. 'We must have as much good English blood in this country as we possibly can,' Marks argued in defence of the scheme. Views such as these mirrored Milnerite sentiment about the political desirability of adjusting the population ratio between Boer and Brit in favour of the latter.[13]

At the end of the war, Bertha went on a hiring campaign for Zwartkoppies in Britain. She was assisted by the South African Expansion Committee, a London-based organisation, endorsed by Milner, which helped recruit domestic servants for affluent households in the Transvaal, and by W. F. Bailey, an Anglo–Irish friend of her husband, who, as a senior official in the Irish Land Commission, was particularly well-placed to help. It would seem that Bertha and Sammy, like many of their contemporaries, preferred Irish girls, who were commonly believed to be 'stronger and less liable to illness than Scotch or English girls'.[14]

Bertha acted under detailed instruction from her husband. As the household manuals of the age (like Mrs Beeton's) advised, she was to spell out to potential recruits precisely what would be required of them. They were to be warned that Zwartkoppies was twelve miles out of Pretoria and two and a half miles from the nearest railway station, and that they would be allowed to go into town only once a month. The female servants were to be told they would be required to wear caps, and 'that they must not say they will not do this and that, after they had come out here'. (As Sammy well knew, white housemaids often balked at performing household tasks they had willingly undertaken in England when they discovered that these were considered 'Kaffir work' in South Africa.) The prospective employees were also to be warned that 'there should be no grumbling' if there was something special on a Sunday, as there were seldom visitors during the week. Something special, of course, meant one of Sammy's regular afternoon-long lunches on Sundays for a score or more guests.[15]

Bertha Marks was less convivial than Sammy. Her feelings about Sundays at Zwartkoppies and about her husband's gregariousness which she did not share, were expressed, possibly for the first and only time, in a remarkable letter to him, written while holidaying at Taormina in 1906. Italy seems to have had the same liberating effect on the 44-year-old Bertha as it did on any of E. M. Forster's young heroines. It encouraged her to cast off restraint and inhibition

and to express feelings and resentments which had been suppressed for a very·
long time. The outburst was triggered by a hectoring letter from her husband
in which he reminded her in a rough and patronising fashion of her domestic
responsibilities and warned her to keep her recruitment of servants within strict
bounds:

I do not need to remind you that you have gone to Europe to recover your health. . . .
When you have done this I would like you to come back here and take some of the
responsibilities of the house off my shoulders. I have no time to look after such things,
as I have more than enough to do with the business. When times are good one can leave
business to itself occasionally but that cannot be done under present circumstances. I have
not seen things so bad in South Africa ever since I have been here. . . . You must not bring
out a whole regiment of servants with you this time. You must be content with half a
regiment in these bad times.[16]

The provocative tone of the letter unloosed a torrent of long-repressed feeling.
Bertha replied:

we shall be busy tomorrow and the next day packing as I have booked to leave here very
early Wednesday morning May 2nd, although by the various letters I get from England,
likewise by the news in the Papers I am afraid I am not doing a wise thing as regards
myself to push on too quickly but as your letters have worried me to such an extent that
I feel I cannot think of my health any longer and therefore must risk the consequences.
I have been ever so much better the last week or so, as no doubt Dr Kay may tell you as
I generally send him a list weekly. I am indeed sorry to hear that things are so bad in
S Africa and hope to hear soon that times have improved. There is no news as all the days
are spent all alike. Everybody has nearly left this Hotel as people move on after this time
of the year to other ones. Each place has its season.

   Re Servants. So you already feel the responsibility of house keeping and I hope you will
now believe what worry it has been to me so much that I should be glad if one never had
to engage another servant. I had more than enough of it during the last year and
considering how ill I was I think I had very little consideration shown to me.

   While you are on the topic of servants I wish to know exactly what staff of servants you
consider should be enough to engage for Swartkopje, as I shall go and see the
Immigration People and ask them to keep so many applicants places open to send out
about Sep[tember] the necessary staff. This all requires some consideration. Do you
happen to remember that *3 years* ago when you were in England you always spoke about
the great expenses at Swartkopje and that when we got back you would take good care
that you would not entertain a lot of people on Sundays[.] I must say you kept well to
your word as I dont consider my home there has ever been my home it has been an Hotel
and I have been the Housekeeper which is a good billet for a Wife. I myself am sick of
those Sunday Parties, as few of them were of any interest to me but it meant work worry
and plenty of extra money to Pay at the end of the month which you do not take into
consideration. Re the servant question that is my reason for alluding to the above, as if
we are to keep less servants[,] less weekend *entertaining must be done.* As we have lived
hitherto that place with all the extra work those Sundays make, re extra Silver taken out,
Glass China and Linen used, all that has to be put in order for the next week end we cannot
do with less than the following servants.

   A Cook and Kitchenmaid[,] a Butler and someone to help him, 2 Housemaids and
1 Housemaid and not counting the necessary Kaffirs to do all the childrens quarters and

wait upon them at meals etc. Then the Laundry requires people and Mostert is not
certainly able to see to the Dairy and my Poultry as it will be required on my return.

Then a Gov[erness] for Doll[,] a nurse for Phil and a maid for myself. I have had
enough inconvenience not having one with me all this time. Re a Butler you had better
see if you can get one there . . . or shall I bring one out. All this you must be sure and reply
as soon as possible as all *this means a lot of work for me.*

. . . I often wonder if you really read my letters because if you dont I need only write
short letters in future.

. . . As I am not sure what you really do with my letters[,] what I would say to you
re Joey and Girlie I shall ask George [Falcke] to read to you. It is not as if he or Phil Levy
do not know *all* you have typed to me.

I have had a warm dressing gown sent out to you as I know you need one for
Johannesburg so I hope I have done right in that respect.[17]

Sammy, deeply anxious about the current economic recession and its likely
effects on his firm and on his personal finances, responded that he thought his
wife's staffing requisition for Zwartkoppies a trifle excessive: 'As to servants,
this is a matter which entirely affects you. It is in your province to see that the
house is properly conducted but I think you must agree with me that it is not
necessary to keep an establishment of 12 white women.' Bertha should recruit
four to six servants in the first instance; if more were needed later, these could
easily be found.[18]

Bertha was clearly emboldened by her expression of defiance. Once she
reached London, on the same visit to Europe, she challenged her husband on the
subject of her alleged extravagance. When he appeared to be ignoring a request
for additional money, she fumed with exasperation:

I regret very much that you place me in such an awkward position and will not reply
to my question re Money. How am I to pay my way and who is to pay all the bills. . . .
It is absurd that you ignore the subject as to whom shall I look to for it if not you. Have
you any idea what a hundred and one little expenses crop up during a month besides bare
living and hotel bills. I am just waiting to see if I do not get some sensible and satisfactory
answer to various questions I have asked you . . . in tomorrow's mail and after that I shall
be compelled to draw on the London office as I shall be practically penniless in a few days
and I cannot draw blood from a stone. Believe me I can *prove* that none of the money that
you gave me when we came home last March has been spent *on myself* up to now[,] I mean
personally. But some of course will have to be before I return. If you only knew how tired
and worried I am over such unsatisfactory affairs, you would be more reasonable and see
matters in a proper way and as most husbands do to their wives. So as you wont give me
any satisfactory answer, you must not blame me afterwards. I am very sorry to see from
Phil's (my brothers) letter to me last mail which was a scorcher that your imagination has
doubled and trebled itself since I left and I must say that I thank you from the bottom of
my heart for making me appear such a spendthrift in his eyes. But I shall certainly clear
myself in his eyes on my return. How could you tell him such an untruth that I spend a
thousand a month. I shall prove very very differently to that on my return. I shall show
him figures which will then convince him. Have you ever counted what my expenses
have been to keep Swaartkopje and your Johannesburg house for the last two years. But
I know when I say that all the money that ever has been placed to my credit in the Bank
has gone to pay for all the necessary household expenses and scarcely any of that for
myself and if you do not provide for my personal requirements and children's befitting

Sam Marks wife[,] who is to [do] that is all I want to know and on my return for both our peace of minds we shall have to go thoroughly into this matter and decide upon such course so that neither you nor I have to constantly bicker and talk on this subject. It worries me more than you . . . because you have always the needful to fall back upon and I have no idea where to get my next shilling if it does not come from you and I think if you will only reason the matter out you will agree with me that I am placed in a very unpleasant and unsatisfactory position. Enough of this. I hope you are keeping quite well.[20]

Sammy's reply to this volcanic outpouring of pent-up anger and frustration, of intense but impotent resentment of her total dependence on her husband, like other women of her class and times, was again conciliatory if evasive. The issue, he wrote, was best left till she returned to Zwartkoppies; 'good things will keep.' Unfortunately we have no record of the promised discussion.[21]

For all the crowds that came on Sundays to Zwartkoppies and for all the servants that surrounded her, Bertha felt very isolated at Zwartkoppies. She had come from a large Anglo–Jewish family living in a growing and vital urban Jewish community. From the very start of their marriage her husband was often away on business, sometimes for days or even weeks at a time. Zwartkoppies was physically isolated; it was an uncomfortable twelve-mile carriage drive of close to two hours from Pretoria. There were seldom visitors during the week, and social custom required that she keep a proper social distance from her servants and employees. Bertha and her children seldom visited Pretoria. Dollie, the youngest daughter, recalls that trips to town were special occasions. Once a year they would ride into Pretoria for their much-awaited annual treat, the Christmas pantomime. For months before, Bertha and Sammy's rumbustious children would be brought to order by adult threats that the treat would be cancelled unless they quietened down. When the time came they would travel into town by cart, stopping on the hill at Silverton to give the horses a breather.

While Zwartkoppies was paradise for her husband, a haven from the turmoil of the world, it was a gilded cage for Bertha, a place of loneliness where her husband left her 'so much alone'. Her increasingly frequent trips 'home' to England and her extended annual stays at the coast during the holiday season, either in Durban or at their holiday home at Muizenberg, were clearly a relief from the isolation of Zwartkoppies. She had difficulty in returning to Zwartkoppies after these forays into the world. Her procrastination over her returns to Africa from England, with the repeated postponements of her departure dates, was for her husband at first amusing and then very annoying. Joking with his daughter about a delayed return, Marks wrote: 'you'll sail within about 8 days after you receive this that is to say if mother does not have some shopping to do, and change her mind, and postpone the voyage for another month or so.'[22]

Bertha occupied her time at Zwartkoppies with her household responsibilities and with recreational activities considered appropriate to the Victorian lady, plus a few that were a little less conventional. Bertha loved gardening. With the assistance of an Austrian horticulturist (who was also adept at catching snakes with a forked stick and converting their skins into purses and belts), she created a Victorian English garden on the veld. Orders for plants, bulbs and seeds were regularly placed with a nursery in Kent, and these were sent out in batches, week by week, in accordance with the season. Her rose garden has recently been excavated and is being restored to its former glory, complete with the Victorian varieties of rose, Baroness Rothschild, Sultan Zanzibar, Anna de Diesbach and the like, which it once contained and which have since disappeared from South Africa. Bertha loved flowers and even after the family moved to a very much smaller house in Johannesburg in 1909 she saw that it was filled with blooms sent specially from Zwartkoppies in a laundry skip.[23]

The library at Zwartkoppies, now frozen in time, attests that Bertha was an avid reader. Her tastes ran to the popular novelists of the age; the Zwartkoppies library contained sets of the novels of Marie Corelli, Wilkie Collins, Ouida and others. Her husband, who cared little for fiction, sniffed at these. His tastes were rather more serious and ran to periodical articles on industries and inventions and to books on farming, mining, irrigation and the South African Question. Besides practical manuals with such compelling titles as *Wire. Its Manufacture and Uses* and *Australasian Sheep and Wool*, the large library at Zwartkoppies also held copies of the Koran, Adam Smith's *Wealth of Nations*, Charles Darwin's *Descent of Man*, Krafft-Ebing's *Psychopathia Sexualis*, Olive Schreiner's *Story of an African Farm*, Rudyard Kipling's *Jungle Book* and Edward Lear's *Book of Nonsense*. Marks probably left the last three to his wife and children. He preferred browsing through the collected speeches of Disraeli, Gladstone and John Bright which he ordered from an Edinburgh bookseller, Winston Churchill's biography of Randolph Churchill which he ordered from London, and a book titled *England and the English* which he ordered from Maskew Miller in Cape Town. Marks also subscribed to the *Nineteenth Century*, a serious monthly magazine, to the 'illustrated papers' and to a selection of South African newspapers, including the *Star*, the *Cape Times*, the *Cape Argus* and the *Sunday Times*.

A passionate autodidact, Marks saw reading as essentially educative, a means of improving one's 'stock of knowledge'. He repeatedly urged his eldest son Louis to read 'good and useful books and remember what you read'. He gave similar advice, tinged with moral anxiety, to his oldest daughter Girlie when she was 11: 'I am glad you like reading but you should let your mother or your Governess select suitable books for you, otherwise your reading may do you more harm than good.' Marks felt that 'Reading is a grand thing and one should devote as much time to it as possible.' His great regret was that he had insufficient time for it. In his late fifties his eyes weakened and he found that after fifteen minutes of reading they would begin to water. In his old age he enjoyed having his youngest daughter Dolly read to him. She recalls that he enjoyed a serious literary diet but 'nothing light'.[24]

Besides reading and gardening, Bertha Marks also rode about the farm and rowed on the large dam a short distance from the house in the boats her husband had specially imported. According to Dolly, her mother often played billiards in the grand billiard room adjoining the library at Zwartkoppies. Her father would come to watch rather than to play for his own game was shaky. Sammy was never much of a sportsman but he did enjoy a few hands of bezique, a card-game for two, with young Dolly, and in his sixties played the occasional game of bowls in Pretoria with other local notables, including T. W. Beckett, A. Johnston and J. J. Kirkness; his bowling handicap was a lowly eight.[25]

Reading, riding and rowing were Bertha's pastimes; poultry-keeping was her passion. Her pure-bred fowls, fed dried locusts when available, regularly won prizes at the shows. Her expertise was acknowledged by the new agricultural department of the Milner administration, which bought breeding eggs for the government estate at Tzaneen and distributed eggs as well on her behalf, free of charge, to 'families of the poorer classes'. The Zwartkoppies Poultry Farm was an expensive pursuit and the subject of gentle teasing by her husband and children; Sammy used to joke that each egg at the table had cost him £1. Unfortunately Bertha's chicken runs were eventually destroyed by fire and were not replaced.[26]

Bertha's isolation had deepened after the war with her husband's increasingly frequent absences in Johannesburg. With the closure of the Hatherley distillery during the war, the Vereeniging Estates company and later African and European became the focal concerns of the firm. Both were headquartered in Johannesburg and Marks was consequently obliged to spend most of the working week in the city, returning to Zwartkoppies for the weekend only. For five years between 1903 and 1908 he commuted backwards and forwards, leading a bachelor existence reminiscent of his Kimberley days for most of the week. First he rented accommodation in Wolmarans Street close to town, then moved to rustic Parktown, the elite suburb further north which he far preferred, as it approximated more closely to Zwartkoppies: 'I like living at Parktown as the air is so fresh in the morning and I can go about for a walk around the garden instead of being cooped up as I was at Wolmarans St.' Marks, already in his early sixties, grew very weary of this routine. 'You cannot expect me to live in Johannesburg by myself', he complained to Isaac Lewis, 'and leave my family at Zwartkopje as I have done for a good many years. I cannot altogether forgo home comforts and it is unreasonable to expect me to live as an exile from my family.'[27]

After Sir Edwin Dunning resigned as managing director of African and European in 1909, the Marks family at last moved from Zwartkoppies and took occupation of his company house at 5 St David's Place, Parktown. Because this was 'woefully insufficient', Marks added a number of rooms and charged the firm for the alterations. When Isaac Lewis apppeared to query this, Marks lost his temper. Time and time again, he raged, he had passed up offers of comfortable homes at bargain prices out of deference to Lewis's wish that no money be withdrawn from the hard-pressed partnership: 'It was the desire not to draw on the firm that induced me to patch up the house now occupied by me and endeavour to make it habitable for it is not fit for my family to live in and was built by a Dutchman. Why my stable at Zwartkopje is 50 per cent better than my present residence. . . . I feel that after 38 years of slaving I am entitled to have a comfortable residence for myself and my wife and children.'

Characteristically, he hastened to add: 'Pray do not think that I am annoyed with you, it is with myself I feel vexed and I blame myself entirely.'[28]

Marks's ill-temper probably owed something to regret at leaving his beloved Zwartkoppies. Bertha, on the other hand, seems to have welcomed the move for it represented a liberation from the physical and social isolation of country living and from the demands of managing a very large household. Johannesburg offered the opportunity to mix more readily with women of her own class and background, and to move a little way beyond the domestic sphere to exercise her talent for organisation on a broader stage. For Bertha, and other upper-middle-class Jewish housewives in Johannesburg, this was a new age in which the still powerful constraints imposed upon them by the Victorian ideal of the 'perfect lady' – the 'ideal of the completely leisured, completely ornamental, completely helpless and dependent middle-class wife or daughter' – were slowly yielding ground to the greater latitude associated with the *fin de siècle* notion of the 'new woman'. Bertha and her peers were what the historian Riva Krut calls 'domestic feminists', women who did not necessarily share the views of the militant feminists and suffragists of their time – in fact, often roundly condemned these – but who in their daily lives increasingly practised a tacit feminism of a cautious sort. While domesticity and the household were still emphasised, it became more acceptable for a 'lady' to move beyond the hearth and enter public life, albeit on a limited and strictly feminine basis.[29]

Besides joining the Johannesburg Country Club Bertha enlisted, together with her social peers, in the Jewish Ladies' Communal League, an organisation founded after the war to encourage women to play a more active part in Jewish communal life. The League's chief concern was the establishment and management of the first Jewish orphanage in South Africa, a project to which Bertha and Sammy contributed generously in both cash and kind. Bertha gave money while Sammy donated 650 trees from the Vaal River plantation and the roofing tiles. Trees and building material, it seems, were his favourite form of charitable donation.[30]

But Bertha was more than a wealthy patroness; she played an active part in the affairs of the League and the running of the orphanage. During her busy and sociable Johannesburg years she presided at League meetings, chaired the building committee of the orphanage, canvassed donations from her wealthy acquaintances, and organised the League's fancy dress ball, then one of the most popular ways of raising funds. These were splendid social occasions. The *South African Jewish Chronicle* singled out Bertha Marks at the annual Simchas Torah ball at the Wanderers Hall in Johannesburg in 1912. Bertha was 'beautifully gowned' in black satin embroidered with sequins with a fish-tail train and wore a 'lovely' string of pearls. Significantly, she was escorted by her now grown-up sons rather than by her husband, who had no fondness for such occasions.[31]

Marks's oldest sons completed their education in the decade after the South African War. His expectations of the expensive public school education he had provided for his boys – that it would make English 'gentlemen' of them – were fulfilled but in an unexpected and rather disquieting way, as Marks discovered when Louis, his oldest son, now 18, visited South Africa in the middle of 1904.

The visit, the first since he had left for England as an 8-year-old in 1894, was peculiarly upsetting for his father. As Marks discovered to his dismay, Louis was estranged from his immigrant father and indifferent to his mercantile and industrial concerns. The public school ethos which Louis had so successfully absorbed, and which had been the *raison d'être* for sending him to Harrow, was at odds with the spirit of entrepreneurship and commerce that animated his father. So upset was Marks that he spoke impulsively about bringing his children back from England to be educated in the Transvaal. As he wrote to his partner Isaac Lewis:

After ripe consideration I have come to the conviction that children sent thousands of miles away from their parents to be educated cannot have that sympathy with their parents and their relations which they should have, this is only natural because they are left almost entirely to strangers, are away from home influence and lose touch with the ideas and aspirations of their parents, moreover they are not in sympathy with the business which their fathers have built up for themselves and which they are constantly planning to extend for the benefit of their children. Taking these facts into consideration I have determined to build a school if necessary on my farm and get out 2 or 3 competent teachers . . . so that the children may be under my personal supervision and have home influences, that they may see and appreciate what I am doing and learn that all my efforts are made with the sole object of furthering their future welfare. The expense of what I propose to do will not be much more than that incurred in Europe. It is rather late in the day to carry out my idea as I am grown old and my children are big, but still I feel that I am doing what is right.

Possibly you may think that I have reason to be dissatisfied with Louis or that he is misbehaving himself. Let me assure you such is not the case. I am in the highest degree pleased with him, his conduct has been exemplary and he is quite content to remain at home preferring this to going about.[32]

Indeed, this was part of the problem. Marks had asked his son repeatedly to go with him to Johannesburg and elsewhere on his business rounds, but Louis preferred to remain at Zwartkoppies. On mature reflection Marks recognised the impracticality of setting up a farm school for his children at Zwartkoppies and left his sons at public school in England. As the poignant letter to Lewis suggests, he was beginning to sense that he had unwittingly undercut his own efforts to create an enduring inheritance for his children. With the best intentions in the world he had provided his sons with an education that unsuited them to take over the reins of an industrial barony.

As a result of his education abroad Louis Marks had become 'Y. L.', the 'Young Lord', the deflating nickname given to him by his cousin George Falcke when he returned from Europe, a nickname which stuck with him for life. Pompous and self-important though he was, Louis had the grace to accept the nickname in good part and later incorporated it into his telegraphic address in Johannesburg.[33]

For Marks, as for his gentile and Jewish contemporaries, the education of daughters was less of a priority than the education of sons. A boy should be taught a profession, a girl the genteel accomplishments that would help to make her 'a perfect lady', the feminine equivalent of the 'gentleman'. Education beyond this point was likely to be wasted: 'in my opinion', he wrote to his oldest daughter, 'more than 75% of the education for Girls is thrown away.' Yet, for all his scepticism, he was prepared to spend lavishly on their schooling.[34]

Like her brothers, though at a later age, Gertrude Miriam Marks, nicknamed Girlie or Gai, was sent to a private school in England, Highfield in Golders Green, one of a crop of girls' schools established to cater for the new fashion of sending young ladies to public school. Marks, who was more protective even of his daughters than he was of his sons, was none too enthusiastic about the idea, and would have preferred Girlie to remain at home with a private tutor. But he allowed himself to be persuaded by his wife and daughter.[35]

A bright, exuberant girl, commended by her headmistress for her 'unfailing flow of fun and good spirits', Girlie was clearly her father's favourite child. The letters he wrote to her while she was away in England were far less perfunctory than those to her brothers. They were suffused with warmth, affection and gruff tenderness, salted with chaff and good humour and only lightly dosed with advice and admonition.[36] Writing sixteen months before the Wright brothers' first flight, he teased:

I received your letter and can see from it that you are as naughty a little girl as ever, and I expect your mother allows you to be so.

I hope you do not overlook the days, hours, and minutes for your lessons, as it seems to me from what you write that you are thinking of nothing else but excitement and pleasure. . . . I think Miss Forsyth is a great deal to blame for it. Tell her if she does not work you up, I won't give you two a farm for horsebreeding and on which to break in horses. I think a flying-machine worked by electricity, which is to be gathered in the atmosphere will be much better for both of you, as it will go so much quicker.[37]

Studying some photographs Girlie had sent from school: 'In the one of Miss Forsyth and yourself, I can see you are pretending to be very deep in study with Miss Forsyth, but that it was as much as you could do to abstain from laughing. I expect now that you have been travelling over Germany and other parts of the continent there will not even be a chance to keep you in order with an iron chain.'[38]

Writing more sternly than usual: 'I have received your letter and was very glad to see from it that you are still in very good health and also full of mischief and I hope you will continue so. However, although I always like to see you light-hearted and a little harmlessly mischievous, you must not forget that there is a limit to everything, especially as you are now already 16 years of age, as you yourself say, and 6,000 miles away from your mother and father you have not got them to guide you in what is wrong and what is right.'[39]

Answering a complaint that his letters were too short: 'Now I would like you to tell me what I can write you about Blouses? I do not wear them. Dancing I have forgotten and all other kinds of nonsense I have never known!! So therefore when I write you a short note you must always bear in mind that your Daddy is thinking about you and that he does not know what to tell you except that you must always be a perfect lady and work hard and learn everything that is useful for the sake of your future. No doubt mother writes you very long letters about her chickens and pigeons, parrots, cows, butter and so forth, which is not in my department. My department, as you know, is mining and farming.'[40]

Girlie had a musical talent her father enjoyed and her mother wished to develop further. She played the violin and sang well, and Bertha hoped that she would continue her training in Dresden or Paris. Her father was less certain about the value of this: 'I feel quite sure you do not wish to become a Prima Donna, and I only want you to have all the accomplishments that a very nice young lady should have, and I am sure you must have nearly all that already, as I am highly satisfied with you, and I hope that you have the same high opinion of yourself.' Nevertheless, he was quite willing to indulge his wife, and reassured his daughter that he would cheerfully bear the cost of the scheme: 'Do not worry about the expenditure and think it would be less if you came home. I arranged all that a good many years ago, when I determined to give my children a good education and to make them children of whom any one might be proud.'[41]

Dolly, the younger daughter, was the first to attend school in South Africa. After the family moved from Zwartkoppies to Johannesburg in 1909 she and Phil, the youngest child, went to St Andrew's and Parktown Preparatory respectively, before following their older siblings to school in England. The quality of education in the Transvaal had clearly risen by 1910 to a level Marks considered personally acceptable.[42]

Besides Sammy and Bertha and their servants and children, the Marks household at Zwartkoppies also included one other figure of note. This was John Murray, an elderly and educated but impecunious Scot who lived with the Marks family for over two decades. Born in Aberdeenshire in 1834, he had arrived at Zwartkoppies in the early 1880s. Marks had originally hired Murray as a transport-rider but had so enjoyed his company that he had invited him to take up residence at Zwartkoppies, and had given him marginal land to work on a share basis at nearby Hatherley. Murray grew mealies, oats and potatoes, though with little success: 'as long as I have known him,' Marks wrote in 1897, 'he has never yet reared anything; but that, of course, is the fault of the ground.' Early in the war Murray had one of his better yields of potatoes, but these were picked out of the ground by famished Argyle and Sutherland Highlanders; 'Uncle John' – understandably – 'was very wild with them'.

Murray's farming exploits and Murray himself were part of the family folklore, discussed in the weekly letters between Marks and his children at school in England. Murray was the Marks children's adopted uncle, who took them on regular Sunday drives around the neighbourhood, allowing each in turn a chance to drive. 'Uncle John' was clearly more than just an unusual *bywoner*; amiable and well-read, he doubled as Marks's gentleman companion. As an autodidact Marks had a thirst for information and discussion, and this Murray, who lived in the house with the family, provided. Murray acted as Marks's reader just as his nephew George Falcke acted as his amanuensis. 'Kindly read these books through carefully and communicate to me anything that you think would interest me therein,' Marks instructed, handing over a parcel which included British consular reports on North and South America,

guides for intending settlers in Argentina, California, Ceylon and the West
Indies, and a text on family budgeting. Murray's household 'duties' extended no
further. Throughout his lengthy stay he was treated with consideration and
respect by his fond host: 'Your kindness to him,' Murray's relatives wrote after
his death in 1905, 'we hold in most grateful remembrance. . . .'[43]

The other regular at Zwartkoppies, though not resident like Murray, was Dr
Kay, the family doctor. James Alexander Kay was five years younger than
Marks. Born in Plymouth in 1849, he studied medicine in Scotland but failed to
complete his studies. For ten years he served as an unqualified medical officer on
whaling ships in the southern oceans. When one of these called at Durban in 1879
at the start of the Anglo–Zulu War, Kay jumped ship and joined the Royal Army
Medical Corps. After the campaign ended he was stationed in Pretoria, where
he remained till the Transvaal reverted to Boer rule in 1881 after the Transvaal
War. He then went back to Britain but returned to South Africa shortly
afterwards. He had taken a liking to Pretoria and when he heard that the Boers,
who were desperately short of professional men, would register anyone who
had satisfactory practical experience of medicine and surgery whatever his lack
of formal qualifications, he returned to the Boer capital to set up his shingle as
a general practitioner.

Kay became the Marks family doctor as well as medical officer to the
Hatherley distillery. Before the railways opened he would ride out from Pretoria
to examine his patients at Zwartkoppies or Hatherley, a long and rough journey.
On his return to Pretoria after this strenuous round trip, he would dispense the
necessary medicines. If Marks was at his Pretoria office for the day, he would
take the medicines home with him. On one such occasion, early in their
relationship, Marks failed to deliver the medicine through some misunderstanding. When Kay, who was a very forthright individual, unintimidated by
authority or wealth, next met Marks he gave him a tongue-lashing. This earned
Marks's respect and Kay subsequently became a close friend.

Kay, a hospitable and generous person, was financially reckless like two other
of Marks's old friends, Jimmy Sivewright and Alois Hugo Nellmapius. Kay's
personal finances were chronically disordered. Though he had the leading
practice in Pretoria, worth at least £3,000 per annum, the Standard Bank judged
him a poor risk. 'Has a first class practice but lives extravagantly and is heavily
in debt,' the bank wrote in 1893. 'We attach very little value to his name.' Marks
repeatedly bailed out Kay as he did his other friends. Kay's Pretoria home,
Jellalabad Villa, which was worth £5,000 and was in Mrs Kay's name, was
bonded to Marks for £4,000. Marks also saw to the education of Kay's children,
including the medical training of his son.

On the eve of the South African War, Kay, a fervent jingo like many of the
Uitlanders, did some freelance spying for the British. Fearing arrest, he fled to
Natal, boarding the south-bound train disguised as a woman. He was trapped
in Ladysmith during the siege in early 1900 but returned to Pretoria later in the
year with Roberts's victorious army, acting, surprisingly, as a war correspondent rather than as a doctor. He then resumed private practice in Pretoria,
serving the Marks family as before. Like many a Victorian doctor he was very

censorious and authoritarian. He was particularly critical of Bertha Marks. When her 7-year-old son Teddy had fits and developed an emotional disorder in 1901–2, Sammy kept a medical report from her in which Dr Kay insinuated unfairly that she was somehow to blame. 'She is very neurotic and highly excitable, and does not rear her children in a commendable manner; when quite young, even from four and five years of age they are taken to theatres, and any excitement that is likely to amuse them, and they have their evening meal as late as six o'clock and generally have meat before going to bed.' The report clearly says more about Kay's severe traditional views on child-rearing than it does about Bertha's responsibility for her son's condition.

When Bertha became seriously ill three years later, Kay again found much of which he disapproved. Writing to the patient's husband rather than directly to the patient, he complained: 'It appears to me that Mrs. Marks does not understand how very serious her condition is. I thought that I had spoken so strongly to her as well as to yourself that you both fully recognised that every care and precaution was essential to her recovery, yet I find that a day or two ago Mrs. Marks wore a very light blouse, and again last night she did not leave the dinner table until past nine o'clock. I do not wish to cause any unpleasantness, nor any panic, but it is my duty to tell you that it is quite impossible for Mrs. Marks to recover altogether. With *care* and *strict attention* to orders she may live many years and enjoy a *quiet* life. . . .'

Sammy Marks received equally short shrift from the outspoken doctor. When in December 1909 Marks threatened to cut short a rest-cure at the Caledon mineral baths, after a bout of rheumatism, Kay wrote from Pretoria: 'Surely you don't intend to return for the present. If you do I shall say right out that you deserve to get worse. I'm sure if you don't get this attack quite out of your system you will be in for a bad time but it is no use preaching.' Duly chastened, Marks stayed on at the Caledon Baths.[44]

In a period when illness was rife and standards of medical knowledge were low, Marks's health was generally good, at least until he reached old age. After a near-fatal bout of camp fever at Kimberley in 1882 when he was 38 years old, he seems to have avoided major illness until he reached his sixties, though he was plagued by rheumatism from his early forties. Dr Kay gave him a clean bill of health at the end of the South African War when he was 58 years old: Marks was 'a singularly strong and robust man who has had little or no illness through life, excepting Muscular Rheumatism and Influenza.' From his youth he had led a vigorous life and he continued to do so into his sixties. Marks drank very little and abhorred smoking. His prescription for healthy eating is best summarised in a letter of advice he wrote to a Jewish friend, Mrs Max Langerman of Johannesburg, who was recuperating at the seaside at Muizenberg from illness. She should rise at 6 and drink a glass of fresh milk while reading the newspaper. 'After that a little fresh air will be very beneficial and then a nice and refreshing toilet.' She should be very 'particular' about her breakfast and insist on poached or boiled eggs rather than fried eggs: the cook of the Alexander Hotel would use the same pan to fry ham and eggs for the other guests, and Mrs Langerman (whose husband was the first chairman of the Transvaal Jewish Board of

Deputies) would surely not approve. At 11 in the morning she should take a good glass of port, beaten with a fresh egg and some finely ground sugar, and at 12.30 strong beef tea, that favourite Edwardian pick-me-up. Lunch should consist of some baked fish, and half a grilled chicken with a nice salad. At 4 she should have tea with thinly buttered toast. Some light soup with a little maizena (cornflour) added in would be very refreshing at dinner time. 'For the rest I must leave you to take what you fancy best, but you must always be careful not to take too heavy pastry as I presume you go to bed about 10 o'clock and it would therefore not do you 'any good at all.'[45]

In his sixties Marks's health deteriorated sharply. He had suffered from rheumatism from his early forties but 'my old enemy' now became far more severe; on some days '[I] could hardly move myself'. During 1907 he felt below par for months on end; 'taking myself all round, I regret to say that I do not feel A.1, still like the Old Working Horse I go on pulling.' In 1908 he fell very seriously ill. He was confined to bed for a fortnight and lost a great deal of weight. While the diagnoses of Dr Kay of Pretoria and Dr Davies of Johannesburg veered between 'rheumatic gout' and Kidney or Bright's disease, they did agree that their patient should travel to Europe to take the cure at Carlsbad. Whatever the curative powers of the waters, the break from the severe stresses of business life seemed to have helped, if only temporarily. But for the rest of his life Marks continued to experience savage bouts of rheumatism, which interfered on occasion with his work. Marks tried 'electrical treatment' for relief from his discomfort. His daughter Dollie recalls how his butler Maclaren helped him use a large wooden 'hot box' fitted with numerous electric lamps. Sammy would sit in this, perspiring heavily, with only his head sticking out. Besides this prescribed treatment, he also improvised his own personal remedy for rheumatism. When he felt the first signs of an imminent attack he would order his motor car and go for a drive over very rough roads. After a thorough shaking, he would return home, apparently relieved of much of his pain.[46]

The deterioration in Marks's health in the post-war years coincided, as we have seen, with enforced and unwelcome changes in his domestic arrangements and with severe difficulties in his business life. It coincided too with a crisis of faith within the Marks household.

XI

Sammy Marks the Jew

Sammy Marks faced a series of daunting challenges during the post-war era: the need to adapt to a new and less pliable political order; to reconstruct his business in an age of recession; and, finally, to reorder his domestic arrangements. At the same time that his wife Bertha was questioning these, Sammy was confronted with a challenge from his oldest daughter, Girlie, to his religious beliefs. Girlie asked very uncomfortable questions about the meaning of his core identity – his Jewishness.

Sammy Marks was the prototype of the modern South African Jew. Though nominally orthodox, Marks's Judaism, like that of many of his South African Jewish contemporaries and his Jewish social peers in England, deviated substantially from the norms of the Eastern European *shtetl*. While he had been born into a traditional Lithuanian Jewish community, he had left while still young and had spent his impressionable early adult years in a more liberal English Jewish environment, where orthodoxy had adapted to the requirements of a modern industrial society. After leaving Sheffield, he had spent years on the frontier of Jewish settlement in South Africa where strict orthodoxy, even had he wished to practise it, was impracticable. For lengthy periods of time he had lived beyond the reach of the communal support systems so necessary to a rigorous orthodox Jewish existence. Following his brief spell as a pedlar or smous, an occupation which took him to remote places where strict observance of the Jewish dietary laws was extremely difficult, he had arrived in Kimberley well before the establishment of an organised Jewish community. Then, in the early 1880s, he had once again crossed the South African Jewish frontier, settling in the Transvaal which was as yet uncolonised by orthodox Judaism – hence the need to bring a *mohel* all the way from Kimberley to Pretoria to circumcise his first-born son in 1885.

Marks's marriage into a well-established Anglo–Jewish family had hastened, if anything, the drift away from the strict orthodoxy of his *shtetl* childhood. Though her father, Tobias Guttmann, had been both president and treasurer of the Sheffield Hebrew Congregation, Bertha Marks's orthodoxy seems to have been of the lukewarm, anglicised variety so characteristic of the Jewish elite in Victorian England. From the very start of their marriage, the Jewish dietary laws were less than strictly enforced in the kitchen at Zwartkoppies. Bertha's first grocery list included an order for two dozen lobster, which together with all other shellfish are forbidden food in Jewish law. Sammy himself clearly enjoyed shellfish. The Marks papers include a letter of thanks to his old Cape friend Jimmy Sivewright for a gift of 'very good' crayfish and a payment of £9.7s.6d. he personally made in 1896 to the Cape Canning Company for six cases of 'preserved crayfish'. The papers also include receipts from non-kosher as well as kosher butcheries. The City Kosher Meat Market in Johannesburg supplied kosher tongue, polony and smoked beef, while the Connaught Butcheries in Pretoria made regular deliveries of *treyf*, or non-kosher meat.[1]

Like many of her Anglo–Jewish contemporaries, Bertha celebrated Christmas. 'Christmas is drawing close and we are all very busy preparing for it,' Marks reported in December 1896 to Louis and Montie at school in England. 'Mother especially has very little time to spare.' She had already purchased 'quite an army of Turkies [sic]', presumably for the staff Christmas dinners which were part of Zwartkoppies' annual round. At Christmas-time gifts and greetings were exchanged between parents and children, and on one occasion at least, Louis was rebuked by his father for forgetting to do so: 'I wonder if he has got somebody whom he thinks is more entitled or more in need of presents than his own people.' Dolly Maisels still recalls the large Christmas parties at Zwartkoppies and the concerts she and her siblings 'had to perform much against our will' for the adults in the dining-room, which was specially converted for the purpose.[2]

The Marks household kept relatively few of the principal Jewish observances. Friday night had no special significance for the Marks family. Instead Sunday lunch was the great occasion of the week. Marks appears to have worked on Saturdays. Here he was clearly in the company of the great majority of his Jewish contemporaries in South Africa: as early as 1911 the *South African Jewish Chronicle* complained that only the 'minutest minority' still kept the Sabbath. Marks seems to have attended synagogue infrequently. Since he lived well out of town and travelled a great deal on business, opportunities to attend synagogue would have been limited even had he been eager to do so. The Marks family did, however, celebrate the Passover and the High Festivals, though these were more often spent at home than at the communal services in Pretoria: 'As usual we spent the New Year out at Zwartkoppie and had two very pleasant days,' Marks wrote to his sons in 1897. 'We were all out at Zwartkoppies and kept the day [of Atonement] in a quiet way,' he told a nephew a few weeks later. Similarly the family observed the Jewish rites of passage. Marks took care to see that his sons were circumcised on precisely the day prescribed by Jewish law, 'as in matters like this I prefer being exact'. Their *bar mitzvahs* were celebrated but with little fuss. Neither parent was present when Louis and Joe read their portions from the Law while at school in England.[3]

Sammy Marks's letters suggest that then, as now, the rites of passage, the Passover and the High Festivals were the most enduring of Jewish observances. When all else was left behind, these were retained, even if only in a modified form, perhaps more as symbols of Jewish identity than for their religious content. For Marks and many other anglicised Jews, Judaism had become more a matter of personal identity than of religious conviction. 'My father was not religious,' Marks's daughter Dolly Maisels explains, 'he was a very staunch Jew but he wasn't a religious one.' In an age when most Jewish magnates in the Transvaal preferred to distance themselves from their ethnic origins, Marks was very conscious, and openly proud, of his membership of a 'Nation . . . more than 6000 years old'. As his advice to Louis when he left for Harrow before the South African War attests, Marks encouraged his children and nephews to take the same pride in their Jewishness. On another occasion, he promised a football and pump to a nephew who had 'challenged another boy to mortal combat in the cause of [his] religion, which is noble'.[4]

With pride in Jewishness went a sense of kinship with Jews elsewhere and a concern for their plight. Marks shared the dismay of Jews everywhere when in the 1890s Captain Alfred Dreyfus was falsely accused of treason in France, publicly dishonoured and unjustly imprisoned on Devil's Island. Again, Marks, like many other Jews in the West in the late nineteenth and early twentieth centuries, felt a strong sense of solidarity with his oppressed brethren in Eastern Europe. Since the beginning of the 1880s the Jews of the Russian empire had been the victims of recurrent bouts of mob violence. These pogroms often had tacit official approval: Jews were convenient scapegoats for the ills of a cancerous empire. When in 1906, after the abortive revolution of the previous year, Russian Jews were the targets of yet another wave of anti-Jewish rioting, Marks volunteered to assist some of those who found their way to the Transvaal. Marks offered to provide farming land for between five and ten refugee families. The ground would be rent-free for five years and Marks would loan each family a furrow plough and six plough animals. He would also provide each family with a month's rations at his own expense plus six goats to supply them with milk. The offer was not unconditional though. 'It must be clearly understood', he wrote, 'that the heads of the families I am prepared to assist . . . must be thorough and experienced farmers and not too old. I do not desire my offer to be taken advantage of on behalf of those who have devoted themselves entirely to the study of Talmud nor of those who have walked the streets discussing politics.' Marks's half-jest reveals a great deal about his notion of the ideal Jew. He was sceptical both of those orthodox Jews who had taken refuge from a hostile world in traditional learning and of their diametrical opposites, those Jewish modernists who had wholly abandoned orthodoxy and forsaken Judaism for revolutionary politics. His ideal, plainly, was the Jew like himself: a practical man, fully engaged with the modern world, but religiously orthodox in sentiment if not necessarily in practice.[5]

With ethnic pride and solidarity went a complete rejection of intermarriage or of any negation of Jewish identity. In 1905 Sammy's favourite child, Girlie, then a 15-year-old at an Anglican boarding-school in England, announced that she wished to be baptised. Her father was 'greatly shocked'. His nephew George Falcke recalls that 'he was distracted with grief and was inconsolable'. Conversion, like intermarriage, was wholly unacceptable to orthodox Jewish opinion both in South Africa and in Britain. This was an age when orthodox parents would sit *shivah* – in mourning – for a child lost to the Jewish faith through intermarriage. Arrangements were hurriedly made through the Lewis family, to bring Girlie home at once. She was escorted to Pretoria in June by a chaperone who then caught the return steamer to England. Girlie spent the next months at Zwartkoppies practising the violin and her singing and 'working hard at fencing', while her father gingerly skirted round the question that was uppermost in both their thoughts. Marks's hopes that removal from an Anglican environment and a period at home would have the 'desired effect' were disappointed. Girlie remained obdurate. After months of deadlock her parents decided that she would return to England with her cousin Miriam Levy and her mother, who would arrange suitable accommodation for the two girls and private tuition for Girlie. Bertha left for England with little guidance from her husband, who clearly found it very difficult to discuss such a painful subject. As she wrote on board ship to him: 'I also want you please (as you never give one the satisfaction of talking personally over any matters) to let me know exactly your wishes re Girlie.'

Arriving in London in early 1906, Bertha sought the assistance of Dr Adler, the Chief Rabbi of the British Empire, who advised that Girlie 'should live in a *nice* Jewish family . . . where she will see what real Judaism is without it being forced upon her'. Despite Adler's assistance Bertha experienced great difficulty in finding the right home: 'I am as yet worried to death trying to find a *suitable Jewish family* with the proper accommodation for Girlie and Miriam,' she wrote to her husband. 'All the families so far are certainly not the class I would like a child of mine to mix with. I dont know if you can understand the difficulty because as a rule rich Yidden do not need to take in strangers and the others who want to I consider are too common and what we must now guard against is putting her with a family where she would be disgusted with the Yidden. . . . As far as terms go even if I have to pay high it will be better for Girlie to live with a good class of Jewish people.' After placing an advertisement she found the Lewy family of Westbourne Square, who, she was pleased to note, 'visit only with high class Yidden', the Montagus and Samuels. Bertha arranged that the girls would have two bedrooms and a private sitting-room, with board, for ten guineas per week.[6]

Girlie's spiritual crisis continued unabated for the next few months; in the midst of it her father wrote a letter (which has unfortunately not survived) expressing what he had found so difficult to say when Girlie had been in Pretoria. Girlie responded by questioning the meaning and content of his Jewishness:

Thanks for last weeks letter. It is a beautiful letter, and the foundation of your ideas are quite right – but father have you carried them out?

In your letter, you say it is the children's duty to be guided by the example of their parents, also to follow implicitly the religion of their parents; but I do not know what is your religion, you were born a Jew and married a Jewess, saying that, one has said all. I have never heard any religion from either you or *Mother*, the fear of God has never been taught me, neither have either of you ever told what is right or wrong; having no example to follow, I sought one for myself, which has guided and helped me, when human help was *not* given. When I discussed the subject with mother at Naples, and asked her if she had ever tried to gain my confidence, she laughed at me and said 'Why what confidence can you have.' Father you must know, children form opinions and thoughts just the same as you older ones, for are we not all the children of God.

. . . You had me out and did not speak, Father how could you put a question like that aside? Why don't you realise it means my life to me?[7]

One consequence of Girlie's religious crisis and her narrowly averted apostasy was that her father and mother rewrote their will in 1906, introducing a Jewish faith clause, a feature found in other wills of this period: 'The Testators declared it to be their express will and desire that, should any of their children contract a marriage with a person belonging to any other than the Jewish faith or live as man and wife without being married with any person whatsoever, their said administrators and trustees for the time being shall regard such child as if he or she shall have died on the day of his or her marriage. . . .'[8]

While on holiday in Muizenberg a few years later, Marks discussed the question of apostasy with the very distinguished Rabbi Landau of Johannesburg. Landau asked Marks to commit his views to paper, presumably for use as ammunition in the fight against apostasy. Marks wrote:

Apostasy is in my opinion an act of cowardice. The Jew who embraces another religion rarely, if ever, does so out of conviction. Apostasy is as a rule intended to serve selfish motives, social or political ends. It is thus a moral crime. Besides the fact that among Jews it severs the last link that knits the apostate to his near relatives, it often harms the cause of the whole Jewish community. Its disastrous consequences are therefore incalculable and cannot be sufficiently deplored.[9]

In an accompanying letter Marks noted:

I have always held the same opinion on the subject . . . and in fact the last 40 years I have spent in South Africa have strengthened my opinions and sentiments on this subject. During the above period I have had the privilege of meeting some of the oldest nobility of Great Britain and also of many of the other European countries. Amongst whom I have entertained in my house, in the early days in Kimberley, Sir Bartle Frere and his Staff and in the Transvaal no lesser personages than the Prince of Teck, Lords Roberts, Chesham, Milner and Selborne and a great many of the other English Generals. And whenever I have had the pleasure of conversing with these gentlemen I have never for one moment allowed myself to forget that I also belong to a very old stock, and have acquainted these people of that fact.[10]

According to George Falcke, intermarriage remained Marks's great dread for the rest of his life. As Falcke wrote after Marks's death: 'Mr. Marks has over and over again expressed himself to me to the effect that such marriages invariably end in unhappiness and he was always haunted by the fear that his children might marry out of the faith.'[11]

Though his personal orthodoxy was of a diluted kind, Marks, unlike other Jewish magnates in the Transvaal, placed great value on formal affiliation to the Jewish community. For many years he held concurrent memberships in congregations at opposite ends of the country. In 1874 he joined the Cape Town Hebrew Congregation, the mother community of South African Jewry, and though seldom in Cape Town, remained a member for the rest of his life. Similarly he kept his membership of the Kimberley congregation after he moved to Pretoria in 1882, though he resigned a few years after in protest against the community's niggardly treatment of its minister. When a congregation was established in Johannesburg in 1887, Marks agreed to join and to contribute £100 towards the costs of building the first synagogue on the Witwatersrand. After the community split in 1891, as many others did in their early years, Marks resigned, refusing to belong to a 'quarrelsome congregation', though he subsequently joined the breakaway group who formed the new Johannesburg Hebrew Congregation.[12]

Marks had a special relationship with the Jewish community of Pretoria, his 'home' congregation. Though individual Jews had lived in the Boer capital since the 1860s, the local community only began to take shape with the discovery of gold on the Rand and the consequent influx of Jews to the Transvaal. As in Johannesburg the first communal initiative was the establishment of a Jewish burial ground. The community obtained land from the government and erected a 'handsome' iron gate, paid for by Marks, to prevent cattle trampling the graves. The congregation held its first formal meeting in July 1890. Marks does not appear to have been present. The congregation developed rather slowly in the years that followed, compared especially with the mushrooming Jewish community on the Rand which by the end of the decade was already 12,000 strong. Pretoria's synagogue, as elsewhere the focal point of Jewish communal life, was completed only in 1898. Marks supplied the bricks and 'an electric light installation with beautiful electroliers'. The congregation appointed its first minister shortly afterwards. He served for less than a year before the outbreak of war sent most of the capital's two thousand Jews to the coast as refugees.[13]

Other than making substantial donations, Marks does not seem to have played an active part in the life of the community during the 1890s. He attended a general meeting of the congregation for the first time in May 1899, a fact considered of sufficient note to be recorded in the minutes. These do not, however, indicate the position he took in the lengthy discussion at the meeting about the desirability of forming 'a mixed choir for beautifying the services in the Synagogue', a radical departure that would have been anathema to the more traditionally minded Eastern European members.[14] One might speculate, though, that Marks would have favoured anything which strengthened the modernist Anglo–Jewish orientation of the Pretoria congregation. The active part he played in the recruitment of an English minister at the end of the war, and in the establishment of a communal school run on secular and modernist lines, would suggest that while Marks had been born into a traditional East European Jewish community, he had been fully absorbed by the turn of the century into the anglicised elite who set the tone of Jewish life in the Transvaal in its early years.

After the war Marks played a more active role in the shaping of the Pretoria Jewish community. When communal life revived in 1902, the congregation's first priority was the appointment of a spiritual leader, who would double also as *mohel* and cantor. Marks helped to recruit a suitable candidate, significantly an Anglo–Jewish minister, the Reverend M. Rosenberg of Liverpool, and paid £50 towards his removal expenses.[15] This rabbinic Jack-of-all-trades was also expected to make suitable arrangements for the education of the Jewish children of Pretoria, a cause very close to Marks's heart. Rosenberg found that many of the children attended church schools and that their knowledge of Hebrew was predictably meagre. To prevent the inevitable dilution of their Jewishness, he proposed, with Marks's support, to establish a school that would provide both a secular and a Jewish education, though the emphasis, significantly, was to be on the former. With 'his accustomed liberality' Marks offered to provide the ground and to pay all the building costs. The total value of the gift was about £7,000. Once the school, which was named after his mother Miriam, had opened, Marks met its running expenses. He also provided small extras such as fruit, school picnics and swimming lessons for the children, and oak trees for their playground. Marks estimated in April 1907 that the school cost him £600 per annum. It was money well spent. As Rosenberg reported to Chief Rabbi Adler in England, the school was a 'great success. . . . It is almost unnecessary for me to add that this happy state is almost entirely due to our presiding genius and Chairman Mr. Marks.' The school had attracted 125 pupils, Rosenberg happily recounted, and very few Jewish children remained at the local convent school.

From the start, the Miriam Marks School admitted gentile children and continued to do so, on Marks's insistence, despite the objections of some members of the community who felt that the presence of these pupils and of gentile teachers diluted the Jewish character of the school. Marks's stand was of a piece with his secular outlook and his broad tolerance of other religions. 'Politics and religion do not pay any dividends in this world,' he was fond of repeating.[16]

Shortly after the commissioning of the school, Marks made another decisive intervention in the life of the local Jewish community, this time to save it from bankruptcy. Before the war the congregation had borrowed £4,000 from a local finance company to build its lovely 'antique Moorish' synagogue. With the wartime departure of most of its members, and the commercial recession that followed their return, the congregation experienced the greatest difficulty in meeting its interest payments, which by early 1903 were £480 in arrears. When the exasperated creditors eventually gave notice of the cancellation of the bond the community faced the ignominious prospect of a forced sale of its synagogue. To avert disgrace the congregation turned in desperation to its richest member. Marks agreed to contribute £2,000 if the rest of the community would pay the other half of the money owing. Marks also insisted that the title-deeds of the property be redrawn to prevent the synagogue ever being put at risk again. The property could never again be mortgaged nor could it be sold. Marks's reward was the honorary life presidency of the congregation bestowed in 1905.[17]

In a recessionary climate, when many of its members struggled for economic survival and could barely afford to pay their annual synagogue dues, the Jewish community depended on the generosity of its few wealthy members. In 1906 the Pretoria Hebrew Congregation was forced to reduce its annual subscription

from eight to five guineas per member. By contrast, Marks paid an annual fee
of £105. In addition, he and Bertha made generous donations to the synagogue
for specific purposes: £50 to the Burial Society in 1905; £101 in 1907 for the
painting of the synagogue, a job which, unfortunately, was very badly done;
and, in 1908, a set of *Etzchayim*, a multi-volume cabbalistic or mystical text.
Such generosity was expected automatically of the wealthy. When in 1906
Marks refused to exceed his offer of £2,000 to the synagogue and failed to
persuade his wealthy Johannesburg friends to donate an additional £1,000 to the
struggling Pretoria congregation, he was berated, *in absentia,* at a general
meeting by a disgruntled member of the community, a Mr Lichtenstein:

> Referring to Mr. Marks' promise, the speaker remarked that in his opinion he had failed
> to carry out same, as he thought that if Mr. Marks had made an effort to collect £1,000
> from his friends he undoubtedly would have succeeded in raising this amount. In his
> unprejudiced opinion Mr. Marks failed to help the Congregation in that spirit which
> could be expected from a man of his position and the only thing now left to the
> Congregation is to make an appeal to some of the most influential Coreligionists on the
> Rand and elsewhere for assistance and if this should fail then an appeal should be made
> to Lord Rothschild as it would be an everlasting disgrace to Judaism that a Synagogue
> should be sold by auction.[18]

Despite his move to Johannesburg in early 1909, Marks continued to intervene
in the affairs of the Pretoria Jewish community. When the congregation dragged
its heels about appointing a new minister he withheld his sizeable annual
subscription and threatened to resign his membership if an appointment was not
speedily made. This dire threat, made in person at a special general meeting
called at his request, had a salutary effect and the congregation appointed a new
minister in October 1909. In 1910 Girlie Marks, who a few years before had been
on the verge of apostasy, donated 36 prayer books for the use of children
attending the Sabbath classes, while her father agreed to contribute £5 for every
£50 the Pretoria congregation spent in renovating its synagogue.[19]

Once in Johannesburg Marks attended the Park Synagogue of the Johannesburg Hebrew Congregation, the synagogue which at least apocryphally had
been opened in 1892 by Marks's old friend and religious sparring partner,
President Kruger, in the name of Jesus Christ. As was expected of a leading
congregant, Marks made a generous donation when the congregation erected its
magnificent Byzantine-style Great Synagogue in Wolmarans Street in 1914.
Marks gave the bricks for the synagogue which was modelled on the Hagia
Sophia in Istanbul; these were manufactured at his brick and tile works in
Vereeniging. When the synagogue was officially opened, Marks, as the most
renowned member of the Johannesburg Jewish community – indeed of the
South African Jewish community – presented the keys of the synagogue to
Rabbi Landau, its distinguished spiritual leader. The Great Synagogue,
presently the seat of the Chief Rabbinate of South Africa, has remained the
Marks family synagogue until today.[20]

Other than his synagogue membership Marks was not an active participant in
any of the host of organisations that his fellow Jews established in the Transvaal,

though he could generally be relied upon for a substantial donation. This was more a question of a lack of time than a lack of interest. When he was invited, for example, to form a local committee in 1902 of the London-based Jewish Association for the Protection of Girls and Women, he expressed his 'entire sympathy' with its efforts to combat the 'infamous' international white slave trade, then a grave source of concern for Jewish communities world-wide. Marks felt that the most effective way to combat the 'abominable traffic' was to run to earth the 'miserable wretches' who abducted women for purposes of prostitution 'and live by the fruits of their debasement'. But while he was very willing to give advice and assistance, he was not prepared to serve on a committee: 'my time being so fully occupied that I should not be able to devote to the object in view the attention it merits.'[21]

Similarly when Marks was asked in 1904 to serve as honorary vice-president of the Herzl Zionist Society of Johannesburg, one of the many Zionist groupings formed in the wake of Theodor Herzl's call in 1896 for the establishment of an independent Jewish state, he once again politely declined on the grounds of shortage of time. He did, however, make donations to Zionist societies when these were solicited (he gave ten guineas to the Pretoria Zionist Association in 1904) and took off a day from work – no mean sacrifice for someone as industrious as Marks – to entertain David Wolffsohn at Zwart-koppies when the 'great Zionist' leader toured South Africa in 1906. These were polite gestures, though, the behavior expected of a community leader, rather than expressions of enthusiasm for the idea of a Jewish state. Like many members of the Anglo–Jewish elite in the early part of this century, Marks had no commitment to the Zionist cause. As Dolly Marks recalls: 'father was never a Zionist. . . . He wasn't anti-Zionist but he just wasn't interested. South Africa was his home where he had made his life and that is what he loved.'[22]

Marks was not present at the inaugural meeting in Johannesburg of the Jewish Board of Deputies for the Transvaal and Natal which was held in July 1903, and never served on that representative body despite his standing both within the Jewish community and in society at large. He did, however, support its efforts to protect the public interests of the local Jewish community. In conjunction with the Board he made urgent representations in 1904 to Milner, the High Commissioner, to rescind a deportation order against sixteen Russian Jews who had been arrested for residing in Pretoria without the required permits. Milner, Marks was presently informed, agreed to make 'a very liberal concession' in this particular instance 'in deference to representations from yourself and other gentlemen possessing his confidence', though he warned that no further breaches of the law would be condoned. Again, when Jewish interests appeared to be threatened in 1912 by the restrictive terms of a draft immigration bill aimed at limiting Indian immigration to the Union of South Africa, Marks lobbied his old friends Piet Grobler, now MP for Rustenburg, and Jan Smuts, the responsible minister. 'What I particularly wish to avoid', Marks wrote, 'is that my people should receive, under the proposed Bill, the same treatment as is meted out to Coolies.' The bill was duly amended to Marks's satisfaction.[23]

While Marks kept few of the multitude of Jewish religious laws and practices, his behaviour was nevertheless conditioned to a considerable degree by the Jewish values he had absorbed in the *shtetl* during his early years. Amongst these was the importance attached to the obligations of child to parent, chief of which was support in old age. After Marks left Russia at the age of 17, he saw little of his father, who predeceased him by only twelve years. Marks made few trips to Europe, while his father, a member of the more sedentary, older generation, who reached adulthood long before the great migration of the 1880s and 1890s, seldom ventured beyond the neighbouring districts. Though Marks had only very limited physical contact with his father after he left home, he clearly took his filial responsibilities very seriously as a succession of letters demonstrates. 'Please ask London to forward my Old man £25, if they have not already done so, as I see that the winter season is setting in and they look like having hard times after the Cholera,' he wrote in 1892.[24] 'If you have not already done so, and as the wintry weather is setting in,' he wrote to Lewis in 1894, 'you might send my Father a few pounds with which to purchase a few necessary comforts.'[25] 'I gather from the papers that they have had a very severe winter in Russia,' he wrote in 1897, 'and in consequence the people are having a very rough time of it. I shall therefore be pleased if you will remit to my father starting from the 1st January last £2 per week and a little extra for the coming passover festival, say a sum not exceeding £10. Kindly also send him for the poor of our town the sum of £33.6.8.'[26]

Mordechai Feit Marks, a man much like his son, 'full of fun' and 'more lively than many young men', was the channel for Sammy's benefactions to his home village. On his son's behalf, the old man dispensed alms to the needy, gave generous wedding presents to poor couples, funded the building of a *talmud torah* – a communal school for orphan and pauper children – and paid off part of the debt it soon accumulated. All this was in addition to a spectacular gift from the firm of Lewis and Marks of close to £1,000 for the rebuilding of the Neustadt synagogue, an enormous sum given the purchasing power of the pound sterling in a poor Russian village.

Mordechai Marks won considerable social esteem – earned much *yiches* – through his son's achievements in Africa and through the largesse he dispensed on his behalf, so much so that he got swept away on occasion on a tide of exuberant liberality. 'Regarding my father,' Marks complained half-jestingly to a kinsman, S. L. Heymann, 'I do not know what the old man thinks. He gets money from Lewis and from you, and it seems to me that he wants me to keep the whole town, which is rather too much to expect from an old man like me. I wrote to Lewis a short while back to pay my father £20 extra in addition to his usual allowance, and I expect he got it all right, and it is no use my sending him more money. The old chap does not know the value of money and also has a lot of scoundrels surrounding him.'

When Mordechai died in 1908 at the age of 92, his will revealed that despite his slender means, he had made a large number of bequests. His testament stated that should his estate be insufficient to cover these, he looked to his son Samuel to make up any deficiencies. Marks duly performed this final act of filial piety, and at the same time made provision for his stepmother, his father's third wife, so that she would 'want for nothing'. S. L. Heymann, who made the necessary arrangements, agreed that £1 per week was 'as much as she will require to live in that comfort usually understood in that part of the World'.

Marks, already well into his sixties, was philosophical about his nonagenarian father's death – and about his own mortality of which it was a reminder: 'It does no good to sorrow overmuch, because we cannot live for ever. We all have to go sooner or later. It is only a matter of time, and I can assure you it does not frighten me in any way.'[27]

The values Marks acquired in the *shtetl* as a youth also guided his relations with his extended family in later life. In this milieu cardinal importance was attached to family ties. There was a compelling obligation to aid one's siblings and their children if help was needed and if one was in a position to do so. 'It is always assumed', write the ethnographers of *shtetl* life, 'that those who can will do, and those who have will give.' If, for example, parents were unable to support their children, then their more prosperous kinsmen were expected to come to the rescue. Marks, as by far the most successful member of his family, was quite naturally the focus of such expectations. It was automatically assumed that he would aid his brothers and sisters and their children.[28]

Marks helped his brothers to find jobs in businesses with which he was connected and then loaded them with older-brotherly advice, drawn from his own experience and reflecting something of his own personality. He wrote to Joe, who managed the Kimberley Mining Company in the early 1880s: 'The only thing that I must remind you about is, that you should try to agree with everybody, even sometimes if they say or do anything wrong, and never be too proud to ask or take anybodys advise [*sic*].' His advice to Ellia on managing a diamond mine was that 'he must always write to the point, and represent good things with bad ones, exactly as they stand . . . but never under or overvalue anything.'[29]

Marks was equally solicitous of his sisters' welfare. Both Fanny and Krena had unsatisfactory husbands who were unable to provide adequately for their wives and children. Marks supported his sisters financially, housed them, educated their children, paid their medical expenses and protected them as best as he could against their husbands' fecklessness – and worse.

Fanny Levy and her husband Abraham, a diamond buyer, lived in Kimberley for 'a long time, long enough for her worthy husband to drop all his money there'. When they moved to Cape Town in the mid-nineties, Marks bought them a house and furnished it at his own expense, though he insisted that Levy pass a bond in his favour for the full amount. This was clearly a sensible precaution. Abraham was a feckless speculator, whom Marks had to save from sequestration some years later to spare his sister humiliation and disgrace.[30]

Krena Abromowitz was in a worse plight. Twice married with four children from her first marriage to Judah Falcke and five from her second, she was abandoned for a time, it would seem, by her ne'er-do-well second husband. When Mr Abromowitz returned and 'installed' himself in the house her brother Sammy had bought her in Cape Town, Sammy imposed certain conditions:

Of course it appears to be only correct that a husband should live under the same roof as his wife and children, but then there are certain obligations on the part of the husband, chief among which are that he shall provide a house and maintenance for his wife and children, and this you have failed to do. However I have no objection to you remaining in the house provided you observe certain conditions and conduct yourself decently.

1st you must give up your old habits, some of which I think it is desirable that I should enumerate. One is drink which is obnoxious to others and bad for yourself. Second you must not use any obscene language in the house, in the first place for the sake of your children and in the second for the sake of my sister.

Should his brother-in-law misbehave, Marks would have him ejected from the house, bring Krena to the Transvaal, 'and leave you and the children to do the best you can'.[31]

Besides regular monthly remittances, ranging between twelve and forty pounds over the years, Marks sent his sisters handsome £100 Jewish New Year gifts and met contingency expenses such as the costs of Fanny's trip to Europe for an eye operation. Marks also arranged and paid for their children's education, acting in place of their weak fathers. The old-world expectation that one should see to the future of one's nephews and nieces if their parents were unable to provide, was adapted to South African circumstances. Marks went to considerable effort and expense, not always rewarded, to see that his young relatives received a schooling which would make 'gentlemen' of them, and a vocational training which would equip them for the modern business world.[32]

Marks sent Fanny Levy's Harry to Grey College in Bloemfontein, then on to England to continue his education. 'I shall not like Harry to be wasting a single day in walking about doing nothing,' Marks wrote to his father-in-law, who was asked to make the necessary arrangements. When the boy showed an interest in a career in engineering and spoke of attending Glasgow University, Marks unhesitatingly promised his support. No less than William Preece, the Engineer-in-Chief of the British government's telegraph department and an old friend of Jimmy Sivewright's, was asked to keep an eye on Harry, 'and to see whether it will be possible to make a man of him. I may mention', Marks added, 'that I am willing to go to almost any expense to attain this end.'

Harry flopped. Stronger on bluff than on performance, and averse to hard work, he returned to South Africa without a qualification. Marks arranged for him to serve an apprenticeship with H. E. V. Pickstone, pioneer of the Cape fruit industry, with a view to a position in Marks's farming business, but Harry simply failed to turn up, pretending years later that he had never been told of the offer – 'the whole affair is a conspiracy against me by some jealous party,' he explained. After a lengthy silence, he wrote to his long-suffering uncle demanding a 'billet'.

The position I find myself in today is so unnatural that I sometimes imagine I am only dreaming. Fancy the nephew of a millionaire finding himself at a loss for a career! I repeat again that it is unnatural in the extreme. Why, you could search the whole World through and would not come across a similar case to my own, unless the individual in question is utterly worthless and a veritable vagabond to boot.

People who know me remark 'Oh you're alright being a nephew of Marks' if only they knew?

Faced with this extreme example of the traditional expectation that the rich relative should help, Marks, his patience finally exhausted, simply refused.[33]

Phil Levy, Harry's younger brother, was less of a disappointment. After a period at Grey, he was sent to a Jewish schoolmaster in Tiel, a small town in Holland, where Marks hoped he would learn German, French and 'good Hollandsch' as well as Yiddish so that he could correspond easily with his parents in Cape Town and his grandfather in Russia. Besides modern languages, which Marks felt were an essential part of a commercial training, Phil was also to study bookkeeping, shorthand and typewriting. Marks insisted that his nephew write him a proper letter at least once a fortnight, not simply a postcard. 'I do not like to see correspondence carried on by postcard,' Marks wrote after receiving one from his nephew, 'and if you have not enough spending money to buy stamps, I shall send you a little more'. Besides meeting all his schooling and living expenses, Marks also sent Phil occasional gifts of money, as he did to his own children and his other nephews and nieces. Phil received £6, for example, from his thoughtful if demanding uncle in August 1898 'to take two friends to Amsterdam for Queen Wilhelmina's coronation festivities'.[34]

After Phil completed his training in Tiel, Marks arranged for a year in a 'good London office where he will have plenty of hard work of a useful nature and where the discipline is somewhat severe, so that he may arrive here equipped with business ideas.' He was not to neglect his languages, though: 'It took a lot of time and money to get all the Knowledge into your head and you must not lose it again for the sake of a little practice. If you are not quite proficient, especially in the languages when you come out I shall be very cross for having spent so much money in vain.' When Phil at last returned to South Africa, he was taken into his uncle's office – almost his predestined fate – and served in time as Marks's confidential secretary. He followed in the footsteps of George Falcke, one of the unfortunate Krena Abromowitz's sons by her first marriage, and Marks's favourite nephew.[35]

George went via Beaufort College at St Leonards-on-Sea in England, a 'Collegiate and Commercial Establishment' which also prepared him as part of its wide-ranging services for his *bar mitzvah*, to the school at Tiel in Holland. Like Phil Levy, he studied a combination of modern languages and commercial subjects. Besides the usual small gifts of spending money, his uncle also offered to pay for a holiday in England, Germany and France, believing 'that young people derive great benefits from travel, both mentally and bodily'. George was a very diligent pupil and a dutiful boy who consulted his uncle, if only belatedly, about the major decisions of adolescence. 'Now about smoking. Its rather late in the day to consult me,' Marks wrote, 'but if you think your health and studies will benefit by it you may continue, if not, I say dont smoke, as I have done without it. It is a habit, when once acquired, it is very difficult to drop.'

When George returned to South Africa to work for his uncle's firm, he proved just as dutiful. As Marks reported to his partner: 'Falcke worked very hard here

in Pretoria, till midnight often, early in the mornings, on Sundays and holidays.
. . . he does not deal in shares or options, or in ground and he does not sell our
cables for a drink, as he drinks very little.' Falcke's reward was increasing
responsibility and trust. On Lewis's instructions, Falcke was appointed to
various directorships the firm had in its pocket. He became his uncle's secretary
and confidant, wrote and read his most personal and private letters, including
those to and from Bertha Marks, and held his signing power at the bank. He also
acted as Marks's surrogate on business trips when he was too ill to travel. George
Falcke was the model confidential secretary. He was sensible, tactful, especially
in his dealings with his employer's family, entirely trustworthy and discreet. He
would take dictation from his uncle in Pitman's shorthand and render this into
grammatical English before reading it back. As he later recalled, his uncle
'would at once pull [him] up . . . if he left out anything, especially some of his
old sayings and similes, which were sometimes very difficult to work in'.
George Falcke had impressive language skills; he could correspond in French,
German, Yiddish and Dutch, besides his native English. Long after his eventual
retirement he regularly spent his mornings reading foreign books and journals
to practise these.[36]

George's brothers were less academic. They were brought out from Russia
before the South African War by their uncle Sammy who helped set them up in
business at Viljoensdrift on his Vaal River estate. By his grace they ran a
concession store cum bakery cum butchery (renowned locally for the excellence
of its beef sausages), which serviced the Cornelia colliery. In return for exclusive
trading rights on the mine, they paid the Vereeniging Estates a rental of 1s. per
'working boy' each month. When they had saved £500 they sent this to their
uncle asking him to invest it for them in shares. He sent their cheque back to
them by return of post with their signatures crossed out. The next time he met
them, he gave them a severe dressing-down: 'You mustn't buy other people's
shares. You must sell your own,' he lectured.[37]

Marks's nieces did not get the same degree of attention as his nephews. In an
age when the education of girls was considered much less of a priority than that
of boys, Marks was reluctant to pay for their schooling beyond the limits he felt
appropriate. Disputing his sister Fanny's plans for her daughter Dora's further
education, he wrote:

It is no use having balloons if you cannot travel in them and it is likewise no use educating
your children to too high a degree if you cannot make use of their talents. I am not
preaching to you because I believe that in some things you are a great deal smarter than
I am, and I do not think I am altogether bereft of brains. I think if your Girl can write a
good English letter and can do some other useful things which are good enough and is
[sic] required by people of the middle class it is ample for her. When girls are too highly
educated their parents and surroundings are at a discount. At least this is what I have seen
in my life time and I am not a chicken anymore.[38]

Marks's generosity reached far beyond his extended family. His wide-ranging
and extensive philanthrophy was rooted in the culture of the *shtetl* where *tsdokeh*,
or charity, was the cardinal virtue, and second only in importance to religious

scholarship as a source of social esteem. While *tsdokeh* was expected of everyone, Marks, as a man of wealth, had special obligations: the Jewish version of *noblesse oblige* dictated that he had an added burden of responsibility because of his good fortune. These inherited expectations meshed with similar expectations in the gentile Anglo–Saxon world in which Marks spent his adult years. Increasingly in the nineteenth century it was felt that the man of wealth should practise philanthrophy; public regard came more and more to depend on public displays of generosity.

Beyond any cultural expectations, beyond any social considerations, Marks was instinctively, impulsively, compulsively generous, given to the spontaneous and uncalculated act of kindness. In a letter apologising to Sivewright for not cabling, he explained that just as he was about to pay for the cable, 'a poor devil came in at the door and told me he was hard up, and so I had to give him the few shillings which I had intended to spend on the cable to you'.[39]

Marks derived an almost visceral pleasure from giving: 'You know when people can afford to do anything of that kind,' he wrote to his daughter about a donation she planned, 'they should not neglect doing it, because I think the giver gets more pleasure from the giving that [sic] the receiver gets from receiving.'[40] He certainly expected little in return for his generosity, much of which was on the quiet. Warned by Jimmy Sivewright that he would get nothing in return for helping a particular individual, Marks wrote: 'This is nothing fresh to me. I have put myself out for a good many thousands of people (not hundreds) in my life time, and up to the present I can count on my fingers all the returns I have received. Its a great blessing I can manage without them, and I never expect any returns.'[41]

Marks was eager to instil his sense of *noblesse oblige,* his feelings of charity, in his offspring. In the *shtetl*, children were encouraged to practise *tsdokeh*, were 'trained to the habit of giving'. A father would, for example, allow his son to dole out the weekly alms to the *shnorer*, the professional beggar, rather than giving these directly himself. Marks tried to do the same, to teach his children, albeit in a secular idiom, the virtue of *tsdokeh*. Writing to Girlie, then living in England, he instructed: 'I should also like you to subscribe a little to assist people who are poorer than yourself. There is no need to give a lot, but you can at least give 5/- or 10/- a month. . . . You must not forget that Orphans and Widows and people who cannot help themselves, must be helped by those who have, and are able to do so, as we do not live in this world only to eat and drink and enjoy ourselves. Perhaps we are meant to be the keepers of those who cannot keep themselves, and therefore if we do not assist them we may be robbing them.'[42]

Marks's generosity took a variety of forms. Education was perhaps the favourite cause. Having had so little himself, Marks, like many other Jewish immigrants, placed a particularly high value on education, which, he believed, 'comes above everything'. Besides endowing the Chair of Hebrew at the South African College, underwriting the Miriam Marks School in Pretoria, and subsidising schooling at Vereeniging and Hatherley, Marks met numerous individual requests for assistance: '[I] have spent a good deal during the last 25 years', he wrote in 1894, 'in the education of children, whose fathers have not been as fortunate as myself. . . .'[43]

Marks's civic donations focused on Pretoria. He gave two globes, one terrestrial and one celestial, to the State Library before the war. After the war he provided a thousand trees for a new park in Pretoria. He also donated a cast-iron fountain which was ordered from the Victorian builder's vade-mecum, the encyclopaedic catalogue of Walter MacFarlane's Saracen foundry in Glasgow. The fountain was cast in Scotland and shipped out to South Africa in sections for re-assembly in Pretoria. It is a grandiloquent monument to Edwardian taste. Désirée Picton-Seymour, doyenne of South African architectural historians, describes it as 'a masterpiece of cast iron, with four seated women, representing art, science, literature and commerce contemplating a large pool. Above them rises a colonnade supporting a basin with writhing dolphins spewing forth water; putti and lion masks also pour forth jets of water.' This grand fountain was erected originally in Church Square as a politically neutral replacement for the Kruger statue which had become an embarrassment during the war. At the official opening in 1906 the mayoress of Pretoria set the water in motion with a golden key specially made for the occasion. But the fountain had only a brief tenure of Church Square. In 1910 Pretoria's prosaic city fathers decided to remake the square as a tram terminus. Marks's splendid cast-iron fantasy was exiled to an obscure corner of the Pretoria zoo.[44]

Marks, who had a very broad range of interests, served on the committee of the Zoological Gardens, which had been founded shortly before the war, and of the museum associated with it. One of his pleasant duties was a regular tour of inspection of the gardens. Marks took turns with his fellow committee members to visit the zoo to see that all was in order at what after the war became the favourite gathering place for respectable Pretorians. The associated Transvaal Museum was the recipient of one of Marks's more exotic donations, a gift acknowledged in a charming note from the director, Dr J. W. B. Gunning: 'I have very great pleasure in thanking you for the very kind presentation of a 7 foot Crocodile. To my pleasant surprise I found that it was stuffed, and I can assure you that it is a welcome addition to the Museum.'[45]

There were no corresponding gifts, whimsical or otherwise, to Johannesburg, despite a decade and a half of residence in the city, and the transfer to Johannesburg of the firm's South African head office after the South African War. This reflects Marks's lack of enthusiasm for a city to which he moved very reluctantly, as well as his long-term personal identification with Pretoria. He was, however, an enthusiastic supporter of the activities of the Witwatersrand Agricultural Society, which was founded in 1894 to promote progressive farming, a cause close to his heart. Marks contributed £100 to the costs of the first show in 1895 which his firm used as a shop-window for its products: jam and gin from Eerste Fabrieken, bricks and coal from Vereeniging. When the society was relaunched a few years after the war, Sammy once again made a handsome cash contribution and also served on the council of the society. Marks's eventual reward was election as an honorary vice-president of the society in 1911. Even Bertha was drawn into the activities of the society, and judged and exhibited in the needlework and homecrafts section of the show – appropriate accomplishments for the mistress of a middle-class Edwardian home.[46]

There were also innumerable calls on Marks's generosity by indigent whites, especially in times of recession, for Marks had a country-wide reputation for open-handedness. At times these requests became overwhelming and exasperating: 'however willing I might be to assist you,' he wrote to an ex-official of the Transvaal Republic during the long post-war recession, 'I really cannot pension all the old people in the Country. I have a good number of pensioners already and really cannot do any more.'[47]

Marks's legendary generosity to Jewish causes has already been described. He was similarly generous, though on a lesser scale, when it came to Christian calls on his pocket-book; donations were made even-handedly to Anglican, Catholic, Dutch Reformed and Methodist causes. These donations reflect his broad tolerance in matters of faith, a value acquired during an adulthood in a liberal English milieu. They are also indicative of Marks's position and that of the Jew in general in gentile society in South Africa at the turn of the century. The Jew was not the pariah he had been, and still was, in the Pale of Settlement. He increasingly regarded himself, and was regarded by others, as a South African of Jewish extraction who could be reasonably expected to support all good causes, irrespective of their religious character. What was unthinkable in *der heim* – Jewish support for Christian religious causes – was now perfectly normal and reasonable. The Jew could be called upon to donate the copper stand and stone pedestal for the baptismal font in the Vereenigde Kerk in Rustenburg, 'knowing your liberality in giving for religious and charitable purposes'. After all, the Jew had already offered to donate 60,000 bricks for the construction of a Dutch Reformed Church in Vereeniging.[48]

Then there was the small change of philanthropy: the cash donations; the cups and prizes; the endless tickets to balls he avoided attending; and the token memberships of societies at whose meetings he never appeared. Like his wealthy peers, Marks received endless calls for support from the host of Anglo–Saxon voluntary organisations – standard-bearers of British cultural imperialism – that sprang up in the Transvaal Colony after the South African War. Marks made donations to everything from the Transvaal Trout Acclimatisation Society to the Transvaal Rifle Association, which aimed 'to gradually instil in the whole white population of South Africa the desire to take up rifle practice as a pastime . . . from the point of view of its utility in the case of emergency' – a goal Marks, who shared the current anxieties about a general native rising, would have endorsed. Marks also gave five guineas to the Witwatersrand Cambrian Society in 1906 to buy the prize for the essay competition at its annual eisteddfod. The title of the essay – 'To what extent do Welshmen retain their national characteristics in South Africa' – betrayed the sort of ethnic anxiety about assimilation into a dominant culture and consequent loss of identity that Marks as a Jew would have easily understood, if personally only partly shared.

Marks belonged, at least nominally, to a wide range of organisations, including the Freemasons, the Pretoria Volunteer Corps, the Geological Society of South Africa, and the South African Association for the Advancement of Science. While these memberships were largely a disguised form of donation, one of the minor costs of fame and fortune, they were, together with the adoption of a gentry life-style at Zwartkoppies and the education of his children at English public schools, part of a personal drive towards assimilation into the dominant Anglo–Saxon culture. At the same time they were also a measure of the success of these efforts and of Sammy Marks's acceptance into a middle-class gentile society which was not always welcoming of people of Sammy's faith and which often practised a veiled antisemitism.[49]

A further measure of Marks's success in this regard were the invitations he received to join the gentlemen's clubs in the towns where he did business. Though Marks was not a clubman by nature, membership of the Pretoria Club, the Rand Club in Johannesburg, the English Club at Lourenço Marques, and of the very exclusive City Club in Cape Town was yet another welcome badge of social respectability. But membership of an even more exclusive club still awaited him. In 1910 Sammy Marks, the former fugitive from the *shtetl* and one-time smous, reached the apogee of acceptance and recognition. He was invited to join the newest, but none the less the most prestigious, club in the land: the Senate of the first parliament of the Union of South Africa.[50]

The Jewish Synagogue in Pretoria (Photo: Sammy Marks Museum)

XII

Senator and Steelmaker, 1908–1919

Sammy Marks played little part in the protracted discussions and negotiations that preceded the union of the four South African colonies in 1910. Unlike most of his white countrymen who became wildly euphoric at the prospect, Marks had no enthusiasm for the idea, about which indeed he had very serious reservations. These were expressed in a letter to Louis Botha in October 1908, dictated aboard the *Kenilworth Castle*, two days out of Cape Town, on his return from taking the 'cure' in Europe. Marks's fellow passengers, he wrote, were 'politicians' from the Cape, Natal, Rhodesia and Britain; the chief topic of conversation for the past fifteen days had been 'the grand unification of South Africa'. All were caught up in the euphoria of the moment and agreed that 'nothing else but unification is advisable for the future welfare of South Africa without any consideration', Marks added, 'as to which State is going to pay the highest price for the glory of it'.

Marks was one of the few dissenters: 'My opinion is that unless there is something very pressing, Unification should not be adopted at once but that at least from five to ten years longer of waiting would do no harm.' In the interim the coastal colonies could reduce their indebtedness, thus sparing the Transvaal 'a heavy burden'. However, if Botha and his colleagues were still convinced that now was the time for unification, there were certain considerations he hoped they would bear in mind. The Transvaal's war debt of £35 million should be renegotiated; 'it should not be left to be repaid by our children, as a good deal of that money has been used to conquer us.' This was a far cry from Marks's jingoism of a few years before! Rhodesia should be incorporated at once in the proposed Union; if left out, a united South Africa would have to pay a heavy price for its inclusion at a later time. Moreover, Britain should hand over the 'natives' of the High Commission Territories to the white people of South Africa. But before doing so, it should disarm the Basuto, thus leaving a united South Africa the sole source of arms and ammunition in the region. 'After that all fears of a native rising would slowly and surely die out.' Unless the native question was finally settled in this way, it would revive, possibly in a more severe form, under a future British government. 'The Exeter Hall people, the parsons and all the old ladies in Great Britain instead of looking after their own poor people, will scream and worry themselves over the poor natives in South Africa, whom they think are being so badly treated!!' A final thought: why not draw on outside expertise in drafting a charter for a united South Africa? Canadian experts would be able to warn against the mistakes made when their country was united.[1]

After his arrival in Cape Town, and further discussion with many people about unification, Marks wrote another discouraging letter to Botha, warning him, by means of a biblical analogy, of the dangers of union and specifically of the political risks he ran by making Cape Town the capital and leaving his Transvaal power-base unattended:

I was very strongly reminded of what I used to read in the Old Bible when I was a boy. You will remember that when the Jews received the ten Commandments on Mount Sinai, they all with one voice said to Moses they were prepared to accept the responsibility, and I daresay it would have been dangerous for any one Israelite present on that day to have said anything else. Similarly with the people of this Country and Unification.

When Moses went up the Mountain to receive the Commandments and left his people although only for a short time, you know what happened, and I suppose since then that is the reason my Countrymen are so fond of Gold!!

. . . I am very much afraid that if our General becomes Prime Minister of the United South Africa and goes awayfrom the Transvaal to live in Cape Town there will be great danger for the People in this Country to be left alone, just the same as my people when Moses went away and left them that time I have mentioned, especially as you know yourself there are any number of false prophets here now as it was in those days.

Why not then make Vereeniging the capital of the Union, a note in one of Marks's letterbooks suggests?[2]

Marks was also concerned that adequate provision be made for expanding northwards. As he wrote in January 1909 to Sir Percy FitzPatrick, a member of the Transvaal delegation to the National Convention, 'I only hope that when the "Loving Knot" is to be tied, none of you will try to make it too tight.' As a businessman with extensive interests beyond the borders of the four colonies, he was anxious that no obstacle be created to the future territorial expansion of the Union: 'we expect to expand and you know the risk we run if that is not allowed for.'[3]

Other than dishing out these dollops of advice, Marks was a spectator, not a player, at the making of Union. Once the negotiations were complete, though, and Selborne and the colonial premiers left for England to secure the endorsement of the British parliament, Marks played a small part in selling the new constitution to British public opinion. In June 1909 he asked an English friend, Sir Hugh Gilzean-Reid, a provincial newspaper proprietor and a former Liberal member of parliament, to pass the word to his Liberal colleagues that they ought not to insist on constitutional guarantees for the protection of the 'coloured races' of South Africa. 'We in South Africa have proved to the civilized world within the last 39 years that we are not such murderers nor such fools, neither are we cowards nor lazy. . . . If we were trusted with the management of all coloured races within this country England would never regret it, and moreover she would save lives, money, and jealousy to say nothing of disagreements.'[4]

As it happened, the Liberal government chose to follow advice of this kind and to ignore black South African protest against the racial exclusivism of the draft constitution. Once union on the white colonists' terms was a *fait accompli,* it remained to be decided whether it should be led by a northener or a southerner. The choice of first prime minister of the Union lay between John X. Merriman of the Cape and Louis Botha of the Transvaal.

Marks had known both candidates for many years. He had dealt with Merriman while still in Kimberley, and had been a close witness to Botha's growth in stature since 1899. Marks's personal preference was for his fellow Transvaler for besides provincial loyalty, he, like many others, found Botha by far the more agreeable personality. Marks shared his old friend Jimmy Sivewright's disdain for Merriman.

On 27 January 1910 Marks spent a few hours in conversation with Botha, in the course of which they discussed Merriman's attempt to outmanoeuvre his northern rival. Marks urged Botha to stand his ground – 'the whole of the Transvaal', he reminded the General, 'expected him to be the first Prime Minister.' Shortly after, Marks travelled to Cape Town where he made discreet enquiries, at Botha's behest it seems, about Merriman's efforts to win the nomination. Within days Marks returned to Pretoria where he reported to Botha that Merriman and his allies were 'using all the influence they can bring to bear' to induce the Liberal government in Britain to instruct the Governor-General to appoint Merriman rather than Botha. Alarmed, Botha asked Marks to cable his London office to take steps 'to frustrate Merriman's little scheme'. Lewis was to pass the word to his influential English contacts, including the Baron Rothschild. Botha was confident that if the King, whom he had met a few years before, came to hear what was afoot, he would not allow it.

Marks followed his cable with a letter explaining why he had agreed to become involved despite Lewis's constant urgings that he 'leave politics alone'. The choice of premier, he felt, was a question of vital concern to 'all who have invested their money in this country'. It was of the utmost importance that 'a strong representative of the Transvaal such as Botha' be chosen. 'Botha will carry the Dutch with him and if Merriman should, unfortunately, be elected he will do his utmost to prevent one six pence being spent on improvements here and we should certainly be taxed inordinately to pay off the £54,000,000 debt of the Cape Colony. Furthermore no encouragement would be offered for the establishment of industries in this country[;] all influences would be at work to render this difficult if not impossible.' Botha, on the other hand, strongly favoured the promotion of local industry, in fact had promised Marks that a large sum would be earmarked in the budget for bonus payments to those, like Lewis and Marks, who were eager to establish 'sound industries'.

The prospect of increased taxation and of a premier unsympathetic to Transvaal industry jolted Marks's normally politically passive partner into action. A few weeks later Lewis was able to cable that he had been informed 'in strictest confidence' that the Governor-General would 'almost certainly' send for Botha. Marks passed on the good news to the General.

To strengthen Botha's position still further, Marks wrote also to his friend Sir Hugh Gilzean-Reid, requesting that he put Marks's views on the candidates to Viscount Gladstone, the Governor-General elect, who would make the final decision on his arrival in South Africa. Gilzean-Reid presented Marks's views 'with all their native force and authority': Marks warned the British government against making 'the irreparable error' of appointing Merriman, whose failure as a businessman cast doubts on his competence and whose loyalty to the Empire was suspect. 'He has never been a true patriot in the interests of those he represented, nor has he shown unalloyed devotion to the Flag.' Botha, by contrast, stood 'head and shoulders' above the rest. 'He is the one man who would command the respect of all and his loyalty to the Crown has been sufficiently proved.'

Botha was duly nominated by Gladstone as the first premier of the Union. While it is unlikely that Marks's intervention was in any way decisive – Botha was the clear favourite from the start, both in England and in South Africa – it presumably helped to strengthen the perception of the Liberal Party, and in particular of the new Governor-General who was charged with making the choice, that Louis Botha was the best man.[5]

The story had a sequel some months later. Returning home after a visit to Lourenço Marques in late September 1910, Marks received a message that he should break his journey in Pretoria as General Botha wished to see him 'urgently'. The prime minister told Marks the Cabinet had decided that he should be offered a seat in the upper house of the Union parliament, which was due to meet in Cape Town shortly for the first time. 'Impossible,' Marks responded. How could he take off two or three months at a time from his business? Botha, persuasive as ever, immediately appealed to Marks's sense of loyalty. 'He then said that he had reckoned on me and that I must not leave him in the lurch, but it was my duty to help him.' Cornered, Marks searched for an escape. Before he could agree, he told Botha, he would have to cable London for his partner's consent.

Marks begged Lewis to go at once to Sir Richard Solomon, the Union's first High Commissioner in London and a trusted adviser to the new government, to ask him to cable Botha that the firm of Lewis and Marks could not afford to have one of its partners immobilised in Cape Town when it had pressing business in Johannesburg and increasingly in Rhodesia. Lewis balked. Rather than rushing off to see the High Commissioner, he cabled by return that Marks should accept the appointment. Pressured by his partner and also by Jan Smuts and other cabinet ministers, Marks's resistance collapsed, though he warned Botha that he would serve for no more than one year.[6]

In the same week, Marks at last came out of the political closet, and after years of discretion, openly aligned himself with a political party. Sir George Farrar, one of the leaders of the opposition and a fellow mining magnate, called on Marks during the week, and after talking 'a good deal of nonsense', asked Marks to subscribe to his party's election fund. When Marks refused, Farrar 'became very wrathful and was not complimentary. . . . I told him that he was at liberty to think what he liked but he must understand that I was a friend of the Government. This did not please him. . . .'[7]

Marks's elevation to the Senate, at the age of 66, recognised and rewarded both a long and supportive association with the Boer leadership over almost four decades and a distinguished business career. It was presumably also a reward for services rendered during the contest for the premiership. Marks's appointment delighted his Jewish compatriots, symbolising as it did the large measure of acceptance they had achieved in South African society. The *South African Jewish Chronicle* hailed the choice: 'Our Jewish Senator', a man whose 'invaluable advice and assistance have been sought and obtained by the highest in the land', would not only serve 'the new South African Nation' with distinction, but would also protect Jewish interests in parliament if these were ever threatened.[8]

At the end of the month Sammy, Bertha, Louis and Girlie went down to Cape Town for the opening of parliament, leaving the younger children at home in the Transvaal. Marks felt rather self-conscious and not a little foolish in his new and unaccustomed role as a parliamentarian. As he wrote to an old friend, 'no doubt you will come to the conclusion that the old saying is true: "No fool is such a fool as an old fool." And that is exactly what I consider I am. I have no business to be down here, but now that I am here I must try and keep myself occupied.' Marks's uneasiness and his boredom with parliament's protracted proceedings were readily apparent to cynical observers like Patrick Duncan: 'Sammy Marks is much perplexed by Parliamentary procedure. He says "it is a funny way of doing business" and is already tired of the legislator's seat. It certainly is not his job.'[9]

For someone as active and industrious as Marks, and as accustomed to rapid decision-making, the leisurely rhythms of parliamentary life, with its interminable discussion, must have been a severe trial. Though Marks had long experience of politicking, his métier had always been backstairs lobbying, not debating in the chamber. For the next ten years, while he voted conscientiously with the government, he seldom intervened in debate. He was frequently absent from parliament and clearly had neither political ambition nor a passion for politics. As he wrote from Cape Town during the 1911 session: 'All the news here at present is political. And all the politics put together is not worth the penny newspapers that record it.'[10]

Marks's silent decade in the Senate was also the culmination of his business career. It was a decade in which he resolved some of the major difficulties that had beset the firm since the South African War and realised the ambition of a lifetime. But it was also a decade in which Lewis and Marks came to suffer severe financial embarrassment.

Vereeniging Estates, the central pillar of Lewis and Marks's business, had been badly damaged by the crisis of overproduction that shook the Highveld coal industry after the war. Cut-throat competition for customers had forced down prices and slashed profit margins. Worse still, Vereeniging Estates could no longer depend after 1904 on the Cape railway contract as it had before and since the war. The Cape took greatly reduced amounts at low prices and offered one-year contracts only. One solution was to find a steady customer to replace the Cape railways, a client that could be relied upon to take a large volume of coal every year without fail. But where was this model customer to be found? There was little point in looking to the railways or to the gold mines, the principal existing consumers of coal in the region. In a market where prices were slipping, neither could be expected to bind themselves to any long-term agreements with the collieries.[11]

The answer was to create a source of demand under the direct control of Lewis and Marks. A decade before, Marks had proposed that they use the mountain of duff coal their customers would not accept, to generate electricity at the Vaal for transmission to the mines at the Rand. As Marks reluctantly conceded at the time, the idea was probably premature then. But now its time had come. The energy needs of the gold-mining industry, still relatively modest in the early 1890s, had soared in the interim. The industry had switched very largely from outcrop to deep-level mining, which meant hauling great quantities of ore to the surface from workings deep below the ground. In addition, the labour crisis that followed the war – the relative scarcity of unskilled workers at the wages the industry was prepared to offer – had focused attention on the merits of limited mechanisation. Machine-drilling would need fewer workmen than hand-drilling, but would require additional supplies of power.

The existing sources of power barely met these needs. Most gold mines were equipped with steam engines; some drew electricity from two small power stations at Brakpan and Germiston, while a handful had their own electric generators. None of these sources were particularly efficient or economical. There was clearly an opening for the establishment of a large central power station which could supply power more efficiently than the steam engine, and more cheaply than the small power station, by applying economies of scale.[12]

In January 1906 Marks wrote to the Chamber of Mines suggesting that a central power station be established at the Vaal River. Vereeniging was an ideal site: it had unlimited reserves of coal and all the water a power station would need for cooling purposes; it was also reasonably close to the Rand, and had cheap stone, timber and bricks for building the station. At the same time the Vereeniging Estates applied for government support in obtaining way-leaves for a transmission line between the Vaal and Johannesburg.[13]

The chief competition came from an Anglo–German concern, the Victoria Falls Power Company, jointly controlled by the late Cecil John Rhodes's Chartered Company and AEG, the German concern which dominated the market in power-generating equipment. This company proposed nothing less than harnessing the power of the mighty Victoria Falls and transmitting this 600 miles overland to distant Johannesburg, a visionary conception first and fittingly suggested to Rhodes by the adventure novelist H. Rider Haggard. This grand design, which would have been vitiated by severe energy losses along the transmission line and a shortage of water at the Falls during the dry season, was rapidly abandoned for a more sensible, if more prosaic scheme: the construction of a power station on the Rand itself.[14]

Neither Lewis and Marks nor the Victoria Falls company wanted a destructive competition for the Rand market for electric power. Both sides believed that a monopoly would be the most efficient and profitable way of generating and distributing electrical power on the Witwatersrand. Consequently, they struck a deal which left the Falls company the field, but fully compensated Lewis and Marks. In return for withdrawing their scheme, Vereeniging Estates was to receive 20,000 fully paid ordinary shares in the Victoria Falls company and a seat on its board. More important, the Falls people undertook to build a large power station at the Vaal once they had successfully established their first major station on the Rand; the Vereeniging power station would draw all its coal from Marks's nearby colliery.[15]

The deal was almost too good to be true. In 1909 the Victoria Falls company tried to renege on its undertaking to build its second major plant at the Vaal. Isaac Lewis threatened litigation; the Falls company offered £500,000 compensation for the cancellation of the agreement. Lewis refused, insisting they honour their undertaking. After much tussling, the Falls company capitulated, and signed a modified agreement.[16]

The chastened Victoria Falls company agreed to proceed without further delay with the building of a power station at Vereeniging. To sweeten the pill, Lewis and Marks, in turn, undertook to find one-third of the necessary capital, no great hardship considering the potential rewards to their Vaal River collieries. These were contracted to supply a minimum of 200,000 tons per annum for a period of fourteen years at a guaranteed profit of 1s. per ton, a dream contract which provided the long-term security of demand and profitability Marks had worked so hard to secure since the early 1890s.[17]

Once the contract was assured, Marks lobbied his friends in and about government for the necessary state approval for the construction of a major power station and set of transmission lines. After talking to Botha and Smuts he could report that 'they all promise to do their best for us'. When the required legislation came before the Transvaal parliament in 1910, Marks, the master lobbyist, did his 'utmost to assist the passage of the bill. . . . I need hardly say that I saw every member of the Government and also all the leading members of Het Volk.' He might have added that he had also won assurances from the leaders of the Progressives, the opposition in the Transvaal parliament, that they would not hold up the legislation. The bill went through despite the hostility of rival colliery-owners who correctly feared that the erection of major power stations at the Vaal and elsewhere would cost them their direct sales to the gold mines.[18]

The Vereeniging power station, a giant by the standards of Marks's age, a 40,000-kilowatt midget by the standards of ours, was finally operational in 1912. Not only was it a triumph for Marks as a colliery-owner, but also for Marks as an industrial visionary, for it was a leap forward towards the realisation of a thirty-year-old dream, the creation of a South African Sheffield on the Vaal. The power station would 'soon attract other industries,' he wrote; 'owing to the advantage of having power near an inexhaustible supply of water Factories will soon be established.'[19]

And so they were. Like Sammy Marks, Henry Horace Wright, a one-time shift boss on the Premier diamond mine, had long dreamed of establishing a native steel industry. Son of an English iron-master, he immigrated to South Africa in the mid-1890s. In 1903, after the South African War, he discovered a large iron-ore deposit at Magnet Heights in the Lydenburg district of the Transvaal. When he brought this to the attention of the Milner administration and asked for its aid in exploiting the deposit, the response was less than helpful. The mining houses and the local representatives of English and American steel firms he approached were equally wary of his scheme – 'you may as well try and freeze a snowball in Hades,' he recounted some years later, 'as try and get people to support an industry in another country.'[20]

When economic prospects brightened in 1908, Wright tried again. He travelled to Britain and hawked his idea around the steel industry, but, just as before, the steel-masters 'did not burst into beautiful fits of enthusiasm'. Investment of this sort in a wholly untried area seemed too risky; besides, why help launch a concern which might ultimately compete with their own products?[21] Wright was turned down too by Wernher Beit, which, like the rest of the gold-mining industry, was not overly concerned with promoting secondary industrialisation in the Transvaal. After months of disappointment and frustration, Wright at last found a backer who was prepared not only to invest capital in the scheme, but to provide a site and use his considerable influence to win vitally needed government support for the venture.[22]

Sammy Marks felt that the time was at last ripe to fulfil his great ambition. All his previous attempts to establish a local iron and steel industry had been frustrated by the political and economic uncertainties and difficulties that had beset the country since the 1880s. Now, with a government in power in the Transvaal apparently sympathetic to industrialisation, and with South Africa on the brink of unification and better times, there was at last a solid prospect of success.

If the steel industry were to be drawn to Vereeniging, Marks argued, it would be of far greater benefit to Vereeniging Estates than even the erection of a power station. Other industries would gravitate there once a steel works was established, and Vereeniging would become, as Marks had long dreamed, a 'centre of great industries'. Lewis, who by his own admission was generally less eager than his partner to invest in industry in the Transvaal and who had always vetoed similar proposals in the past, was more receptive this time. Iron and steel-making would be an 'excellent business' for Vereeniging, he wrote. 'I am every bit as keen as you to get good industrial concerns established at Vereeniging . . . and shall continue to sound its praises as an ideal site for Works for all that I am worth.' But while both were enthusiastic about the proposition, they none the less agreed that they should not take more than a 10 per cent stake in the venture. The firm's tight financial position simply did not allow a larger exposure to the considerable risks associated with a novel undertaking of this sort.[23]

To minimise these risks, the scheme Marks and Wright proposed was deliberately limited in scope. They were not planning to establish an integrated iron and steel works that would first produce pig-iron from iron-ore, and then convert this into steel. The size of the local market simply did not warrant such heavy capital expenditure, nor was sufficient known about the iron-ores of the Transvaal. Instead they planned to set up a more modest plant at Vereeniging, which would simply convert scrap iron into finished steel. After a quarter century of industrialisation, there were large accumulations of scrap in the Transvaal, which had been cast off by the railways and the mining industry. While some of this had recently been exported to Europe at knock-down prices, ample quantities remained and more would certainly be generated in the future for use as a cheap raw material in the manufacture of steel.

Though restricted in scope, the scheme was nevertheless more ambitious than anything of a similar kind that had been attempted before in South Africa. The South African Iron and Steel Company, later renamed the Union Steel Corporation of South Africa, would have a capital of £250,000; £85,000 of this would be spent on the erection of a plant capable of producing 15,000 tons of iron and steel per annum; £36,000 would serve as working capital; and the rest would be a reserve for later issue.

Marks and Wright took care to see that their promotion was beyond reproach. Besides a few shares allocated to Wright, there was nothing of the large-scale, free handout of shares to vendors and promoters which was such a notorious feature of South African company promotion in Johannesburg's early years. Similarly, the choice of directors was beyond criticism: there were no aristocratic passengers of the sort who often adorned company boards in this great age of dubious flotations. As the promoters proudly noted, the directors were 'all practical business men' – financiers, English iron-masters and steelmakers, including Frederick Siemens, the world-renowned authority on steel production.

For all its ambitiousness, the promoters felt confident the venture was commercially viable. They calculated that the local market was more than large enough to absorb all of the company's proposed output. The Transvaal alone imported over £1,250,000 of steel and iron annually; the company would surely win a profitable slice of this even in the face of competition from the powerful British steel industry, the traditional supplier to the South African market. It would do this by underselling the imported product.

How was this possible? How could a small and infant industry undercut the products of one long-established and enjoying all the advantages of the economies of scale? The promoters acknowledged that their overseas competitors had certain important advantages, but claimed that there were compensating factors which swung the balance in favour of local manufacture. They accepted that the costs of production would be higher in South Africa than in England, but, they believed, not cripplingly so. Some of the raw materials would have to be imported at considerable cost. Pig-iron, in particular, which would be smelted with the scrap to improve the quality of the end product; the price of this would soar after a long sea and rail journey. On the other hand, scrap iron was plentiful and inexpensive, and Vereeniging coal, for fuel rather than metallurgical purposes, was cheaper than the coal delivered to the English steel works. The costs of skilled labour would be higher at Vereeniging. Forty or more workmen would have to be specially imported from Sheffield and paid double the going rate in England. On the other hand, cheap black labour would be available for many of the 'rougher operations'.

The admitted cost advantages of the English manufacturers would be outweighed, though, by the benefits of proximity to the market. The sea and rail journey to the Rand from England added as much as £7. 7s. 0d. per ton to the price of imported iron and steel; Vereeniging, only 36 miles from Johannesburg, would pay a fraction of this in railage charges. It would thus be able to deliver its finished products to its customers at a competitive price and still rack up a handsome profit of at least £5 per ton, even on a relatively small annual output of 6,000 tons – or at least so the consulting engineers assured the promoters.[24]

Before the scheme could be launched publicly, a guarantee of state support was essential. Everything hinged on the promoters' securing the railway's huge stockpile of scrap and on the measures the state would be prepared to take to protect an infant industry facing fierce foreign competition. In October 1909 Marks took the scheme to Jan Smuts who, with Botha, was the dominant figure in the Transvaal government, and asked for the support of the state. To win this, he assured Smuts that this was no fly-by-night speculation, 'that if we go in for this concern it will be business and not merely talk. . . .' Smuts was very sympathetic. 'He himself can see that works of this kind should and must be established in this Country, and he is also satisfied that Government will have to protect the business . . . up till now they had been forced to fight for other things but now that they have obtained them their idea is to see businesses and Industries established throughout this Country, so therefore the Government will be willing to assist but without granting any concessions whatsoever.'[25]

The necessary agreement was signed in June 1911 by Horace Wright for the promoters and by Jan Smuts for the government. The agreement made few demands on the concessionaires for the government was all too aware of the difficulties of raising funds for a scheme of this sort and was consequently reluctant to jeopardise the project by insisting on any conditions that would frighten off capital. All it asked was that the company establish a works to process scrap iron the railways would supply. Some 15,000 tons would be delivered at £1 per ton in the first year; the company would have to take a minimum of 500 tons per annum for the following fifteen years and would also have a preferential right to purchase all railway scrap beyond this annual minimum. The company was also required to work local iron-ores, a far riskier and more costly exercise than working up scrap, but this obligation was made as light as possible. Three years after it started manufacturing it would have to carry out experiments, but only experiments, with the smelting and treatment of local ores. But even this was subject to a range of provisos which effectively let the company off the hook.

Finally, the government guaranteed a market for the iron and steel goods produced by the company. The railways – with the mines, the largest consumer of iron and steel goods in the country – undertook to place its orders with the company, subject to its producing goods of an acceptable quality at a satisfactory price. As Marks acknowledged, when discussing the flotation of the company, 'If this is not an inducement to hold out to people, I do not know what is.'[26]

Though the agreement was signed in June 1911 by Wright and Smuts, it only became public knowledge many months later. When its existence was discovered, there was an immediate outcry in parliament. The government was accused of going behind parliament's back and creating an undesirable monopoly. The executive had granted valuable privileges to a member of parliament, it was alleged, without the consent of the legislature. Senator Marks had been awarded exclusive rights to government scrap iron and to state custom which would effectively eliminate any competing effort to establish a local steel industry. Furthermore, the government had done nothing to ensure that the contractor would make proper use of local ores and thus lay the foundations of a genuine national steel industry. Instead, all that the government had helped to create was 'a pettifogging . . . scrap iron shop'.[27]

At Smuts's suggestion a parliamentary select committee was appointed to investigate the charges against the government and the contractors. Marks made one of his rare public appearances before this body, which was chaired by his friend Sir Thomas Cullinan, the diamond magnate; ordinarily, Marks preferred to operate less visibly and more discreetly. He adamantly denied the charges: 'I wish you to understand that it is not a monopoly. . . . I call it encouragement from the Government.' He insisted too that the intention was to move rapidly from the smelting of scrap to the smelting of South African iron-ore, agreeing with a sympathetic and supportive Cullinan that scrap was only a 'secondary consideration'. Marks also promised to train and employ white youths at the steel works, an attractive prospect for white legislators at a time when unskilled and impoverished whites were deserting the countryside in large numbers for the towns. Vereeniging was particularly well placed for training youngsters, he noted paternalistically; 'it is away from town, and there will not be the temptations there that would otherwise be present.'[28]

Cullinan's select committee exonerated the government, finding that the steel agreement was a fair one, that it did not constitute a monopoly and that it would foster the development of a South African iron and steel industry. These findings were endorsed by parliament despite a thundering denunciation of the contract by John X. Merriman, the great parliamentarian, at his most devastatingly censorious: 'All I can say is in the circumstances a gross wrong has been done to this country. . . . A more inept contract, bad in principle – thoroughly bad in principle – and unsound in its provisions, he had never seen. It began with a proposal to sell railway iron scrap and *had developed into a monopoly* that was going to end in disaster to this country.'[29] Merriman's broadside was quoted approvingly in the Johannesburg *Star*, which also published a cartoon that lampooned the putative steel monopoly. Marks, the embryonic steel magnate, is shown as a giant magnet drawing to himself a heap of assorted scrap metal, pots, barbed wire, chains, etc. Marks gleefully framed the cartoon and hung it on a wall at Zwartkoppies. He was less blithe though about his rough treatment at the hands of his fellow parliamentarians. Despite his vindication, Marks seethed with righteous indignation. True to character,

however, he chose to vent his anger – and his general sense of frustration with
parliamentary politics and procedure – in a private letter to his partner but
maintain an equable front in public: 'Irresponsible fools in Parliament get up and
make silly statements which, although they are not of much importance cause
a lot of annoyance and unnecessary delay in the business of Parliament. The
opposition here causes a lot of obstruction by their tactics and do whatever they
can to throw obstacles, however stupidly conceived, in the way of the party in
power.'[30]

Union Steel's shares were placed privately rather than publicly, and remained
unlisted for the rest of the decade. The new corporation soon faced the teething
problems inseparable from a project of its scale and novelty. There were delays
in starting up; there were technical headaches; there were management blunders;
and there were labour difficulties. (The workmen imported from abroad were
not 'consistent workers . . . and addicted to drink'.) The first ingot of steel
produced in South Africa was cast at the Union Steel works on 1 September 1913
but production subsequently fell well short of the original targets, pointing to
the necessity of extensive and expensive re-equipment. And contrary to original
expectations, Union Steel found no ready market for the very limited range of
goods it produced. All in all, its prospects in mid-1914 were none too bright. But
they were soon to be transformed by events in the Balkans.[31]

The shockwaves of the great diplomatic crisis in Europe precipitated by the
assassination of the Archduke Franz Ferdinand in Sarajevo on 28 June 1914
reached even the remote South African backveld. General 'Koos' de la Rey,
Sammy Marks's old friend, was caught up in the general excitement. He was
profoundly influenced by a local seer, 'Siener' van Rensburg, 'a simple and
illiterate farmer' who had persuaded many in the western districts of the
Transvaal of the power of his prophetic gifts. During the South African War,
Van Rensburg had served as travelling prophet to De la Rey's wandering
commandos. The story went that they had relied on him to alert them to the
presence of 'Khakies', British troops, in the neighbourhood; if 'Siener' van
Rensburg said there were none, the Boers had not bothered to place sentries
around their camp.

Years before the outbreak of the First World War, Van Rensburg had a much
publicised vision in which he saw a half-dozen bulls, including a grey one and
a red, engaging in mortal combat. After a bloody struggle the grey bull had
emerged victorious. According to his custom Van Rensburg left the interpretation to his audience. As a government commission later explained, 'his
"visions" were invariably symbolic and mysterious; they possessed an
adaptability of character that was truly Delphic.' When the European crisis came
to a head in mid-1914, the prophecy of the bull fight was dusted off and widely
discussed amongst the Boers. Van Rensburg's disciples took the bulls to signify
the great nations of Europe; the victorious grey bull was Germany, the mauled
and defeated red bull Britain. The vision bolstered the belief of a great number
of the Empire's reluctant Boer subjects that Germany was predestined to win the
European war. Many, including De la Rey, felt the time had at last come to
regain the independence they had surrendered at Vereeniging twelve years

before. De la Rey's conviction that the moment had arrived was strengthened, it seems, by another of Van Rensburg's Delphic visions. The prophet had seen the number 15 on a dark cloud which issued blood; next he saw De la Rey returning home without his hat; immediately after came a carriage covered with flowers. The prophet was uncertain as to what all of this meant. It might signify, he ventured, some high honour for De la Rey.

After the declaration of war on 4 August 1914, secret orders went out to the Boers of the western Transvaal to assemble at Treurfontein, a farm sixteen miles from the town of Lichtenburg, on Saturday 15 August. They were to come armed and fully equipped for active serve – with horse, rifle, cartridges and provisions. At Treurfontein they would be addressed by their great Boer War leader, 'Oom Koos' de la Rey; they would then raise the Vierkleur, the standard of their lost Republic, and would march on Potchefstroom, the original capital of the Transvaal. The 15th would be 'the day of liberation'. The Union government was 'finished', 'Siener' van Rensburg assured his followers. Not a shot would be fired; the revolution would be complete and bloodless.

The government caught wind of the meeting from loyalists in the Lichtenburg district. The meeting clearly posed a great threat to public order. Botha and Smuts knew that De la Rey, who possessed 'an unrivalled influence' in the western Transvaal, held the key to the situation. As a commision of inquiry later put it, 'his attitude at the meeting would sway the mass of his adherents and decide the question of peace or war'. Marks was inspanned to calm his old friend. He, together with Botha and Smuts, was to wrestle with Van Rensburg for De la Rey's soul. His was to be the voice of reason countering the seductive unreason of Van Rensburg's prophecies.[32]

Some eight hundred Boers, gripped by a millenarian excitement, waited for De la Rey at Treurfontein on Saturday 15 August. They had come in carts and on horseback to usher in the rebirth of the Republics. Instead, thanks in part to Marks's persuasion, the meeting was a great anti-climax. Rather than a dramatic arrival on horseback to lead a revolutionary cavalcade to Potchefstroom, the hero of the hour, De la Rey, made a more prosaic entrance by motor car with his old Jewish friend, Sammy Marks. As he climbed out he was surrounded by excited well-wishers eager to shake his hand. He mounted a stack of bagged mealies and for the next half-hour spoke to the expectant crowd before him about the need for patience and calm, hardly the message they had come to hear. At the end of the speech, a journalist reported, there was 'a prolonged and unusual silence'. Instead of a call to arms De la Rey had urged his audience to wait upon events. At the end of the meeting De la Rey rode away, as he had come, in the motor car with Sammy Marks. Despite their disappointment the crowd mustered a cheer for their hero – and then dispersed quietly to their homes. Afterwards Marks issued a reassuring, if somewhat wishful, statement to the press that the government could rely on the loyalty of the district.[33]

Marks, Smuts and Botha had kept De la Rey from acting rashly, at least for the moment. Their triumph was shortlived, though, for De la Rey remained in an agitated state of mind. Botha's decision to invade German South West Africa in support of the imperial war effort pushed him, once again, to the brink of rebellion. On 15 September, exactly a month after the misfire at Treurfontein, De la Rey set out from Pretoria for a meeting with disaffected army officers in Potchefstroom. Passing through Johannesburg, De la Rey's car failed to stop at a police roadblock set up to apprehend the notorious Foster gang, a band of violent criminals whom the police were hunting on the Witwatersrand. De la Rey was struck and killed by a shot from one of the policemen. His death, blamed on the government, fuelled the rebellion that followed.

The 1914 Rebellion divided Afrikanerdom. 'Half our tenants have been commandeered by the Government', Marks reported, 'and the other half has joined the Rebels.' The northern Free State, the region of which the Vereeniging Estates formed a part, was the epicentre of the rebellion. When Marks tried to arrange war and riot insurance for the Estates' 1,200 head of cattle and its 15,000 sheep – a tempting target for the rebels – he failed because the insurers insisted that the company kraal all of its stock – in Marks's view, an impossible condition. Instead the company relied on protection by the government forces. Vereeniging became a base for operations against the local rebels led by General de Wet, the great Boer War hero (and a debtor of the Lewis and Marks partnership). Marks arranged hospital accommodation for government troops and provided ground at Vereeniging for their wagons and animals. 'Naturally I gave them all possible assistance . . . and I think this is a good exchange for the provision of protection,' he wrote to Lewis.[34]

In the event the company lost only about a hundred hamels – castrated rams – to the rebels. Once the Rebellion was crushed by the government and De Wet captured, Marks's rebel tenants slunk back to their farms. For a while Marks considered punitive action against them but then thought better of it. In such troubled times it was hard to find suitable tenants for his farms. 'I have half a mind to turn them off,' he wrote to his partner, 'but, of course, we must not throw away dirty water before we can replace it with clean water.' Marks did insist, though, that the imprisoned General De Wet immediately repay the loan that the partners had made him over a decade before at the end of the South African War.[35]

Patriots by adoption, Sammy Marks and Isaac Lewis fully identified with the British cause during the First World War, dutifully contributing to the unending wartime appeals for funds. In October 1914, for example, Lewis donated £1,000 on behalf of the partners to a fund founded to provide 'comforts' for the Union's sick and wounded; at the same time Vereeniging Estates gave £196 and 752 tons of coal to the government as its contribution towards a planned hospital ship. Isaac Lewis grumbled about the incessant demands on the partners' purse, the endless stream of callers who came to the firm's offices soliciting donations. Marks, far more generous by nature than his partner, joked that the only way they could evade these demands was by closing down their offices![36]

With the patriotic tide running high, Louis, Joe and Teddy Marks, Sammy's oldest sons, joined the army as did numbers of his staff. As patriotic employers Lewis and Marks placed those with dependants on half pay. Joe Marks served in the artillery while Teddy Marks participated in General Smuts's arduous campaign against the Germans in East Africa. (The Marks papers contain a

Central News Agency receipt for a subscription to the *Sunday Times* by Trooper T. Marks of the Animal Advance Base, Transport Depot, Lines of Communication, A.P.O. Kilindini.)[37]

Marks attempted to induce his black tenants to follow suit. Blacks were reluctant recruits for the imperial war effort; when the South African Native Labour Contingent was raised midway through the war for service on the Western Front, it fell well short of its recruiting targets. To spur enlistment Marks visited the large 'colony of natives' living on Brakfontein, an African and European farm in the Rustenburg district, and promised the chief that the dependants of those of his followers who volunteered for service in France could remain on the farm without paying any rent as long as their husbands and sons were away at war. The offer was open to anyone wishing to settle on the farm. Marks proposed extending the arrangement to his other farms, and wrote to the prime minister, Louis Botha, seeking his endorsement. The government, however, had reservations: the arrangement was acceptable only so long as the offer was restricted to Marks's existing tenants on Brakfontein and his other farms. If it were extended to blacks not presently resident on Marks's farms, it might contravene either the recently passed Natives Land Act of 1913 or the Transvaal's Squatter Law of 1895.[38]

Like the South African War of 1899–1902, the First World War was bad for business, at least initially. Marks's brick and tile works at Vereeniging was forced to close as the construction industry came to a halt; farming was badly disrupted by the Rebellion and by the campaign in German South West Africa; and Union Steel's re-equipment programme was seriously delayed as its British suppliers turned from civilian production to production for the war effort.[39]

At the outbreak of war, credit dried up overnight as the London money market went into a state of shock. Lewis and Marks, heavily committed because of the founding of Union Steel and the expansion of the coal works at Vereeniging, struggled desperately to meet its financial obligations. The firm faced a debtor's nightmare. It was unable to realise assets because the stock market was dead; it was unable to borrow fresh funds because the banks it approached were themselves running for cover. Isaac Lewis wrung his hands: 'It seems a waste of time coming up to the City and it is depressing as well, for, although one comes up and puts the best face on it, one all along feels one's helplessness and impotence. Still, we must go on hoping that things will gradually improve: and, after all, we are very much better off than any of the other combatants so I suppose it is not fair to grumble too much.' Lewis urged Marks to find tenants for their farms and to press their South African debtors for repayment, even small debtors like General De Wet and Sir James Molteno, the Speaker of the Union parliament: every little bit would help to reduce the firm's overdraft.[40]

By late 1915 the firm was in a desperate plight. Heavily borrowed, it was close to losing its credit-worthiness. For three anxious weeks in September, Isaac Lewis scrambled around to find funds to cover the quarterly interest due on the firm's outstanding loans. Though all that was immediately needed was £8,000, he had the 'greatest difficulty possible' in arranging a credit facility. The Union of London and Smiths Bank – to which Lewis and Marks already owed close to £400,000 – eventually obliged, but insisted that the firm lodge its Rand mining shares at the bank as additional security. Much to Lewis's chagrin, the bank also demanded that he pledge the title-deeds of Bedgebury, his beloved country estate in Kent. This was a 'terrible blow' to Lewis: 'I will leave you to imagine', he told Marks, 'what my feelings are at having to make such a sacrifice.' Marks was equally upset: 'Although I do not constantly write on the subject you must not conclude that I do not worry very much. The position is like a nightmare to me but let us hope that better times are in store for us.'[41]

Much of the trouble seems to have stemmed from the activities of the firm's Diamond Branch, a joint venture Lewis and Marks had established six years before the war with the wrong Oppenheimer – Bernhard, the older, less successful brother of Ernest Oppenheimer. Like Ernest, Bernhard had served an apprenticeship in the diamond business with the London house of Dunkelsbuhler, but there their ways had parted. Ernest remained with Dunkelsbuhler for many years and eventually became a partner; the house of Dunkelsbuhler helped him to form the Anglo American Corporation in 1917. Bernhard, on the other hand, left Dunkelsbuhler when in his early forties and in 1908 became managing director of Lewis and Marks's new Diamond Branch. This was an attempt by Lewis and Marks to re-establish themselves as a significant presence in the world of diamond trading, the business which had formed the basis of their original fortune but which they had abandoned some two decades before when Cecil Rhodes's De Beers company and its allies in the diamond trade, the Diamond Syndicate, had established a stranglehold over the international diamond market.

Bernhard Oppenheimer's brief before the war was to deal in diamonds in competition with the Syndicate; Lewis and Marks's role in the joint venture was to provide the necessary capital. This proved a very hazardous and burdensome undertaking. The Diamond Branch was capital-hungry: it was obliged to carry a large stock of diamonds and to grant generous credit to its customers, forcing it to rely heavily on bank credit. The parent firm, Lewis and Marks, ultimately bore the risk. Before the war the Lewis and Marks partners signed bank guarantees on the Diamond Branch's behalf amounting to no less than £270,000. The collapse of the international diamond market at the outbreak of the war left the Diamond Branch stranded with no means of meeting its financial commitments. As a last resort Lewis and Marks were forced to approach the Bank of England, which agreed to cover the outstanding bills of the Diamond Branch till the end of the war.[42]

While Marks's fortunes depended on the success or failure of the Diamond Branch, he had little say in its affairs. Bernhard Oppenheimer ran the Diamond Branch from London. He had two buyers based at Kimberley who operated independently of Sammy Marks and of the Lewis and Marks office in Johannesburg. Isaac Lewis in London, rather than Sammy Marks in South Africa, kept a watching brief on the venture and arranged the necessary financing. Marks's role in an operation that had such an impact on his pocketbook was restricted to lobbying on its behalf.

In 1915 South African forces commanded by the prime minister, General Louis Botha, conquered German South West Africa. The spoils of war included deposits of alluvial diamonds which had been discovered in the bleak southern reaches of the territory only six years before the war. Lewis and Marks had toyed at the time with the idea of investing in South West African diamond-mining. Arrangements had been made, and then cancelled, to send Hans Merensky, the German geologist who many years later discovered the great platinum deposits of the Transvaal bushveld and the diamond deposits at the mouth of the Orange River, to investigate. Marks had felt that it would be very difficult to control the diamond operation from Johannesburg. South West Africa was a tedious and time-consuming rail and sea journey from his office. Besides, the territory was 'uncivilised and unhealthy', a surprising objection on the part of someone who had spent a lifetime rushing around the fever-ridden Transvaal lowveld.

By the outbreak of the First World War, Marks had clearly come to regret his earlier hesitancy, for German South West Africa had become an important competitor with De Beers and the Premier mine. Botha's invasion of the territory in 1915 seemed to offer Marks an opportunity to make good his earlier omission and to establish a commanding position for the firm's flagging Diamond Branch in the international diamond trade. The South West Africa campaign was still under way when Marks sought out General Smuts, Botha's deputy, in his office at the Union Buildings on Union Day at the end of May. Despite the public holiday Smuts was at his desk and patiently heard out Marks's request for a stake in the South West African diamond industry. When Botha returned to Pretoria in triumph two months later, Marks sat next to Smuts at the celebratory luncheon and engaged him in a long conversation about the South West African diamonds. Smuts was a little less patient when Marks once again visited his office at the Union Buildings a few weeks later: 'he begged of me to allow business discussion of any kind to stand over for the present as he was extremely busy, and from what I could see he appeared to have a great abundance of work before him.' Marks, who was always tenacious when he sensed profit, was quite unabashed. He promised Lewis that he would make another attempt the next week 'to occupy a little of his [Smuts's] time' about the diamonds.

Besides Smuts, Marks also badgered the prime minister himself, as well as F. S. Malan, the Minister of Mines and Industries, and David Graaff, his unloved associate from the Imperial Cold Storage fiasco who was now Minister of Finance. What Marks sought, unsuccessfully, was the right to market the diamonds the Union government now controlled in South West Africa, an arrangement which would have propelled Lewis and Marks's Diamond Branch into the front rank of the international diamond trade. Instead this prized right was acquired by the powerful Diamond Syndicate which had dominated the trade for years.[43]

Besides touting for the South West African diamonds, Marks devoted a great deal of attention during the war to his infant steel concern. In its first years Union Steel had struggled to find its feet. The World War was its salvation, effectively insulating it against foreign competition for the duration. The wartime shortage of shipping meant that South African consumers of steel were forced to rely in large measure on their local producer rather than on their traditional overseas suppliers. Output and sales at Union Steel expanded dramatically. These rose from just under 2,000 tons, valued at £23,604, in 1914, to over 8,000 tons valued at just under £250,000 in 1918. The surge in demand for its products led eventually to a shortage of scrap, the raw material on which Union Steel relied.[44]

Though the company consistently denied that it made surplus profits as defined in its contract with the state, and insisted therefore that it was under no obligation to conduct trials of local iron-ore, it nevertheless spent £60,000 on experiments. This was prompted partly by a desire to please government and public opinion, which were very keen to see the country's natural resources properly exploited; partly by the wartime scarcity of scrap, which posed a threat to continuity of production in the future; but very largely by Marks's enthusiasm for the idea. As his right-hand man at Union Steel explained later, the company undertook the experiments because 'Senator Marks . . . was very keen to go into this thing'.

In preparation for the experiment the company conducted a search for suitable iron-ore. Altogether 282 samples were submitted in response to its advertise-ments, and these were analysed at a laboratory specially built for the purpose by an experienced chemist who had worked at English iron works. The 58 most promising properties were then inspected and large samples obtained from the best of these. The very best came from Kromdraai, a farm near Warmbaths, some 140 miles from Vereeniging, which Lewis and Marks had acquired in 1911; its iron-ore proved to be of 'phenomenal richness'.

The next step was the design of an experimental blast furnace by Professor G. H. Stanley of the University of the Witwatersrand. The design for a small furnace capable of producing 10-15 tons per day was submitted to and approved by Marks. Coke was the next problem. Vereeniging coal was unsuitable for this purpose and management were unaware of a satisfactory alternative source of supply. They seriously considered having charcoal made from the waste timber of the wattle district of Natal, but the costs of railage were prohibitive. Just when the situation seemed hopeless, it was discovered that successful experiments had been made at Vryheid in Natal with the production of good quality coke from coal.

The furnace, which cost £40,000, began operations in October 1918, the month before the Armistice, but rapidly ran into technical difficulties. Work was also very seriously disrupted by the great influenza epidemic which struck soon after. After a better run, Marks and the business manager of Union Steel took two ingots to an engineering works in Johannesburg and had the iron planed in their presence. 'We asked for an opinion on the quality of the iron and we were told it was excellent, and they would be well satisfied if we could give them stuff of that character. Mr. Marks was delighted, his expression showed what he felt about it and he gave the fitter ten shillings on the spot to get a drink with. He lived for this thing.'[45]

For Marks it was the culmination of a 37-year-old dream. At last he had produced iron from native Highveld ore – his great ambition ever since he had first visited the Transvaal, then little more than a benighted rural backwater, in 1881. But for all the excitement of the moment, for all the sense of achievement, Marks knew that this was really only a beginning. The Vereeniging furnace was small and experimental; the next step towards the creation of a full-blown South African steel industry – a costly and very risky step at that – would have to be the construction of an integrated steel works, producing steel on a large scale. Negotiations began in late 1919; Sammy Marks died – on 18 February 1920 – before his bold initiative could bear fruit.[46]

A contemporary newspaper satirises the controversial grant to Sammy Marks in 1911 of a government scrap iron concession (The Star, 12 June 1912)

XIII

Sammy Marks:
The Haimisher Mensh,
1844–1920

In his seriocomic lexicon, *The Joys of Yiddish*, Leo Rosten explains that a *haimisher mensh* is 'someone with whom you can take your shoes off, or let your hair down'. *Haimish* comes from the German word *heim* – home – and means 'informal, cosy, and warm; . . . unpretentious; putting on no airs; unspoiled by office or honours.' *Mensh* comes from the German word for 'person', but means a lot more. A *mensh* is someone who is 'upright, honourable [and] decent . . . someone to admire and emulate.' Eastern European Jews placed a great value on being a *mensh* as they also did on being *haimish*. As Rosten often heard in his childhood, 'The finest thing you can say about a man is that he is a *mensh*.'[1]

Sammy Marks's South African Jewish contemporaries greatly admired his success. He was a symbol of what could be achieved in the new country. A Jew could leave the oppression and poverty of Russia and arrive in South Africa without capital, without contacts and with poor English, and yet achieve enormous worldly success and recognition. But Marks's wealth was only part of the reason for the esteem in which he was held. There were other Jews who had made their fortunes in South Africa but who were regarded with indifference or even faint hostility by their fellow Jews. Besides his wealth and success, Marks owed his special place in the Jewish community's esteem to two things: the fact that unlike some of his wealthy Jewish peers he strongly and unambiguously identified throughout his life with Jewishness and with local Jewry, and, equally important, that despite his wealth and fame, he had remained a *haimisher mensh*.[2]

'In person short, every movement denoting restless activity, his face was redeemed from plainness by the extraordinary play of feature, and the almost habitual humour flashing into the expression. A countenance fascinating to watch because of the thoughtful mind which animated it.'[3] During his life Marks had mocked his own plainness. Once overhearing a fellow member of parliament remarking to another that 'There goes old Sammy! I should like to have his money,' he wheeled round and asked, 'Would you like to have my face too?'[4]

His dress was as plain as his physical appearance. As was customary amongst his affluent contemporaries, Marks ordered his clothes from English tailors and bootmakers who kept details of his measurements and used their discretion in filling his orders. He bought in bulk and by broad category. In September 1900, for example, shortly before Lord Roberts visited Zwartkoppies, he ordered two dozen shirts and six dozen pocket handkerchiefs, and in January 1901, a long overcoat, reaching to his ankles. After the Boers cleared out his wardrobe in early 1902 he was forced to send for three or four suits of clothes, three or four pairs of boots, two dozen each of socks, ties and handkerchiefs, a dozen changes of underlinen and half-a-dozen night-shirts and pyjamas. (Marks grumbled that the underlinen Lewis sent out was both too large and too thin.) In these and a series of other bulk orders Marks made little attempt to give more precise detail about his clothing requirements; this is in marked contrast with the great care he often took in placing orders for other items. Marks's tastes in clothes were simple. He was very critical of those his wife bought for him while she was away in England, resisting her attempts to update his wardrobe. He preferred his old overcoat to the one she sent from London: 'I do not at all like the colours,' he wrote, 'and would not wear it even in far off Africa.' Thanking Bertha for a navy-blue dressing-gown which had cost ten guineas, he noted rather ungraciously that 'a gown costing 50/- would have answered the purpose just as well. Please do not go and buy things for me at those fancy places, as you know that I am not a fancy man.' [5]

Sammy Marks had an engaging modesty. He was very *haimish*, very homely and unpretentious in manner. He disliked swagger and conceit, what the Victorians called 'side'. Recommending an employee to him once, his partner Isaac Lewis wrote: 'He is a good fellow, without the side and bluster which I know you object to in some people. . . .' Marks practised the self-mockery which was so much part of Eastern European Jewish humour. When an absurd rumour circulated in London in early 1899 that Marks was a possible candidate for the presidency of the Transvaal, he wrote to an English friend: 'Since my return [from England] I have given up the idea of aspiring to Presidential honours, and have developed an ambition to become Lord Mayor of London.' Replying to a letter from his daughter Girlie during the South African War, Marks, who played at most the occasional poor game of billiards, wrote: 'I certainly am a great sportsman as you know and am anxious to learn the new games you speak of. I am having flannels made for the game of "ping-pong".' [6]

In an acutely status-conscious age Marks put on none of the airs of his upper-class peers, affected none of the offensive snobbishness of his contemporaries: 'he was easily the most approachable and friendly of all our leaders of men,' an acquaintance recalled after his death. As he advised his oldest son, Louis:

you must always try and be a gentleman: that is not to say that you must only act as a gentleman to those whom you like, but also to those whom you dislike, as the world is very wide and people of business are always likely to meet all sorts and conditions. You must therefore train yourself to be a gentleman alike to old and young, rich and poor, and of whatever nationality, even a kaffir who is black and nearest to an animal. By doing this you will find that the world will think well of you, and you will always have influence amongst people.[7]

As his advice to his son suggests, Marks's geniality often masked acute ethnic prejudice. He was by no means immune to the currents of racism and xenophobia that swirled about him. He covertly possessed a full set of the dominant ethnic stereotypes of his age. The Portuguese, with whom he had had frustrating dealings at Delagoa Bay, were, inevitably, lethargic and 'slow'. They 'are never in a great hurry', he told Isaac Lewis. As he once joked at a luncheon given in his honour by the Governor-General of Mozambique, three things were essential in dealing with the Portuguese: 'First: to live as long as Methuselah; Second: to have the patience of Job; and Third: to possess the purse of a Rothschild.' As much as Marks admired and liked the English and aspired to their way of life, he felt, as many others did during the heyday of Victoria's empire, that the English were stubborn and arrogant. 'Like the majority of Englishmen,' he complained of a manager at his glassworks, 'Parker imagines he has nothing to learn.'

Marks, who had grown up on the Russo–Prussian border, had a lifelong prejudice against Germans, which was presumably reinforced by the increasing imperial competition between Britain, the country with which he so closely identified, and Kaiser Wilhelm's Germany. Time and again he warned his partner of the dangers of dealing with Germans. 'I have already asked you by all that is holy to have nothing to do with Germans,' he wrote in 1894. In 1904, after he had himself been misled by his German agents at Delagoa Bay, he noted plaintively: 'Our experience here again illustrates how circumspect one must be in one's dealings with Germans and how deceitful they are.' When his son Louis studied in Germany in 1905, he warned him against German students in particular and against Germans in general:

They drink any amount of beer and there is also no end of swagger and tall talk about them, but all this does not become an English gentleman. I must tell you, and I do not keep it a secret, that I utterly dislike Germans. They are as deceitful as every egg is full of yoke, and in all my travels and business dealings I have found very few of them whose word I can take without tying them up in black and white. . . . They are exceedingly nice people among their own nationalities but they can prove very dangerous to strangers.

Hollanders were equally untrustworthy. Marks shared the popular prejudice against Hollanders in the Transvaal, provoked by Kruger's heavy reliance on imported Dutch officials. 'As regards . . . what any Hollander tells you in the future,' he instructed Isaac Lewis, 'if you can put it all down on soft paper, you might afterwards find that soft paper useful. They are people I care to say very little about.'[8]

Marks's views about the Boers amongst whom he spent the greater part of his life were more ambivalent. 'Now, there isn't a more open-hearted class of people than the real old Dutch people,' he wrote shortly after the South African

War. 'They are charitable, hospitable, and so forth. . . .' They were also simple and unspoilt. Explaining why Louis Botha would be unaffected by the fêting he received in London in 1907, Marks wrote: 'You know that an Afrikander is quite satisfied if he gets some Biltong and mealies and a glass of water!' Marks perceived the Boer as a natural pioneer, ever willing to trek northwards 'when he can get Game to shoot'. But he was a poor farmer. When the rinderpest swept through the Transvaal in 1896, Marks, a progressive farmer himself, felt little sympathy for his Boer neighbours. 'I cannot say that I sympathise with them as they are a lazy good-for-nothing lot and absolutely abhor work.'[9]

Like many other English-speaking colonists in South Africa, Marks shared the illiberal Boer view of blacks. Like many other colonists he claimed a special understanding of the 'native mind' unavailable to critics of South African native policy in Britain. Because he had employed large numbers of Africans ever since the 1870s he claimed to 'have had ample opportunity of gaining a thorough insight into the character of the natives and gauging his wants'. This knowledge seems to have largely consisted of the conventional views of his age. His letters contain the standard colonial images of black indolence and barbarism. Blacks were 'savages', 'a lot of good-for-nothing lazy rascals', and less than fully human. The 'native mind' differed markedly from the white. A letter in 1907 to his old wartime patron and protector, General John Maxwell, captures the flavour of his very conventional perceptions:

It is a great pity that some of those good people on your side did not come out and stay beside the Natives, even for twelve months, and they would then learn what a troublesome lot they are and how backward they are in falling in with our views of civilisation. In my opinion it will take a good many years because my experience tells me the native has no sympathy and no gratitude and no feelings. They must grow very slowly by a little education in reading and writing and by gradual pressure to bring home the fact that every human being must do a little work on the land in which he lives and this the Native has not yet realised.

You yourself are aware that Bigamy is carried on to a very great extent. Every Native that has 2 or 3 wives makes slaves of them. He lies about in his Kraal while his wives till the ground and make Kaffir Beer for him. He and his Chums talk politics all day long and their politics consist in wondering how to get the better of the white man and how to steal his Cattle.

Similar negative colonial sentiments were expressed in a letter to the plantation manager on his Pienaarsport farm: 'Further, natives, even the best of them, can never be trusted to do a certain piece of work without some supervision. It is not enough to tell a native to go and do some work, you must see that he does it, otherwise he will take about three days to do what should only take him about half a day. That is my experience during the last forty years in this country.'[10]

Whatever his innermost feelings, outwardly Marks was even-tempered and genial, a natural diplomat and conciliator, who dealt skilfully and tactfully with German employees and Boer generals, Portuguese officials and African sharecroppers. 'I never willingly pick a quarrel with anybody,' he wrote to Isaac Lewis. His view was that 'it is an advantage to be on good terms with everybody', however much one privately despised the individual or group.

Characteristically, though he lived in a litigious age when the likes of J. B. Robinson kept the legal fraternity in a flourishing condition, Marks avoided litigation and public quarrelling. 'I think we can congratulate ourselves', he wrote to Isaac Lewis in 1904, 'on having been singularly free from law suits in the past.'[11]

Marks reserved his occasional eruptions for those upon whose friendship and support he could absolutely depend. For the rest, he kept up an amiable front, however great the provocation. He quarrelled furiously with his partner Isaac Lewis and constantly railed at his brother Ellia Marks who managed the Vaal River property during the 1890s. Frustrated at Ellia's failure to make a promised delivery of firebricks, he wrote: 'You seem to content yourself like a mad Frenchman with lifting your arms and shrugging your shoulders. Now, my dear Ellia, I have been trained and have always found it best to keep my word and when that is given I feel as much bound as though I had signed and had my signature witnessed by two people . . . is what you have done management or is it child's play[?]' When Ellia, who was less diplomatic and genial than his brother, quarrelled with the station master at Vereeniging, Sammy wrote: 'Now, my dear Ellia, if you would try and make as many friends as you do enemies you would perhaps find that your business would run a little more smoothly.'[12]

Marks himself made friends with considerable ease. His modesty, his hospitality, his generosity and kindness, his warmth, good cheer and good humour attracted many. Marks, one of these recalled, had a 'gift for the apt retort'. He enjoyed exchanging banter with his friends and acquaintances. This was mostly good-natured and inoffensive stuff but occasionally there was a sting in the tail. When he heard, after Rhodes's death, that Abe Bailey vainly believed that the mantle of the Great Cecil had descended upon him, he told the Cape millionaire, who had taken over both Rhodes's Muizenberg house and his parliamentary constituency, that 'I have dealt in old clothes myself and you can take it from me they never fit'. When Marks asked his brother Ellia why there was no water on one of their properties, Ellia replied: 'I have not got Moses' Rod.' To this Marks retorted sharply: 'I am aware of that but as far as we are concerned, we have Balaam's Ass.' Asked why he had not acquired a title as many others had during the unseemly and mercenary scramble for honours in the years after the South African War, he explained: 'Well, when I have a little money to spare, I like to buy myself a piece of ground.'

Sometimes Marks's sense of humour, like his friend Paul Kruger's, took a droll turn. A pig belonging to a Jewish acquaintance wandered onto Marks's property and began feasting on his mealies. Marks had his black employees kill the trespasser and remove the carcase for their own use. When the owner later complained and asked for reparation, Marks replied: 'At the time I had no idea it was your pig, or would have had it carefully prepared to present it to you at the Passover Feast, which I believe is close at hand. I was not aware that such a valuable pig, which you value at £10, could be found in the Transvaal, especially kept by one of the Chosen People.' Marks's quips often had a Jewish theme.

He chose to defuse latent hostility on the part of his gentile acquaintances by making a joke of their antisemitic barbs. When he was asked, for example, why Jews were so fond of money, he said the answer was quite simple. When Moses went up Mount Sinai to receive the Ten Commandments, he was absent for forty days and for forty nights. On his return he found the Hebrews worshipping a golden calf. Moses took this away from them, ground it into dust and made them drink it in their water. Somehow, Marks ended, the taste still lingered with their descendants. On another occasion, when asked by a Christian friend why so many Jews were flat-footed, Sammy replied: 'I daresay you would suffer from the same defect if your ancestors had been compelled to wander around in the desert for forty years.' [13]

Marks's geniality was only one of an array of personal attributes that made him a successful businessman. His personality was particularly well adapted to the rigours of entrepreneurship. Throughout his career he was willing to take large risks. His life is a testimony to this. At the age of 17 he left the security and familiarity of home for England without any useful skills or visible means of support. Later he emigrated to distant South Africa with a set of knives as the sum total of his capital. He trekked from Cape Town to the remote diamond fields with a wagon-load of goods. He set up a factory in a rural backwater. He repeatedly risked his shirt on land, mineral and industrial speculations. Defying the conventional wisdom, he eventually established a steel works on the Highveld.

He was an incurable optimist who was undaunted by either the possibility or the actual experience of failure. He showed remarkable resilience in the face of repeated setbacks. Project after project either was stillborn or foundered after a promising start, yet he continued to dream and to venture: 'as you know I am always very sanguine,' he told his more cautious partner Isaac Lewis. Marks accepted failure philosophically. As he blithely informed Lewis midway through their partnership: 'I admit that I have made lots of mistakes in the past, for which we have had to pay, and if I remain in this business I shall make many more mistakes in the future, as there is no one who does not make mistakes, but I think if you will compare my mistakes with my successes then you will find that I am still to the good.' Marks refused to dwell morbidly on past failures: 'You must not cry over spilt milk,' he told his war friend, General Pole-Carew. 'It may perhaps turn yet into good Cream Cheese or even Butter.' (Like other non-native English-speakers, Marks enjoyed the commonplaces of his adopted tongue, 'the good old English language', but he was in the habit of reworking these stale saws in fresh and appealing ways. Thus, for example, when he rebuked an employee for disclosing company secrets, he told him that 'There is an old saying that "you should never let your right hand know what your left hand does".')[14]

Marks was justifiably proud of his own perseverance. As he once boasted to a Cape railway official during the difficult early years of the Cape coal contract: ' I have wonderful staying power, and where others get tired, I put on more steam. . . .' The dark side of this was a deep reluctance to cut his losses and abandon dying projects which had little hope of survival. When his Lourenço

Marques Wharf Company went aground during the post-war regional recession, Marks continued to clutch onto it. This prompted the Corner House, the dominant Rand mining house of the age – who were his partners in the concern and who were reluctant to throw good money after bad – to complain that 'Mr. Marks does not seem to be quite able to make up his mind to cut a loss'. Marks was instinctively a buyer, not a seller. Once acquired, he was loth to part with assets.[15]

Marks had prodigious energy and his work-rate was phenomenal. 'I am somewhat like a flying trapeze,' he joked, 'always moving.' Throughout his Transvaal years he was a frenetic traveller, chasing around the countryside in pursuit of business possibilities. 'As usual I am flying all over the Country,' he wrote shortly before his fiftieth birthday; 'there is no rest for the wicked.' In the days before the railways, this meant long and uncomfortable trips by coach or cart, snugly covered in his waterproofed Scottish plaid travelling rugs. It meant arduous and sometimes hazardous journeys on horseback along rough tracks in all weathers. Racing once to Barberton in the rainy season to pay expiring claim licences, he came to a river swollen by floodwaters. Rather than turning back and risking the loss of the claims, he plunged in and waded across, holding on to the tail of his horse. Marks's relentless travelling also meant endless nights in 'not very agreeable' hotels, or what passed for these in remote villages and towns in late-nineteenth-century South Africa. 'When I do business I am never in a hurry,' he teased a licensed victualler. 'The only time I am in a hurry is, when I am away from home and staying at a strange hotel, because I am afraid of fleas.' Yet when he was at home, he felt a compulsion to be out at the office or the factory, and working. As George Falcke put it: 'He found remaining at home irksome unless he had congenial company there and would proceed to the office to keep himself occcupied.' 'I do plenty of work,' Marks himself wrote when he turned 60. 'I get up, and start at six o'clock every morning, work till late on Saturday afternoons and a little on Sundays. . . .'

Marks was a notoriously early riser. His preferred routine, when visiting the Vereeniging Estates, was to take the night train from Pretoria which arrived at Viljoensdrift station at 4 in the morning, then walk to his estate manager's home for coffee and breakfast, before setting off on a dawn patrol of the property. He would scurry ahead of the often younger officials accompanying him, scramble over the mountains of scrap at the steel works and wander around for hours underground at the mines. He made late-night inspections, too, at Eerste Fabrieken, often appearing at the distillery between midnight and 1 o'clock in the morning to check on the distilling.

Marks's hectic routine left little time for leisure. On the rare occasions he took vacations, these were soon converted into busman's holidays. When he holidayed in Muizenberg, he relaxed by inspecting and purchasing Cape properties. On his infrequent returns to Europe his chief recreation was touring factories to collect fresh ideas for possible use at home. As Marks's secretary later recalled, 'he simply had to keep going at full speed; there was some force within him which impelled him to ceaseless activity. Had he retired years ago before his death it would have meant that he would have declined. He was not working for wealth, but he had to find an outlet for his ceaseless energy. He often remarked that a man could only eat three meals a day and wear one suit of clothes at a time.'

His wife, Bertha, was less admiring, however, of this single-minded dedication to work and business than his secretary: 'sometimes I think it is a great pity for yourself,' she wrote while holidaying alone in Durban, 'that there is really nothing in the World that you do take a pleasure in outside Business. After all one has one life only. It is quite right to work hard, but at the same time there is not one man in a million who does not sometimes enjoy a little mild recreation, which is one of the very best nerve tonics.'

Marks's workaholicism was not just temperamental; it was elevated into a central tenet of his personal belief system. He held the Jewish equivalent of the Protestant work ethic, ceaselessly preaching to his children and his nephews the gospel of hard work, which was one of the articles of faith of the Victorian middle class to which he belonged: 'when you grow up to be a big man in business,' he wrote to his son Teddy, then all of 9 years of age, 'you will understand it is business first and pleasure afterwards.' Writing to his surrogate nephew Henry Lewis, Isaac Lewis's son and heir, he stressed that work was a good in itself, not merely a means of enrichment, and that wealth won through personal effort was more rewarding and satisfying than unearned wealth:

My advice is to get your father to put you into business with first rate people, not Germans, so that you may have a good business training, for although your father and Uncles are rich, you must not run away with the idea that it is not necessary for you to work.

I have always found it is far more pleasant to spend a £5 note that you have earned yourself, than twice that amount given to you by another.

Not for Marks, then, the life of the idle rich: hard work gave life its meaning and purpose. But there was a heavy price to be paid, as Marks was the first to acknowledge. Looking back on his long career, he believed that he had sacrificed self, and family to some degree, to work and duty to the firm. Writing to Isaac Lewis late in life, he complained that in all the decades of their partnership he had taken very few holidays or 'pleasure trips'. 'I have even stinted myself in going over to Europe to look after the interests of my Children, although it was my duty, as it is the duty of every Father towards his own Children.'

Marks began to slow down in his late sixties, though only by his own hyperkinetic standards. Rushing through Johannesburg in March 1912, en route from Cape Town to Lourenço Marques to interview the Governor-General of Mozambique, he received a phone-call to come urgently to Vereeniging on Union Steel business. Somewhat annoyed, he protested: 'I cannot at my age, go flying all over the country as I used to in my younger days. . . . In the early days I was at the beck and call of everybody and would at a moment's notice board a stage coach or mount a horse and hurry off but this I cannot do now.' The minute-books of his companies suggest that despite this protestation, he still did.[16]

Along with the energy went curiosity and imagination. Marks had the thirst for information of the self-educated, and a receptivity to knowledge whatever its source. As he enthused after an informative conversation with the new lime-burner on his Vaal River estate: 'I always find one can learn something from everybody. . . .' When his daughter squabbled with his nephew, he wrote: 'You say that George is supposed to have finished learning; no one is supposed to have finished learning however old he may be and I can assure you I learn something nearly every day.'[17]

Marks was feverishly creative. As he confided to his old friend and fellow schemer, Jimmy Sivewright, 'I have a great many ideas and fancies in my head.' For decades he bombarded his more staid and 'sensible' partners with volleys of proposals, many of which they simply overlooked, much to his chagrin. 'I believe there are a good many suggestions of mine in your office which you would appear to have ignored,' he complained to Isaac Lewis in 1894. 'I think it shows ingratitude to be a trait in your nature because you must remember that all these little suggestions, before I present them to you, have occupied my brain during a sleepless night. . . .' Marks suspected, probably correctly, that his partners thought that some of his suggestions were 'mad ideas'. Nevertheless he kept up his bombardment. 'I always have looked ahead,' he proudly confessed to Isaac Lewis, 'and I suppose I always shall.' This, he wryly joked, was his 'unfortunate lot in this world'. Marks was a business visionary. Like all the boldest entrepreneurs he had a capacity to conjure up schemes out of apparent nothingness, to recognise the potential of what seemed to others the most unpromising of places, to conceive schemes which at first appeared preposterous to the less imaginative, and to see the factory on the bare veld.[18]

Besides his fascination with the grand design, Marks also had a great eye for detail. Reminiscing about the early days, an old Vereeniging hand recollected that Marks's 'active interest in everything was endless'. He recalled seeing his employer marching into the store-room at the colliery and remonstrating with the storekeeper about poorly fitting bolts; the storekeeper was to get his 'boy' to make sure they fitted. The Marks papers include a lengthy letter to Lewis, written when Vereeniging Estates was already a well-established public company with a large management complement, explaining why shovels with cow mouths were preferable to square-nosed shovels. As Marks wrote of himself to one of his managers: 'As you are aware I am in the habit of looking here there and everywhere and always thinking.'[19]

The corollary of all of this, however, was that Marks was a demanding and sometimes trying employer. He found it difficult to delegate and leave his subordinates be, and, like many a hard-driven person, expected the same relentless effort from his employees as he did from himself. Perhaps George Falcke was talking of himself and of his own relationship with his uncle when he later wrote: 'One of his secretaries at Johannesburg, who had commenced his business career with him and who was expert at interpreting him, became so useful that he had very little leisure. The more competency he displayed, the more onerous became his duties, until they were well-nigh overwhelming, necessitating his working every day in the week including Sundays and Public holidays and almost every night.'[20]

As their business grew after the South African War, Lewis and Marks employed a string of senior executives to supply the professional skills the partners thought they lacked and to broaden their management team. Marks had an uncomfortable relationship with these new men, some of them specially imported from England. Despite appointing them at high salaries to run major areas of his operation, Marks continued, as he had always done, to involve himself directly in every aspect of the business. Some of the senior managers seem to have strongly resented this interference. Marks, in turn, suspected that his Anglo–Saxon managers were secretly contemptuous of the thick accents and alien manners of their employers, and that some harboured antisemitic feeling. 'Like a good many other Christians,' he wrote of one senior employee, ' he does not love the tribe of Levy.'

Marks was very sensitive to the real or imagined condescension of his superior English employees. He feared that these men were mocking him and Isaac Lewis behind their backs. In his mid-seventies, Marks complained to Lewis that though Dunning, Villiers and Hodges, present and past senior managers of the business, had all done well out of the firm, they were none the less very hostile to the partners: 'I do not think any one of the three had or has a good word for us and we were and are dubbed by them even as ignorant low mean selfish people.' The behavior of Hodges, general manager of Vereeniging Estates during the 1910s, was particularly galling. Marks visited the estate with a Professor Buchanan in June 1919 to inspect the collieries. 'After my departure', Marks complained to Lewis, 'the language used by Hodges to the Professor, and the manner in which he spoke of both you and me, was most abominable, so much so, that I do not think such words worthy of repetition here. . . .' Whatever these words might have been, Marks continued to work closely with Hodges. Shortly afterwards they took a trip together to inspect coal-bearing ground in the eastern Transvaal.

When, a short while after, Lewis suggested that they engage a leading but unnamed Rhodesian figure – probably Sir Drummond Chaplin, Administrator of the territory – on the grounds of his political influence, Marks vetoed the suggestion. Why employ yet another senior person who would sneer at his employers? 'I appreciate that our interests are expanding and that we are both getting older and require further assistance, but I do not wish to employ anybody who will look down upon us.' [21]

Sammy Marks the business partner was no easier than Sammy Marks the employer. His partnership with Isaac Lewis was as important, as enduring and as stormy on occasion as his relationship with his wife. The partnership was founded in 1870 when Sammy was 26 and Isaac 21 and they both hawked goods around Cape Town, and continued for half a century till Marks's death in 1920. It was not an easy alliance: as this biography has indicated, Sammy Marks and Isaac Lewis were a quarrelsome duo. Sammy, normally so careful and conciliatory in his dealings with people, frequently let fly at his distant partner. It would seem that the effort of remaining calm and controlled under the severe stresses and strains of conducting a high-risk business proved too much for him at times, and that he required the emotional release of an outburst against his partner – the safest possible outlet for his pent-up frustrations given the solidity and strength of their relationship.

Scattered throughout Sammy's letters to Isaac are barbs directed at his partner: 'if I had the patience of a Job, and the temper of an Angel I could not stand it. You grumble when I do not write and you grumble when I do write. . . . ' 'Judging from your letter I am afraid that you think I am altogether blind and deaf to everything. . . . ' 'You may rest assured that we do not lose sight of these matters, but we cannot perform impossibilities here as is done on your side.' 'I do not know why you should treat the advice I give gratis always as so much nonsense. . . . Is it because . . . I have not about sixteen letters after my name? I intend to keep my advice in future, so that you will not be troubled again.' [22]

Lewis, generally more restrained than his partner, struck back occasionally: 'I have read your remarks . . . very carefully and I must say I don't quite follow your complaints. You had the thing in your hands and attended to it yourself and I wasn't even there. . . . It seems very clear to me that whenever there is a doubt about anything on your side you always pounce upon me and at once come to the conclusion that I must have done it. I would really like you to look into matters a bit more carefully before you write such stupid things of this kind, and not take for granted all that people tell you.'[23]

As this letter hints, part of the problem was the tyranny of distance, the inherent difficulties of conducting a partnership at long range in an age when travel was still relatively slow. For the most part the partnership rested on the exchange of letters and cables, often prepared by others, rather than on face-to-face interchanges. Without the corrective of ready access to the partner there was ample room for misunderstanding. Marks sometimes felt that Lewis was allowing too much latitude to those who corresponded in his name; he felt insulted that junior employees in London were so presumptuous as to chide him anonymously under the protection of his partner's signature. By contrast, he prided himself on taking considerable care with his own correspondence. Isaac Lewis, on the other hand, sometimes found that there were opaque references in Sammy's letters, cryptic comments which were hard to decipher at 6,000 miles' range. As Marks joked about Lewis's baffled responses, 'he sometimes calls my letters conundrums'.

Distance sometimes led to comic misunderstandings. When in 1882 Isaac Lewis bought a new house, Marks very generously sent caseloads of African curios as a gift, but failed to properly identify who had sent them, much to Lewis's bewilderment. 'About the cases of horns and curiosities,' Marks belatedly explained to his bemused partner who had been landed with curios he apparently detested, 'you don't know and can't make out the madman who did such a thing and I am glad to say, it was myself. The reason I sent them to you was, because I heard you had a nice big house, and I thought an assortment of that sort would show off a few rooms if they were well polished and put together; and the remainder you could have given away to some friends.'

Both Sammy and Isaac felt the need for more direct communication; both felt frustrated by their heavy dependence on the written or cabled word. As Marks noted after a particularly angry outburst: 'Please excuse me writing as I have done. As I have told you already, when you are here we can do more in an hour's talking than in six months' writing.'[24]

Another chronic source of strain within the partnership was Sammy Marks's territorial imperative. Marks regarded South Africa as his sphere of influence within the partnership. He was enormously resentful of any attempt – real or imagined – by his partner to encroach on what he took to be his preserve. This led to frequent outbursts. Writing in 1896, after Lewis had made a fairly innocuous suggestion about the distillery at Hatherley: 'If you or anybody else think you can manage things better in South Africa than I do then I am quite willing to relinquish the management here in your favour, but it is rather hard for a man 53 years of age, who has spent 17 years in the country, and who has constantly watched all the different concerns from the very start, to be referred to a report some three weeks old when I mentioned the subject a year ago. It is like drinking sour milk.'[25]

Writing during the South African War to explain why he had sent a 'sharp' cable to Lewis: 'This is not the first time I have been slighted in the correspondence and things written in your name which I know do not come from you. Your people seem to be under the impression that London office is not only in a position to regulate its own affairs unaided but is also able to dictate to us what should be done in Africa and this notwithstanding that circumstances very often arise of which you cannot have the slightest conception. Our first deed of partnership was entered into as far back as 1870 and you should have found out before this that I am incompetent.' Again, in 1908, in a marvellously mixed metaphor: 'You cannot look across 6,000 miles of water and see where the shoe pinches.'[26]

More important than Sammy's territorial sensitivities as a source of tension within the partnership were the major differences in temperament and in approach to business of the two partners. Thomas Leslie, one of the pioneers of Vereeniging who had known both Sammy and Isaac since the 1880s, wrote in his unpublished reminiscences: 'It was an extraordinary combination. Of Mr Lewis I shall say little. I did not admire him. I had the idea that he was all for money and money only. Naturally, with my long association with the firm, I was well known to him and he always tried to create an impression on me of his ability which as far as the instinct for successful finance was concerned was considerable, but he lacked the milk of human kindness, and was childishly jealous of the popularity of his partner. . . . Sam Marks was in character diametrically opposite, the remarkable success of the firm may have been due to the combination.'[27]

The Marks–Lewis corrrespondence suggests that Marks was warm and sociable; Lewis was cool and reserved. Marks was ebullient and enthusiastic; Lewis was dour and cautious. Marks was generous; Lewis was tight-fisted. Marks had wide-ranging and insatiable curiosity; Lewis had few interests outside business and family life. Marks maintained a high public profile; Lewis was 'never a great public figure'. Marks was a 'buyer' who sold only reluctantly; Lewis was a 'seller' who typically bought only with reluctance.[28]

'Why is it that they never attempt to sell or realise anything even when they get the opportunity,' Lewis complained to Marks of the failure of his Pretoria office to sell certain shares. 'I think whenever you get the chance of selling anything, especially shares, you should always take advantage of it, as in addition to the actual sale of the stuff, it would give us a little encouragement to see that something in the way of realising is done on your side instead of always buying. You ought to cultivate the art of selling as well as that of buying.' Marks cheerfully acknowledged the charge. 'You know very well that I never interfere in share-dealing transactions. I am a buyer, but not a seller.'[29]

Unlike Sammy but like many others who made their fortunes at Kimberley or on the Rand, Isaac Lewis preferred living in England to living in South Africa. London and the Home Counties seemed far more attractive than bleak mining camps and bare veld. Lewis came to England initially, at the beginning of the 1880s, for practical reasons. If the partnership was to continue to prosper it needed a representative in London with ready access to the London Stock Exchange and the Bourse in Paris, and to bankers and financiers in England and on the Continent. While necessity dictated his moving to England, this clearly represented no personal hardship. Lewis rapidly developed a taste for 'the life of a keen City of London businessman' which he 'varied . . . with the life of a country squire'. He bought a succession of 'fine houses' in London, in the burgeoning upper-middle-class suburb of Hampstead and elsewhere. Then, like other upwardly mobile Victorian and Edwardian businessmen, he sought respectability and social status by acquiring a country estate, Bedgebury Park, near Tonbridge in Kent. Despite a century of industrialisation, the ownership of land remained the high road to social respectability and acceptance in England.[30]

Isaac Lewis bought Bedgebury Park from the Beresford Hope family after the death of Lord Beresford. It was a 'splendid estate' which apart from 'a grand old family mansion' and beautiful gardens and parkland, encompassed three villages, a well-stocked lake and an old monastery with its moat still visible. Lewis removed the armorial bearings of the Beresford Hopes – a bronze dragon issuing flames from its mouth – from the entrance gates to the estate and replaced them with his own, 'a muscular bronze arm with a hand grasping a round-nosed shovel'. A cynical visitor from South Africa, Thomas Leslie of Vereeniging, suggested to his host that as he was as unlikely to handle a shovel as the ancestor of the Beresford Hopes was to encounter a dragon, he must have had in mind the 'bronze-coloured Bantu' who were the source of his affluence. To Leslie's dismay the interior of the old monastery had been 'perverted' into store-rooms. The shelves had 'been spiked into the old plastered walls on which could still be seen in rare illuminated Gothic lettering latin prayers, in fresco, painted with such loving care and skill by the monks, one nasty obscene gash deforming "Gloria in excelsis Deo".' Isaac Lewis, Leslie bitterly noted, 'had no sickly sentimentality about him.'[31] And yet, as we have seen, he was anguished when in 1915, at the height of Lewis and Marks's wartime liquidity crisis, he was forced to pledge the title-deeds of Bedgebury Park, as security for a life-saving loan from the Union of London and Smiths Bank. This was a 'terrible blow', he wrote to Marks, who could no doubt easily empathise since he felt equally strongly about Zwartkoppies.[32]

Despite his attachment to Bedgebury Park, Lewis disposed of the estate after the war and returned to Africa at the end of 1919. The woods at Bedgebury were sold to the Crown and the house became a girls' school. Lewis's decision to leave after four decades in England seems to have been both personal and professional. As he grew old, Isaac Lewis found the English winter increasingly 'severe and trying'. Besides, the post-war expansion of the business, which placed an increasing burden on a partner who was himself in his mid-seventies, seemed to require his presence in South Africa. Lewis shipped off much of the antique furniture from Bedgebury as well as its library, and took up residence at Leeuwenhof, the Cape Dutch mansion in the Gardens above Cape Town, which the partners had acquired in the early 1880s. Significantly, Lewis chose Cape Town though it was far from the centre of the firm's business operations. While he was at last prepared to return to South Africa, he was not willing, it seems, to live in Johannesburg, which his wife, Sarah Ann (who died on the eve of their departure), had always disliked. Lewis did, however, build a gracious riverside residence on the Vaal. This later became the Vereeniging Country Club and still later was incorporated into the Riviera Hotel complex. Some while after Lewis's death in 1927 Leeuwenhof was acquired by the state and became the residence of the Administrator of the Cape Province.[33]

A further source of frustration for Marks was the unequal nature of his relationship with Isaac Lewis. The balance of power in their partnership was permanently tilted in Lewis's favour. While Isaac and Sammy and Isaac's brother Barnet Lewis were theoretically equal partners, in practice Isaac could always rely on his brother's vote if matters ever came to a head. As Sammy noted resentfully, 'you are two partners against one, and when you come to this country you are always furnished with Barnet's Power-of-Attorney that you can always outvote me.'[34]

Other than guaranteeing his brother ascendancy in the partnership, Barnet seems to have played only a minor role in the business. After Lewis and Marks closed their Kimberley office in the late 1880s he returned to London, where he played second fiddle to his more capable older brother. Barnet – once described by the Standard Bank as 'a respectable but ignorant man, and not possessed of very good business habits' – took little part in the unending dialogue between the London and South African offices of the partnership. 'I know that you are a man of very few words,' Marks wrote apologetically in one of his very rare letters to the partnership's third man, 'and that you do not care for writing or receiving letters. Therefore I will be very brief.'[35]

Sammy Marks and Barnet Lewis were never very fond of each other. In the early 1880s they squabbled bitterly over the mounting costs of setting up the distillery at Hatherley; in the 1890s they fought over a not inconsequential sum of £10,000 that Sammy claimed Barnet owed him. And Sammy never let Barnet forget he had ridiculed his proposal that the partnership buy seven farms on the Witwatersrand in 1885, a year before the great discovery. Marks, it seems, found Barnet Lewis, a life-long bachelor who lived next door but one to the former Liberal prime minister Lord Rosebery in Berkeley Square, a very unsympathetic character – liverish, unhelpful and complaining. 'I know that Barnet does not like to be bothered with family affairs,' Marks wrote to Isaac Lewis, while struggling to make practical arrangements through the London office for his children's education abroad; '[this] is only natural as he does not understand them.'[36]

For all the strains within the partnership, it nevertheless was a highly successful one, as the business empire which the partners created bore testimony. There was a creative tension within the partnership that allowed Isaac Lewis and Sammy Marks to accomplish more together than they could have accomplished separately. Theirs were opposed but complementary talents. Sammy was the creative force, the propeller that drove the partnership; Isaac was the stabilising presence, the rudder that kept the partnership on an even keel and prevented shipwreck.

However much anger and frustration was expressed at times, the Lewis and Marks partnership was nevertheless a stable and enduring union. Sammy and Isaac were bound together inextricably by deep mutual respect, by real mutual affection and concern, by mutual trust, by a lifetime of shared experience, and above all, by a very powerful sense that whatever their occasional differences, their interests basically coincided and would continue to do so as long as they lived. As Sammy put it in a letter to Isaac: 'You once wrote me that what is good for you is good for me. I agree with you.'[37]

Isaac accurately captured the quality of the partnership – its resilience and strength – when he wrote: 'You must bear in mind that however strained that relationship may for a moment unfortunately become, or whatever may for a time come between us, that relationship, as I have often told you, is stronger than marriage and cannot be broken or severed by a mere disagreement on a matter of business, or simply by the tittle-tattle of outsiders, and whatever the course of business may bring us it is you and I who have to stand the brunt of it for better or for worse.'[38]

Sammy Marks and Isaac Lewis were partners for half a century. Their partnership survived through wars and recessions, dramatic setbacks and disasters. It endured despite their temperamental differences, their bitter quarrels, their mutual resentments and their damaging failures. When all is said and done, their partnership was indeed stronger than marriage. It was broken only, in February 1920, by the death of one of the partners.

XIV

Epilogue:
'Overtaken by Nemesis'

Marks died of a stomach ailment at the Lady Dudley Nursing Home in Johannesburg on 18 February 1920 at the age of 75 years and 7 months. True to character, he was fully engaged in work till shortly before his death. Up to two months previously, he had regularly chaired board meetings of the Vereeniging Estates and of African and European. As late as their December meetings he had won approval for a scheme to build accommodation for young foresters at Maccauvlei and was given authority to investigate and negotiate for an alluvial diamond prospect in the western Transvaal. Marks refused 'to grow old physically': some two months before his death he spent an hour and a half scrambling around underground at the South Rand colliery inspecting all its workings. Even in the nursing home during his final illness he was preoccupied with business. Beckoning Isaac Lewis over to his bedside, he whispered that it looked like a severe winter was on its way and made his partner promise that fodder would be laid in for the cattle.[1]

Though he had lived in Johanesburg for over a decade, Marks was interred in the Jewish cemetery in the capital in accordance with an eleventh-hour codicil to his will. 'I wish to be buried at Pretoria,' he had recorded, 'and desire that the funeral shall be as simple as possible without wreaths or flowers, as I wish to be buried as I have lived without ostentation or parade.' Pretoria was chosen because of his long association with the city and its Jewish community.

The funeral was conducted with all the simplicity of the orthodox Jewish burial rite. The *Star* reported that the funeral procession was a lengthy one and that all along the route businesses were closed as a mark of respect to the deceased. Prime Minister Jan Smuts, Marks's old friend, was present, as were representatives of the Senate, the Department of Agriculture, the Licensed Victuallers and other organisations reflecting the remarkable diversity of his career. Marks was interred in a plain deal coffin. His unadorned, horizontal gravestone is fenced in with a simple railing prepared by the blacksmiths at Union Steel as a token of their regard for their late employer.[2]

The news of Marks's death was received with general regret by South African Jewry, to whom he had become a symbol of what could be achieved in the new country. As the *South African Jewish Chronicle* wrote: 'The whole career of the late Mr. Marks shows the possibility of the individual rising above the circumstances of his birth and accomplishing great things, in despite [sic] of his early environment. The one time *tocher* becomes a millionaire and not a millionaire whose whole life was wrapped up in the amassing of wealth. . . .'[3] The Reverend A. P. Bender of the mother congregation in Cape Town paid special tribute to Marks during a synagogue service, as did the chairman, Mr Harris, at the next meeting of the synagogue committee. Marks, Harris said, was 'one of the most prominent and distinguished Jews in South Africa and a Knight of Industry of the Country'. The committee arranged to send a telegram of condolence to his family and then rose as a mark of their respect. [4]

Marks's estate was far smaller than had been popularly anticipated. A preliminary figure of £297,000 was published soon after his death but this had to be revised drastically afterwards to take full account of the heavy liabilities of the estate. As Patrick Duncan wrote to Lady Selborne: 'It is like having one's idols thrown down to find that old Sammy was not a millionaire. What is left for us to believe in.' The small proportions of the estate, at least by Randlord standards, reflect the heavy losses sustained by the firm of Lewis and Marks in its ill-fated diamond-trading and diamond-cutting ventures. The shares Marks held in the firm were meant to be his major asset, but these were greatly devalued by hefty guarantees the firm had signed on behalf of the Diamond Branch and of a large diamond-cutting works at Brighton that Bernhard Oppenheimer had established at the end of the war. Beyond the firm's diamond debacle, the relative modesty of Marks's estate also reflects his long-term failure to establish a major beachhead in gold-mining, for many decades the most profitable form of South African investment and the highroad to personal fortune in the turn-of-the-century Transvaal.[5]

Sammy Marks's complex testamentary arrangements were to prove a source of enduring difficulty for his executors and heirs as well as for the administrators of the Trust which is still operative at the present time, seven decades after his death. As Patrick Duncan noted: 'Poor old man. He has been overtaken by the nemesis that usually descends on those who try to defeat fate by keeping control of their possessions after they have left this world.'[6]

The first of the problems was the disquieting discovery after Marks's death that there were two potentially conflicting wills. In 1892 Sammy and Bertha had drawn up a comprehensive joint will to which Sammy had added a codicil in 1897 and again in 1899, days before the outbreak of the South African War. In 1906 Sammy and Bertha had redrafted their joint will, revoking the earlier one. Prompted by the threatened conversion of their daughter Girlie to Christianity, a very disturbing prospect for Jews of Bertha and Sammy's generation, this will included a forfeiture clause which disinherited any child marrying out of the Jewish faith or living as man and wife with any person whatsoever without being married.

In January 1913, while lying seriously ill in his Parktown house awaiting an operation, Marks, who was not far short of the biblically allotted three score and ten years, gave further thought to the future. He sent for his attorney, Mr R.

Bowman of Bowman and Gilfillan, and instructed him to draw up a codicil empowering his executors to invest the funds of his estate in securities other than British government stock. He also wanted to cancel Isaac Lewis's appointment as one of his executors and as guardian of his minor children, presumably because Lewis himself was getting on in years. Before drawing up the codicil, Bowman asked to see his client's will. Bertha was sent from the bedroom to fetch the document which was kept in her safe together with her jewellery, private papers and letters. Rather vague about such matters and anxious about her husband's impending operation, Bertha took the first envelope she found, a closed envelope bearing the words 'the last will of Samuel Marks'. Bowman, a Johannesburg attorney, who had drawn up neither of the previous wills, both of which had been prepared by Pretoria notaries while the Marks family still lived at Zwartkoppies, opened the envelope and found that it contained a will drawn up in 1892 with two codicils dating respectively from 1897 and 1899. He then drew up the new codicil Marks required, prefacing it with a note that it was a codicil to the 1892 will. Marks, who was seriously ill, failed to pick up the discrepancy when the codicil was read out to him. He then signed the document, which unintentionally revived the old will that had been superseded by that of 1906.

Subsequent codicils, drawn up in 1913 and 1920 by D. F. Gilfillan, Bowman's partner, simply compounded the error. All referred back to the 1892 will. No mention was made of the 1906 will. Indeed, Bowman and Gillfillan had no knowledge of its existence till after Marks's death in February 1920, when Gilfillan was summonsed to the Parktown house by his widow. Bertha handed him a fistful of sealed envelopes from the safe in her bedroom. One of these contained the 1892 will and the 1913 codicil; the other, marked 'Will S. Marks', and bearing the stamp of a firm of Pretoria lawyers on its flap, contained the 1906 will. Neither Bertha nor any of her children could throw light on this disconcerting discovery. As Gilfillan later attested, 'the widow had no recollection of any of the wills nor had any of the children present any information regarding their father's will.'

Which will was to prevail? The 1892 will, revoked in 1906 but revived by the preface to the 1913 codicil? The 1906 will which had never been formally revoked? Or were both to be discounted and Marks declared intestate? This muddle was taken to the Transvaal Supreme Court for a ruling. In a Solomonic judgment it declared that both wills were valid and should be read together, but that wherever the two were in conflict, the 1892 will was to prevail for it, paradoxically, was the more recent of the two wills, having been revived in 1913. In law at least, if not in common sense, the old will of 1892 was equivalent to a new will of 1913 vintage, and therefore carried more weight than the 1906 will.[7] The two-will saga was the first of a series of applications to the courts by the Marks estate. These were to become grist to the mill of the legal profession as well as the stuff of scholarly texts on the law of succession.

Meanwhile there were legacies to be distributed. The arrangements Marks made in his wills and codicils clearly reflect his personal concerns and priorities. His acute sense of responsibility for his extended family, part of his own inheritance from the *shtetl*, is strikingly evident in the detailed provision he made for the well-being of his siblings and their children. Thus in 1897 he attached a lengthy and complex codicil to his 1892 will, aimed at protecting his sister Fanny Levy against the financial imprudence of her husband and at ensuring the education of her offspring. In an extended codicil dictated from his sickbed in 1913, he provided for the continuation for a number of months after his death of the monthly allowances of £20 and £40 paid respectively to his sisters Krena Abromowitz and Fanny Levy. In the same codicil he left a house in Cape Town to his favourite nephew George Falcke, a monthly allowance of £5 to his favourite niece Miriam Levy, who at this time lived with the Marks family, and shares in Lewis and Marks Ltd to George, Miriam and her brothers. At the same time he directed that his executors were not to press his brother Ellia Marks for repayment of the debt he owed him, and that any money eventually reclaimed should be invested on behalf of Eli Marks's son. In the last codicil he dictated before his death, he amended the provision he had previously made for his surviving sister Krena Abromowitz: she should be paid her monthly allowance for the rest of her life, not just for six months after his death.

Marks made only limited bequests beyond his family circle and none of these were spelt out in the intricate detail of the bequests to his kinsmen. Agnes Strachan and Molly McCarthy, two of the household staff, were to receive £50 each, as was his chauffeur R. J. Willmer. Japie Kok and James Potts the handyman at Zwartkoppies, H. Hilse at Hatherley, and Otto Brandmuller, the long-serving German forester at Maccauvlei – perhaps Marks's favourite employee – were to be given £100 apiece.

The Miriam Marks School in Pretoria, the Jewish day school Marks had founded in 1904 and named after his late mother, was granted a perpetual annuity at the rate of £20 per month. This equalled the regular subsidy he was paying the school at the time of his death. Corresponding gifts were made to Jewish institutions in Johannesburg. The Jewish Aged Home and the South African Jewish Orphanage, Bertha Marks's favourite charity, were each to receive £250, while the Jewish Guild, which was planning a new building, was to be supplied with Marks's favourite gift in kind, bricks of 'the best quality' the Vereeniging Brick and Tile Company produced. In addition, £1,000 went to the new university in Johannesburg: the interest on this sum was to be used to fund a Chair of Hebrew. The university college at Pretoria was to receive the same amount in five annual instalments of £200 each; these were to be used to maintain a bursary Marks had awarded before his death.[8]

The press compared these modest public benefactions unfavourably with the provisions of Cecil Rhodes's will and with the Beit bequests. 'Do South African millionaires do as much as they might for the country in which they made their millions?' asked the *Sunday Times*. 'The late Mr. Marks's provisions for the advancement of public institutions in South Africa could be covered by a very poor man, amounting as they do, to a matter of £3,000.' It would seem that, like many others, Marks chose to make very generous public benefactions during his lifetime but to leave his estate basically intact to his heirs.[9]

Once provision had been made for the legacies, the balance of the assets was to pass to Marks's descendants, subject though to a set of conditions which left his immediate heirs little room for manoeuvre. In terms of Marks's 1892 will his children's inheritance was burdened with a *fidei-commissum*. They were only to receive the interest on their inheritance during their lifetimes; after their deaths, the capital sum, excluding the farm Zwartkoppies, was to devolve on their children free and unencumbered. Those who were to administer the estate's assets were straitjacketed by severe restrictions on their powers of investment. None of the fixed properties Marks owned at his death were to be sold during the lifetime of any of his children; only after the demise of the last survivor could the administrators dispose of any land or building, again with the exception of Zwartkoppies. Free monies were to be invested in British government stock or Consols, the hardy standby of all cautious Victorian investors.

These restricted powers of investment were amended to a limited degree in the codicils to the will. Once the regional political order had stabilised after Union, Marks gave his future executors permission to invest the free funds of his estate in South African government stock. He also allowed an exception to the embargo on the sale of fixed property: after his death his undeveloped properties in Cape Town were to be sold off and the proceeds invested in the erection of buildings on his vacant erven in Pretoria, a long-standing ambition.

As this provision suggests, Marks had a long-term investment strategy in mind for his estate. He continued to believe till the end that he had made adequate provision both for the support of his widow and children, and for the future development of the estate's core properties. His heirs discovered otherwise after his death. As his sons Louis and Joe attested in an affidavit submitted to the Supreme Court in 1927: 'Our father believed there would be ample funds in his estate to carry out his desire that buildings should be erected on the vacant erven in Pretoria, and to provide an ample income for our Mother and his children, we declare that shortly before his death he called us and our brothers and sisters together and informed us that we and our Mother would be well provided for on his death as the funds in his estate were very considerable. This is far from being the case, and we can only assume that he must have believed that his assets were of far greater value than they have since proved to be.'[10]

By the time this affidavit was submitted, the executors had already sold off a string of properties to pay the legacies and meet the liabilities of the estate. With the Master's permission, they had disposed of some of the farms and Pretoria erven, as well as the Cape Town properties (including Hatherley House, the family's holiday home in Muizenberg, for £4,250) which Marks had hoped would finance building operations in Pretoria. Contrary to his expectations, the sale left little over for this purpose. Without this redevelopment, the prospects of the remaining properties were unappealing. Under the circumstances the executors felt that the interests of the heirs would be best served by engineering the removal of the restriction on the alienation of the fixed property of the estate, selling all of this off, and reinvesting the proceeds in government securities. When they approached the Supreme Court, however, their application was denied. The restraint on the sale of fixed property was left intact. For decades after, Marks's executors and administrators struggled with a portfolio of undeveloped properties and of aging buildings which were difficult to let and needed costly maintenance. These never yielded anything approximating to a satisfactory return on the capital they represented. The prime example was a valuable block of ground, opposite what is now the State Opera House in Church Street, Pretoria. In 1965, more than four decades after Marks's death, this underutilised, partly vacant central city site was eventually expropriated by the Pretoria City Council, involving the Marks Trust in prolonged litigation to obtain adequate compensation.[11]

While Marks lumped most of his assets together in his wills, his beloved Zwartkoppies was singled out for special treatment and subjected to conditions that were even more restrictive than those applied to the rest of his fixed properties. In his 1892 will Marks stated that it was his 'express will and desire' that Zwartkoppies 'be burdened with the entail of *fidei-commissum*' for three generations; only after the demise of the last of his great-grandchildren would his descendants be free to sell the property. His widow Bertha was to have the right of occupation as long as she lived. The right of occupation was extended in the 1906 will, drawn up when the older children were on the threshold of adulthood. Should Bertha remarry or fail to live at Zwartkoppies after her husband's death, the children were to have the right to 'free residence' on the estate. The eldest son was to have first choice of 'Zwartkoppies Hall', the 'great house' Marks had built on the estate, while the other sons and the daughters (while they remained unmarried) could occupy one of the four other houses on the property. After the death of all the sons, Zwartkoppies was 'to serve as a free residence for the eldest legitimate male descendant in each generation'.

The dream of continued family occupation of Zwartkoppies for generations to come in the style of the English landed classes was never properly fulfilled. Just as in Marks's lifetime, the lure of Johannesburg proved too strong and the attractions of farming and of country living too slight. Zwartkoppies was simply too isolated and inconvenient. After her husband's death, Bertha exercised her right of occupation at Zwartkoppies. She gave up the Parktown house and took up residence, at least formally, at Zwartkoppies. In practice she spent much of her time travelling both locally and abroad as she had during the last decades of her married life. She died on 28 October 1934 at the age of 72 at the Carlton Hotel in Johannesburg where she had been staying for some time. She too is buried in the old Jewish cemetery in Pretoria, beside her husband.[12]

While Bertha travelled at home and abroad, the 'great house' at Zwartkoppies was occupied by Joseph Marks, known by the family as 'Mark II' because of his strong resemblance to his father. Trained as an agronomist and the only son with a professional qualification, Joe supervised the farming of Zwartkoppies on behalf of the Marks estate while himself farming nearby Pienaarspoort, which his father had given to him and to his older brother Louis when he was 15 years old, subject to a *fidei-commissum* in favour of their children. After a period of sustained losses on farming operations at Zwartkoppies in the 1920s, the executors of the Marks estate agreed to lease the farm to Joe, who insisted that it could be run at a profit. Joe remained at Zwartkoppies till the early 1930s when he followed the rest of the family to Johannesburg. The house was now a serious burden on the Marks estate as funds for its maintenance and renovation were scarce. Nothing came of suggestions that it be let as a sanatorium, convalescent home or school, or of pre-war and wartime offers to, the Pretoria Jewish community and the Red Cross respectively.

At the end of the Second World War, Joe, who had served in the artillery, returned to Zwartkoppies where he remained till his death in 1975. His widow Kirsty stayed on in the house until she took seriously ill in 1977. Since it was quite apparent that no members of the family wished to live permanently at Zwartkoppies, a search began for a suitable tenant for what was now an aging structure in a deteriorating condition. The large house was offered to the Jewish community of Pretoria as an old-age home or school, to the army as a convalescent home, and finally to a hotel group, without any success.

The ideal tenant presented itself almost by chance. In September 1980 the National Cultural History and Open-air Museum, based in Pretoria, asked the Marks Trust whether it could purchase forty hectares of Zwartkoppies farmland as a site for an open-air museum. The chairman of the Marks Trust, Neill Maisels, Sammy Marks's oldest grandson, explained that it was not possible to do so because the property was entailed in terms of Marks's will and suggested instead that the Museum consider leasing and restoring the house and its immediate grounds and purchasing its contents.

Neill Maisels recognised that the 'great house' at Zwartkoppies had the makings of a remarkable museum. Here was a wealthy upper-class, late-Victorian residence captured in amber. Its Victorian and Edwardian furnishings, its glassware and ornaments, and its collections of silver, crockery and china were basically intact, little changed since the death of the owner more than half a century before, requiring only sensitive and skilled restoration. The splendid library was as Marks had left it decades before: a Victorian gentleman's library, with leather-bound sets of the standards and a wealth of well-thumbed contemporary volumes, reflecting Marks's interests in practical matters and in the issues of the day. There were also handsomely bound sets of the Jewish festival prayer books and valuable items of Africana. A spacious billiard room, with decorated ceilings and a ring of leather benches for the spectators, still housed the billiard table on which family and guests had played in the 1890s. The entrance hall with its grand teak staircase still bore the signs of Marks's gift for political juggling: photographs of British generals and Boer leaders looked down on marble busts of Cecil John Rhodes and Sir Bartle Frere, while the visitors' book balanced Lord Milner's signature with Reitz's and De la Rey's.

The basic problem was one of finance: the National Museum had very limited funds. Once again the solution presented itself almost by chance. In February 1983, while the Museum staff were still negotiating with the Marks Trust, Neill Maisels and Mendel Kaplan, a Johannesburg businessman and philanthropist, were discussing the possible transfer of Sammy Marks's private papers from the strongroom at Zwartkoppies to the safe-keeping of the Isaac and Jessie Kaplan Centre for Jewish Studies and Research at the University of Cape Town.

Visiting Zwartkoppies, Mendel Kaplan was told of the museum project; when approached by the National Cultural History and Open-air Museum, he offered to contribute through his family foundation half the cost of the moveables the National Museum wished to purchase from the Trust. With this seed-money secured, an agreement for the establishment of the Sammy Marks Museum at Zwartkoppies Hall was finally signed in May 1984. After over two years of painstaking restoration, the Sammy Marks Museum finally opened in November 1986 in the presence of Sammy Marks's only surviving child, his daughter Dolly Maisels. Two and a half years later, in March 1989, Zwartkoppies was declared a national monument.[13]

While Zwartkoppies and Marks's other fixed properties were undoubtedly valuable, the most important legacy Marks left his heirs was his share of Lewis and Marks Ltd, the private company he and the Lewis brothers had established in 1911 to take over the bulk of the assets of their partnership. In 1920, at the time of Sammy Marks's death, Lewis and Marks Ltd still held five-sixths of the shares of the African and European Investment Company. The latter's unimpressive performance since its foundation in 1904, its failure to pay a single dividend in sixteen years, had made it virtually unmarketable on the stock exchange. For all that, it remained a valuable investment, asset rich if income poor. Besides its one-million-acre landholding in the Union, it held a third of a million acres in Bechuanaland and a large block of Vereeniging Estates shares.[14]

To safeguard his family's interest in Lewis and Marks Ltd and, by extension, in African and European and in Vereeniging Estates, Marks left instructions in a codicil to his will a fortnight before he died that his eldest son Louis should succeed him as a permanent director of the controlling private company. The following day he added a further instruction to ensure a strong and abiding Marks family presence in the business. In terms of his powers as a permanent director Louis was to appoint one of his brothers as a co-director of Lewis and Marks Ltd; 'while any brother of his is living there shall always be one of his brothers associated with him as a director in the Company.'

Louis, who was 34 when his father died, was joined in the business by his brothers Joe and Ted, aged only 28 and 25 respectively. After Isaac Lewis died at his Leeuwenhof home in Cape Town in 1927, seven years after his cousin and partner, control of the business passed to this younger generation. Louis and Ted ran the group together with Roy Lewis, Isaac's son, while Joe Marks, the professional agronomist, limited himself to its extensive ranching and farming operations. The Lewis and Marks group prospered under this new direction, aided by the discovery in 1926 of alluvial diamonds on certain of the Lichtenburg farms Sammy Marks had acquired decades earlier. This windfall enabled African and European to pay its first dividend in a quarter of a century. It also enabled Louis Marks, a popular figure in Johannesburg mining circles, who always wore a red carnation in his buttonhole, to finance the expansion of the group's mining interests, both in its traditional area of strength – coal-mining – and in its traditional area of weakness – gold-mining.

In 1936 the group's expanded coal interests were combined to form the Amalgamated Collieries of South Africa Ltd, a coal-mining giant which controlled the Cornelia and Springfield collieries near Vereeniging, the Largo colliery near Springs and the Schoongezicht colliery near Witbank, besides holding valuable undeveloped coal rights in the Witbank and Vereeniging districts. Under the new scheme Sammy Marks's Vereeniging Estates ceased to be the group's principal operating company and became instead an investment and property-holding company, though it continued to run sheep on its many farms and to exploit Brandmuller's great plantation at Maccauvlei.

Further expansion and modernisation, including the opening of the Bertha shaft on the Vereeniging property, made the Lewis and Marks group one of the dominant forces in the South African coal-mining industry. Together with the rest of the industry it grew apace during the Second World War, exporting mountains of coal to the Mediterranean theatre of war as well as supplying South Africa's rapidly industrialising wartime economy. Towards the end of the war the Lewis and Marks group was producing close to one-third of the total coal output of the Union of South Africa.[15]

Besides developing the group's traditional business, the younger generation at Lewis and Marks also took steps to rectify the long-term structural weakness of the group: the lack of a significant presence in gold-mining, South Africa's premier industry. South Africa's departure from the gold standard in 1932, and the consequent rise in the gold price, had revived the fortunes of a flagging mining industry and set off an exploration boom of unprecedented proportions which would vastly enlarge the geographical scope of the industry. Drilling on the far west Rand and the discovery of the extremely rich Carbon Leader and Ventersdorp Contact reefs proved the existence of a massive extension of the Witwatersrand deposits to the west, the West Wits Line. Drilling even further to the west, in the Klerksdorp area, led to the rediscovery of a gold-field, first exploited in the late 1880s, but largely neglected since.

These successes raised the possibility that Witwatersrand deposits might occur even further away from the Central Rand, the original place of discovery. In the mid-1930s the search was extended across the Vaal River into the north-western Free State, first close to the river, then deeper into the veld. All the major mining houses joined in a scramble for options over land. Large sums of money passed hands (neatly supplementing local farming incomes) and boreholes were sunk by the score and then abandoned, as farm after farm proved valueless. Two of the principal players in the hunt for a new Witwatersrand were Louis Marks and Sir Abe Bailey, his father's old rival and occasional partner in land speculation. In 1937 Bailey established Western Holdings Ltd, an exploration company which acquired options and began test-drilling in an area due south of the small northern Free State town of Odendaalsrus.

African and European took up a large number of shares in Western Holdings and was granted representation on its board. At the same time African and European was very active on its own account. It took up options over 56,000 acres of land in the same district, amassing a large and solid block abutting on the ground held by Western Holdings. It, too, initiated a drilling programme. In April 1939 Bailey's Western Holdings struck a payable reef at a depth of 1,143 feet in a borehole on the farm St Helena. This was the Basal Reef, the reef on which the second greatest gold-field in mining history was to be based. Soon after, African and European also struck gold.

The results of the Western Holdings and African and European boreholes excited mining insiders, who recognised the significance of these finds. Ernest Oppenheimer of the Anglo American Corporation, which had had little successs with its own exploration efforts in the Orange Free State, moved energetically and aggressively during the war years to secure a decisive stake in what he foresaw would become a major gold-field. In January 1941 a friendly approach was made to Louis Marks. Would African and European allow Anglo American a share in its Odendaalsrus discovery? Louis's response was very cool: 'At the present time . . . they did not have it in mind that it was either necessary or advisable to take in any partners . . . finance was no problem, either at the present time or when they went to flotation. . . .'

Rebuffed but undeterred, Ernest Oppenheimer changed his tack. In early 1942 he bought the controlling shareholding in the South African Townships, Mining and Finance Corporation from the estate of Sir Abe Bailey who had died in August 1940. This in turn gave him control of Western Holdings and a large portion of the prospective gold-field. With it, too, came a foothold in African and European. South African Townships held 93,630 shares in the Marks company, a stake which, it seems, was subsequently enlarged by Oppenheimer through purchases on the open market. For the moment, though, Lewis and Marks still held a controlling share in the company.

Once Oppenheimer established a strong presence at Odendaalsrus through the acquisition of Western Holdings, Anglo and African and European were drawn together inexorably. Cooperation made good sense: the costs of establishing an industrial infrastructure in a remote corner of the Free State, far from the established urban centres, were bound to be high; sharing these would lighten the financial burden, particularly for the less-well-endowed Lewis and Marks interest. In 1943 Anglo American and African and European reached agreement on the sinking of a number of joint boreholes and on participation rights in any resulting ventures. Oppenheimer and his chief lieutenant, R. B. Haggart, joined the board of African and European while African and European, in turn, was granted representation on the board of the Orange Free State Investment Trust, the holding company for Oppenheimer's interests on the new gold-field.

Yet for all the *toenadering* and closer association between the two companies, African and European remained an independent concern, pursuing a vigorous programme of systematic drilling to establish the hidden contours of Block 7, the compact group of farms it held so firmly, with a view to establishing African and European-controlled mines on these. At its fortieth annual general meeting in June 1945, Louis Marks, its chairman, announced that 47 boreholes had already been completed and that a further 11 were still being drilled. The results were overwhelmingly positive. 'I think we are justified', he trumpeted, 'in making our plans to go ahead promptly with the negotiation of mining leases and the provision of finance for the new areas relying on the Government to see that we get a fair deal . . . we have proved the positive areas to be valuable and it appears that the area is sufficiently large for the eventual establishment of three mines on the scale usually visualised here on the Rand.'

But within a few months of this confident assertion of independence, Louis, together with his brothers and the Lewis family, had performed a remarkable about-turn and sold out their controlling interest to Ernest Oppenheimer. In September 1945 Anglo American announced that it had purchased 149,850 shares with a nominal value of £1 each in Lewis and Marks Ltd, just 150 shares short of the total issued capital of the firm. Lewis and Marks, the announcement added, had a large shareholding in African and European. These, together with the shares Anglo already held in African and European, meant that Anglo now assumed control of that company. By mutual agreement, the old directors, Louis Marks and his brothers and associates, were to resign from the boards of Lewis and Marks Ltd and of African and European and so make way for Sir Ernest's men.

Sammy's and Isaac's heirs had sold their birthright for just over £1,500,000, the Marks family receiving £762,397, the Lewis clan £774,189. Their motives are hard to fathom and cannot be established with any degree of certainty. Little direct evidence is available: the papers of Lewis and Marks Ltd were destroyed after the Anglo American take-over; the minute-books of African and European and of the Anglo American Corporation are unrevealing, as are the minutes of the Marks estate which were usually very full. The correspondence book of the Marks estate for the critical period is missing; and the chief parties to the deal are no longer alive.[16]

The entry for Ernest Oppenheimer in the *Dictionary of South African Biography* implies that the heirs to African and European abdicated in favour of Anglo because they 'had neither the resources nor the expertise' to develop their Free State gold properties. This view ignores the sterling performance of the Lewis and Marks group during the 1930s and early 1940s. It also exaggerates the difficulties of mobilising the resources needed to develop the new gold-field. With such a promising asset firmly in its grasp, a well-established mining house like Lewis and Marks could undoubtedly have raised the capital required. The queue of potential backers included Anglo itself.[17]

The answer to the conundrum might possibly lie in the personalities and personal circumstances of the two heirs most directly involved in the management of the Lewis and Marks group of companies: Louis and Ted Marks. In 1945 Louis Marks was in his sixtieth year. It might well be that after a lifetime in the family business, he and his younger brother Ted no longer had the energy and sense of commitment which the launching of such a huge new enterprise required. Selling out spared them the enormous expenditure of effort and time the opening of a new gold-field would unavoidably demand. It also spared them the colossal financial risks inevitably associated with a project of this magnitude and kind. The contrast with their late father, who was still enthusiastically and energetically pursuing expensive and risky new projects shortly before his death, could not be more striking.

Then again, Louis and Ted's willingness to sell out might have had to do with their home circumstances. Teddy was childless and Louis had a daughter.

Neither had a male heir, a son to whom they could pass the business. This might possibly have vitiated their commitment to keeping the business within the family. Under the circumstances, Oppenheimer's attractive cash offer, which at one blow not only unburdened them of all responsibility but also considerably increased their personal income, might have seemed irresistible. Because of the onerous restrictions Marks's will had imposed on the deployment of the estate's assets, his heirs' income from the estate had previously been severely limited. The total revenue of the estate in 1945 was £14,705, including a dividend of £2,485 from Lewis and Marks Ltd; the total net distribution to the six beneficiaries was only £4,704. Once the net proceeds from the sale of Lewis and Marks Ltd to Anglo were invested in government stock (as the will required), the net distributable income of the Marks estate trebled to £13,516.[18]

While the motives for the sale are obscure and uncertain, its consequences and significance are not. In the years that followed the sale, Sir Ernest Oppenheimer, an energetic and bold entrepreneur in the Sammy Marks mould, built a great gold-field, second only to the Witwatersrand, on the mining ground he had bought from the Lewis and Marks heirs for a fraction of its ultimate value. In the late 1940s three mining companies were formed to exploit African and European's Block 7 – Welkom, President Steyn and President Brand. The two 'Presidents' became star performers on the Free State gold-fields, pillars of the House of Oppenheimer. As an additional bonus, the coal companies and coal rights that came to Anglo as a by-product of its purchase of African and European and its gold farms have ensured Anglo American's dominance of the South African coal-mining industry till the present.

On the eve of the Lewis and Marks group's greatest triumph, the fulfilment at long last of Sammy and Isaac's dream of establishing a major presence in the gold-mining industry, their heirs had thrown it all away. To borrow a phrase, they had snatched defeat from the jaws of victory.

Their abdication meant they had converted hard assets of enduring value, shares in mining, industrial and land companies, into an asset – cash – highly vulnerable to the ravages of inflation. It also meant the disappearance of the family name from the roll-call of South African business. Since the 1870s Lewis and Marks had been a fixture in local business life. After buying the firm, Ernest Oppenheimer changed its name to Free State Mines Selection Limited. This act symbolised the final dissolution of the remarkable empire Sammy Marks had bequeathed to his descendants; his unintended heir would be Sir Ernest Oppenheimer.

Sammy Marks would certainly have been dismayed at the prospect. He would have been equally dismayed at the fate of his lineage. Marks was very proud of being Jewish. He was also immensely proud of the country of his adoption. Most of his descendants, however, have left both faith and country, casualties of deeper social and political currents sweeping late-twentieth-century South African Jewry. The Jewish faith clause in Marks's 1906 will was essentially a failure, if not in form, certainly in spirit. From the start his sons were unhappy with the restrictions he had attempted to place on their choice of marriage partner. Within a year of their father's death, Joe and Ted Marks approached the Supreme Court for a ruling on the validity of the clause. The court upheld the Jewish faith clause but interpreted it in a broad and liberal fashion of which Marks, who had had a horror of intermarriage between Jew and gentile, would hardly have approved. The court ruled that the conditions of the clause would be satisfied if the intended marriage partner 'has been admitted to the Jewish religious community at the date of the marriage'. In practice this opened the way to marriage with gentile women: so long as the bride had been formally converted to Judaism before the wedding day, there was no danger of disinheritance. In the years that followed, Louis, Joe and Ted all ensured that their gentile fiancées were converted before their wedding day. The fourth and youngest son, Phil, never married. Neither did Girlie, Sammy's older daughter, whose threatened apostasy in 1906 had precipitated the introduction of the Jewish faith clause into her father's will.

The Jewish faith clause had a further airing in the courts in the next generation. In 1951 one of Sammy Marks' grandchildren married out of the Jewish faith. Some time after her weddding the fear arose that the forfeiture clause might well apply to generations beyond the first. The Marks estate and the granddaughter concerned sought an interpretation from the Supreme Court. The bench ruled that the Jewish faith clause was meant to bind not only Sammy Marks's children, but his remoter descendants as well. The basis of this judgment was the 'extremely strong sentiment for the Jewish faith' which the clause itself was held to demonstrate. When the issue was taken to Bloemfontein, the Appeal Court reversed the decision of the lower court. It dismissed arguments about Marks's religious views and conjecture about his wishes, and insisted instead on a strict reading of the wording of the clause: the Jewish faith clause spoke only of children; therefore, it only applied to Marks's children, not to his remoter issue.[19]

Today very few of Marks's descendants have remained within the Jewish fold. It is doubtful that even had the Jewish faith clause specified more than one generation that it would have halted the drift away from Judaism within the family, which was part, after all, of a general movement within Western Jewry in this century towards assimilation and loss of Jewish identity. The diluted Judaism of the Marks household clearly played an important part in this process, providing the initial impetus towards the family's eventual assimilation. Significantly, the only descendants of Sammy Marks who have remained strongly Jewish (besides one of Joe Marks's grandson's) are the members of one half of the Maisels line of descent. Unlike her siblings, Dolly Marks married into an orthodox Jewish family. Her late husband, Rael Maisels, a successful Johannesburg surgeon, came from a family who had immigrated to South Africa from Lithuania long after Sammy Marks made the journey and were far closer to their traditional roots than the Marks family.

But like their more assimilated cousins, the Maisels great-grandchildren have settled far from Sammy Marks's Transvaal. Marks had pioneered Jewish immigration to South Africa in the nineteenth century. His conspicuous success in a range of spheres, in mining, agriculture as well as industry, had encouraged many of his Lithuanian Jewish *landsleit* – fellow countrymen – to turn south for

Africa rather than head west for America as many others had done. His great-grandchildren, who were not immune to the turbulence of their times, joined in the reversal of that flow in the late twentieth century and they, like many others, left South Africa for countries with less uncertain futures.

Marks had pioneered Jewish settlement in the Transvaal in the 1880s. He was one of the founders of what was to become a remarkably vital Jewish community. The departure of the last of his great-grandchildren from the country a century later signified the irreversible decline of that community in the 1980s and the end of an era – the Jewish century in the Transvaal – which had begun with Sammy Marks's arrival in Kruger's Pretoria in 1881.

But although his heirs are widely dispersed and his business empire has long since crumbled, Marks lives on, both in fond if inaccurate popular memory and in the enduring economic structures he helped create. The South African industrial economy of the late twentieth century rests on foundations that Sammy Marks and his contemporaries laid. Diamonds, coal, electricity, steel, all of these and more, were part of the legacy of a young Jewish immigrant who stepped ashore in Cape Town in 1868 with little more than a case of knives, a visionary imagination and an unquenchable optimism.

Sammy Marks shortly before his death, with Bertha and son-in-law Israel Maisels (Photo: Mrs Dolly Maisels)

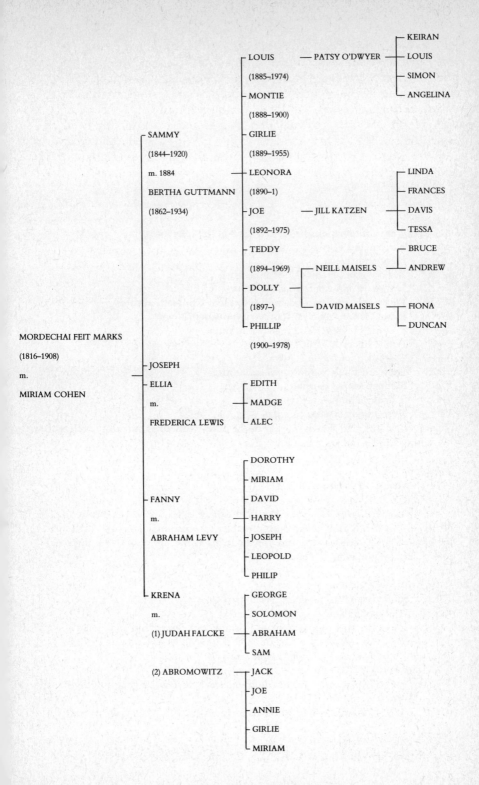

MORDECHAI FEIT MARKS
(1816–1908)
m.
MIRIAM COHEN

SAMMY
(1844–1920)
m. 1884
BERTHA GUTTMANN
(1862–1934)

LOUIS
(1885–1974) — PATSY O'DWYER — KEIRAN
— LOUIS
— SIMON
— ANGELINA

MONTIE
(1888–1900)

GIRLIE
(1889–1955)

LEONORA
(1890–1)

JOE
(1892–1975) — JILL KATZEN — LINDA
— FRANCES
— DAVIS
— TESSA

TEDDY
(1894–1969)

DOLLY
(1897–) — NEILL MAISELS — BRUCE
— ANDREW
— DAVID MAISELS — FIONA
— DUNCAN

PHILLIP
(1900–1978)

JOSEPH

ELLIA
m.
FREDERICA LEWIS — EDITH
— MADGE
— ALEC

FANNY
m.
ABRAHAM LEVY — DOROTHY
— MIRIAM
— DAVID
— HARRY
— JOSEPH
— LEOPOLD
— PHILIP

KRENA
m.
(1) JUDAH FALCKE — GEORGE
— SOLOMON
— ABRAHAM
— SAM

(2) ABROMOWITZ — JACK
— JOE
— ANNIE
— GIRLIE
— MIRIAM

References

The following abbreviations have been used in the references:

AE   African and European minutes
BH   *Barberton Herald*
BRA   Barlow Rand archives, Johannesburg
DSAB   *Dictionary of South African Biography*
JCI   Johannesburg Consolidated Investment Company records
JHA   James Henry archives, University of Cape Town
PHC   Pretoria Hebrew Congregation minutes
PRO   Public Records Office, London
SAJC   *South African Jewish Chronicle*
SBA   Standard Bank archives, Johannesburg
SM   Sammy Marks papers
TA   Transvaal archives, Pretoria
VE   Vereeniging Estates minutes

Wherever 'Marks' and 'Lewis' appear in the notes without an initial, the reference is to Sammy Marks and Isaac Lewis.

Preface
   1. *The Review of Reviews* 29.6.04.
   2. *SAJC* 9.6.05.
   3. SM/B2/12: Marks–H. Lewis 1.9.95, 8.8.96; SM/B2/20: Marks–Lewis 13.8.04, 30.10.04. 'Samuel Marks writes with difficulty', his bank manager reported in 1900, 'and I have never seen his signature for the firm.' (SBA, INSP 1/1/144: Inspection report, Pretoria branch, September 1900)

I. Beyond the Pale
   1. For information on Neustadt, see Sudarsky *et al.*
   2. Simonowitz: 25–6.
   3. For life in the *shtetl*, see Gitelman; Roskies; and Zborowski and Herzog.
   4. SM/B2/29: Marks–Lewis 25.4.08; SM/B2/1: Marks–J. Dumont 29.12.81.
   5. See Zborowski and Herzog for the values of the *shtetl*.
   6. Stanislawski: 27.
   7. For the conscription of Jewish children, see Stanislawski: ch.1; Pinkus: 20; and Vital: 37–41.
   8. SM/B2/21: Marks–H. Hamilton 10.3.05; SM/B2/17: Marks–W. F. Bailey 22.3.01.
   9. SM/B2/20: Marks–F. Levy 11.2.05.
   10. Leslie: 39; Williams: 176, 267, 269; Pollard: 118–19, 125.

11. Information from E. Isaacs, Sheffield; Leslie: 39; Falcke: 1.
12. Leslie: 39.
13. Leslie: 39–40.
14. Leslie: 40; [London] *Jewish Chronicle* 12.4.95, 28.6.95.
15. Turner's *Kimberley . . . Directory and Guide*: 58.
16. Cohen: 66–7.
17. Saron and Hotz: 116–120.
18. Trollope: 9, 358, 370, 371.
19. SM/B2/1: Marks–Inspector of Bultfontein Diggings 29.3.81.
20. Turrell, 1982: 128; Worger, 1982: 36–7.
21. Worger, 1982: 37, 133.
22. SBA, INSP 1/1/84: Inspection report, Kimberley branch, 31.12.77; SBA, INSP 1/1/85: Inspection report, Kimberley branch, 15.3.79.
23. Turrell, 1982: 139; Worger, 1982: 46; JHA: Half-yearly report, General Manager, Standard Bank, 6.8.80.
24. Turrell, 1982: 139, 177; JHA: Half-yearly reports, General Manager, Standard Bank, 6.8.80, 11.2.81; SBA, INSP 1/1/85: Inspection report, Kimberley branch, 12.11.81.
25. SBA, INSP 1/1/85: Inspection report, Kimberley branch, 12.11.81; SM/B2/1: Lewis–[?] 17.2.81.
26. SM/B2/1: Marks–Lewis 12.1.81; De Klerk: 10, 77.
27. JHA: Half-yearly reports, General Manager, Standard Bank, 13.2.80, 6.8.80; Turrell, 1982: 23–4, 27.
28. SM/B2/1: Lewis–[?] 17.2.81, Marks–J. Wernher 28.4.81; SBA, INSP 1/1/85: Inspection report, Kimberley branch, 12.11.81; Turrell, 1982: 191, 473, 477, 490.
29. Leigh: 13–17; Young: 107, 109; *DSAB* II: 718–20.
30. Turrell, 1982: 30, 39, 177; Worger, 1982: 110; SM/B2/1: Marks–Lewis 23.6.81.
31. SM/B2/1: Stow and Caldecott–South African and Orange Free State Coal and Mineral Mining Association 5.7.81; SM/B2/2: Marks–I. and B. Lewis 1.2.82; SM/B2/3: Marks–B. Lewis 3.7.82; SM/B2/4: H. Cohen–B. Lewis 2.12.82.
32. Stander: 1–2; Leigh: 17; SM/B2/1: Marks–Lewis 14.7.81.
33. SM/B2/1: Marks–Lewis 21.4.81, 19.5.81, Marks–J. Wernher 28.4.81.
34. SM/B2/1: Marks–Lewis 7.7.81, 21.7.81, 27.7.81, Marks–South African and Orange Free State Coal and Mineral Mining Association 1.9.81; TA, R3108/81: Marks and J. Dumont–President and Members of Triumvirate 13.8.81, Registrar of Deeds–State Secretary 17.8.81.
35. SM/B2/1: Lewis–J. Brasch 30.12.80, Marks–Lewis 7.7.81, 27.7.81, Marks–Simpson and Schappert 12.9.81; TA, R10526/96: Marks–President and Executive Council 7.8.96. For Kruger as a land speculator, see D. W. Kruger, *Paul Kruger*, I, pp.76–80.
36. SM/B2/1: Marks–Lewis 12.10.81; Kaye: 18–19; *DSAB* IV: 404–5.
37. Leslie: 35–7; Jeppe, 1881; Trollope: 297–301.
38. SM/B2/29: Marks–J. Sivewright 3.4.08.
39. SM/B2/1: Marks–G. W. Stow 31.8.81, Marks–South African and Orange Free State Coal and Mineral Mining Association 1.9.81, Marks–J. Richardson 14.9.81, Marks–F. Herz 26.10.81 , Marks–Spengler 24.10.81.
40. SM/B2/1: Marks–Lewis 1.9.81, 3.11.81, Marks–J. Wernher 6.9.81, Marks–F. Herz 26.10.81, Marks–S. Paddon 3.11.81.
41. SM/B2/1: Marks–Lewis 1.9.81, 26.10.81.
42. SM/B2/1: Marks–Lewis 7.7.81; SM/B2/3: Marks–Lewis 29.5.82.
43. SM/B2/1: Marks–Lewis 21.4.81, 19.5.81, 27.7.81, Marks–J. Wernher 28.4.81, Marks–J. Richardson 28.4.81, Marks–Robey and Co. 14.7.81, H. W. P. Steeds–Lewis 4.8.81.
44. SM/B2/2: Marks–I. and B. Lewis 16.2.82; Cohen: 144; SM/B2/1: Marks–Lewis

26.10.81, 17.11.81; A9–1882, Report of the Select Committee on Illicit Diamond
Buying in Griqualand West: 40.
    45. A9–1882: 20–1, 42.
    46. SM/B2/1: Marks–Lewis 17.11.81.
    47. A9–1882: 27; SM/B2/1: Marks–Lewis 3.6.81; SM/B2/2: Marks–I. and B. Lewis
9.2.82.
    48. A9–1882: 27; SM/B2/1: Marks–Lewis 30.11.81, Marks–J. Dumont 30.11.81,
Marks–I. and B. Lewis 12.1.82, 9.2.82, Marks–S. W. Paddon 30.11.81, 26.1.82.
    49. SM/B2/1: Marks–Lewis 8.9.81, Marks–J. X. Merriman 10.10.81,
Marks–S. W. Paddon 30.11.81; SM/B2/2: Anglo-French D.M.C., Phoenix D.M.C.,
Kimberley M.C.–J. X. Merriman 8.3.82, Marks–Lewis 10.5.82, H. W. P. Steeds–
Lewis 22.6.82. See Turrell and Worger for a discussion of the process of
proletarianisation amongst white diggers.
    50. SM/B2/1: Marks–Lewis 12.10.81.
    51. *Buitengewoon Staats-Courant* 18.10.81.
    52. SM/B2/1: Marks–Lewis 20.10.81, Marks–Simpson and Schappert 22.10.81.
    53. SM/B2/1: Marks–Simpson and Schappert 22.10.81.
    54. SM/B2/1: Marks–J. Dumont 30.11.81, Marks–Lewis 26.1.82.
    55. SM/B2/1: Marks–I. and B. Lewis 15.12.81, 18.1.82.
    56. SM/B2/1: Marks–J. Dumont 30.11.81; SM/B2/3: Marks–Durham 14.8.82.
    57. SM/B2/1: Marks–J. Dumont 20.10.81, Marks–F. Herz 26.10.81, Marks–Lewis
20.10.81.
    58. SM/B2/1: Marks–S. Lewis 28.9.81.
    59. SM/B2/1: Marks–Lewis 24.11.81; SM/B2/2: Marks–F. Lewis 9.2.82,
Marks–S. Cohen 16.2.82, H. W. P. Steeds–I. and B. Lewis 23.3.82, 30.3.82;
SM/B2/3: Marks–Lewis 29.5.82; Matthews: 100–1.
    60. A9–1882: 19–44. See Turrell and Worger for the Diamond Trade Act and its
aftermath.
    61. SM/B2/2: Marks–Lewis 14.9.82; SM/B2/3: Marks–J. Robertson 19.6.82,
Marks–Lewis 26.6.82.

II. Founding the First Factory
    1. SM/B2/3: Marks–B. Lewis 19.6.82.
    2. Cd. 625, Report of the Transvaal Concessions Commission, 1901: 231–2;
SM/B5: Simpson and Schappert–Lewis and Marks 6.12.81; SM/B2/3: Marks–Lewis
5.6.82, Marks–H. S. Caldecott 5.6.82; SM/B2/2: Marks–Lewis 31.8.82.
    3. SM/B2/3: Marks–Lewis 29.5.82.
    4. SM/B2/2: Marks–Lewis 10.5.82; SM/B2/3: Marks–B. Lewis 26.6.82.
    5. SM/B2/3: Marks–B. Lewis 3.7.82, Marks–Lewis 19.6.82, 10.7.82,
Marks–S. W. Paddon 10.7.82.
    6. SM/B2/3: Marks–E. Marks 8.10.82.
    7. SM/B5: A. H. Nellmapius–F. Schuster 7.3.82; SM/B2/3: Marks–Lewis 23.10.82;
SM/B2/3: Marks–B. Lewis 23.10.82.
    8. SM/B2/3: Marks–Lewis 19.6.82, Marks–B. Lewis 12.6.82, 19.6.82, 24.7.82,
Marks–L. Daly 12.6.82, Leslie: 23.
    9. SM/B2/3: Marks–Lewis 19.6.82, Marks–B. Lewis 19.6.82; Leslie: 24–5.
    10. SM/B2/3: Marks–J. Betz 26.6.82, Marks–Lewis 8.10.82; SM/B5: A. H.
Nellmapius–F. Schuster 7.3.82; SM/B2/4: Marks–Lewis 20.12.82, 3.2.83, 14.4.83.
    11. SM/B2/3: Marks–B. Lewis 10.7.82, 24.7.82, Marks–Lewis 19.6.82, 6.11.82,
13.11.82; SM/B2/4: Marks–Lewis 2.12.82; Leslie: 23.
    12. SM/B2/3: Marks–Lewis and Marks, London 26.6.82, Marks–B. Lewis 24.7.82,
Marks–T. Schuster 21.8.82, Marks–A. H. Nellmapius 21.8.82.

13. SM/B2/3: Marks–B. Lewis 24.7.82; SM/B2/4: Marks–Lewis 2.12.82; SM/B2/5: Marks–B. Lewis 24.6.83.

14. SM/B5: J. Betz–Marks 10.9.82, F. Schuster–Marks 10.9.82; SM/B2/4: Marks–B. Lewis 14.4.83.

15. SM/B2/3: Marks–J. Betz 14.8.82, 21.8.82.

16. TA, R6859/82: Lewis and Marks–State Secretary 11.12.82; SM/B2/3: Marks–A. H. Nellmapius 27.8.82, Marks–Lewis 13.11.82, Marks–J. Marks 29.5.82, Marks–Managing Directors, South African and Orange Free State Coal and Mineral Mining Association 19.6.82, H. W. P. Steeds–Lewis 13.7.82; SM/B2/4: Marks–B. Lewis 9.12.82, 13.1.83; SM/B5: A. H. Nellmapius–Marks September 1882; Kaye: 40–1; Maylam: 130.

17. SM/B2/4: Marks–Lewis 23.12.82, 10.2.83.

18. SM/B2/3: Marks–J. Wernher 7.10.82, Marks–B. Lewis 6.11.82.

19. SM/B2/1: G. W. Stow–South African and Orange Free State Coal and Mineral Mining Association 9.1.82, 12.1.82; SM/B2/2: Marks–I. and B. Lewis 22.2.82.

20. SM/B2/2: Marks–Bond and Tamblyn 10.4.82, H. W. P. Steeds–Lewis 29.6.82; SM/B2/3: Marks–G. Bulman 11.6.82; SM/B5: W. Ward–Marks 11.6.82.

21. SM/B2/3: Marks–South African and Orange Free State Coal and Mineral Mining Association 29.5.82.

22. SM/B2/3: Marks–Lewis 29.5.82.

23. SM/B2/3: Marks–South African and Orange Free State Coal and Mineral Mining Association 29.5.82, Marks–J. Richardson 5.6.82, Marks–Lewis 29.5.82, 3.7.82.

24. SM/B2/2: H. W. P. Steeds–Lewis 29.6.82, 6.7.82, 13.7.82; SM/B2/3: Marks–H. W. P. Steeds 10.7.82; SM/B5: C. Herz–Marks 28.10.82; Worger, 1982: 194.

25. SM/B2/3: Marks–G. Bulman 5.6.82, Marks–B. Lewis 6.11.82; SM/B2/4: Marks–G. Bulman 9.12.82.

26. SM/B2/4: Marks–G. Bulman 9.12.82, 23.12.82; SM/B5: L. Herz–Marks 25.11.82, 15.12.82.

27. SM/B2/1: Marks–Spengler 24.10.81; SM/B2/3: Marks–G. Bulman 24.7.82; SM/B2/4: Marks–G. Bulman 24.2.83; SM/B2/6: Marks–Lewis 8.11.85, Marks–L. Herz 8.11.95, Marks–H. H. Fraser [undated–probably July or August 1886]; SM/B5: H. H. Fraser–Marks 5.7.84, 28.9.95. For landowner preference for black sharecroppers over white bywoners, see Keegan: 30–2.

28. SM/B2/3: Marks–J. Betz 26.6.82, 3.7.82, Marks–Pilditch 21.8.82, Marks–R. W. H. Giddy 13.11.82, Marks–Lewis 8.10.82; SM/B2/4: Marks–M. Maercker 7.12.87.

29. SM/B2/3: Marks–Maria [?] 5.6.82, Marks–F. Lewis 5.6.82, Marks–Lewis 6.11.82, 13.11.82.

30. SM/B2/3: Marks–Lewis 6.11.82; SM/B2/4: Marks–B. Lewis 2.12.82, Marks–Lewis 2.12.82, 20.12.82.

31. SM/B2/4: H. Cohen–B. Lewis 2.12.82, Marks–Lewis 2.12.82, 20.1.83, 27.1.83.

32. SM/B2/4: H. Cohen–B. Lewis 30.12.82, Marks–B. Lewis 7.1.83, 13.1.83.

33. SM/B2/4: Marks–R. W. H. Giddy 17.2.83, Marks–Lewis 10.2.83, 25.3.83.

34. SM/B2/4: Marks–B. Lewis 9.4.83, Marks–Hadfields' Steel Foundry 28.4.83, Marks–Lewis 6.5.83.

35. SM/B2/10: Marks–Lewis 23.9.94.

36. SM/B2/4: Marks–Lewis 6.5.83.

37. SM/B2/4: Marks–Lewis 6.5.83.

38. SM/B2/5: Marks–B. Lewis 27.5.83.

39. SM/B2/3: Marks–Lewis 6.11.82; SM/B2/4: Marks–Lewis 6.5.83.

40. SM/B2/5: Marks–B. Lewis 27.5.83; *Transvaal Advertiser* 9.6.83; *De Volksstem* 9.6.83; H.W. Struben: 187; Ferreira: 19–20.

41. Cd. 625, Report of the Transvaal Concessions Commission, 1901: 232.

42. SM/B2/5: Marks–I. and B. Lewis 5.11.83; *BH* 2.8.87; Kaye: 43–4; Rosenthal, 1945.

43. SM/B2/5: Marks–Lewis 8.1.84; SM/B2/6: Marks–Lewis 30.3.85, 6.4.85, 18.5.85, Marks–J. Marks 18.5.85; SM/B2/27: Marks–Lewis 4.5.08.

44. SM/E1: Marks–H. O. Arnold Forster 31.10.00; SM/C4: Deed of Transfer No. 1884/221; Falcke: 3.

45. SM/B2/1: Marks–J. Wernher 29.12.81; SM/B2/5: Marks–F. Lewis 16.6.83.

46. SM/A1: Marriage settlement 15.12.84; SM/B5: T. D. Jones–Marks 25.5.85.

47. SM/B2/6: Marks–Adler Bros. 13.3.85.

48. SM/F8: receipt R. W. Winfield and Co. 3.12.84; SM/B2/6: Marks–Adler Bros. 14.3.85, 20.3.85, 26.3.85, H. W. P. Steeds–Adler Bros. 14.7.85; SM/B5: Adler Bros.–Marks 30.7.85, 6.8.85.

49. SM/B2/6: Marks–Jewish Congregation, Kimberley 23.11.85.

50. SM/B2/6: Marks–F. Schuster 8.3.86; Wits, Struben Family papers: H. W. Struben–L. Lys 2.8.85.

51. SM/B3: Lewis–Marks 27.8.85.

52. TA, R1428/85: Marks–President 20.3.85, State Secretary–Under State Secretary 21.3.85; SM/B2/6: Marks–Lewis 28.9.85, 13.10.85.

53. SM/B2/6: Marks–Lewis 20.4.85, 5.5.85; SM/B3: Lewis–Marks 25.5.85; SM/B5: Marks–A. H. Nellmapius 5.5.85, Lewis–A. H. Nellmapius 25.6.85.

54. Coetzee: 46–7.

55. SM/B5: A. H. Nellmapius–Marks 26.7.85, Memorandum on loan required for the South African Republic; SM/B3: Marks–Lewis 1.8.85, Lewis–Marks 27.8.85.

56. SBA, INSP 1/1/143: Inspection report, Pretoria branch, 5.3.85.

57. SM/B2/6: Marks–Lewis 6.4.85, 23.11.85.

III. Gold, Gin and Coal

1. Mathers: 256–64; R. Struben: 238; H. W. Struben: 191–8.

2. SM/B2/6: Marks–J. Lewis 10.8.85, 31.8.85, H. W. P. Steeds–Lewis 10.8.85, Marks–Lewis 10.8.85; SM/B2/10: Marks–Lewis 18.11.94; SM/B2/15: Marks–Lewis 13.11.98; SM/B2/32: Marks–Lewis 26.8.09.

3. SM/B2/3: Marks–Lewis 29.5.82, Marks–B. Lewis 12.6.82; SM/B2/4: Marks–Lewis 2.12.82.

4. SM/B2/5: Marks–Giddy 2.6.83, 10.3.84, Marks–Ward 24.3.84.

5. Mathers: 75, 114; SBA, INSP 1/1/84: Inspection report, Kimberley branch, 31.12.77.

6. Graumann: 11; SM/B2/6: Marks–Dumont [?] 23.11.85, Marks–Lewis 23.11.85.

7. SM/B2/6: Marks–Lewis 21.12.85.

8. SM/B2/6: Marks–Lewis 6.10.85; TA, R6500/85: Memorandum of terms proposed for a concession for the construction of certain railways.

9. TA, URB art. 3, 5.1.86; Kotze, II: 63, 68–9.

10. SM/B2/18: Marks–Dr Smartt 20.8.02; Kotze, II: 68–70.

11. SBA, INSP 1/1/143: Inspection report, Pretoria branch, 1.1.86.

12. TA, R1972/86: Robey and Company, Lewis and Marks–President and Executive Council April 1886; Mouton: 190; SM/B2/6: Account of disbursements by S. Marks during 1885 and 1886.

13. SM/B2/6: Marks–J. Dumont 15.2.86, 4.6.86; TA, R2387/86: Marks, F. Clench and Oriental Company–President and Executive Council 22.5.86; TA, R3780/86: State Attorney–State Secretary 23.10.86.

14. *BH* 3.8.86, 7.9.86; Mathers: 132–5.

15. *BH* 15.2.87; *Gold Fields Times* 15.2.87.

16. JHA: March 1887; *BH* 8.3.87, 15.3.87, 26.8.87, 28.8.88, 18.9.88.

17. Curle: 111; Graumann: 13, 49.

18. *BH* 27.3.88; JHA: Half-yearly report, August 1888.

19. *Volksstem* 21.8.88; *BH* 28.8.88, 27.11.88.

20. *BH* 28.8.88, 4.9.88.

21. *BH* 6.11.88, 20.11.88, 27.11.88; *South African Mining and Engineering Journal* 25.12.1964; Cd. 624, Report of the Transvaal Concessions Commission, 1901: 136.

22. *BH* 8.3.89, 27.6.90; SM/B3: Lewis–Marks 19.11.88, 25.1.89.

23. SM/B2/10: Marks–Lewis 21.4.94; SM/B2/15: Marks–Lewis 13.11.98.

24. TA, R5267/88: Petition Johannesburg inhabitants, June 1888.

25. TA, R7696/87: Lewis and Marks–State Secretary November 1887, Contract J. D. Weilbach and Lewis and Marks 17.10.87, Leyds–State Secretary 5.12.87; TA, R2535/88: Lewis and Marks–President and Executive Council 21.3.88; TA, R4893/88: Lewis and Marks–State Secretary 4.6.88, State Secretary–Under State Secretary 5.6.88; TA, R5244/88: Lewis and Marks–State Secretary 14.6.88.

26. Sawyer, 1889–90: 171.

27. SM/B5: Lewis and Marks–J. Fowler and Co. 29.11.89.

28. SM/B2/18: Marks–Dr Smartt 20.8.02; Falcke: 6.

29. A6–1893, Report of the Select Committee on Coal for Railway Purposes: 70.

30. G52A–1891, Report on Trials of Free State Coal: 3–6; G64–1893, Copies of Correspondence relative to Supply of Coal and Trials of Coal: 49–50.

31. SM/B2/7: Marks–J. Sivewright 24.9.92; SM/B2/8: Marks–J. Sivewright 5.3.92: SM/B5: J. Sivewright–Marks 21.9.92; Cape Hansard: 9.6.92.

32. Cape Hansard: 9.6.92, 10.7.93; SM/B2/7: J. Sivewright–Marks September[?] 1892.

33. Cape Hansard: 10.7.93, 21.7.93.

34. SM/B2/8: Marks–J. Sivewright 4.8.93; SM/B2/7: Marks–Lewis 27.8.93.

35. SBA, GMO 3/2/1/1: Standard Bank, Cape Town–Standard Bank, London 7.8.95; SM/B2/10: Marks–Borckenhagen 9.6.94, Marks–J. Sivewright 20.6.94, 29.6.94; *Transvaal Critic* 23.4.97; SBA, GMO 3/1/34: Standard Bank, Cape Town–Standard Bank, London 5.10.98.

36. SM/B2/11: Marks–J. G. Fraser 16.1.95.

37. TA, R15562/91: Lewis and Marks–State Secretary 21.12.91; TA, R15580/91: Inspector of Prisons–State Attorney 26.2.92.

38. SM/B2/7: Marks–T. R. Price 1.12.92, Marks–E. Marks 8.12.92; SM/B2/12: Marks–Lewis 16.2.96; SM/B2/13: Marks–A. M. Miller 23.12.96.

39. SM/B2/11: Marks–E. Marks 17.7.95; SM/B2/13: Marks–E. Marks 14.2.96; Sawyer, 1889–90: 168.

40. SM/B2/7: Marks–E. Marks 24.1.93.

41. SM/B2/11: Marks–E. Marks 1.12.95.

42. SM/B2/9: Marks–T. R. Price 3.12.94; SM/B2/10: Marks–T. R. Price 13.5.94, Marks–H. Crawford 30.9.94; SM/B2/11: Marks–E. Marks 23.12.95.

43. SM/B2/7: Marks–Lewis 17.3.93; SM/B2/8: Marks–South African and Orange Free State Coal and Mineral Mining Association 17.7.91; SM/B2/10: Marks–Lewis 13.1.95; SM/B2/12: Marks–Lewis 3.11.95; Leigh: 146.

44. SM/B2/12: Marks–Lewis 3.11.95; SM/B2/7: Marks–J. Sivewright 15.10.92.

45. SM/B2/7: Marks–J. Sivewright 15.10.92, Marks–H. Crawford 2.11.92.

46. SM/B2/7: Marks–Lewis 30.9.93, 17.2.94, Report by A. E. H. Coffey 14.10.93; SM/B2/12: Marks–Lewis 9.8.96.

47. *Mines of the Transvaal*, 1909–10: 625; SM/B2/8: Marks–South African and Orange Free State Coal and Mineral Mining Association 17.7.91.

48. SM/B2/8: Marks–South African and Orange Free State Coal and Mineral Mining Association 17.7.91; SM/B2/7: Marks–Lewis 1.2.93; SM/B2/9: Marks–E. Marks 19.11.94; SM/B2/10: Marks–E. Marks 13.10.94; Leslie: 174–5.
49. SM/B2/8: Marks–South African and Orange Free State Coal and Mineral Mining Association 17.7.91; Leslie: 87, 174; *Vereeniging–Vanderbijlpark News* 1.3.55.
50. SM/B2/12: Marks–Lewis 23.11.95.
51. Sawyer, 1889: 12.
52. SM/B2/7: Marks–Lewis 20.9.92.
53. SM/B2/10: Marks–Lewis 28.10.94, Marks–E. Marks 28.10.94; SM/B2/12: Marks–Lewis 23.11.95; SM/B2/15: Marks–I.[?] C. Fawcett 8.3.97.
54. SM/B2/7: Marks–Lewis 9.9.93.
55. SM/B2/8: Marks–T. Guttmann 20.8.92; SM/B2/7: Marks–J. Sivewright 5.10.93, Marks–Lewis 1.11.93; SM/B2/10: Marks–Lewis 2.2.95.
56. SM/B2/8: Marks–South African and Orange Free State Coal and Mineral Mining Association 17.7.91; TA, R3722/82: Simpson and Schappert–State Secretary 30.6.82.
57. TA, R13347/89: Agreement between Government and South African and Orange Free State Coal and Mineral Mining Association 23.12.89.
58. Leslie: 85–6. See A. J. Christopher: 102 and 157, on the ubiquity of the grid pattern in nineteenth-century South African urban 'planning'.
59. VE: 3.3.04.
60. Leslie: 85–6; SM/B2/7: Marks–Lewis 20.9.92.
61. Churchill: 76–8.
62. Van Onselen, I: 53; Cd. 624, Report of Transvaal Concessions Commission, part II: 72; Cd. 625, Report of Transvaal Concessions Commission, part III: 233–5.
63. SM/B2/10: Marks–Lewis 10.8.94.
64. SM/B2/7: Marks–Lewis 17.11.92; SM/B2/10: Marks–Lewis 14.10.94; Falcke: 3.
65. SM/B2/7: Marks–Mrs Nellmapius 10.12.92.
66. SM/B2/10: Marks–Lewis 10.8.94.
67. SM/B2/7: Marks–S. L. Heymann 24.4.93.
68. Longlands *Pretoria Directory* for 1899: 31; SBA, INSP 1/1/144: Pretoria branch, Inspection report, September 1890; SM/B2/15: Marks–Lewis 26.8.97; SM/B2/20: Marks–Lewis 10.12.04, 11.12.04; JHA: LO/GM 29.4.80, Falcke: 18–19.
69. SM/B2/7: Marks–Secretary, Eerste Fabrieken 6.11.91, Marks–Lewis 7.7.93; SM/B2/12: Marks–Lewis 15.11.96; SM/B3: Lewis–Marks 18.3.04; *DSAB* III: 180–1; SBA,GMO 3/1/22: Standard Bank, Cape Town–Standard Bank, London 25.7.88; SBA, INSP 1/1/144: Inspection report, Pretoria branch, September 1892, Pretoria liabilities 9.3.92; SBA, INSP 1/1/145: Pretoria branch, report on obligants 16.10.97.
70. SM/B2/12: Marks–Lewis 13.10.95; SM/B3: Lewis–Marks 6.6.95; Davenport-Hines and Van Helten: 42, 44–5.
71. SM/F4: Profit and loss accounts for half-years ending 30.6.94, 30.6.95 and 31.12.95, Balance-sheets for half-years ending 30.6.94 and 31.12.95.
72. SM/B2/12: Marks–Lewis 1.12.95; SM/F3.2: Journal 1892–1902.
73. SM/B2/12: Marks–Lewis 13.10.95.
74. SM/B2/12: Marks–I. Lewis 10.11.95, 23.11.95.
75. SBA, INSP 1/1/143: Inspection report, Pretoria branch 1.1.86; SM/B2/12: Marks–Lewis 22.9.95, 22.9.95, 6.10.95; SM/B5: P. J. Joubert–Lewis and Marks 22.4.95; Mouton: 206–7.
76. SM/B2/11: Marks–J. H. de la Rey 7.8.95; SM/B2/13: J. P. H. Faure–J. H. de la Rey 26.2.96, Marks–J. H. de la Rey 11.12.96; TA, A681(2): Marks–H. Greef 19.2.86, Marks–A. Visser 19.2.96.
77. SM/B2/10: Marks–Lewis 23.9.94.
78. Alexander: 78; BRA, HE 64: J. H. Hammond–A. Beit 22.4.98.

79. SBA, GMO 3/1/30: Standard Bank, Cape Town–Standard Bank, London 19.9.94, 30.1.95, 13.3.95; SBA, INSP 1/1/102: Inspection report, Lourenço Marques branch, 31.8.96; INSP 1/1/241: Inspection report, Lourenço Marques branch,1.2.02; SM/B2/10: Marks–Lewis 21.4.94, 5.8.94.

80. SBA, INSP 1/1/102: Inspection report, Lourenço Marques branch, 26.7.97.

81. *De Kaap Annual*, 1895: 67–8.

82. JCI, minutes: 27.7.95; JCI, Annual Report 1897: 21. For Dr Somershields see SM/B2/17: Marks–J. Sivewright 21.5.01 and Alexander: 75; SBA, INSP 1/1/85: Inspection report, Kimberley branch, 2.11.82.

83. SM/B2/12: Marks–Lewis 24.8.95.

84. SM/B2/12: Marks–Lewis 1.12.95, 2.2.96.

85. SM/C1: Title-deeds to Cape Town properties; SM/F2.4: Ledger 1888–96; SM/B2/11: Marks–Secretary, City Club 6.1.96.

86. SM/B2/11: Marks–Lewis 22.12.95.

IV. The Transvaal from Within

1. Phillips: 113.

2. SM/B2/12: Marks–[?] 3.2.96; SM/B2/17: Marks–A. Malan 22.11.00; SM/B2/15: Marks–W. G. Soper 15.2.97; Marais: 100–1.

3. Phillips: 121; Hammond: 31–2.

4. SM/B2/10: Marks–H. Crawford 30.9.94.

5. SM/B2/10: Marks–H. Crawford 30.9.94; SM/B2/12: Marks–Lewis 19.1.96; SM/B3: Marks–Lewis 17.1.96, 19.1.96; SM/B5: J. Sivewright–Marks 9.1.96[?], 30.1.96.

6. SM/B3: Lewis–Marks 20.1.96, 23.1.96, 25.1.96.

7. SM/B3: Marks–Lewis 25.1.96; SM/B2/12: Marks–Lewis 9.2.96.

8. SM/B3: Lewis–Marks 27.1.96; Marais: 110.

9. SM/B3: Marks–Lewis 25.1.96.

10. SM/B5: J. Sivewright–Marks 30.1.96.

11. SM/B3: Lewis–Marks 15.2.96.

12. SM/B2/16: Marks–Lewis 5.8.99; Marais: 110, n.8; SM/B2/12: Marks–Lewis 23.2.96.

13. SM/B2/12: Marks–Lewis 24.1.96.

14. SM/B2/12: Marks–Lewis 23.2.96; Rhodes University, Gold Fields collection: E. B. Birkenruth–Marks 14.2.96, E. B. Birkenruth–Chairman and Board, C.G.F.S.A. 22.2.96.

15. SM/B2/12: Marks–Lewis 2.2.96, Marks–[?] 3.2.96.

16. SM/B2/15: Marks–W. G. Soper 10.4.97.

17. TA, LA 256(1): M. White–W. J. Leyds 18.4.96; Falcke: 9.

18. SM/D6: B. Dawson–Lewis and Marks 20.4.96, 14.7.96.

19. SM/B2/12: Marks–M. Berkowitz 16.8.96; TA, R8745/96: Lewis and Marks–State Secretary 6.7.96.

20. BRA, HE 174: G. Rouliot–J. Wernher 9.8.96.

21. SM/B2/12: Marks–Lewis 8.8.96; TA, R10526/96: Marks–President and Executive Council 7.8.96.

22. SM/B2/12: Marks–P. Levy[?] 16.8.96.

23. SM/B2/12: Marks–Lewis 14.8.96.

24. SM/B2/12: Marks–Lewis 8.8.96.

25. SM/B3: Lewis–Marks 4.9.96; TA, R10526/96: Marks–President and Executive Council 7.8.96; TA, R13998/97: S. Evans–State Secretary 24.9.97.

26. TA, A681(1): Secretary's report 31.12.96; Cd. 625, Report of the Transvaal Concessions Commission, 1901: 235; Van Onselen, I: 53.

27. SM/B2/12: Marks–Lewis 8.8.96, 12.9.96.

28. TA, A681(1): J. P. H. Faure–S. L. Heymann 18.12.96, J. P. H. Faure–
F. M. Joseph 15.1.97.

29. BRA, HE 174: G. Rouliot–J. Wernher 9.8.96, 21.9.96; TA, A681(1):
J. P. H. Faure–Lewis and Marks 23.1.97.

30. TA, A681(2): J. P. H. Faure–S. Evans 2.2.98; BRA, HE 65: Wernher Beit–
H. Eckstein and Co. 28.7.98, 6.8.98, 12.8.98, 28.10.98, 9.12.98; SM/B2/15: Marks–
E. Vincent 21.8.98.

31. TA, R13998/97: J. N. de Jongh and J. P. H. Faure–President and Executive
Council 30.9.97, State Attorney–State Secretary 25.11.97, Report Government
Commission into Liquor Question, 1898; SM/B2/15: Marks–Lewis 31.7.98;
SM/B2/16: Marks–Lewis 11.6.99, 18.6.99; SM/B3: Lewis–Marks 7.4.99, 19.5.99,
2.6.99.

32. TA, A681(2): J. P. H. Faure–Lewis and Marks 17.1.98; TA, R13998/97: Report
by W. Y. Campbell on the State Alcohol Question, Report Government Commission
into Liquor Question, 1898; TA, TVR 127: Marks and J. P. H. Faure–Chairman
Second Volksraad 28.6.97.

33. SM/B2/12: Marks–Lewis 12.9.96; SM/B2/15: Marks–Lewis 14.8.97; TA,
A681(1): J. P. H. Faure–Lewis and Marks 4.12.96.

34. SM/B2/16: Marks–Lewis 7.5.99.

35. SM/B2/12: Marks–Lewis 9.8.86. For a history of the breweries, see Cox, 1984.

36. SM/B2/12: Marks–Lewis 9.8.86, 6.9.96.

37. SM/B2/12: Marks–Lewis 8.8.96, 13.9.96; TA, A681(1): A. H. Coffey–Lewis
and Marks 9.10.96.

38. SM/B2/12: Marks–Lewis 9.8.86, 12.9.96; SM/B2/15: Marks–Lewis 27.6.97,
31.7.98; SM/B2/15: Marks–Lewis 28.8.98, 4.9.98.

39. TA, A681(2): J. P. H. Faure–Lewis and Marks 10.1.98, 17.1.98, 7.3.98,
J. P. H. Faure–F. M. Joseph 15.4.98.

40. SM/B2/15: Marks–Lewis 1.5.98, 4.9.98; Cd. 625, Report of the Transvaal
Concessions Commission, 1901: 235; TA, A681(2): J. P. H. Faure–Lewis
and Marks 26.3.98.

41. SM/B2/15: Marks–Lewis 13.7.98, 21.8.98; SM/B2/16: Marks–Lewis 30.4.99;
SM/B3: Lewis–Marks 5.5.99.

42. SM/B2/10: Marks–Lewis 5.8.94, 16.9.94.

43. SBA, INSP 1/1/145: Inspection report, Pretoria branch, 3.8.96; SM/B2/12:
Marks–Lewis 1.2.96, 6.9.96.

44. SM/B3: Lewis–Marks 9.10.96.

45. SM/B2/12: Marks–L. and M. Marks 29.11.96; SM/B2/13: Marks–
J. N. Heymann 23.11.96.

46. SM/B2/12: Marks–Lewis 31.1.97, Marks–B. Dawson 21.1.97; SM/B2/15:
Marks–B. Dawson 12.6.97; SM/B4: Lewis and Marks–Marks 8.1.97; TA, A681(1):
J. P. H. Faure–Secretary, Hatherley Distillery 25.3.97.

47. SM/B2/15: Marks–Lewis 27.6.97; TA, A681(1): Report of secretary of Eerste
Fabrieken for half-year ending 31.12.96.

48. SM/B4: Lewis and Marks–Marks 8.1.97; TA, A1707: Manager, glass factory [?]
– Lewis and Marks[?] n.d.; SM/B2/15: Marks–Lewis 28.8.98, 4.9.98.

49. TA, A1707: J. P. H. Faure–Lewis and Marks 12.6.99.

50. TA, A1707: J. P. H. Faure[?]–Lewis and Marks 8.10.98, J. P. H. Faure–Lewis
and Marks 24.10.98, 29.5.99; SM/B2/12: Marks–M.[?] Meursing 19.12.96.

51. TA, R355/96: Lewis and Marks–President and Executive Council 17.1.96; TA,
R10526/96: Marks–President and Executive Council 7.8.96; SM/B2/9: Marks–
T. Sheldon 25.9.94; SM/B2/12: Marks–L. and M. Marks 29.11.96; SM/B2/15:

Marks–L. and M. Marks 21.3.97, Marks–Lewis 24.4.98; SBA, INSP 1/1/145: Pretoria branch, Report on obligants, 3.8.96; Falcke: 4.

52. SM/B2/9: Marks–A. Chambers 25.8.94, 13.9.94; SM/B2/12: Marks–Lewis 6.10.95, 5.9.96, Marks–W. Bailey 30.1.97; SM/B2/15: Marks–W. G. Soper 15.2.97, Marks–Lewis 7.2.97, 4.7.97, 22.11.97; SM/B3: Lewis–Marks 4.8.99; SBA, GMO 3/1/32: Standard Bank, Cape Town–Standard Bank, London 15.4.96; SBA, GMO 3/1/34: Standard Bank, Cape Town–Standard Bank, London 15.3.99; SBA, INSP 1/1/8: Barberton branch, Inspection reports 7.12.96, 4.12.97; BRA, HE 131: H. Eckstein–Wernher Beit 6.2.99; BRA, HE 140: J. P. FitzPatrick–Wernher Beit 12.8.97; *Mines of the Transvaal*, 1909–10: 535; *Mines of Africa*, 1914–15: 495; *SAMJ* 14.9.12.

53. SM/B2/7: Marks–Lewis 27.10.93, 1.11.93; SM/B2/10: Marks–Lewis 29.12.94; SM/B2/12: Marks–Lewis 8.9.95, 22.9.95, 7.11.96; SM/B3: Lewis–Marks 6.6.95.

54. SM/B3: Lewis–Marks 6.6.95.

55. SM/B3: Lewis–Marks 9.10.96; SM/B2/12: Marks–Lewis 7.11.96; SM/B5: Vereeniging Estates, Limited.

56. SM/B2/11: Marks–Chief Marais 20.8.95; SM/B2/12: Marks–W. F. Bailey 17.12.96, Marks–Lewis 20.12.96; SM/B2/16: Marks–Lewis 27.8.99, 10.9.99; SM/B2/20: Marks–Lewis 29.11.03; SM/B5: A. A. Whitehorn–Lewis 5.3.99; Trapido, 1986: 340, 346; Keegan, 1986: 59, 73; South African Coal and Mineral Mining Association, photographic album. See Trapido, 1986 for a fine account of peasant agriculture on the Vereeniging Estates both before and after the South African War, as well as Tim Keegan's masterly account of rural transformation on the southern Highveld in the late nineteenth and early twentieth centuries.

57. SM/B2/12: Marks–Lewis 13.9.96; SM/B2/13: Marks–President and Executive Council 23.12.96; SM/B2/16: Marks–Lewis 9.4.99, 23.4.99, 28.5.99; Trapido: 342; Leslie: 174–5.

58. SM/B2/15: Marks–Lewis 24.4.98, 1.5.98, 5.5.98, 1.7.98, 10.7.98; TA, R5472/98: Lewis and Marks–President and Executive Council 30.4.98; BRA, HE 64: Wernher Beit–H. Eckstein and Co. 26.5.98.

59. Cd. 625, Transvaal Concessions Commission, 1901: 236–7; Richards: 4–7; SM/B2/12: Marks–Lewis 18.10.86, 25.10.96, 7.11.96; SM/B3: Lewis–Marks 9.10.96; SM/D6: B. Dawson–Lewis and Marks 20.4.96, 14.7.96.

60. SM/B3: Lewis–Marks 19.5.99.

V. Courting Kruger

1. SM/B2/7: Marks–C. Joubert 23.9.93, Marks–H. Crawford 14.5.90, 7.6.90; SM/B2/8: Marks–Lewis 27.4.92, Marks–B. Marks 9.12.92.

2. SM/F2.4: ledger 1892–6; SM/F2.5: ledger 1896–9; SM/B2/7: Marks– H. Crawford 30.6.93, 14.10.93, Marks–Lewis 9.9.93, 30.9.93; SM/B2/15: Marks– A. Hird 28.2.97.

3. BRA, HE 3: M. H. Spence–H. Eckstein 19.2.92; SM/F2.4: ledger 1892–6; SM/F2.5: ledger 1896–9; *Land en Volk* 6.7.98.

4. SM/B2/12: Marks–Lewis 23.2.96.

5. SM/B2/12: Marks–Lewis 17.11.95, 12.9.96.

6. SM/B2/12: Marks–B. Marks 9.8.96; SM/B2/15: Marks–J. Lewis 23.5.98.

7. SM/B2/12: Marks–M. Berkowitz 13.9.96; SM/B2/15: Marks–L. and M. Marks 10.10.97; SM/B2/16: Marks–L. and M. Marks 27.11.98; TA, A356(a): M. Marks– S. J. P. Kruger 16.9.98.

8. SM/B2/9: Marks–F. C. Eloff 20.1.94, Marks–L. Marks 12.5.94; SM/B2/13: Marks–Mrs Kruger 12.8.96; SM/B2/16: Marks–M. Marks 7.5.99; SM/B2/18: Marks–G. Marks 25.7.01.

9. SM/B2/8: Marks–Lewis 27.4.92; SM/B2/9: Marks–F. C. Eloff 7.8.94; SM/F2.4: ledger 1892–6; SM/F2.5: ledger 1896–9; SM/B2/15: Marks–J. Lewis 12.6.98; Grobler: 14, 44, 74–6; Buttery: 230–2.

10. SM/B2/12: Marks–Lewis 27.9.96; SM/B2/16: Marks–Lewis 30.4.99, 7.5.99; Kruger, I: 79; BRA, HE66: Agreement Kruger and Geduld Syndicate, 20.12.98.

11. SM/B2/11: Marks–W. J. Leyds 27.8.95; TA, R8130/95 Marks–President and Executive Council 20.8.95; SM/B2/12: State Secretary–Marks 5.9.95; SM/B2/14: Marks–Lewis and Marks, London 21.2.97; TA, R8130/95: Marks–A. van Wouw 7.10.96; TA, RA6658/98: A. van Wouw–L. A. F. H. van Wouw 1898; TA, R17110/98: Marks–President and Executive Council 27.12.98; SM/B2/16: Marks–Lewis 17.9.99; Breytenbach, 1979: 5–26.

12. Becklake: 28; Engelbrecht: 77; SM/B2/13: Marks–C. Butters 25.2.96, 14.3.96. The Africana Museum in Johannesburg has specimens of the golden tickeys on display. Bertha Marks's will mentions a golden bracelet set with five of the coins.

13. SM/B2/10: Marks–Lewis 26.4.94; Mathers: 237–8; *Star* 22.11.90; Hugo: 20–1.

14. *Star* 21.12.21.

15. Batts: 20; SM/B2/34: Marks–Lewis 20.6.10.

16. Leslie: 85.

17. SM/B2/15: Marks–Lewis 10.7.98; SM/B2/16: Marks–Lewis 20.8.99; *Star* 15.8.99; Gordon: 10, 24, 137; Saron and Hotz: 187, 198, 204–5; Simonowitz: 89. See Mendelsohn, 1991 for an account of Kruger's relationship with another useful Jewish burgher, Emanuel Mendelssohn, owner of the pro-Kruger *Standard and Diggers' News*.

18. TA, R7136/97: Marks–President and Executive Council 14.5.97.

19. SM/B2/1: Marks–J. Dumont 3.11.81; SM/B3: Marks–Lewis 1.8.85, Lewis–Marks 27.8.85.

20. SM/B2/8: Marks–Lewis 30.3.92; SBA, GMO 3/1/28: Standard Bank, Cape Town–Standard Bank, London 22.6.92, 29.6.92, 7.9.92; SBA, GMO 3/1/29: Standard Bank, Cape Town–Standard Bank, London 17.4.93, 17.5.93.

21. SM/B5: Marks–President and Executive Council 14.3.96; SM/B2/12: Marks–Lewis 14.8.96.

22. SBA, GMO 3/1/33: Standard Bank, Cape Town–Standard Bank, London 19.5.97, 2.6.97, 23.6.97, 30.6.97, 14.7.97; SBA, GMO 3/1/34: Standard Bank, Cape Town–Standard Bank, London 21.9.98; PRO, African (South) 543: C. Greene–A. Milner 16.3.98; *Land en Volk* 8.12.97, 15.6.98.

23. SM/B2/15: Marks–Lewis 13.7.98, 4.9.98, 2.10.98; PRO, African (South) 543: C. Greene–A. Milner 16.3.98; TA, EVR 183: Secret session of Eerste Volksraad 16.9.98; BRA, HE 65: Wernher Beit–H. Eckstein and Co. 10.6.98; SBA, GMO 3/1/34: Standard Bank, Cape Town–Standard Bank, London 21.9.98.

24. TA, R8726/91: Lewis and Marks–Commandant-General 15.7.91, 4.3.92, Commandant-General–Lewis and Marks 19.1.92; SM/B2/8: Marks–Lewis 27.4.92.

25. SM/B2/10: Marks–Lewis 30.9.94, 25.11.94.

26. Maylam: 93–6.

27. SM/B2/7: Marks–Lewis 15.12.93; SM/B2/10: Marks–Lewis and Marks, London 24.6.94, Marks–Lewis 5.8.94; BRA, HE 277: Report of Directors, Swaziland Corporation, 1902; Crush: 183–97.

28. SM/B2/9: Marks–J. A. Johnstone 21.7.94, Marks–L. Marks 12.8.94; SM/B2/10: Marks–J. Thorburn August 1894, A. M. Miller–Marks 1.8.94, Marks–J. Sivewright 10.8.94, Marks–Lewis 14.10.94.

29. JHA: Standard Bank, Cape Town–Standard Bank, London 26.8.08; SM/B2/12: Marks–Lewis 1.12.95, 2.2.96; SM/B2/16 Marks–Lewis 11.12.98.

30. SM/B2/16: Marks–Lewis 11.12.98, 16.4.99, 17.5.99; SM/B3: Lewis–Marks 25.8.99.

31. Gutsche: 38; Buttery: 227. See also [London] *Jewish Chronicle* 25.12.96 for Paul Kruger's praise of Marks at the opening of the glass factory.

32. SM/B2/7: Marks–Lewis 6.10.93; SM/B2/15: Marks–W. G. Soper 1.5.97, 15.2.97, Marks–E. Vincent 4.9.98; Jeeves: 322; PRO, African (South) 532: British Agent, Pretoria–High Commissioner, Cape Town 12.1.97. For intervention on behalf of Gold Fields company, see chapter 4.

33. SM/B2/1: Marks–Lewis 12.5.81; SM/B2/10: Marks–Lewis 26.4.94, 19.11.94; SM/B2/12: Marks–Lewis 6.10.95; SM/B2/15: Marks–Lewis 12.6.98; JCI letterbook 3: JCI, London–JCI, Johannesburg 15.12.96.

34. SM/B2/12: Marks–Lewis 22.8.96; SM/B2/15: Marks–Lewis 7.8.98, Marks–E. Vincent 4.9.98; BRA, HE 57: Wernher Beit–H. Eckstein and Co. 31.10.91; BRA, HE 58: J. Wernher–L. Phillips 21.10.92; BRA, HE 140: J. P. FitzPatrick–J. Wernher 28.6.97, J. P. FitzPatrick–A. Beit 5.7.97; Duminy and Guest, 1976: 78; Fraser and Jeeves: 105.

35. SM/B2/7: Marks–Crawford 11.11.90, Marks–Lewis 24.9.92; SM/B2/10: Marks–Lewis 21.4.94, Marks–J. Sivewright 13.10.94, Marks–Lewis 14.10.94; SM/B2/12: Marks–W. F. Bailey 30.1.97; SM/B2/15: Marks–Lewis 26.6.98; SM/B2/16: Marks–Lewis 27.8.99; SM/B2/18: Marks–Lewis 9.5.02, 14.6.02, Marks–Dr Smartt 20.8.02; SM/B3: Lewis–Marks 5.5.99; SM/B5: W. M. Martin–Marks 5.10.07; Falcke: 4–6.

VI. Country House on the Highveld

1. [London] *Jewish Chronicle* 17.3.99; SM/B2/12: Marks–J. Morley 29.8.96, Marks–J. Lewis 4.10.96; SM/B2/15: Marks–L. and M. Marks 28.11.97.

2. Buttery: 226; SM/B2/6: Marks–Lewis 1.3.86; SM/B2/7: Marks–H. Crawford 11.11.90, 8.11.92; Falcke: 4–6; *DSAB* II: 546.

3. Wright: 157–8; Innes: 131–2; SM/B2/11: Marks–Lewis and Marks, London 23.6.95.

4. Falcke 16–17; Dollie Maisels recollections; Zwartkoppies household inventory.

5. SM/B2/7: Marks–A. H. Nellmapius 5.5.90; SM/B2/8: Marks–H. Eckstein 11.8.92, Marks–Milburn Manufacturing Company 18.3.93, 11.11.93; SM/B2/11: Marks–L. Marks 17.11.95; SM/B2/12: Marks–L. Marks 30.9.95, Marks–L. and M. Marks 22.1.96; SM/B2/13: Marks–John Roberts and Coy 19.11.96, Marks–W. P. Fraser 11.9.96; SM/F1.2: cashbook 1884–91; D. Maisels: 28.

6. SM/B2/9: Marks–L. Marks 16.7.94, Marks–N. Stephens 20.6.94; SM/B2/11: April 1895, account for polishing orchestron and billiard table; SM/B2/12: Marks–L. and M. Marks 30.8.96, 19.9.96, 1.11.96, 22.11.96, 29.11.96; SM/B2/16: Marks–H. Lewis 13.5.99.

7. SM/B2/9: Marks–G. Genth 1.2.94; SM/B2/11: Marks–E. Tidmarsh 4.5.95, B. Marks–L. Marks 21.4.95; SM/B2/13: Marks–L. Marks 15.8.96; SM/B2/15: Marks–L. and M. Marks 22.2.97; SM/B2/16: Marks–M. Marks 28.5.99, 13.8.99; SM/E1: Marks–H. O. Arnold Forster 31.10.00; Falcke: 3.

8. SM/B2/12: Marks–H. Lewis 16.8.96; SM/B2/13: Marks–H. E. V. Pickstone 17.8.96; SM/B2/18: Marks–J. Marks 5.12.01.

9. Buttery: 226–7.

10. SM/B2/3: Marks–S. Sacke 6.11.82; information from N. Maisels.

11. SM/B2/15: Marks–W. F. Bailey 21.2.97, Marks–L. and M. Marks 14.3.97, 28.3.97, Marks–J. Lewis 8.3.97.

12. Information from N. Maisels.

13. Falcke: 19; D. Maisels: 12.

14. SM/B2/9: Marks–L. Marks 12.5.94; SM/B2/12: Marks–L. and M. Marks 15.11.96, 3.1.97; SM/B2/16: Marks–M. Marks 13.5.99; D. Maisels: 12.

15. Krut: 108; SM/B2/11: Marks–Prof. Preece 16.6.95.
16. SM/B2/17: Marks–B. Marks 15.9.00.
17. SM/B2/10: Marks–M. Berkowitz 5.5.94; SM/B2/17: Marks–B. Marks 15.9.00.
18. SM/B2/9: Marks–L. Marks 16.7.94.
19. SM/B2/12: Marks–J. Lewis 21.9.95.
20. SM/B2/15: Marks–M. Berkowitz 29.1.98.
21. SM/B2/15: Marks–M. Berkowitz 5.9.97.
22. SM/B2/16: Marks–L. Marks 11.12.98; SM/B2/17: Marks–L. Marks 25.4.01, Marks–C. Sankey 4.6.01. For Karl Marx's interest in 'discoveries in the field of electrical science', see Friedrich Engels's eulogy at Marx's funeral, reproduced in H. Peterson, *A Treasury of the World's Great Speeches*, New York, 1954.
23. SM/B2/16: Marks–L. Marks 11.12.98.
24. SM/B2/16: Marks–M. Berkowitz 11.12.98.
25. SM/B2/16: Marks–M. Berkowitz 9.4.99, 4.6.99, Marks–L. Marks 30.7.99; SM/A2: School reports; information from N. Maisels.

VII. Between the Lines
1. SM/B2/12: Marks–Lewis 12.10.96; SM/B5: J. Sivewright–Marks 18.8.97; SM/B2/15: Marks–Lewis and Marks 13.9.97; SM/B2/16 Marks–Lewis 9.4.99; SM/F2: ledger 1896–9.
2. SM/B2/15: Marks–J. Lewis 5.6.97; SM/B2/17: Marks–P. Levy 11.4.01.
3. SM/B2/16: Marks–J. Jansen and Company 16.4.99.
4. SM/B5: Lewis–Marks 13.6.99; SM/B3: Lewis–Marks 16.6.99; SM/B2/16: Marks–Lewis 18.6.99.
5. SM/B5: Lewis–Marks 11.7.99; SM/B3: Lewis–Marks 14.7.99.
6. SM/B2/16: Marks–A. Fischer 23.6.99.
7. SM/B2/16: Marks–L. L. Michell 24.6.99.
8. SM/B2/16: Marks–Lewis 25.6.99.
9. SM/B2/16: Marks–Lewis 9.7.99; Hofmeyr: 543.
10. Marais: 303–5.
11. SM/B2/16: Marks–S. Lewis 5.8.99.
12. SM/B2/16: Marks–Lewis 30.7.99, 5.8.99.
13. SM/B2/16: Marks–Lewis 5.8.99; Mouton: 214–15
14. SM/B2/16: Marks–Lewis 5.8.99, 20.8.99, 10.9.99, 17.9.99; Marais: 315–6.
15. SM/B2/16: Marks–Lewis 20.8.99, 27.8.99; SM/B3: Lewis–Marks 21.1.99.
16. SM/B2/16: Marks–M. Marks 10.9.99.
17. SM/B2/16: Marks–W. F. Bailey 15.9.99, Marks–L. Marks 15.9.99, Marks–S. Lewis 24.9.99.
18. SM/B2/16: Marks–W. G. Soper 3.9.99, Marks–Lewis 17.9.99, 24.9.99; SM/E1: Acting-Commandant-General–Marks n.d.; TA, R12918/99: Lewis and Marks–Commandant-General 12.9.99; TA, CR6935/99: J. P. H. Faure–Commandant-General 21.9.99.
19. SM/B2/16: Marks–Lewis 17.9.99; SM/B3: Draft letter to Kruger 21.9.99.
20. SM/B2/16: Marks–J. Sivewright 24.9.99, Marks–P. Levy 13.8.99, Marks–M. Marks 24.9.99, Marks–B. Marks 5.10.99.
21. SM/B2/16: Marks–J. Sivewright 30.9.99.
22. SM/B2/16: Marks–P. Levy 19.10.99.
23. SM/B5: Secretary, Medical Commission–Marks 21.2.00, 10.4.00; Theron: 38-9, 43.
24. SM/B5: Corporal Todd–[?], c/o Lewis and Marks, Pretoria 2.1.00, W. Vaughan–Marks 21.3.00.
25. Theron: 215; SM/B2/16: Marks–P. Levy 9.12.99, Marks–M. Marks 19.3.00.
26. SM/B2/16: Marks–J. Sivewright 12.5.00, Marks–P. Levy 9.12.99.

27. SM/B2/16: Marks–A. Hird, 19.10.99, Marks–L. Marks 24.1.00, 2.2.00, Marks–M. Marks 24.1.00, 17.2.00, 19.3.00.

28. SM/B2/16: Marks–M. Marks 24.1.00, 28.4.00.

29. SM/B2/16: Marks–L. Marks 2.2.00, 17.2.00, 6.4.00, Marks–L. and M. Marks 24.3.00.

30. SBA, GMO 3/1/35: Standard Bank, Cape Town–Standard Bank, London 13.12.99, 27.12.99.

31. Theron: 34, 249; TA, R2719X/99, Landdrost, Pretoria–State Secretary 19.12.99; SM/B5: H. Smits–Lewis and Marks 4.4.00, Marks–State Secretary n.d.

32. SM/B2/17: H. Crawford–S. Evans 12.3.01, 13.3.01, Marks–S. Evans 11.3.01, Statement by W. E. Hollard 13.3.01; Cammack: 377–8, 426–7; Kruger: 255.

33. Van der Merwe: 59–60; Grundlingh: 58–9.

34. Girouard: 39.

35. Leigh: 45.

36. SM/B2/17: Marks–P. Grobler 27.2.01, Marks–A. D.W. Wolmarans 11.4.01; TA, MGP 979/01: Marks–Military Governor, Pretoria 13.2.01; TA, R8287/00: Lewis and Marks–Proviand Commissie der Z.A.R. 16.5.00.

37. Theron: 264–6; Hancock, I: 538; Amery, IV: 274–5; Du Preez: 90–1; SM/E1: Marks–L. Botha 31.10.00.

38. SM/B2/18: Marks–Lewis 5.6.02.

39. SM/B2/17: Marks–P. Levy 17.10.00; Hancock, I: 560–1.

40. SM/B2/16: Marks–Lewis 17.7.00, Marks–L. Marks 6.9.00; SM/B2/17: Marks–Lewis 1.2.01; TA, CJC 614/1413: Marks–Compensation Officer 5.10.00, Sworn affidavits S. Marks, 6.11.00 and 21.8.01.

41. TA, CJC 614/1413: J. P. H. Faure–Military Governor, Pretoria 24.7.00.

42. SM/B2/17: Marks–Lewis 20.9.00.

43. SM/B3: Lewis–Marks 8.6.00; SM/B2/17: Marks–L. Marks 19.10.00, Marks–P. Levy 17.10.00.

44. SM/B2/17: Marks–G. Marks 26.9.00, Marks–B. Marks 4.12.00; SM/B4.4: Lewis and Marks, Johannesburg–Lewis and Marks, Pretoria 16.8.00; May: 10–1.

45. SM/B2/17: Marks–G. Marks 26.9.00, 11.12.00, Marks–M. Marks 20.11.00, Marks–A. Hird 19.12.00.

46. SM/B2/16: Marks–L. Marks 6.9.00, Marks–Lewis 17.7.00; SM/B2/17: Marks–B. Marks 11.12.00.

47. Batts: 193–4, 198; SM/B4.4: J. N. de Jongh–Lewis and Marks, Pretoria 26.7.00, 10.8.00, Lewis and Marks, Johannesburg–Lewis and Marks, Pretoria 7.8.00; SM/B2/33: Marks–Dr Landau 11.12.10.

48. SM/B5: J. G. Maxwell–Marks 29.9.00; Pakenham: 448.

49. SM/B2/17: Marks–Countess of Airlie 20.3.01, Marks–G. Arthur 16.5.01.

50. SM/B2/17: Marks–Lord Roberts 2.10.00.

51. SM/E1: Marks–J. H. de la Rey 6.10.00.

52. SM/E1: Marks–L. Botha 31.10.00.

53. SM/E1: H. S. Bosman–E. Rooth 3.11.00, Bosman–Marks, Rooth, J. S. Smit, C. J. Joubert and others 5.11.00; TA, M681, Roberts papers: J. G. Maxwell–Lord Roberts 7.11.00.

54. TA, M681, Roberts papers: A. H. Malan–Marks 10.11.00; May: 123.

55. SM/B2/17: Marks–A. Malan 22.11.00.

56. SM/B3: Lewis–Marks 24.8.00; SM/B2/16: Marks–L. Marks 13.9.00; SM/B2/17: Marks–J. Lewis 17.10.00, Marks–M. Berkowitz 17.10.00, Marks–B. Marks 11.12.00, 13.12.00, 18.12.00, Marks–L. Marks 18.12.00, 16.1.01, Marks–B.Lewis 9.1.01.

57. SM/B2/17: Marks–J. Lewis 27.12.00.

58. SM/B2/18: Marks–L. Marks 17.7.01, 12.4.02, Marks–Lewis 22.3.02;
SM/B2/17: Marks–G. Arthur 22.3.01, Marks–B. Marks 13.2.01, Marks–Lewis
8.2.01, 18.4.01; SM/E3: Pass 6.9.00; Falcke: 16; Spies: 83.
59. SM/B2/17: Marks–Lewis 8.2.01.
60. SM/B2/17: Marks–Lewis 19.12.00.
61. SM/B2/17: Marks–Lewis 19.12.00.
62. SM/B2/17: Marks–J. Marks 26.9.00, Marks–D. Marks 26.9.00, Marks–B.
Marks 4.6.01, 26.6.01, Marks–T. Marks 17.4.01; SM/B2/18: Marks–B. Marks 7.8.01,
Marks–A. Hird 23.7.01.
63. SM/B2/17: Marks–G. Marks 16.1.01, Marks–J. Marks 23.1.01, Marks–L.
Marks 23.1.01, Marks–A. Hird 29.3.01; TA, MGP 2366A/01: Civil Commissioner,
Pretoria–Military Governor, Pretoria 27.2.01, Military Governor, Pretoria–Marks
4.3.01.
64. SM/B2/17: Marks–Lewis 8.2.01, Marks–H. Lewis 22.2.01, Marks–M. Marks
11.12.00, Marks–G. Marks 20.3.01, Marks–B. Marks 21.3.01; SM/B5: J. G.
Maxwell–Marks 11.6.01; Arthur: 84-7, 93; Spies: 65, 74–5.
65. TA, MGP 1368A/01: ADC Vereeniging–Military Governor, Pretoria 29.1.01;
TA, MGP 979A/01: DC Heidelberg–Military Governor, Pretoria 8.2.01; TA, MGP
2660/01: A. R. Hoskins–Commissioner of Police 6.3.01.
66. SM/B2/17: Marks–H. Lewis 9.1.01; SM/B5: Kitchener–Marks n.d.;
Breytenbach: 26–7.
67. TA, MGP 979/01: Marks–Military Governor, Pretoria 13.2.01.
68. TA, MGP 2012/00: Marks–Military Governor, Pretoria 13.8.00.
69. TA, IOMG 925A/01: Marks–Major Hoskins 19.2.01; TA, MGP 973A/01:
Assistant to Military Governor, Pretoria–Marks 6.2.01; SM/B2/17: Marks–P. Grobler
4.1.01, 27.2.01, Marks–Major Hoskins 28.2.01, A. D. W. Wolmarans–Marks
11.1.01, 18.1.01, Marks–A. D. W. Wolmarans 13.2.01, 20.2.01, 5.6.01; SM/B2/18:
Marks–Mrs Grobler 29.8.01.
70. SM/B2/17: Marks–P. Grobler 27.2.01, Marks–B. Marks 27.2.01, Marks–
W. Wilson 3.4.01; TA, CJC 614/1413: Sworn affidavit, S. Marks 28.5.01.
71. SM/B2/17: Marks–B. Marks 7.3.01, 29.5.01, Marks–J. Marks 3.4.01.
72. TA, MGP 1368A/01: Captain Bentinck–Military Governor, Pretoria 29.1.01;
TA, MGP 979/01: Marks–Military Governor, Pretoria 13.2.01.
73. SM/B2/17: Marks–A. D. W. Wolmarans 11.4.01; TA, MGP 3788B/01: Lewis
and Marks–Military Governor, Pretoria 12.4.01; TA, CJC 2428: Affidavits
T. E. Ferreira and J. Torrance July 1901.
74. SM/B2/18: Marks–L. Marks 3.10.01; Amery, VI: 22.
75. TA, MGP 16624B/01: H. Crawford–Military Governor, Pretoria 10.12.01,
11.12.01, Deposition by D. J. Haumann; SM/B2/18: Marks–Lewis 29.1.02; TA,
PMO 2924/02: F. R. de Bertodano–R. M. Poore 11.12.01, Depositions by Geelbooi,
Jack and George Falcke; TA, MGP 1099A/02: J. G. Maxwell–Provost Marshal
20.12.01.
76. SM/B2/18: Marks–L. Marks 9.12.01, Marks–J. Lewis 6.1.02, Marks–J. Marks
16.1.02.
77. SM/B2/18: Marks–Lewis 7.2.02, 22.2.02; SM/B3: L. Marks–Lewis 1.3.02.
78. SM/B2/18: Marks–Lewis 26.3.02, 12.4.02, Marks–S. Lewis 27.3.02; SM/B3:
L. Marks–Lewis 10.3.02, Lewis–Marks 4.4.02; SM/B5: J. Murray–L. Marks January
1903[?].
79. SM/E1: Marks–Lewis 17.4.02.
80. SM/B2/18: Marks–Lewis 9.5.02; SM/E1: Marks–Lewis 21.5.02.
81. SM/E1: Marks–Lewis 21.5.02.
82. See Kestell, 1976 and Kestell and Van Velden for accounts of the peace
conference at Vereeniging.

83. SM/B2/18: Marks–Lewis 13.6.02, 21.6.02.

VIII. Keeping the Peace
1. SM/B2/18: Marks–J. Marks 6.6.02, Marks–Lewis 5.6.02.
2. SM/B2/18: Marks–J. Marks 6.6.02, Marks–Lewis 6.6.02, 13.6.02.
3. SM/B2/18: Marks–Lewis 21.6.02.
4. SM/B2/18: Marks–L. Marks 11.7.02.
5. SM/B2/18: Marks–L. Marks 21.6.02, Marks–Lewis 5.7.02; SM/G2.3: ledger 1901–9.
6. FitzPatrick: 214–16.
7. SM/B2/18: Marks–Lewis 20.7.02.
8. SM/B2/18: Marks–Lewis 22.7.02.
9. SM/B2/18: Marks–Lewis 5.6.02.
10. SM/B2/18: Marks–Lewis 21.6.92, 24.7.02, 5.7.02, Marks–G. Marks 18.7.02, 27.7.02, Marks–J. N. de Jongh 20.7.02, J. N. de Jongh–Marks 18.7.02.
11. SM/B2/18: Marks–Lewis 20.7.02, 22.7.02, 24.7.02, 12.9.02; SM/B3: Lewis–J. H. de la Rey 15.8.02, Lewis–Marks 19.9.02.
12. SM/B2/18: Marks–Lewis 9.5.02.
13. SM/B2/18: Marks–W. F. Bailey 7.8.02.
14. SM/B5: J. Chamberlain–Wrench 25.9.02.
15. SM/B2/20: Marks–H. G. Reid 4.2.05; SM/B2/18: Marks–Lewis 9.5.02; SM/B2/21: Marks–Col. H. Hamilton 10.3.05.
16. Watts: 50–1; UCT, BC831, B3: Milner–Lady Chaplin n.d.
17. SM/B2/18: Marks–W. F. Bailey 7.8.02; SM/B2/20: Marks–J. Sivewright 18.6.04.
18. SM/B2/18: Marks–Lewis 16.8.02.
19. SM/B2/20: Marks–Lewis 8.10.04.
20. SM/B2/34: Marks–Lewis 21.5.10.
21. SM/B2/20: Marks–Lewis 13.12.03; SM/B2/25: Marks–Lewis 27.8.06, 17.11.06.
22. SM/B2/18: Marks–W. F. Bailey 29.12.02; SM/B5: Marks–J. H. de la Rey 22.1.03; SM/B2/18: Marks–W. F. Bailey 29.12.02.
23. SM/B2/21: Marks–J. H. de la Rey 6.5.04; SM/B5: Marks–J. H. de la Rey 21.8.05.
24. SM/B2/21: Marks–Maj. Deane 10.3.05, Marks–B. Cohen 31.3.05.
25. Denoon: 216; SM/B2/17: Marks–Lewis 20.9.00.
26. SM/B2/21: Marks–Col. H. Hamilton 10.3.05.
27. SM/B2/21: Marks–Col. H. Hamilton 1.7.05.
28. SM/B2/21: Marks–J. G. Torrance 8.8.05; Leslie: 187.
29. SM/B5: Marks–J. H. de la Rey 21.8.05, P. H. Kerr–Marks 13.12.05, A. C. MacDonald–P. Duncan 12.12.05, P. Duncan–Selborne 13.12.05, Selborne–Marks 15.12.05.
30. SM/B5: Marks–J. H. de la Rey 21.8.05.
31. SM/B5: Selborne–Marks 22.8.05.
32. SM/B5: Marks–J. H. de la Rey 3.8.05, 21.8.05, J. H. de la Rey–Marks 12.8.05, 30.8.05.
33. SM/B5: Selborne–Marks 27.12.05, 24.1.06, 5.3.06, 9.11.06, 30.11.06, Lord Howick–Marks 11.1.06; SM/B2/24: Marks–Selborne 15.3.06.
34. SM/B5: Selborne–Marks 30.11.06, 6.12.06, 16.5.07; SM/B2/27: Marks–Selborne 4.12.06.
35. SM/B2/21: Lewis and Marks–Governor, Transvaal and Orange River Colony 16.11.05; SM/B5: Selborne–Marks 12.12.05, 14.6.06, 18.12.06, 31.1.07, 1.3.07, 8.3.07; SM/B3: Lewis–Marks 8.12.06; SM/B2/25: Marks–Lewis 8.11.06, 22.11.06,

23.11.06, 3.1.07.

36. SM/B2/20: Marks–H. Hamilton 8.2.06, Marks–H. D. Lewis 19.11.04; SM/B2/21: Marks–E. Marks 21.10.05, Marks–Selborne 22.12.05; SM/B2/24: Marks–Selborne 30.12.05, 27.2.06; SM/B5: Selborne–Marks 16.5.06, Marks– E. Cameron 19.3.08.

37. SM/B2/29: Marks–B. F. Cabral 24.8.07, 6.12.07, 3.2.08; SM/B5: D. O. Malcolm–Marks 6.8.07, Selborne–Marks 20.8.07, B. Marks–Marks 15.8.07, 16.8.07; SAJC 16.8.07; Rosenthal ms.: 156–7.

38. SM/B2/25: Marks–J. Sivewright 8.10.06, 12.11.06. See also SM/B2/20: Marks–Col. H. Hamilton 8.2.06.

39. SM/B2/21: Marks–Col. H. Hamilton 2.9.04.

40. SM/B2/22: Marks–Lewis 21.12.04; SM/B3: Lewis–Marks 21.9.06; SM/B5: H. Webber–Marks 14.12.05.

41. SM/B3: Lewis–Marks 20.7.06, 8.11.06; SM/B2/25: Marks–Lewis 8.11.06.

42. SM/B2/25: Marks–Lewis 13.10.06, 8.11.06; SM/B2/22: Marks–Lewis 23.8.06.

43. SM/B2/25: Marks–Lewis 2.11.06; SM/B3: Lewis–Marks 21.12.06.

44. SM/B3: Marks–Lewis 22.12.06, Lewis–Marks 28.12.06; SM/B2/25: Marks– Lewis 22.12.06.

45. SM/B2/27: Marks–G. Farrar 22.1.07; SM/B2/28: Marks–Lewis 1.2.07; SM/B5: G. Farrar–Marks 18.1.07, J. C. Smuts–Marks 10.2.07.

IX. Reconstructing the Business

1. SM/B2/18: Marks–Lewis 30.8.01, 14.2.02.

2. SM/B3: Lewis–Marks 28.9.01, 31.5.02; SM/B2/18: Marks–Lewis 19.4.02, 12.9.02.

3. SM/B2/17: Marks–Lewis 25.4.01, 17.5.01; SM/B3: Lewis–Marks 18.1.02.

4. SM/B2/17: Marks–Lewis 18.4.01; SM/B2/18: Marks–Lewis 9.5.02, 29.5.02, 12.9.02; Pretoria News 6.4.85.

5. SM/B2/18: Marks–Lewis 12.4.02.

6. SM/B2/18: Marks–Lewis 24.12.01, 18.8.02.

7. UCT, Baker collection: Plans of Marks residence, Muizenberg; SM/B5: B. Marks–Marks 13.6.02.

8. SM/B5: H. Baker–Marks 28.10.02, 30.10.02.

9. SM/B2/20: Marks–Lewis 11.11.03, 19.11.03; Seaside News 30.5.03, cited in Tredgold: 136–7; Cape Argus 3.6.03.

10. SM/B2/20: Marks–Lewis 24.12.03, 25.2.04; SM/B3: Lewis–Marks 6.2.04, 11.3.04; African World Annual, 1903: 25.

11. SM/B2/22: Marks–Lewis 7.4.04; SM/B3: Lewis–Marks 18.3.04; AE: Prospectus of the African and European Investment Company, 1904.

12. SM/B3: Lewis–Marks 11.5.01.

13. SM/B2/18: Marks–W. F. Bailey 23.8.02.

14. SM/B5: J. Chamberlain–Wrench 25.9.02.

15. DSAB I: 872; SC9–1912, Select Committee on Scrap Iron Agreement: 121; TA, IOP 39: Burns-Bigg notebook; SM/B2/12: Marks–Lewis 23.11.95; SM/B2/20: Marks–Lewis 28.12.03; SM/B3: Lewis–Marks 6.2.04, A. de Vere Hunt–L. Weinthal 27.2.04, L. Weinthal–Lewis 29.2.04.

16. SM/B2/20: Marks–Lewis 12.3.04; SM/B2/21: Marks–T. W. Smartt 15.4.04, Marks–Messrs Baker and Massey 30.6.04; Marks–Commissioner of Crown Lands and Public Works 11.3.05; SM/B2/22: T. W. Smartt–Marks 13.5.04.

17. SM/B5: W. M. Martin–Marks 6.7.07, J. Jansen–Marks 22.2.06, 2.3.06; SM/B2/22: J. Langermann–Marks 22.3.04.

18. SM/B2/17: Marks–Lewis 2.5.01; Transvaal Mines Department, Annual Report

of Government Mining Engineer 1906/7, facing p. 16; Watts: 50.

19. *African World Annual*, 1903: 74.

20. SM/B2/18: Marks–Lewis 12.9.02; *African World Annual*, 1916: 273.

21. SM/B2/22: Marks–Lewis 16.3.05, 28.6.06.

22. SM/B2/22: Marks–Lewis 16.3.05, 30.3.05, 7.4.05.

23. SM/B2/18: Marks–Lewis 7.8.01; SM/B2/22: Marks–Lewis 5.5.04, 28.6.06, 4.8.04; SM/B2/25: Marks–Lewis 26.10.06, 1.11.06; SM/B2/28: Marks–Lewis 9.1.08, 2.4.08; SM/B3: Lewis–Marks 26.10.06.

24. SM/B3: Lewis–Marks 10.8.01, 20.9.01, 3.10.01; SM/B2/18: Marks–Lewis 5.9.01; SBA, GMO 3/2/1/2: Standard Bank, Cape Town–Standard Bank, London 11.2.02; VE: 20.9.04, 30.9.04, 19.12.05, 10.12.07; SM/B2/22: Marks–Lewis 19.10.04, 17.11.04; SM/B2/28: Marks–Lewis 16.8.07.

25. VE: 18.10.04, 6.12.04, 7.2.05, 21.2.05, 22.5.06, 5.6.06; SM/B2/22: Marks–Lewis 20.10.04, 17.11.04; SM/B2/20: Marks–Lewis 3.12.04.

26. SM/B2/29: Marks–Lewis 21.10.07, 11.1.08.

27. BRA, HE 88: H. Eckstein and Co.–Wernher Beit 14.11.04, 24.12.04; BRA, HE 89: H. Eckstein and Co.–Wernher Beit 19.2.06; Anglo American, TCC minute book: 12.12.05, 7.4.08, 7.12.09; JCI, T1: African and European–JCI 5.2.07.

28. Cd. 1897, Transvaal Labour Commission: evidence E. Hopper; SM/B2/20: Report on Lourenço Marques Wharf Company by H. F. Strange and S. Marks 16.1.04.

29. SM/B2/20: Report on Lourenço Marques Wharf Company by H. F. Strange and S. Marks 16.1.04; SBA, INSP 1/1/241: Inspection report, Standard Bank, Lourenço Marques 21.2.05; *African World Annual*, 1905: 97–8; UG 33–1921, Report of the Coal Commission: 5; SM/B2/21: Marks–B. F. Cabral 17.2.05; SM/B2/20: Marks–B. F. Cabral 15.1.04, 14.4.06.

30. SM/B2/22: Marks–Lewis 7.4.05; SM/B2/29: Marks–J. Sivewright 7.10.07.

31. SM/B2/21: Marks–H. Hamilton 2.9.04.

32. *The Review of Reviews* June 1904.

33. TA, NA 2210/02: F. F. Collins–Controller of Passports, Johannesburg, n.d. and 23.1.03.

34. VE: 26.1.04.

35. SM/B2/21: Marks–J. N. de Jongh 7.7.04.

36. Jeeves: 27, 165; VE: 10.5.04, 31.5.04.

37. VE: 7.1.04.

38. VE: 26.1.04, 2.2.04, 13.2.04, 3.3.04, 26.4.04, 10.5.04, 19.5.04, 5.8.04, 4.10.04; SM/B2/29: Marks–B. F. Cabral 7.12.08.

39. VE: 12.4.04, 19.5.04, 6.12.04, 15.8.05, 22.8.05, 3.11.08, 26.7.10.

40. SM/B2/21: Marks–I. Kok 30.3.04; VE: 19.5.04, 22.11.04, 29.9.08, 29.9.08, 7.10.08, 10.11.08, 17.11.08, 3.5.10.

41. VE: 29.3.04, 5.4.04, 31.8.04, 13.9.04, 20.9.04, 30.9.04, 4.10.04. For a discussion of labour stabilisation in the pre- and post-war mining industry, see Jeeves: 32, 256.

42. VE: 11.10.04. In October 1902 Vereeniging Estates reported: 'The Natives are principally Red Kaffirs or Mxosas from the British Kaffraria in the Cape Colony, Basutos and Baralongs, Makhatlas, etc., from Kimberley and Indwe.' (TA, NA 2210/02: J. N. de Jongh–Secy WNLA 28.10.02.)

43. VE: 11.10.04, 29.11.04, 17.7.06, 11.9.06; SM/B2/24: Marks–B. Cohen 27.3.06; SM/B5: B. Cohen–Marks 5.5.06, 31.5.06; TA, GEN 757/06: Selborne–Elgin 16.7.06; PRO, FO 367/19: J. Baldwin–Selborne 13.7.06.

44. VE: 15.3.04, 26.4.04, 31.5.04, 6.9.04, 13.9.04.

45. SM/B2/24: Marks–I. M. Kok 10.3.06; VE: 13.3.06, 20.3.06.

46. SM/B2/22: Marks–Lewis 12.3.04, 9.6.04, 17.6.04, 14.7.04, 4.8.04; VE: 7.6.04; Mitchell: 81–7.

47. SM/B2/28: Lewis–Marks 17.5.07, Marks–Lewis 29.5.07.

48. SM/B2/16: Marks–Lewis 23.4.99; SM/B2/21: Marks–J. C. Wernher 19.8.05; SM/B2/22: Marks–Lewis 16.3.04, 17.11.04, 25.11.04, 30.3.05, 13.4.05; SM/B3: Lewis–Marks 31.5.02; SM/B5: J. C. Wernher–Marks 15.9.05; BRA, HE 265: H. Eckstein–Wernher Beit 2.2.05, Lewis–F. Eckstein 16.6.04; *Mines of the Transvaal,* 1909–10: 195–200; AE prospectus 1904. Richardson and Van Helten, 1984: 329–36 provides a very useful account of the development of mining on the Far East Rand.

49. Helme: 42–3, 73, 86–9; *Mines of the Transvaal,* 1904: 502; Green: 8; *African World Annual,* 1903, 1906.

50. SM/B2/15: Marks–L. and M. Marks 13.2.98, 13.3.98, 17.4.98, Marks–W. F. Bailey 12.2.98, Marks–Lewis 3.3.98, 12.6.98, 13.7.98, 24.7.98, 7.8.98, 23.10.98; SBA, INSP 1/1/145: Inspection report, Pretoria branch, 21.1.99.

51. SM/B2/15: Marks–Lewis 24.4.98, Marks–W. F. Bailey 23.4.98; SM/B3: Marks–Lewis 1.8.01; *African World* 6.12.02, 20.6.03.

52. AE: 5.7.06, 28.11.06, 1.5.07; SM/B3: Lewis–Marks 27.10.06.

53. SM/B2/25: Marks–Lewis 20.8.06.

54. *African World Annual,* 1906; *Mines of Africa,* 1914–15: 463–5; SM/B2/21: Marks–J. G. Fraser 28.4.04; SM/B2/22: J. G. Fraser–Marks 30.4.04, Lewis–Marks 29.5.06, Marks–Lewis 3.8.06, 12.8.06, 18.8.06, 23.8.06, 30.8.06, 14.9.06; SM/B2/25: Marks–Lewis 16.6.06, 20.8.06; SM/B2/28: Marks–Lewis 28.2.07; SM/B3: Lewis–Marks 9.6.06, 12.7.06, 20.7.06, 25.7.06; AE: 15.11.05, 20.12.05, 5.1.06, 30.5.06, 18.7.06, 22.8.06, 29.8.06.

55. SM/B2/22: Marks–Lewis 12.8.06, 11.10.06; SM/B2/25: Marks–Lewis 26.10.06, 14.1.07; SM/B2/28: Marks–Lewis 6.2.07, 13.5.07; AE: 6.2.07, 15.5.07; Wagner: 324–5.

56. SM/B2/28: Marks–Lewis 13.5.07, 5.6.07.

57. SM/B2/28: Marks–Lewis 24.12.07; SM/B2/29: Marks–Lewis 11.11.07, 2.12.07.

58. Phimister, 1978: 407; Hanson: 38; SM/B3: Annual Report of the South African Supply and Cold Storage Company, 1901; SM/B2/16: Marks–Lewis 18.6.99, 25.6.99; SM/B3: Lewis–Marks 18.10.01, 24.10.01, 18.1.02, 14.3.02, Marks–Lewis 21.11.01.

59. Hanson: 126; Phimister, 1978: 407; SM/B3: Lewis–Marks 17.5.02, 1.8.02; SM/B2/20: Marks–J. Weill 8.1.04, 30.1.04; SM/B2/22: Marks–Lewis 14.7.04, 25.11.04.

60. SM/B2/20: Marks–J.Weill 21.2.04; SM/B2/22: Marks–Lewis 25.11.04; SM/B2/29: Marks–Lewis 29.7.07, Lewis–Marks 2.8.07; SM/B2/32: Marks–Lewis 26.8.09.

61: Rosenthal ms.: 149; *Transvaal Leader* 2.1.08.

62. *Transvaal Leader* 2.1.08; *Vereeniging–Vanderbijlpark News* 1.3.55; VE: 16.6.08, 16.4.10; SM/B2/28: Marks–Lewis 4.5.08; SM/B2/32: Marks–Lewis 23.4.10, 29.4.10, Marks–O. Brandmuller 30.4.10; Rosenthal ms.: 150.

63. For Swaziland, see Crush: 193; BRA, HE 277: H. Eckstein–Wernher Beit 24.8.08. For the Nyassa Company, see JCI letter-book 2: JCI, London–JCI, Johannesburg 1.3.95; SM/B3: Lewis–Marks 28.12.06; Hammond: 215–17; Jeeves: 215, 225–8; Neil-Tomlinson: 109–28; Vail: 397–402. For Bechuanaland and Rhodesia, see AE: 29.11.05, 31.5.06, 20.8.09, 5.1.10, 9.3.10, 10.5.10, 27.12.12; AE: report of directors, 1907. See Phimister, 1976 for a comprehensive account of the reconstruction of the Rhodesian goldmining industry after the South African War.

64. SM/B2/22: Marks–Lewis 17.6.04, 24.7.04; SM/B3: Lewis–Marks 18.3.04.

65. SM/B2/12: Marks–Lewis 8.8.96.

66. SM/B2/22: Marks–Lewis 12.5.04.

67. SM/B2/22: Marks–Lewis 5.7.06, 23.8.06; SM/B3: Lewis–Marks 20.7.06.
68. SM/B2/28: Marks–Lewis 28.11.07; Falcke: 18.
69. SM/B2/20: Marks–Lewis 20.8.04.

X. The Gilded Cage

1. SM/B2/18: Marks–B. Marks 25.7.01.
2. SM/B2/18: Marks–B. Marks 6.6.02.
3. SM/B2/18: Marks–B. Marks 16.8.02, 18.8.02.
4. SM/B2/18: Marks–B. Marks 24.7.02.
5. SM/B2/18: Marks–B. Marks 8.9.02.
6. SM/B2/19: Marks–B. Marks 4.10.02.
7. SM/B2/26: Marks–G. Marks 8.11.06.
8. SM/B2/29: Marks–B. Marks 11.5.08; SM/B2/20: List of jewellery 27.2.06; SM/B5: B. Marks–J. Smith 21.5.07.
9. SM/B2/21: Marks–B. Marks 13.7.04.
10. SBA, INSP 1/1/145: Pretoria branch, Report on obligants, 16.10.97.
11. SM/B2/16: Marks–P. Levy 3.4.99; SM/B2/19: Marks–L. Marks 15.11.02; SM/B2/9: Marks–J. Rabinowitz 1.3.94, Marks–M. Kennedy 12.6.94; SM/B2/13: Marks–M. Marks 15.8.96, Marks–C. A. de R. Labistour 4.12.96; TA, A681(1): J. P. H. Faure–G. Challoner 14.11.96; SM/B2/11: B. Marks–Klegg 20.5.95.
12. SM/B2/17: Marks–W. F. Bailey 30.5.01; SM/B2/18: Marks–W. F. Bailey 31.7.01.
13. SM/B2/18: Marks–W. F. Bailey 2.8.02.
14. SM/B2/18: Marks–W. F. Bailey 2.8.02, Marks–B. Marks 21.8.02; Van Onselen, 1982, II: 11.
15. SM/B2/18: Marks–B. Marks 21.8.02.
16. SM/B2/23: Marks–B. Marks 31.3.06.
17. SM/B5: B. Marks–Marks 29.4.06.
18. SM/B2/24: Marks–B. Marks 28.6.06.
19. SM/B2/23: Marks–B. Marks 8.6.06.
20. SM/B5: B. Marks–Marks 13.7.06.
21. SM/B2/26: Marks–B. Marks 4.8.06.
22. SM/A4: Statement, B. Marks 31.1.98; SM/B2/19: Marks–G. Marks 24.10.02.
23. TA, CEN497, E144: B. Marks–Acting Government Entomologist 13.2.09; SM/B2/8: List of cuttings, July 1891; information from D. Maisels.
24. D. Maisels: 43; SM/B2/17: Marks–A. Hird 31.1.01, Marks–L. Marks 6.2.01, Marks–G. Marks 7.3.01, Marks–J. Marks 17.4.01, Marks–G. Marks 8.5.01; SM/B2/18: Marks–P. Levy 10.10.01; SM/B5: J. Grant–Marks 15.1.09; SM/B2/24: Marks–J. Ayling 23.2.06.
25. SM/B2/23: 11.12.05; information from D. Maisels; D. Maisels: 42; SM/B5: J. Kirkness–Marks 17.1.08, Secretary, Pretoria Bowling Club–Marks n.d.
26. TA, G2040/04: A. C. Macdonald–B. Marks 21.10.04; TA, CEN497, E144: Acting Entomologist–B. Marks 8.3.07; SM/B5: G. Marks–B. Marks 10.5.07; D. Maisels: 23–4.
27. SM/B2/21: Marks–E. Marks 24.8.05; SM/B2/25: Marks–Lewis 14.1.07; SM/B2/32: Marks–Lewis 29.10.09.
28. SM/B2/32: Marks–Lewis 29.10.09.
29. SM/B5: G. Marks–B. Marks n.d.; H. Perkin, *Origins of Modern English Society*, cited in Bradlow: 59; Krut: 193, 222–4.
30. SM/B2/21: Marks–Messrs. Mackintosh and Moffat 26.4.05; SM/B2/24: Marks–O. Brandmuller 4.1.06, G. Falcke–Mrs Langermann 20.3.06.
31. *SAJC* 12.1.12, 15.3.12, 24.5.12, 31.5.12, 25.10.12; Krut: 215.

32. SM/B2/22: Marks–Lewis 23.9.04.
33. D. Maisels: 3.
34. SM/B2/19: Marks–G. Marks 11.2.05; SM/B2/26: Marks–G. Marks 1.3.07.
35. SM/B2/17: Marks–B. Marks 3.1.01; SM/B2/18: Marks–G. Marks 31.7.01.
36. SM/B5: J. C. Metcalfe–B. Marks 12.1.04.
37. SM/B2/19: Marks–G. Marks 16.8.02.
38. SM/B2/19: Marks–G. Marks 13.8.02.
39. SM/B2/19: Marks–G. Marks 3.12.04.
40. SM/B2/19: Marks–G. Marks 11.2.05.
41. SM/B2/21: Marks–E. Marks 4.11.05; SM/B2/26: Marks–M. Levy 6.12.06, Marks–G. Marks 1.3.07, 21.3.07, 15.8.07.
42. Information from N. Maisels.
43. Information from D. Maisels; Falcke: 18; Zwartkoppies photographic collection: photograph of gravestone of John Murray; SM/B2/12: Marks–L. and M. Marks 22.11.96, 24.1.97; SM/B2/15: Marks–H. Lewis 13.6.97; SM/B2/17: Marks–G. Marks 20.11.00; SM/B2/13: Marks–J. Murray 13.1.97; SM/B5: G. Armour–Marks 26.1.06; SBA, INSP 1/1/143: Inspection report, Pretoria branch, 1.1.86.
44. May: 2–3, 10–11; Batts: 24; Falcke: 18; SBA, INSP 1/1/145: Pretoria branch, Liabilities of obligants, 28.2.93, 21.1.99; SM/B2/18: Marks–Lewis 31.5.02; SM/B5: J. A. Kay–Marks 1.10.05, 30.12.09.
45. SM/B2/20: Marks–Mrs Langerman 20.11.04.
46. SM/B2/29: Marks–Lewis 27.9.07, 4.11.07, 6.12.07, 11.1.08, 25.5.08, 29.5.08, Marks–G. A. Hay 13.6.08; SM/B2/28: Marks–Lewis 21.5.08, J. N. de Jongh–Lewis and Marks, London 8.6.08; Falcke: 22.

XI. Sammy Marks the Jew

1. *The Jewish Directory*, 1874: 83; SM/B5: Adler Brothers–Marks 30.7.85; SM/B2/12: Marks–J. Sivewright 6.12.96; SM/B2/13: Marks–Cape Canning Co. 17.11.96; SM/F8: Household receipts.
2. Kokosolakis: 31; SM/B2/12: Marks–L. and M. Marks 6.12.96, 20.12.96; SM/B2/22: Marks–L. Marks 23.12.05; Dolly Maisels: 18. See Endelman, 1985 and 1990 for the diluted orthodoxy of the Jewish elite in Victorian England.
3. Dolly Maisels: 8; *SAJC* 3.2.11; PHC: 7.4.07; SM/B2/15: Marks–L. and M. Marks 3.10.97, Marks–P. Levy 23.10.97; SM/B2/9: Marks–S. L. Heymann 26.12.93; SM/B2/15: Marks–M. Berkowitz 14.8.98. For Marks's non-observance of the Sabbath, see, for example, letterbook SM/B2/5; numerous business letters were dictated on 16.6.83, a Saturday.
4. Dolly Maisels: 8; SM/B2/29: Marks–B. F. Cabral 20.12.07; SM/B2/16: Marks–L. Marks 11.12.98; SM/B2/21: Marks–S. A. Marks 2.6.05. See also Marks's remarks at a general meeting of the Pretoria Hebrew Congregation, reported in *SAJC* 12.4.07.
5. SM/B2/16: Marks–P. Levy 2.7.99; SM/B2/24: Marks–I. H. Guinsberg 18.7.06.
6. N. Maisels: 2; SM/B5: J. R. Metcalfe–G. Marks 12.4.05, B. Marks–Marks 10.3.06, 1.6.06, 8.6.06, 15.6.06, G. Marks–Marks 8.7.06; SM/B2/22: Marks–H. Lewis 13.5.05; SM/B2/21: Marks–E. Marks 4.11.05, Marks–S. Lewis 9.6.05. See Endelman, 1985: 507–8 for contemporary Jewish attitudes to conversion and intermarriage.
7. SM/B5: Girlie Marks–Marks 8.7.06.
8. TA, MHG 43182: Marks wills and codicils.
9. SM/B2/33: Marks–Dr Landau 28.11.10.
10. SM/B2/33: Marks–Dr Landau 11.12.10.

11. Maisels: 2.

12. Abrahams: 34; UCT, Cape Town Hebrew Congregation minutes: 7.3.20; SM/B2/6: Marks–J. Guttmann 20.2.86; *SAJC* 27.11.08; SM/B2/12: Marks–E. Mendelssohn 17.12.91; SM/B2/8: Marks–Secretary, Johannesburg Hebrew Congregation 9.9.93.

13. [London] *Jewish Chronicle* 5.9.90; Simonowitz: 39; [Pretoria] *Press* 17.8.98; Katz: 43–9.

14. PHC: 21.5.99.

15. *SAJC* 7.2.02; PHC: 15.6.02; SM/B2/18: Marks–A. Levy 21.6.02.

16. [London] *Jewish Chronicle* 21.11.02, 24.4.03; *SAJC* 10.4.03; PHC: 3.11.02, 15.2.03, 7.4.07, 9.4.07, 14.4.07, 15.4.07, 26.1.08; SM/B2/18: Marks–Lewis 23.8.02; SM/B2/19: Marks–L. Marks 18.2.05, M. Rosenberg–Dr Adler 15.5.05; SM/B2/21: Marks–O. Brandmuller 26.7.05; SM/B2/23: Marks–T. Marks 23.12.05; *SAJC* 26.4.07, 3.5.07; *Pretoria News* 31.5.07; SM/B2/20: Marks–[?] 15.7.05; Archives of the Chief Rabbinate, London: M. Rosenberg–Dr Adler 29.1.05. My thanks to John Simon for the last reference.

17. [Pretoria] *Press* 17.8.98; PHC: 16.11.02, 18.2.03, 22.5.04, 19.2.05, 1.3.05, 30.7.05, 6.8.05, 7.1.06, 21.1.06, 18.3.06, 21.10.06; SM/B5: E. Freedman–Marks 19.3.06.

18. PHC: 15.1.05, 5.11.05, 7.1.06, 18.3.06, 3.4.07, 25.10.08; SM/B5: E. Freedman–Marks 19.3.06.

19. PHC: 25.7.09, 17.10.09; SM/B5: Marks–Pretoria Hebrew Congregation 9.9.09, Pretoria Hebrew Congregation–Marks 24.8.10.

20. Zwartkoppies library, SM1625: Souvenir programme, Consecration of synagogue, 23.8.14; Norwich: 153. See Mendelsohn, 1991 for a discussion of the Kruger incident. The Great Synagogue in Wolmarans Street remains today the Marks family synagogue. In August 1919, just six months before Sammy Marks died, his younger daughter Dolly married Israel Maisels under its grand dome. Dolly, aged 23, was the only child who married during her father's lifetime. Her older son, Neill Maisels, Sammy Marks's first grandchild, still regularly occupies his grandfather's seat in the synagogue. His two sons, Bruce and Andrew, Sammy Marks's great-grandchildren, had their *bar mitzvahs* at the Great Synagogue and subsequently married there too. Another of Sammy's grandsons, David Maisels, and a great-grandson, David Katzen, also celebrated their *bar mitzvahs* at the 'Great'.

21. SM/B2/18: Marks–Secretary, Jewish Association for the Protection of Girls and Women 7.1.02.

22. SM/B2/21: Marks–G. Trapowski 13.12.04; SM/F1.4: Cashbook 1903–6, 67; SM/B2/26: Marks–M. Levy 6.12.06; Dolly Marks: 23.

23. First Annual Report of the Jewish Board of Deputies for the Transvaal and Natal, 1904; *SAJC* August 1903; SM/B5: Chief Secretary for Permits–Marks 19.5.04; UCT, Smuts Papers, 10, 1912, 38: Marks–P. Grobler 27.2.12.

24. SM/B2/7: Marks–H. Crawford 19.11.92.

25. SM/B2/10: Marks–Lewis 11.11.94.

26. SM/B2/15: Marks–Lewis 7.2.97.

27. Zborowski and Herzog: 298; Shimoni: 8; Falcke: 20–1; SM/B2/7: Marks–H. Crawford 19.11.92; SM/B2/10: Marks–Lewis 11.11.94; SM/B2/12: Marks–Lewis 1.9.95; SM/B2/15: Marks–Lewis 7.2.97; SM/B2/18: Marks–Lewis 24.10.01; SM/B2/20: Marks–S. L. Heymann 7.5.04; SM/B2/29: Marks–Lewis 22.2.08, 28.3.08; SM/B5: S. Good–Marks 28.1.08, S. L. Heymann–Marks 5.3.08.

28. Zborowski and Herzog: 201, 304–5.

29. SM/B2/3: Marks–J. Marks 10.7.82, 24.7.82.

30. SM/B2/7: Marks–T. R. Price 5.3.94; SM/B2/13: Marks–T. J. O'Reilly 25.9.96;

SM/B2/21: Marks–A. Levy 5.12.05; SM/B5: F. Levy–Marks 13.11.07; A. Levy–
Marks 14.11.07.

31. SM/B2/20: Marks–M. Abromovitz 16.11.03.

32. SM/B2/8: Marks–F. Levy 28.12.92; SM/B2/11: Marks–F. Levy 6.11.95;
SM/B2/12: Marks–F. Levy 13.9.95; SM/B5: F. Levy–Marks 13.3.06.

33. SM/B2/8: Marks–J. G. Fraser 5.7.93; SM/B2/9: Marks–E. Marks 15.5.94,
Marks–T. Guttmann 15.7.94; SM/B2/12: Marks–H. Levy 1.9.95, Marks–
W. H. Preece 21.11.96; SM/B2/16: Marks–H. E. V. Pickstone 4.6.99; SM/B5:
H. Levy–Marks 23.10.05, 3.3.06, Marks–L. Levy 5.10.07.

34. SM/B2/12: Marks–A. Hirsch 20.12.96; SM/B2/15: Marks–A. Hirsch 13.5.97,
7.8.97, Marks–P. Levy 25.4.97; SM/B2/16: Marks–P. Levy 7.5.99, Marks–A. Hirsch
21.7.99; SM/B2/18: Marks–P. Levy 22.8.01.

35. SM/B2/18: Marks–J. Sivewright 7.1.01, Marks–P. Levy 5.7.02.

36. SM/B2/7: Marks–A. Hirsch 3.12.92, Marks–G. Falcke 3.12.92; SM/B2/10:
Marks–G. Falcke 20.5.94; SM/B2/18: Marks–Lewis 26.4.02; SM/B2/19: Marks–
L. Marks 18.2.05; SM/B3: Lewis–Marks 17.5.02; SM/B5: P. Bender–Marks 14.12.86,
A. Hirsch–Marks 3.12.91, 7.6.92, Assistant Manager, Standard Bank,
Johannesburg–Marks 5.1.06, B. Marks–Marks 29.4.06; Falcke: 17; Maisels: 3.

37. SM/B2/15: Marks–B. Patlanski 13.3.97; Leigh: 280–1; VE: 18.12.14; SM/B5:
Falcke Bros.–Marks 29.7.06, 25.5.07; Rosenthal ms.: 156.

38. SM/B2/20: Marks–F. Levy 11.2.05.

39. SM/B2/25: Marks–J. Sivewright 1.11.06.

40. SM/B2/26: Marks–G. Marks 7.1.07.

41. SM/B5: C. C. Henkel–Private Secretary, Marks 2.11.07; SM/B2/18: Marks–
J. Sivewright 22.2.02.

42. SM/B2/26: Marks–G. Marks 13.10.06; Zborowski and Herzog: 193.

43. PHC: 7.4.07; Stander: 59; SM/B2/9: Marks–N. Mansvelt 19.11.94; SM/B2/10:
Marks–C. G. Hibbert 27.4.94.

44. [Pretoria] *Press* 8.7.96; SM/B2/21: Marks–O. Brandmuller 11.7.05; SM/B2/23:
Marks–T. Marks 23.4.06; Picton-Seymour, 1977: 290; Picton-Seymour, 1989: 171;
Katz: 111.

45. SM/B5: J. W. B. Gunning–Marks 7.12.07, 15.1.08.

46. SM/B2/11: Marks–J. L. van der Merwe 16.1.95; SM/B5: Secretary,
Witwatersrand Agricultural Society–Lewis and Marks 29.1.97; SM/B2/27: Marks–
L. Phillips 28.12.06; VE: 25.10.10; AE: 25.10.10; [Johannesburg] *Star* 11.11.11;
Gutsche: 23–5, 32, 38, 84, 86, 92, 103, 112, 114, 116, 128.

47. SM/B5: C. C. Henkel–Private Secretary, Marks 2.11.07, Marks–Capt.
Hendriks February 1908.

48. SM/B5: G. J. Rudolph–Marks 26.6.09; SM/B2/8: Marks–M. Hugo 17.10.93.
For examples of donations to church causes, see SM/B2/11: Marks–Mrs Bousfield
6.4.95 (gift of £10 to Anglican-run benevolent society); SM/B4.4: Lewis and Marks,
Johannesburg–Lewis and Marks, Pretoria 7.8.00 (annual subscription of £100 to
Nazareth House); VE: 29.8.05 (free building-stone from VE quarry plus £50 towards
costs of Methodist Church in Vereeniging); AE: 13.9.10 (£50 towards YMCA
building fund); VE: 13.7.14, 20.8.14 (sale at low price of eight erven to N.H.K.
congregation, Vereeniging).

49. SM/B2/21: Marks–H. Gilzean-Reid 11.12.05; SM/B5: Transvaal Trout
Acclimatisation Society–Marks 16.7.10, Transvaal Rifle Association–Marks 8.4.10;
H. Gwynne–Marks 6.9.06. For details of petty donations and token memberships, see
SM/B5: incoming correspondence folders.

50. SM/B2/11: Marks–Secretary, City Club 6.1.96; Atkinson: 16; SM/B5:
Secretary, Rand Club–Marks 6.12.06, Circulars of English Club, 1908–9.

XII. Senator and Steelmaker

1. SM/B2/29: Marks–L. Botha 3.10.08.
2. SM/B2/29: Marks–L. Botha 19.10.08, Memorandum 16.11.08.
3. SM/B2/29: Marks–J. P. FitzPatrick 12.1.09.
4. SM/B2/31: Marks–H. Gilzean-Reid 14.6.09. See also Marks–Gilzean-Reid 5.8.09.
5. SM/B2/32: Marks–Lewis 2.2.10, 3.2.10, 5.3.10; SM/B3: Lewis–Marks 5.2.10, 4.3.10; SM/B5: H. Gilzean-Reid–Marks 31.3.10; *Who Was Who*, 1897–1915: 592; Garson: 32.
6. SM/B2/34: Marks–Lewis 25.9.10, 26.9.10, 30.9.10, 17.10.10, Lewis–Marks 26.9.10.
7. SM/B2/34: Marks–Lewis 30.9.10.
8. *SAJC* 21.10.10.
9. SM/B2/33: Marks–F. J. Dormer 8.11.10; UCT, Duncan papers: P. Duncan–Lady Selborne 30.11.10.
10. SM/B2/36: Marks–Lewis 28.3.11.
11. VE: 20.9.04, 30.9.04, 19.12.05, 10.12.07.
12. For the electrification of the Rand, see R. Christie, 1984.
13. SM/B2/24: Marks–F. D. P. Chaplin 4.1.06; *African World Annual*, December 1906: 280–2; TA, LG112/102: Vereeniging Estates, Limited–Lieutenant-Governor of the Transvaal 13.1.06.
14. *African World Annual*, December 1906; Christie: ch. 3; SM/B2/24: Marks–F. D. P. Chaplin 4.1.06.
15. SM/B3: Lewis–Marks 15.12.06; VE: Report AGM 1907.
16. Christie: 37; VE: 16.3.09, 25.3.09.
17. Christie: 37; VE: Report AGM 1910, Directors' reports 1910 and 1911.
18. SM/B2/29: Marks–Lewis 7.6.09; SM/B2/32: Marks–Lewis 22.10.09, 24.3.10, 15.4.10; Christie: 40–1, 44–5.
19. SM/B2/35: Marks–Lewis 5.2.11; *African World Annual*, December 1912: 340A, 401.
20. SC9–1912, Select Committee on Scrap Iron Agreement: 48–9; SM/B2/35: Marks–Lewis 29.6.11.
21. *African World Annual*, December 1912: 398.
22. BRA, HE 246: Wernher Beit–H. H. Wright and R. Haigh 13.2.09.
23. SM/B2/31: Marks–Lewis 5.7.09; SM/B2/32: Marks–Lewis 8.7.09; SM/B2/32: Marks–Lewis 26.8.09; SM/B3: Lewis–Marks 9.7.09, 26.8.09, 23.9.10.
24. TA, MM4107/13: Prospectus of the South African Iron and Steel Company, 1909; TA, MM811/10: Proposal of the South African Iron and Steel Company for the Erection of a Local Plant for the Manufacture of Iron and Steel, 10.3.10; SC9–1912: Evidence of H. H. Wright; SM/B2/31: Marks–H. Gilzean-Reid 14.6.09.
25. SM/B2/31: Marks–Lewis 11.10.09.
26. SC9–1912, Appendix D: Agreement with H. H. Wright; SM/B2/37: Marks–Lewis 4.1.12.
27. Union of South Africa, House of Assembly Debates, 1912: 6.2.12, 19.3.12.
28. Union of South Africa, House of Assembly Debates, 1912: 19.3.12; SC9–1912: Evidence of S. Marks.
29. Richards: 36–7, 39; *Star* 17.6.12; Union of South Africa, House of Assembly Debates, 1912: 10.6.12.
30. *Star* 12.6.12; SM/B2/40: Marks–Lewis 12.7.12.
31. TA, MM 4107/13: Government Mining Engineer–Secretary for Mines and Industries 20.12.13; Richards: 48–9; SC5B–1920, Seventh Report of the Select Committee on Railways and Harbours, 1920: Evidence of I. Lewis; SM/B3:

L. Marks–Lewis 7.7.14.

32. UG10–1915, Report on the Outbreak of the Rebellion and the Policy of the Government with Regard to Its Suppression: 5–7; UG46–1916, Report of the Judicial Commission of Inquiry into the Causes of and Circumstances Relating to the Recent Rebellion in South Africa: 4–7; *South Africa* 10.4.20.

33. *Cape Times* 19.8.14.

34. SM/B2/40: Marks–Lewis 10.11.14, 1.12.14.

35. SM/B2/40: Marks–Lewis 25.11.14, 9.3.15; AE: 19.12.14; SM/B2/41: Marks–Lewis 25.10.15.

36. SM/B2/40: Marks–Lewis 30.10.14, 25.11.14; VE: 20.10.14, 29.10.14; SM/B3: Lewis–Marks 30.12.14.

37. AE: 8.9.14.

38. TA, NA 10/323: Marks–L. Botha 19.3.17, Secretary of Native Affairs–Marks 23.3.17. See Grundlingh, 1987: 68–74, for reasons for the reluctance of blacks to enlist for war service.

39. SM/B3: Lewis–Marks 22.1.15.

40. SM/B3: Lewis–Marks 22.1.15, 17.4.15.

41. SM/B3: Lewis–Marks 4.10.15; SM/B2/41: Marks–Lewis 25.10.15.

42. SM/B3: Lewis–Marks 8.10.09, 3.12.11, 26.11.14, 18.12.14; Gregory: 48, 110; Marks estate papers: Chantrey, Button and Co.–Lewis 11.10.23.

43. SM/B2/32: Marks–Lewis 17.2.10; SM/B2/40: Marks–Lewis 3.6.15, 4.8.15, 2.9.15; SM/B2/41: Marks–Lewis 25.10.15, 15.12.15, 7.3.16; Gregory: 112.

44. Richards: 51–2; SC5B–1920, Select Committee on Railways and Harbours: 49–61; TA, MM 2147/17: Marks–F. S. Malan 5.6.17; Union Steel, Annual report, 1916: 4–5.

45. SC5B–1920, Select Committee on Railways and Harbours: 49–52, 59, 62–3, 66, 73–4; TA, MM 2147/17: Marks–F. S. Malan 5.6.17, Marks–Government Mining Engineer 14.6.17; Richards: 53–6.

46. SM/B2/41: Marks–Lewis 21.8.19, 9.10.19, Marks–Lewis and Marks 1.11.19. See Richards for the struggle for the steel industry in the 1920s. After Sammy's death, Isaac Lewis was outmanoeuvred by Cornelis Frederik Delfos, founder of the South African Iron and Steel Corporation; in 1930 Iscor acquired control of the Union Steel Corporation.

XIII. Haimisher Mensh

1. Rosten: 151, 240.

2. For Jewish esteem for Marks, see *SAJC* 9.6.05 and 20.2.20.

3. *SAJC* 27.2.20.

4. Falcke: 13.

5. SM/B2/17: Marks–Lewis 20.9.00; SM/B2/18: Marks–B. Marks 25.7.01, 13.6.02; SM/B2/23: Marks–B. Marks 8.6.06.

6. SM/B3: Lewis–Marks 28.12.06; [London] *Jewish Chronicle* 17.3.99; SM/B2/16: Marks–W. G. Soper 16.4.99; SM/B2/18: Marks–G. Marks 21.8.01.

7. *SAJC* 27.2.20; SM/B2/19: Marks–L. Marks (date unclear – either February or March 1903).

8. SM/B2/22: Marks–Lewis 9.2.05; SM/B2/20: Marks–B. F. Cabral 14.4.06; Falcke: 11; SM/B2/12: Marks–B. Dawson 21.1.97; SM/B2/7: Marks–Lewis 11.3.94; SM/B2/22: Marks–Lewis 2.9.04; SM/B2/23: Marks–L. Marks 17.6.05.

9. SM/B2/18: Marks–W. F. Bailey 7.8.02; SM/B2/26: Marks–M. Levy 10.5.07; SM/B2/29: Marks–Lewis 16.8.07; SM/B2/13: Marks–Lewis 25.10.96.

10. SM/B2/15: Marks–W. Pickstone 12.6.98; SM/B2/21 Marks–H. Gilzean–Reid 11.12.05; SM/B2/12: Marks–W. F. Bailey 17.12.96; SM/B2/29: Marks–H. Gilzean–

Reid 7.12.07, Marks–J. G. Maxwell 28.12.07; SM/B5: Marks–A. G. Turner 2.4.07.
   11. SM/B2/12: Marks–Lewis 1.9.95; SM/B2/32: Marks–Lewis 30.7.09; SM/B2/22: Marks–Lewis 7.4.04.
   12. SM/B2/9: Marks–E. Marks 25.8.94, 16.10.94.
   13. Falcke: 12–14; Leslie: 41; SM/B2/20: Marks–H. Gilzean–Reid 4.2.05; SM/B2/7: Marks–A. Bonheim 10.3.92.
   14. SM/B2/12: Marks–Lewis 24.8.95; SM/B2/20: Marks–Lewis 3.12.03; SM/B2/29: Marks–Pole-Carew 20.1.08; TA, A681(2): J. P. H. Faure–F. M. Joseph 26.4.98.
   15. SM/B2/10: Marks–T. R. Price 13.5.94; BRA, HE 88: H. Eckstein–Wernher Beit 13.3.05.
   16. SM/B2/3: Marks–R. W. H. Giddy 13.11.82; SM/B2/7: Marks–Lewis and Marks 24.3.93, Marks–J. Sivewright 1.5.93, Marks–C. B. Elliott 9.5.93; SM/B2/11: Marks–S. Foote 16.10.95; SM/B2/12: Marks–H. Lewis 1.9.95; SM/B2/19: Marks–T. Marks 9.1.04; SM/B2/20: Marks–Lewis 2.4.04; SM/B2/29: Marks–Lewis 20.12.07, 28.12.07; SM/B2/37: Marks–Lewis 25.3.12; SM/B5: L. Heymann–Marks 12.11.06, B. Marks–Marks 8.7.07; Falcke: 15, 19, 20; Rosenthal ms.: 166; *Huisgenoot* 17.8.45.
   17. SM/B2/9: Marks–E. Marks 7.5.94; SM/B2/17: Marks–G. Marks 20.11.00.
   18. SM/B2/25: Marks–J. Sivewright 1.10.06; SM/B2/7: Marks–Lewis 1.2.93, 17.3.93, 17.2.94, Marks–J. Sivewright 1.5.93.
   19. Rosenthal ms.: 166; SM/B2/22: Marks–Lewis 18.3.04; SM/B2/24: Marks–J. W. Barlow 13.1.06.
   20. Falcke: 14–15.
   21. SM/B2/32: Marks–Lewis 10.3.10; SM/B2/41: Marks–Lewis 30.6.19, 1.7.19.
   22. SM/B2/25: Marks–Lewis 13.10.06, 14.1.07; SM/B2/20: Marks–Lewis 16.7.04; SM/B2/8: Marks–Lewis 16.11.93.
   23. SM/B3: Lewis–Marks 2.6.99.
   24. SM/B2/18: Marks–Lewis 22.8.02; SM/B2/17: Marks–Lewis 19.12.00; SM/B2/3: Marks–Lewis 3.7.82; SM/B2/29: Marks–Lewis 28.12.07.
   25. SM/B2/12: Marks–Lewis 7.11.96.
   26. SM/B2/17: Marks–Lewis 19.12.00; SM/B2/29: Marks–Lewis 22.2.08.
   27. Leslie: 40–1.
   28. *Cape Times* 30.3.27.
   29. SM/B3: Lewis–Marks 9.10.96; SM/B2/18: Marks–Lewis 24.3.02.
   30. *Cape Argus* 29.3.27; Lewis, Certificate of Naturalisation, July 1889.
   31. *Cape Argus* 29.3.27; Leslie: 119–20.
   32. SM/B3: Lewis–Marks 4.10.15.
   33. SM/B3: Lewis–Marks 18.2.15; *Cape Argus* 29.3.27; *Cape Times* 30.3.27; De Klerk: 10, 77; Leigh: 91.
   34. SM/B2/14: Marks–Lewis 22.11.97.
   35. SBA, INSP 1/1/85: Inspection report, Kimberley branch, 3.2.80; SM/B2/18: Marks–B. Lewis 2.3.02.
   36: SM/B2/25: Marks–Lewis 27.12.06; SM/B2/7: Marks–B. Lewis 15.4.93, Marks–Lewis 1.11.93; SM/B2/14: Marks–Lewis 22.11.97; SM/B2/18: Marks–B. Lewis 2.3.02, Marks–H. D. Lewis 18.4.03; TA, PS 144/01: J. G. Fraser–Military Governor, Bloemfontein 22.12.00.
   37. SM/B2/7: Marks–Lewis 18.6.93.
   38. SM/B3: Lewis–Marks 20.4.06.

Epilogue
   1. TA, MHG 43182: Marks death notice; AE: 3.12.19; VE: 4.12.19; Falcke: 19, 24.
   2. Katz: 113; *South Africa* 27.3.20; Falcke: 23.

3. *SAJC* 20.2.20.

4. *SAJC* 27.2.20; UCT, Cape Town Hebrew Congregation minutes: 7.3.20.

5. UCT, Duncan papers: P. Duncan–Lady Selborne 19.5.20; *South Africa* 12.6.20; SM/A5: Chantrey, Button and Co.–Lewis 11.10.23; N. Maisels: 15.

6. UCT, Duncan papers: P. Duncan–Lady Selborne 19.5.20.

7. *South African Law Reports*, Transvaal Provincial Division, 1921: 180–202; TA, MHG 43182: Marks wills and codicils; N. Maisels: 7–8.

8. TA, MHG 43182: Marks wills and codicils.

9. *SAJC* 16.4.20: report of *Sunday Times* comments.

10. N. Maisels: 17.

11. *South African Law Reports*, Transvaal Provincial Division, 1927: 318–24; N. Maisels: 12–13, 20.

12. TA, MHG 86653: Death notice Bertha Marks; N. Maisels: 2.

13. N. Maisels: 25–30.

14. N. Maisels: 14, 19; AE: Annual report 1919–20.

15. TA, MHG 43182: Marks wills and codicils; N. Maisels: 4–6; *Optima*, March 1952: 23–4; *Optima*, June 1955: 62–5; *Optima*, December 1955: 133–4; *Mines of Africa*, 1937: 52–7, 813–14; *The Mining Year Book*, 1940: 1–2, 580–1; *South African Mining Year Book*, 1944–5: 35, 191–7.

16. *Optima*, December 1955: 134; *Mines of Africa*, 1938–39: 54D; *South African Mining Year Book*, 1944–5: 193; Gregory: ch.8; Anglo American: Agreement Anglo American and Louis Marks, George Falcke et al., 5.9.45, Press announcement by African and European, London 6.9.45; N. Maisels: 17–20.

17. *DSAB* IV: 433.

18. N. Maisels: 17–18.

19. *South African Law Reports*, Transvaal Provincial Division, 1921: 180–202; *South African Law Reports*, 1957: O'Dwyer v. *Estate Marks and others*; N. Maisels: 22–3.

Bibliography

PRIVATE PAPERS

SAMUEL MARKS PAPERS, UCT
A. *Personal*
Includes naturalisation papers, children's birth certificates, school reports, etc.

B. *Correspondence*
B2 Letterbooks 1–41, 1880–1919
B3 Correspondence between Isaac Lewis and Sammy Marks, 1880–1915
B4 Letters from the firm of Lewis and Marks, 1882–1927
B5 Letters to Sammy Marks
B7 Letters from and to others than Sammy Marks
B8 Letters to Bertha Marks

C. *Property and farming interests*
Includes lists of farms and other properties, title-deeds, maps, etc.

D. *Other business interests*
Includes Lewis and Marks partnership agreements, concessions, business agreements, reports on mines, specifications for machinery, and recipes used in distilling.

E. *Political and other interests*
Includes correspondence showing Marks's involvement in the South African War, and wartime passes, permits and proclamations.

F. *Financial records – S. Marks*
Includes cashbooks, ledgers, journals, balance sheets, promissory notes, cancelled cheques and household receipts.

G. *Financial records – Lewis and Marks*
Includes cashbooks, ledgers, journals, and balance sheets.

H. *Miscellaneous documents*
Includes pamphlets, manufacturers' catalogues and newspaper clippings.

OTHER COLLECTIONS OF PRIVATE PAPERS CONSULTED
African and European Investment Company, minute books and annual reports 1904–20, Anglo American, Johannesburg
Anglo American archives, Johannesburg
Cape Town Hebrew Congregation, minutes 1920, UCT
Patrick Duncan papers, Jagger Library, UCT
H. Eckstein and Company papers, Barlow Rand archives
Eerste Fabrieken, letterbooks 1896–8, Transvaal Archives, Pretoria

FitzPatrick papers, National English Documentation Centre, Grahamstown
Glass Factory, letterbook 1898–9, Transvaal archives, Pretoria
J. Henry archives, Jagger Library, UCT
Johannesburg Consolidated Investment Company records, Johannesburg
Pretoria Hebrew Congregation, minute books
Smuts collection, Jagger Library, UCT
Standard Bank archives, Johannesburg
Struben Family papers, University of the Witwatersrand Library
Transvaal Consolidated Coal Company, minute book 1905–9, Anglo American, Johannesburg
Vereeniging Estates Limited, minute books and annual reports 1903–20, Anglo American, Johannesburg

OFFICIAL RECORDS

TRANSVAAL ARCHIVES
A. *South African Republic*
Commandant-General
State Secretary
Leyds archives

B. *Transvaal Colony*
Colonial Secretary
Colonial Treasurer
Compensation Commisssion
Intelligence Officer to the Military Governor, Pretoria
Lieutenant-Governor of the Transvaal Colony
Military Governor, Pretoria
Political Secretary
Private Secretary of the Governor
Provost Marshal's Office
Secretary for Native Affairs
Transvaal Agricultural Department

C. *Union of South Africa*
Master of the Supreme Court, Pretoria
Secretary for Mines and Industries

CAPE ARCHIVES
Griqualand West

PUBLIC RECORDS OFFICE
Colonial Office
Foreign Office

OFFICIAL PUBLICATIONS

CAPE OF GOOD HOPE
Parliamentary debates, 1891–94
A9–1882, Report of the Select Committee on Illicit Diamond Buying in Griqualand West
G52A–1891, Report on Trials of Free State Coal
A6–1893, Report of the Select Committee on Coal for Railway Purposes
G64–1893, Copies of Correspondence relative to Supply of Coal and Trials of Coal
A11–1894, Correspondence between the Commissioner of Public Works and the Representatives of Messrs. L & M in regard to Coal Supply for Colonial Railways
A5–1899, Report of the Select Committee on Railway Coal

GREAT BRITAIN
Cd. 623, 624, 625, 1901, Report of the Transvaal Concessions Commission
Cd. 1791, 1903, Minutes of Evidence taken before the Royal Commission on the War in South Africa
Cd. 1897, 1904, Report of the Transvaal Labour Commission

TRANSVAAL COLONY
Government Mining Engineer, Annual Report, 1906–7

UNION OF SOUTH AFRICA
House of Assembly Debates, 1912
Senate Debates, 1910–15
SC9–1912, Select Committee on Scrap Iron Agreement
UG10–1915, Report on the Outbreak of the Rebellion and the Policy of the Government with Regard to its Suppression
UG46–1916, Report of the Judicial Commission of Inquiry into the Causes of and Circumstances relating to the Recent Rebellion in South Africa
SC5B–1920, Seventh Report of the Select Committee on Railways and Harbours
UG33–1921, Report of the Coal Commission

PUBLISHED CORRESPONDENCE
Duminy, A. H., and Guest, W. R. (eds.), *FitzPatrick, South African Politician: Selected Papers, 1888–1906* (Johannesburg, 1976)
Fraser, M., and Jeeves, A. (eds.), *All That Glittered: Selected Correspondence of Lionel Phillips, 1890–1924* (Cape Town, 1977)
Hancock, W. K., and Van der Poel, J. (eds.), *Selections from the Smuts Papers*, vol. I (Cambridge, 1966)
Mabin, A., and Conradie, B. (eds.), *The Confidence of the Whole Country: Standard Bank Reports on Economic Conditions in Southern Africa, 1865–1902* (Johannesburg, 1987)
Wright, H. M. (ed.), *Sir James Rose Innes: Selected Correspondence, 1884–1902* (Cape Town, 1972)

NEWSPAPERS, PERIODICALS, ANNUALS
African World Annual, 1903–19
Barberton Herald, 1886–90
Cape Times, 1914
Goldfield News, 1893
[London] *Jewish Chronicle*, 1895, 1896, 1899, 1900, 1905
Land en Volk, 1897, 1898
Mines of Africa, 1914–15, 1937, 1938–9
Mining Year Book, 1940
Optima, 1952, 1955
South Africa, 1920
South African Jewish Chronicle, 1902–12, 1920
South African Law Reports, 1921, 1927, 1957
South African Mining Year Book, 1944–5
Standard and Diggers' News 1894, 1895
Star, 1890, 1891, 1899, 1911, 1912
Statist's Mines of the Transvaal, 1904, 1909–10
Transvaal Advertiser, 1883
De Volksstem, 1883

CONTEMPORARY BOOKS, MEMOIRS, GUIDES, DIRECTORIES
Abercrombie, H. R., *The Secret History of South Africa or Sixty-Five Years in the Transvaal* (Johannesburg, 1951)

Amery, L. S. (ed.), *The Times History of the War in South Africa*, seven vols. (London, 1900–9)

Batts, H. J., *Pretoria from Within during the War 1899–1900* (London, n.d.)

Buttery, J. A., *Why Kruger Made War or Behind the Boer Scenes* (London, 1900)

Bleloch, W., *The New South Africa: Its Value and Development* (London, 1902)

Churchill, R., *Men, Mines and Animals in South Africa* (London, 1893)

Cohen, L., *Reminiscences of Kimberley* (London, 1911)

Curle, J. H., *The Gold Mines of the World* (London, 1899)

FitzPatrick, J. P., *South African Memories* (Johannesburg, 1979)

FitzPatrick, J. P., *The Transvaal from Within* (London, 1900)

Girouard, E. P. C., *History of the Railways during the War in South Africa, 1899–1902* (London, 1903)

Goldmann, C. S., *South African Mines* (London, 1895–6)

Graumann, H., *Rand Riches and South Africa* (Cape Town, n.d.)

Hammond, J. H., *The Truth about the Jameson Raid* (Boston, 1918)

Hatch, F. H., *British Association's Visit to Vereeniging: A Short Account of the Chief Points of Interest* (n.p., 1905)

Hobson, J. A., *The War in South Africa: Its Causes and Effects* (London, 1900)

Hofmeyr, J. H., *The Life of Jan Hendrik Hofmeyr* (Cape Town, 1913)

Innes, J. R., *Autobiography* (Cape Town, 1949)

Jeppe, F., *Transvaal Book Almanac and Directory for 1881* (Pietermaritzburg, 1881)

Kestell, J. D., and Van Velden, D. E., *The Peace Negotiations between the Governments of the South African Republic and the Orange Free State, and the Representatives of the British Government, Which Terminated in the Peace Concluded at Vereeniging on the 31st May, 1902* (London, 1912)

Kestell, J. D., *Through Shot and Flame* (Johannesburg, 1976; reprint of 1903 London edition)

Kotze, J. G., *Memoirs and Reminiscences*, two vols. (Cape Town, 1934, 1941)

Lochhead's Guide, Handbook and Directory of Pretoria, 1913 (Pretoria, 1912; State Library reprint 1980)

Longland's Pretoria Directory for 1899 (Pretoria, 1979; reprint of original)

Mathers, E. P., *The Gold Fields Revisited* (Pretoria, 1970; reprint of 1887 Durban edition)

Matthews, J. W., *Incwadi Yami* (London, 1887)

Men of the Times. Pioneers of the Transvaal and Glimpses of South Africa (Cape Town, 1905)

Phillips, L., *Some Reminiscences* (London, 1924)

Sawyer, A. R., *Coal Mining in South Africa* (Newcastle, n.d.)

Sawyer, A. R., 'The South African Coal-field', *Transactions of the North Staffordshire Institute of Mining and Mechanical Engineering*, 10, 1889–90

Sawyer, A. R., *South African and Orange Free State Coal and Mineral Mining Association Report* (Pretoria, 1889)

Struben, H.W., *Recollections of Adventures 1850–1911* (Cape Town, 1920)

Trollope, A., *South Africa* (Cape Town, 1973; reprint of 1878 London edition, edited by J. H. Davidson)

Turner's Kimberley, Old De Beers, Dutoitspan, Bultfontein and Barkly Directory and Guide (Kimberley, 1878)

Wagner, P. A., *The Diamond Fields of Southern Africa* (Johannesburg, 1914)

Wills, W. H., and Barrett, R. J., *The Anglo-African Who's Who and Biographical Sketch-book 1905* (London, 1905)

Wilson, H. W., *After Pretoria: The Guerilla War* (London, 1902)

Witwatersrand Chamber of Mines, *The Mining Industry: Evidence and Report of the Industrial Commission of Enquiry* (Johannesburg, 1897)

SECONDARY SOURCES

A. BOOKS

Abrahams, I., *The Birth of a Community* (Cape Town, 1955)

Alexander, D., *Holiday in Mozambique: A Guide to the Territory* (Cape Town, 1971)

Allen, V., *Kruger's Pretoria: Buildings and Personalities of the City in the Nineteenth Century* (Cape Town, 1971)

Arkin, M. (ed.), *South African Jewry: A Contemporary Survey* (Cape Town, 1984)

Arthur, G., *General Sir John Maxwell* (London, 1932)

Atkinson, A. K. W., *Old Ivory and Roses: The Pretoria Club* (Pretoria, 1969)

Becklake, J. T., *From Real to Rand: The Story of Money, Medals and Mints in South Africa* (n.p., n.d.)

Beinart, W., Delius, P., and Trapido, S. (eds.), *Putting a Plough to the Ground: Accumulation and Dispossession in Rural South Africa, 1850–1930* (Johannesburg, 1986)

Breytenbach, J. H., *Die Geskiedenis van die Krugerstandbeeld* (Pretoria, 1979)

Buxton, S. C. B., *General Botha* (London, 1924)

Cameron, T., and Spies, S. B. (eds.), *An Illustrated History of South Africa* (Johannesburg, 1986)

Chilvers, H. A., *Out of the Crucible* (London, 1929)

Christie, R., *Electricity, Industry and Class in South Africa* (Albany, 1984)

Christopher, A. J., *Southern Africa* (Folkestone, 1976)

Coetzee, D. J., *Spoorwegontwikkeling in die Suid-Afrikaanse Republiek* (Cape Town, 1940)

Coleman, F. L. (ed.), *Economic History of South Africa* (Pretoria, 1983)

Cunningham, A., *The Strubens and Gold* (Johannesburg, 1987)

Davey, A. M., *The British Pro-Boers* (Cape Town, 1978)

De Klerk, A. J. B., *Leeuwenhof: Die Kronieke van 'n Kaapse Herehuis* (Cape Town, 1954)

Denoon, D. J. N., *A Grand Illusion* (London, 1973)

Dictionary of South African Biography, five vols. (Cape Town and Pretoria, 1968–87)

Duminy, A. H., *The Capitalists and the Outbreak of the Anglo–Boer War* (Durban, 1977)

Duminy, A. H., and Guest, W. R., *Interfering in Politics: A Biography of Sir Percy FitzPatrick* (Johannesburg, 1987)

Dunston, L., *Young Pretoria* (Pretoria, 1975)

Emden, P. H., *Randlords* (London, 1935)

Endelman, T. M., *Radical Assimilation in English Jewish History, 1656–1945* (Bloomington, 1990)

Engelbrecht, C. L., *Money in South Africa* (Cape Town, 1987)

Garson, N. G., *Louis Botha or John X. Merriman: The Choice of South Africa's First Prime Minister* (London, 1969)

Gildea, R., *Barricades and Borders: Europe, 1800–1914* (Oxford, 1987)

Gitelman, Z., *A Century of Ambivalence: The Jews of Russia and the Soviet Union, 1881 to the Present* (London, 1988)

Gordon, C. T., *The Growth of Boer Opposition to Kruger, 1890–95* (Cape Town, 1970)

Green, T., *The World of Diamonds* (London, 1981)

Gregory, T., *Ernest Oppenheimer and the Economic Development of Southern Africa* (Cape Town, 1962)

Grundlingh, A. M., *Die 'Hendsoppers' en 'Joiners'* (Pretoria, 1979)

Grundlingh, A. M., *Fighting Their Own War: South African Blacks and the First World War* (Johannesburg, 1987)

Gutsche, T., *A Very Smart Medal: The Story of the Witwatersrand Agricultural Society* (Cape Town, 1970)

Hammond, R. J., *Portugal and Africa 1815–1910: A Study in Uneconomic Imperialism* (Stanford, 1966)

Hanson, S. G., *Argentine Meat and the British Market* (Stanford, 1938)

Helme, N., *Thomas Major Cullinan* (Johannesburg, 1974)

Hundert, G. D., and Bacon, G. C., *The Jews in Poland and Russia: Bibliographical Essays* (Bloomington, 1984)

Innes, D., *Anglo American and the Rise of Modern South Africa* (Johannesburg, 1984)

Jeeves, A. H., *Migrant Labour in South Africa's Mining Economy: The Struggle for the Gold Mines' Labour Supply, 1890–1920* (Johannesburg, 1985)

Kaye, H., *The Tycoon and the President: The Life and Times of Alois Hugo Nellmapius, 1847–93* (Johannesburg, 1978)

Kaplan, M., *Jewish Roots in the South African Economy* (Cape Town, 1986)

Katz, J. (ed.), *The Story of the Pretoria Jewish Community up to 1930* (Pretoria, 1987)

Katzenellenbogen, S. E., *South Africa and Southern Mozambique: Labour, Railways and Trade in the Making of a Relationship* (Manchester, 1982)

Keegan, T. J., *Rural Transformations in Industrialising South Africa: The Southern Highveld to 1914* (Johannesburg, 1986)

Kennedy, B., *A Tale of Two Mining Cities: Johannesburg and Broken Hill, 1885–1925* (Johannesburg, 1984)

Kruger, D. W., *Paul Kruger*, two vols. (Johannesburg, 1961, 1963)

Kokosolakis, N., *Ethnic Identity and Religion: Tradition and Change in Liverpool Jewry* (Washington, 1982)

Krut, R., 'The Making of a South African Jewish Community in Johannesburg, 1886–1914', in Bozzoli, B. (ed.), *Class, Community and Conflict: South African Perspectives* (Johannesburg, 1987)

Kubicek, R.V., *Economic Imperialism in Theory and Practice: The Case of South African Gold Mining Finance, 1886–1914* (Durham, 1979)

La Hausse, P., *Brewers, Beerhalls and Boycotts: A History of Liquor in South Africa* (Johannesburg, 1988)

Lewsen, P., *John X. Merriman: Paradoxical South African Statesman* (Johannesburg, 1982)

Marais, J. S., *The Fall of Kruger's Republic* (Oxford, 1961)

Marks, S., and Rathbone, R. (eds.), *Industrialisation and Social Change in South Africa: African Class Formation, Culture and Consciousness, 1870–1930* (London, 1982)

May, H. J., *Music of the Guns* (Johannesburg, 1970)

Maylam, P., *A History of the African People of South Africa: From the Early Iron Age to the 1970s* (Cape Town, 1986)

Meiring, P., *Dynamite and Daisies: The Story of Barberton* (Cape Town, 1976)

Mendelsohn, R., 'Oom Paul's Publicist: Emanuel Mendelssohn, Founder of the First Congregation', in Kaplan, M., and Robertson, M. (eds.), *Founders and Followers* (Cape Town, 1991)

Mitchell, B. R., *Economic Development of the British Coal Industry 1880–1914* (Cambridge, 1984)

Newbury, C., *The Diamond Ring: Business, Politics, and Precious Stones in South Africa, 1867–1947* (Oxford, 1989)

Newitt, M., *Portugal in Africa: The Last Hundred Years* (London, 1981)

Pakenham, T., *The Boer War* (Johannesburg, 1982)

Phimister, I. R., *An Economic and Social History of Zimbabwe, 1890–1948: Capital Accumulation and Class Struggle* (London, 1988)

Picton-Seymour, D., *Historical Buildings in South Africa* (Cape Town, 1989)

Picton-Seymour, D., *Victorian Buildings in South Africa including Edwardian and Transvaal Republican Styles 1850–1910* (Cape Town, 1977)

Pinkus, B., *The Jews of the Soviet Union: The History of a National Minority* (Cambridge, 1988)

Pollard, S., 'Sheffield during the Industrial Revolution', in Brucker, G. (ed.), *People and Communities in the Western World*, vol. 2 (Homewood, Ill., 1979)

Richards, C. S., *The Iron and Steel Industry in South Africa* (Johannesburg, 1940)

Richardson, P., *Chinese Mine Labour in the Transvaal* (London, 1982)

Ritchie, W., *The History of the South African College, 1829–1918*, vol. 2 (Cape Town, 1918)

Roberts, B., *Kimberley: Turbulent City* (Cape Town, 1985)

Rosenthal, E., *Milnerton* (Milnerton, 1980)

Rosenthal, E., *Other Men's Millions* (Cape Town, n.d.)

Rosenthal, E., *Southern African Dictionary of National Biography* (London, 1966)

Roskies, D. K., and Roskies, D. G., *The Shtetl Book* (n.p., 1975)

Rosten, L., *The Joys of Yiddish* (Harmondsworth, 1971)

Saron, G., and Hotz, L. (eds.), *The Jews in South Africa: A History* (Cape Town, 1955)

Shimoni, G., *Jews and Zionism: The South African Experience 1910–67* (Cape Town, 1980)

South African Iron and Steel Corporation, *Steel in South Africa* (Parow, 1953)

Spies, S. B., *Methods of Barbarism?: Roberts and Kitchener and Civilians in the Boer Republics, January 1900–May 1902* (Cape Town, 1977)

Stanislawski, M., *Tsar Nicholas I and the Jews: The Transformation of Jewish Society in Russia, 1825–1855* (Philadelphia, 1983)

Struben, R., *Taken at the Flood: The Story of Harry Struben* (Cape Town, 1968)

Sudarsky, M., Katzenellenbogen, U., and Kissin, J., *Lite* (New York, 1951)

Trapido, S., 'Putting a Plough to the Ground: A History of Tenant Production on the Vereeniging Estates, 1896–1920', in Beinart, W., Delius, P., and Trapido, S. (eds.), *Putting a Plough to the Ground: Accumulation and Dispossession in Rural South Africa, 1850–1930* (Johannesburg, 1986)

Trapido, S., 'Reflections on Land, Office and Wealth in the South African Republic, 1850–1900', in Marks, S., and Atmore, A. (eds.), *Economy and Society in Pre-Industrial South Africa* (London, 1980)

Tredgold, A., *Bay Between the Mountains* (Cape Town, 1985)

Turrell, R. V., *Capital and Labour on the Kimberley Diamond Fields, 1871–90* (Cambridge, 1987)

Van der Merwe, N. J., *Marthinus Theunis Steyn: 'n Lewensbeskrywing*, vol. 2 (Cape Town, 1921)

Van der Poel, J., *Railway and Customs Policies in South Africa, 1885–1910* (London, 1933)

Van Onselen, C., *Studies in the Social and Economic History of the Witwatersrand, 1886–1914*, two vols. (Johannesburg, 1982)

Viney, G. E., *Colonial Houses of South Africa* (Cape Town, 1987)

Vital, D., *The Origins of Zionism* (Oxford, 1980)

Warwick, P. (ed.), *The South African War: The Anglo-Boer War, 1899–1902* (London, 1980)

Williams, B., *The Making of Manchester Jewry, 1740–1875* (Manchester, 1976)

Worger, W. H., *South Africa's City of Diamonds: Mine Workers and Monopoly Capitalism, 1867–95* (Johannesburg, 1987)

Young, R. B., *The Life and Work of George William Stow* (London, 1908)

Zborowski, M., and Herzog, E., *Life Is With People: The Culture of the Shtetl* (New York, 1962)

B. ARTICLES

Anon., 'History of Coal in South Africa', *Mining Survey*, 5, 1954

Anon., 'The Origins of Coal Mining in South Africa', *South African Mining and Engineering Journal*, March 1940

Anon. , 'The Triumphs and Trials of Barberton's Sheba Mine', *South African Mining and Engineering Journal*, 1964

Bradlow, E., 'Women at the Cape in the mid-19th Century', *South African Historical Journal*, 19, 1987

Coetzee, N. A., 'John Johnson Kirkness', *Pretoriana*, 86, 1984

Cronjé, B., 'Zwartkoppies Hall, die Huis van Sammy Marks', *Pretoriana*, 87, 1985

Crush, J. S., 'Settler-Estate Production, Monopoly Control, and the Imperial Response: The Case of the Swaziland Corporation Ltd.', *African Economic History*, 8, 1979

Davenport-Hines, R. P. T., and Van Helten, J., 'Edgar Vincent, Viscount D'Abernon and the Eastern Investment Company in London, Constantinople and Johannesburg', *Business History*, 28, 1986

De Jong, C., 'Lewe en Bedryf van Samuel Marks, 1843–1920', *Pretoriana*, 87, 1985

Endelman, T. M., 'Communal Solidarity among the Jewish Elite of Victorian London', *Victorian Studies*, 28, 1985

Ferreira, O. J. O., 'Eerste Fabrieken: Die Beginpunt van Nywerheidsontwikkeling in die Zuid-Afrikaansche Republiek', *Contree*, 15, 1984

Garson, N. G., '"Het Volk": The Botha–Smuts Party in the Transvaal, 1904–11', *Historical Journal*, 9, 1966

Hugo, T., 'The Presidency 1890', *Museum Memo*, 16, 1988

Kaplan, D. E., 'The Politics of Industrial Protection in South Africa, 1910–39', *Journal of Southern African Studies*, 3, 1976

Kruger, D. W., 'Paul Kruger en die Jode', *Jewish Affairs*, November 1960

Marks, S., and Trapido, S., 'Lord Milner and the South African State', *History Workshop*, 8, 1979

Mawby, A. A., 'Capital, Government and Politics in the Transvaal 1900–07, a Revision and a Reversion', *Historical Journal*, 17, 1974

Mendelsohn, R., 'A Mining Magnate at Muizenberg: Sammy Marks and the Cape Town Property Market, 1881–1919', *Cabo*, 4, 1987

Mendelsohn, R., 'The Sammy Marks Collection', *Jagger Journal*, 6, 1985–6

Mouton, J. A., 'Genl. Piet Joubert in die Transvaalse Geskiedenis', *Archives Year Book for South African History*, 1957–I

Neil-Tomlinson, B., 'The Nyassa Chartered Company, 1891–1929', *Journal of African History*, 18, 1977

Phimister, I. R., 'Meat and Monopolies: Beef Cattle in Southern Rhodesia, 1890–1938', *Journal of African History*, 19, 1978

Phimister, I. R., 'The Reconstruction of the Southern Rhodesian Gold Mining Industry, 1903–10', *Economic History Review*, 29, 1976

Pieterse, D.J., 'Die Geskiedenis van die Mynindustrie in Transvaal, 1836–86', *Archives Year Book for South African History*, 1943

Ploeger, J. J., 'Die Maatskappy "Eerste Fabrieken in de Zuid-Afrikaansche Republiek",' *Historia*, 2, 1957

Ploeger, J. J., 'Uit die Geskiedenis van "The South African Republic Fruit and Meat Preserve Works", Eerste Fabrieken', *Pretoriana*, 85, 1984

Richardson, P., and Van Helten, J. J., 'The Development of the South African Gold-Mining Industry, 1895–1918', *Economic History Review*, 37, 1984

Rochlin, S. A., 'Sammy Marks and the Kruger Statue', *Jewish Affairs*, November, 1954

Rosenthal, E., 'Transvaal se Eerste Fabriek', *Die Huisgenoot*, 17.8.45

Smallberger, J. M., 'IDB and the Mining Compound System in the 1880s', *South African Journal of Economics*, 42, 1974

Smith, R. J., 'The Kruger Monument, Church Square, Pretoria', *Africana Notes and News*, 15, 1962

Vail, L., 'Mozambique's Chartered Companies: The Rule of the Feeble', *Journal of African History*, 17, 1976
Watts, B., 'Some Letters from Lord Milner', *Jagger Journal*, 6, 1985–6

C. THESES

Cammack, D. R., 'Class, Politics and War: A Socio-Economic Study of the Uitlanders of the Witwatersrand, 1897–1902' (Ph.D. thesis, University of California, Irvine, 1983)
Du Preez, S., 'Vredespogings gedurende die Anglo-Boereoorlog tot Maart 1901' (M.A. thesis, University of Pretoria, 1976)
Grobler, J. C. H., 'Die Vroeë Politieke Loopbaan van P. G. W. Grobler, 1896–1916' (D.Phil. thesis, University of South Africa, 1979)
Jeeves, A. H., 'The Rand Capitalists in Transvaal Politics, 1892–9' (Ph.D. thesis, Queen's University, 1970)
Kagan, N., 'The Growth and Development of the Municipality of Green Point and Sea Point' (B.A. Honours dissertation, University of Cape Town, 1975)
Krut, R. M., 'Building a Home and a Community: Jews in Johannesburg, 1886–1914' (Ph.D. thesis, University of London, 1985)
Mabin, A. S., 'The Making of Colonial Capitalism: Intensification and Expansion in the Economic Geography of the Cape Colony, South Africa, 1854–1899' (Ph.D. thesis, Simon Fraser University, 1984)
Norwich, R., 'Synagogues on the Witwatersrand and in Pretoria before 1932: Their Origin, Form and Function' (M.Archit. thesis, University of the Witwatersrand, 1988)
Oosthuizen, J., 'General Koos de la Rey en Sy Verhouding tot die Uitlanders' (M.A. thesis, University of Pretoria, 1940)
Oosthuizen, J., 'Jacobus Hercules de la Rey en die Tweede Vryheidsoorlog' (D.Litt. thesis, Potchefstroom University, 1950)
Simonowitz, G., 'The Background to Jewish Immigration to South Africa and the Development of the Jewish Community in the South African Republic, between 1890 and 1902' (B.A. Honours dissertation, University of the Witwatersrand, 1960)
Stander, H., 'Die Ontstaan en Ontwikkeling van Vereeniging, 1882–1912' (M.A. thesis, University of South Africa, 1946)
Theron, B. M., 'A Social History of Pretoria during the First Phase of the Anglo–Boer War: October 1899–June 1900' (M.A. thesis, University of South Africa, 1984)
Turrell, R. V., 'Capital, Class and Monopoly: The Kimberley Diamond Fields, 1871–89' (Ph.D. thesis, University of London, 1982)
Worger, W. H., 'The Making of a Monopoly: Kimberley and the South African Diamond Industry, 1870–95' (Ph.D. thesis, Yale, 1982)

UNPUBLISHED PAPERS AND MSS.

Cox, B., 'From Castle to Casino: The Historical Growth of South African Breweries, 1895–1983', unpublished paper, 1984
Falcke, G., *Sam Marks: A Character Sketch* (Johannesburg, 1948)
Leslie, T. N., *Casual Memories of an Octogenarian* (n.p., n.d.), unpublished ms.
Maisels, Dolly – transcript of interview with M. Robertson
Maisels, S. J. N., *Notes for Epilogue to Sammy Marks Biography* (Johannesburg, 1986)
Mendelsohn, R., '". . . the country is rotten with coal": Sammy Marks and the Highveld Coal Industry, 1880–1910', unpublished paper, South African Historical Society conference, 1989
Rosenthal, E., *The Vereeniging Estates Story*, unpublished ms.

Index

Abromowitz, Krena (*née* Marks, formerly Falcke), sister of SM, 2, 207-8, 209, 252

African and European Investment Company, 158, 178, 180, 189; diamond investments, 173-5; gold investments, 256-9

Afrikaner Bond, 36

agriculture, 4; possibilities for, 27-8, 52, 61; use of steam plough, 52-3, 82-3; *see also* tenant farming

alcohol, 4, 15; illicit trade in, 73-4; manufacture *see* Eerste Fabrieken; concession for, 13, 19-21, 23, 31-2; prohibition on sales, 69-74, 118

Amalgamated Collieries of South Africa Ltd, 256-7

arms trade, 95-6

Bailey, Sir Abe, 110, 238, 257-8

Bailey, W. F., 159, 184

Baker, Sir Herbert, 156-7

Barberton gold fields *see* Sheba mine

Barnato, Barney, 44, 62-3, 84, 98

Barnato Brothers, 85, 98, 174, 175

Bechuanaland, 178

Beckett, T. W., 13-14, 114, 123, 189

beer, 52, 74, *see also* South African Breweries

Beit, Alfred, 42, 44, 83-4, 99, 252

blacks: SM's views of, 18, 52, 81-2, 158, 166, 237

Bosman, Rev. H. S., 127

Botha, Louis, 153-4, 231; SM's relationship with, 141, 215-18; during South African War, 119-21, 126-8, 138; post-war reconciliation, 142-3, 147

Bourke, Edmund, 14, 123

Brandmuller, Otto, 53, 177, 252, 257, *see also* Maccauvlei

Bray, Edwin, 39-40, 42

brickfields, 53-4, 84, *see also* Vereeniging Brick and Tile Company

bywoners, see tenant farming

Cape Government Railways, 47, 164, 166

Cape Town, 21-2; property investments, 10, 63-4, 110-11, 157, 161-2, 253; *see also* Leeuwenhof; Muizenberg

Cape Town Hebrew Congregation, 201-2

Chamber of Mines, 83, 152, 169, 179, 220

Chamberlain, Joseph, 111; relationship with SM, 66-9, 113, 145-8, 159-61

Chaplin, Sir Francis Drummond Percy, 243

Chinese labour, 18-19, 147, 166, 179

Churchill, Lord Randolph, 56, 101

coal mines and mining, 11-12, 14-16, 26-8, 61; labour for, 15, 28, 48-50, 166-70; marketing, 16, 36, 45-8, 51, 62, 164-5; *see also* South African and Orange Free State Coal and Mineral Mining Association; Vereeniging Estates Ltd

Cockroft, Charles William Rufus, 33

Cohen, Edward, Viscount Matalha, 20

Cohen brothers (Ben and Leon), 62, 169

cold storage *see* Imperial Cold Storage Company

Compagnie Française des Mines du Diamants du Cap, 9, 12
concessions, 155; cyanide, 97-8; Delagoa Bay pier, 62, 169; dynamite, 44, 126; iron, 84; liquor, 13, 19-21, 23, 31-2; railway, 36-7, 40-1, 46; tramway, 42, 44; *see also* Nellmapius, A. H
conservation, 56, 61, 104
convict labour, 49
Corner House, 83, 85, 99, 171, 240, *see also* Wernher, Julius; Beit, Alfred
Cornish miners, 19
Crawford, Hugh, 58, 60, 123, 143, 178
Cullinan, Sir Thomas, 171-3, 225
customs union, Cape–Transvaal, 41-2
De Beers, 49, 164, 174, 175, 230, 231, *see also* Rhodes, Cecil John
De Jongh, Jacobus Nicholas, 143-4, 152, 179
Delagoa Bay: harbour, 62, 165, 169; illicit alcohol trade, 73-4; investment in, 61-3, 98, 177; railway project, 35-6, 40-2, 46-7, 61-2, 94; *see also* Mozambique
Delagoa Bay Lands Syndicate, 62-3
De la Rey: SM's friendship with, 61, 141-3; South African War, 119, 125-6, 135-6, 138; post-war reconciliation, 141-3, 147-9; 1914 Rebellion, 226-8
De Wet, Christiaan, 141, 228
diamond mines and mining, 6-10, 17-19, 21-2, 28, 170-4, 256
Diamond Trade Act, 1882, 22
distillery *see* Eerste Fabrieken
Dumont, Jerôme, 12, 14-16
Duncan, Patrick, 149, 219, 250
Dunning, Sir Edwin Harris, 152, 179-80, 189, 243
Du Toit, S. J., 36
Dutoitspan mine, 10, 17, 21
dynamite concession, 44, 126
East Rand Mining Estates Ltd, 171
Eastern Transvaal gold fields, 39-40, 42-4, *see also* Sheba mine
Eckstein, H. and Co., 99
education, 203, 210-12, 241-2, 252; of SM, 2-3, 28-9, 188; of SM's children, 69, 104-9, 117, 123, 181, 183, 188, 190-3, 214; of SM's nephews and nieces, 208-10
Eerste Fabrieken: establishment, 21, 23-6, 28-30; marketing, 30-3, 37, 56-7,

59, 69-76, 118, 212; effect of South African War, 158-9; closure, 178, 189
electricity, 51-2, 177, 220-1
Esselen, Ewald, 86
Falcke, George, nephew of SM, 58, 69, 112, 123, 180, 191; relationship with SM, 193, 201, 209-10, 240, 242, 252
Falcke brothers, 167, 210
farming, tenant *see* tenant farming
Farrar, Sir George, 152-3, 218-19
Fischer, Abraham, 112-13
FitzPatrick, Sir Percy, 99, 216
forestry, 4, 12-13, 53, 176-7, *see also* Maccauvlei
franchise, 112-14
Fraser, John, 11
Gilzean-Reid, Sir Hugh, 216, 218
glass factory, 30, 76-7
Goerz, Adolf, 89
gold mines and mining, 19, 38-40, 42-4, 171, 220, 257-60, *see also* Sheba mine; Witwatersrand gold fields
Graaff, David, 175-6, 231
Grobler, Piet, 89, 97, 133, 205
gunpowder factory, 26
Guttmann, Bertha *see* Marks, Bertha
Guttmann, Tobias, 6, 33, 54, 197
Hammond, John Hays, 65-6
Hatch, Dr Frederick Henry, 179-80
Hatherley Distillery *see* Eerste Fabrieken
Hatherley House *see* Muizenberg holiday home
health: SM, 21, 143, 195-6, 249-50; Bertha Marks, 151, 195, 254; Marks children, 128-9, 181-2, 195
Heller, Henry, 40
Herz, Fils et Compagnie, 11
Het Volk, 153-4
Heymann, S. L., 71, 206-7
Hofmeyr, Jan ('Onze Jan'), 112-13
illicit diamond buying (IDB), 17-18, 21-2
Imperial Cold Storage Company, 175-6, 231
iron and steel industry, 16-17, 54, 69, 84, 160-1, 222-6, 231-3
jam factory, 76, 116, 159
Jameson Raid, 64-9, 94, 98
Joel, Solly, 98, 163
Johannesburg: Jewish community, 202, 204; Lewis and Marks office, 178-81; Marks family moves to, 189-90, 193

Johannesburg Consolidated Investment
    Company, 62, 98, 163, 175
Joubert, C. J., 86-7
Joubert, General Petrus Jacobus, 36, 42,
    60-1, 65, 95-6, 119; relationship with
    Kruger, 87, 93, 114
Joubert, Mrs P. J., 127-8
Judaism, 8, 108, 197-214, 250, 260-1
Kaplan, Mendel, 255-6
Kay, Dr James Alexander, 105, 123,
    143-4, 194-6
Kimberley, 7-10, 21, 28
Kimberley Mining Company, 9-10,
    18-19, 21
Kitchener, Horatio Herbert, 1st Earl
    Kitchener of Khartoum, 131-2, 135-8
Kotze, Sir John Gilbert, Chief Justice,
    41, 67, 69
Kruger, Stephanus Johannes Paulus
    (Paul), 12; relationship with SM, 13,
    26, 54-5, 83, 87-101, 111-14, 120;
    distillery, 31-2, 70-3, 76-7; railway,
    35-6, 40-2, 46-7; statue, 86, 89-90, 132,
    212; Jameson Raid, 66-8; South
    African War, 111-13, 119-20, 132
labour, 27, 49, 53, 77, 130, 166, 178;
    Chinese, 18-19, 147, 166, 179; on coal
    mines, 27-8, 48-50, 167-70; on
    diamond mines, 17-19, 21-2; on gold
    mines, 19, 220
Landau, Rabbi, 201, 204
Leeuwenhof, 10, 22, 247
Levy, Abraham, brother-in-law of SM,
    207
Levy, Fanny (née Marks), sister of SM,
    2, 207, 252
Levy, Harry, nephew of SM, 208-9
Levy, Miriam, niece of SM, 200, 252
Levy, Philip, nephew of SM, 117, 209
Lewis, Barnet, brother of IL, 7, 9, 10;
    and distillery, 20, 24, 29-30, 31, 247;
    and Witwatersrand gold, 38-9, 247;
    relationship with SM, 247-8
Lewis, Frederica, m. Ellia Marks, sister
    of IL, 34
Lewis, Henry, son of IL, 152-3
Lewis, Isaac [IL], 7, 10, 247; character,
    36-7, 56, 76, 84-5, 245-6; financial
    expert, 24, 59-60, 87, 141, 174;
    London office, 10, 20, 87; relationship
    with SM, 30, 76, 144, 235, 238, 242-8;
    see also Lewis and Marks

Lewis, Joseph, brother of IL, 7
Lewis and Marks, 85, 93-5, 97-8, 158-9,
    206, 243, 256; coal interests, 11-12,
    14-16, 26-8, 45, 79, 162-4, 219-20,
    256-7, see also Amalgamated Collieries
    of SA Ltd; South African and Orange
    Free State Coal and Mineral Mining
    Association; Vereeniging Estates;
    diamond interests, 7-10, 17, 21, 170-4,
    230-1, 250, 256; distillery see Eerste
    Fabrieken; gold interests, 38-9, 42-5,
    170, 178, 256-9; Johannesburg office,
    178-81; London office, 10, 20, 87;
    Pretoria office, 57-8, 178; property
    investments, 10, 60, 62-3, 155-8,
    177-8; post-war reconstruction and
    problems, 37-8, 69, 155-6, 180, 197,
    219, 229-30; see also Lewis, Isaac;
    Lewis, Barnet
Leyds, Dr Willem Johannes, 45-6, 69, 84,
    91-2, 126; relationship with SM, 86,
    95, 97
Lippert, Edward, 44, 89, 93
liquor see alcohol; Eerste Fabrieken
Lynch, Thomas, 11
Maccauvlei, 53, 82, 148, 176-7, 249, 252,
    257
Maisels, Dolly (née Marks), daughter of
    SM, 105, 189, 193, 198-9, 205, 256,
    261
Maisels, Neill, 255
Maisels, Rael, 261
Malan, Commandant Abe, 127-8
Marks, Bertha (née Guttmann), wife of
    SM: character and interests, 184-90,
    252; children, 35, 69, 105, 181, 183;
    health, 151, 195, 254; Judaism, 197-8;
    marriage, 33-4, 39, 181-2, 197, 241; at
    Muizenberg, 115, 117-18, 123, 134,
    157; at Zwartkoppies, 103, 181, 187-90
Marks, Dolly see Maisels, Dolly
Marks, Ellia, brother of SM, 2, 7, 11, 34,
    49, 117
Marks, Fanny see Levy, Fanny
Marks, Gertrude Miriam (Girlie),
    daughter of SM, 105, 192-3; and
    Judaism, 197, 199-200, 204, 250, 261
Marks, Joseph, brother of SM, 2, 7, 11,
    21, 33, 34, 207
Marks, Joseph Mordechai (Joe), son of
    SM, 105, 228, 254-6, 261
Marks, Krena see Abromowitz, Krena

Marks, Leonora Josephine, daughter of SM, 105

Marks, Louis, eldest son of SM, 35, 105, 228, 256-61; education, 69, 106-8, 117, 190-1

Marks, Miriam, mother of SM, 2; school named after, 203, 211, 252

Marks, Montague (Montie), son of SM, 105, 107, 117, 128-9

Marks, Mordechai Feit, father of SM, 2, 206-7

Marks, Phillip, son of SM, 105, 118, 193, 261

Marks, Theodore (Teddy), son of SM, 105, 181-2, 195, 228, 256, 259-61

Maxwell, Major-General Sir John, 129, 131-2, 134, 137, 139, 237

McLaren, W. A., 53, 83

Mendelssohn, Rev. Meyer, 35

Merriman, John Xavier, 18-19, 217-18, 225

Meyer, Lucas, 119, 141

Milner, Sir Alfred, 111-13, 138, 140, 143-9, 155, 160, 205

Milnerton, 110, 157, 161

mining industry: relationship with SM, 69-74, 97, 98; *see also* specific types of mining, coal, diamond, gold

Miriam Marks School, 203, 211, 252

Mozambique, 48-9, 73-4, 169, 177-8, *see also* Delagoa Bay

Muizenberg: Marks holiday home (Hatherley House), 115, 118, 123, 134, 156-7, 162, 240, 253

Murray, John, 117, 193-4

Nellmapius, Alois Hugo, 116; concessions, 91, 93; iron, 84; liquor, 13, 19-21, 30-2, 72; railway, 36, 42; relationship with SM, 13, 20-1, 23, 25-6, 31, 161, 194

Neustadt, 1-4, 8, 206

1914 Rebellion, 226-9

Nyassa Company, 177-8

Ohlsson, Anders, 52

Oppenheimer, Bernhard, 230, 250

Oppenheimer, Ernest, 230, 258-60

Paddon brothers, 9, 11

Phillips, Sir Lionel, 97-9

Pickstone, H. E. V., 102, 208

Porges, Jules, 9, 11

Portugal, Crown Prince of, 150-1

Pretoria: SM in, 12-14, 212, 253-4, 349;

Jewish community, 13, 202-4; Lewis and Marks office, 57-8, 178

prohibition on alcohol sales, 69-74, 118

property investments, 60-1, 155-8, 177-8, 253-4; Cape Town, 10, 63-4, 110-11, 157, 161-2, 253; Delagoa Bay, 62-3

railways, 16, 40-1; Cape, 46-8, 164, 166; Delagoa Bay, 35-6, 40-2, 46-7, 61-2, 94

Rand Water Board, 84

Reitz, F. W., 91, 118, 126

Rhodes, Cecil John, 44, 46-7, 65, 86, 93, 110, 175, 220, 238, 252; relationship with SM, 21-2, 98-102; *see also* De Beers

Rhodes Fruit Farms, 102

Rhodesia, 178

Roberts, Frederick Sleigh Roberts, Earl Roberts, 118, 122, 124-5

Roberts Victor Company, 173-4, 176

Robey and Company, 16, 36, 42

Robinson, Sir Hercules, 66

Robinson, J. B., 9, 44, 85, 94-5, 99, 110, 163, 238

Rosenberg, Rev. M., 202-3

Rothschilds, 94, 111-12, 141

Schuster, Ferdinand, 24-5, 28, 31-2

Selborne, William Waldegrave Palmer, 2nd Earl of, 148-51, 169

Senate: SM in, 218-19, 225

sharecroppers, 28, 80-1

Sheba mine, 39-40, 42-4, 78-9, 116; gold tickeys from, 91

Sheffield, 6, 16, 30, 161, 197, 221, 224

Sivewright, Sir James, 46-8, 62-3, 66-7, 84, 110, 175-6, 194

Smit, General N. J., 86-7

Smuts, Jan Christiaan, 97, 111, 137-8, 150, 153-4, 205

Somershields, Dr Oskar, 63

South African and Orange Free State Coal and Mineral Mining Association, 11, 13, 15, 26-8, 50, 52, 79-80, *see also* Vereeniging Estates Ltd

South African Breweries, 52, 77, 98, 157

South African College, Chair of Hebrew, 211

South African Iron and Steel Company, 223, *see also* iron and steel industry; Union Steel Corporation of South Africa

South African Native Labour Contingent, 229

South African Supply and Cold Storage Company, 175
South African War, 130-1, 142-4; SM attempts to avert, 111-15; SM assists Boers, 116, 118, 120-1, 132, 141; SM assists British, 116-17, 121; SM as peacemaker, 119-29, 135-40
Sprigg, Sir Gordon, 66
steel industry see iron and steel industry
Steyn, President Marthinus Theunis, 112, 119, 126
Stokes, Frederick Walter, 31-2, 37
Stow, George William, 11-15, 27
Struben brothers, 38-9
sugar, 30
Swaziland, 49, 96-7, 177-8
tenant farming, 28, 49, 52, 80-2, 158
tickeys, golden, 90-1
timber see forestry; Maccauvlei
tramway, 42-4
Transvaal Chamber of Mines see Chamber of Mines
Transvaal Consolidated Coal Company, 62, 87, 164-5
Transvaal Progressive Association, 152-3
Trench, B. B., 43-4
unification, SM's views on, 215-17
Union Steel Corporation of South Africa, 223, 226, 229, 231-2, see also iron and steel industry
Upington, Sir Thomas, 41
Van Wouw, Anton, 90
Vereeniging, 54-6, 84, 120, 220-3
Vereeniging Brick and Tile Company, 204, 212, 213, 229, 252

Vereeniging Consolidated Mills, 51
Vereeniging Estates Ltd, 80, 180, 189, 222, 256-7; agriculture, 80-3; collieries, 162-70, 212, 219-20, 229, 256-7; in South African War, 119-20, 133; see also South African and Orange Free State Coal and Mineral Mining Association
Vereeniging Milling Company, 51
Victoria Falls Power Company, 220-1
Vincent, Sir Edgar, 59, 63, 71-2
Volkshoop see Eerste Fabrieken
water supply, 51, 83-4
Wernher, Julius, 11-12, 34, 83-4, 99; gold investments, 38, 42, 44, 171; see also Corner House
will of SM, 250-61
Witwatersrand Agricultural Show, 78
Witwatersrand Agricultural Society, 212-13
Witwatersrand gold fields, 14, 43-5, 257; discovery of, 38-9, 42, 247; during South African War, 118-19
Witwatersrand Native Labour Association, 169
Wolmarans, A. D. W., 132-3
World War, First, 227-9, 231
Wright, Henry Horace, 222-5
Zionism, 205
Zwartkoppies Hall, 33, 188; furnishing and building alterations, 34-5, 39, 103-4, 130, 150, 255; as museum, 255-6; during South African War, 121-2, 131-5, 181; staff, 183-6, 252; visitors to, 101-2, 123-5, 131, 134, 140, 150, 205